Fathering through Sport and Leisure

Today's fathers are responding to new expectations about fathering: the remote father of the past has faded and men are now expected to be 'involved' fathers who actively engage with their children. Most turn to leisure and sport to do this, yet in the areas of family studies and men's studies, the leisure component of family life is under-played. This book provides a long overdue and thorough investigation of the relationship between fatherhood, sport, and leisure.

Fathering through Sport and Leisure investigates what fathers actually do in the time they spend with their children. Leading researchers from the fields of sport, leisure and family studies examine the tensions men encounter as they endeavour to meet the new expectations of fatherhood, and the central role that sport and leisure play in overcoming this. Analysed in relation to social trends and current policy debates, this unique collection examines fathering in a wide range of contexts including:

- Parental expectation and youth sports
- Fathers and daughters
- Leisure time and couple time in dual earner families
- Divorce, fatherhood and leisure.

This book shows how contemporary fathers use sport and leisure to engage with their sons and daughters, achieve emotional closeness and fulfil their own expectations of what it means to be a 'good father'. Drawing on research carried out in the UK, Australia, Canada and the United States, this is a crucial text for anybody with an interest in sport and leisure studies, family studies or fatherhood.

Tess Kay is Senior Research Fellow and Deputy Director of the Institute of Youth Sport at Loughborough University, one of the largest research centres dedicated to the study of young people, sport and leisure.

Fathering through Sport and Leisure

Edited by Tess Kay

Routledge
Taylor & Francis Group

LONDON AND NEW YORK

First published 2009
by Routledge
2 Park Square, Milton Park, Abingdon, Oxon, OX14 4RN

Simultaneously published in the USA and Canada
by Routledge
270 Madison Avenue, New York, NY 10016

Routledge is an imprint of the Taylor & Francis Group, an informa business

Typeset in Goudy by
RefineCatch Limited, Bungay, Suffolk
Printed and bound in Great Britain by
CPI Antony Rowe, Chippenham, Wiltshire

British Library Cataloguing in Publication Data
A catalogue record for this book is available from the British Library

Library of Congress Cataloging-in-Publication Data
  Fathering through sport and leisure / edited by Tess Kay.
     p. cm.
  Includes bibliographical references and index.
1. Fatherhood.   2. Father and child.   3. Leisure.   4. Sports.
I. Kay, Tess.
HQ756.F38247 2009
306.874′201—dc22   2009000196

ISBN13: 978–0–415–43868–1 (hbk)
ISBN13: 978–0–415–43870–4 (pbk)
ISBN13: 978–0–203–89070–7 (ebk)

ISBN10: 0–415–43868–3 (hbk)
ISBN10: 0–415–43870–5 (pbk)
ISBN10: 0–203–89070–1 (ebk)

This book is dedicated to the affectionate memory of
Sue Glyptis
1953–1997

Contents

     TESS KAY

8   **Fathers and daughters: negotiating gendered relationships
     in sport**   124
     NICOLE WILLMS

9   **Divorce and recreation: non-resident fathers' leisure
     during parenting time with their children**   145
     ALISHA T. SWINTON, PATTI A. FREEMAN AND RAMON B. ZABRISKIE

10 **Traditional marriages, non-traditional leisure: leisure and
     fathering in the Church of Jesus Christ of Latter-day Saints**   164
     PATTI A. FREEMAN, BIRGITTA BAKER AND RAMON B. ZABRISKIE

11 **Rising to the challenge: fathers' roles in the negotiation of
     couple time**   183
     VERA DYCK AND KERRY DALY

12 **Where are the kids? Researching fathering, sport and
     leisure through children's voices**   200
     RUTH JEANES

13 **Reaching out: widening research into fathering, sport
     and leisure**   215
     TESS KAY

     Endnote   252

     References   255
     Index   283

Figures

Tables

Boxes

Acknowledgements

I have been assisted by many people in bringing this volume together. It has been a wonderful bonus that their help has been accompanied by so much enthusiasm.

My first thanks go to the contributing authors. A number of these originally wrote papers for a themed issue of *Leisure Studies* journal on 'Fathering through leisure'; others joined the writing team subsequently. All have been industrious, patient and good-natured throughout. I thank all of them for their excellent contributions and for engaging in a global email correspondence as we fine-tuned the collection. A special thank you to a number of the 'first wave' authors who were insistent on developing their work further and produced revised or new chapters for this volume.

I thank the editorial board of *Leisure Studies*, then headed by Neil Ravenscroft, who first gave me the opportunity to bring researchers together on this topic; Ken Roberts for permission to reproduce a version of the paper that appears here as 'Fathers and sons: being "Father Angel", and previously appeared in *World Leisure* (Kay, 2007); and Rowman and Littlefield Publishers for permission to reproduce Ralph LaRossa's chapter 'Until the ball glows in the twilight', which previously appeared in Marsiglio, Roy and Fox's *Situated Fathering* (2005). At Routledge Books, Brian Guerin and Simon Whitmore have been skilful managers of both the volume and the editor.

This book was completed alongside my research roles in the Institute of Youth Sport and the School of Sport and Exercise Sciences at Loughborough University. Both provide a stimulating intellectual environment and generously supportive colleagues. I am grateful to the Institute and School for granting the period of study leave during which I have been able to complete the book. This is also an appropriate place to acknowledge the much-appreciated longer-term professional and personal support of Barrie Houlihan and Mary Nevill.

At the start of 2008 I attended the ANZALS conference in Melbourne and visited Griffiths University in Brisbane for a short study visit. My thanks to Peter Brown, Maureen Harrington and Simone Fullagar for hosting my visit to Griffiths which provided extra stimulus for my research in this area, and to ANZALS for accommodating themed sessions on men, masculinities and leisure. These opened up avenues that I hope we will now be able to explore further.

Several people have directly assisted my own research and writing on fatherhood, helped me develop some of my understandings of more diverse family situations, and advised me on content within this book. Liz Such was the first person with whom I worked directly on research into leisure, families and parents and our collaboration did much to stimulate my interests; and Liz and I both owe a debt to Linda Hantrais for the many opportunities she gave us to participate with her in European social policy research. My thanks also to James Lowrey, who undertook the study of football fathers with me; Joanna Welford, who provided research assistance in preparing the final manuscript; John Horne, who provided feedback on the later sections relating to ethnicity; and Louisa Webb, who kindly shared her knowledge of Aboriginal Australians. Rahmanara Chowdhury has gently guided my interest in Muslim family life for some time now and did so again here. I thank her for the many conversations which enhance my life as much as my work.

I recently read in another author's acknowledgements, 'It is always friends who get you through'. It is. Thank you to Ruth Jeanes and Leigh Robinson, experts in that process! Above all, love and thanks to my very best friends, my husband Guy and our daughter Katarina. Between them they have fathering pretty sorted.

This book is dedicated to the memory of Sue Glyptis, former colleague and beloved friend to very many of us. The 'family-tree' of people in sport and leisure studies who were nurtured, encouraged, advised and supported by Sue reaches wide indeed. Were she with us now she would have had her pen out on my manuscript, checking and suggesting and improving – 'glyptifying' it as ever!

Tess Kay
Loughborough
December 2008

Contributors

Birgitta Baker, Ph.D. is a faculty member in the Kinesiology Department at Louisiana State University. She teaches courses in the areas of research, evaluation, and psychosocial aspects of physical activity. Her research interests include psychosocial and environmental predictors of physical activity and familial and cultural influences on leisure and health behaviors.

Jay Coakley is Professor Emeritus of Sociology at the University of Colorado in Colorado Springs, USA. He received a Ph.D. in sociology at the University of Notre Dame and has since taught and done research on play, games, and sports, among other topics in sociology. Dr Coakley has received many teaching, service, and professional awards, and is an internationally respected scholar, author, and journal editor. His text, *Sports in Society: Issues and Controversies* is in its 10th edition with adaptations published in Canada, Australia, and the United Kingdom, and translations in Japanese and Chinese.

Kerry Daly is Associate Dean of Research for the College of Social and Applied Human Sciences at the University of Guelph. He is the Principal Investigator of the Father Involvement Research Alliance in Canada and his current research interests focus on the changing meaning of fatherhood, the way that families negotiate and navigate time pressures in their lives, and the challenges families face in trying to harmonize their work and family life.

Vera Dyck recently completed a post-degree clinical certification in Couple and Family Therapy. She facilitates groups, leads parenting workshops, and offers counselling services to individuals, couples and families in Guelph, Ontario. In working with couples who have children, she seeks to enhance family relationships by strengthening couple bondedness in ways that enhance both fathers' and mothers' individual perceptions of personal power in the negotiation of time choices.

Patti A. Freeman, Ph.D., joined the Recreation Management and Youth Leadership Department at Brigham Young University in 1999. She teaches classes in research and evaluation and directs the Conservation and Outdoor Leadership Training program for undergraduate students. In addition, she teaches a graduate statistics course as well as serving on thesis committees. Her primary research interests include examining attributes of leisure experiences that strengthen individuals and families.

Maureen Harrington has a Ph.D. (Sociology) from U.C. Santa Barbara. After teaching at the University of Ottawa, Canada from 1988 to 1995 in the Department of Leisure Studies she moved to Australia where she has been teaching in the Department of Tourism, Leisure, Hotel and Sport Management at Griffith University. She has written on women's work, leisure and family lives, and gender and family leisure. Her current research is on family leisure, healthy lifestyles and notions of risk.

Ruth Jeanes Ph.D. is a Senior Research Associate at the Institute of Youth Sport at Loughborough University where she works on evaluations of national and international youth sport initiatives. She has specialist expertise in youth sport policy and is currently assessing the use of sport to deliver HIV/AIDS education to young people in Zambia. Ruth is committed to representing young people in research and has developed a number of innovative participatory methods to engage young people actively in the research process.

John Jenkins is a non-resident father of two children who is continuing to explore aspects of leisure and non-resident fatherhood. His interest in this field of research has been inspired by the lack of research on leisure and fatherhood and his own experiences of father–child contact and leisure both as a child and as a parent. John is also Professor of Tourism and Hospitality Management at Southern Cross University Australia.

Tess Kay, Ph.D., has a longstanding involvement in research into sport, leisure and family. She has undertaken studies in the UK, Zambia, India and Brazil for governmental and independent organizations and served on research policy networks for the European Commission. She has a special interest in issues surrounding inclusion, diversity and development and is currently working with sports-based initiatives to promote education among young Muslim women. Tess is Deputy Director of the Institute of Youth Sport, Loughborough University and Managing Editor of *Leisure Studies* journal.

Ralph LaRossa is Professor of Sociology at Georgia State University. He has received grants from the National Science Foundation and National Institutes of Health in support of research on the history of fatherhood and the experience of becoming a father in contemporary society. His most recent work focuses on the social construction of parenthood and the history of fatherhood during and after the Second World War. He also has written on the theorizing process in qualitative research.

Liz Such Ph.D. is a Senior Lecturer in Leisure, Sport and Physical Activity in the School of Health and Social Sciences, University of Bolton. After a five year stretch working as a researcher for the British government, she has returned to her main areas of research interest. These include the relationships between leisure, employment and family life and the role of leisure in the construction of lifestyle and identity. She also has a broad interest in policy relevant research in matters relating to leisure, physical activity, children, the family and the labour market.

Alisha T. Swinton completed her BA (2003) in Recreation Management Youth Leadership, with a minor in Sociology and her Master's in Youth and Family Recreation (2006) from Brigham Young University. Her research most recently examines the family, divorce and parental involvement through leisure. A future goal is to complete a Ph.D. in positive psychology, in order to examine the role of leisure and life satisfaction variables in distressed relationships. Alisha is currently a mother of three children living in Sydney, Australia.

Nicole Willms is currently a Ph.D. candidate in the Department of Sociology at the University of Southern California. Her work focuses on the experiences of female athletes with the goal of expanding ideas about the social construction of gender. She has also recently co-authored an article in *Contexts* examining representations of female athletes on television. She is currently studying the constructions of gender, race/ethnicity and community within Japanese-American basketball leagues in Los Angeles.

Ramon B. Zabriskie, Ph.D., CTRS, is on faculty in the Department of Recreation Management and Youth Leadership at Brigham Young University in Provo, Utah, USA. Prior to entering academia he practiced as a recreation therapist for many years. He currently teaches courses in therapeutic recreation and recreation/leisure studies, and teaches in the Youth and Family Recreation Graduate Program. His primary area of research and scholarship is family leisure functioning.

Introduction

Fathering through sport and leisure

Tess Kay

This book brings together an international collection of research into fathers, sport and leisure. It has its origins in a themed issue of *Leisure Studies* journal published in 2006, which was the first collection of academic papers to focus on the role that leisure plays in men's fathering. That collection is now expanded, updated and diversified and appears here in a rather different form, reflecting a more extensive array of research – into sport as well as leisure – than was available three years ago. Sport and leisure researchers therefore appear to be riding on a tide of interest in fathers and fatherhood. With so much mounting evidence that fathers place leisure at the heart of their parenting, they are ideally poised to contribute to understanding of contemporary fathering.

The role of leisure in family life is by now well-proven. Across four decades scholars have shown the pivotal position leisure plays in building and sustaining family relationships. In the UK, the Rapoports (1975) set out to critically analyse the development of family life across the life cycle and found that 'leisure' was one of the three fundamental domains through which family members individually and collectively constructed their lives. (The others were 'work' and 'family'.) Twenty years later Orthner, Barnett-Morris and Mancini (1994) showed that leisure experiences are the context within which most family members establish and develop their relationships with each other. Since then Shaw and Dawson's (2001) concept of 'purposive leisure' has introduced us to the idea that parents use leisure activities to pursue goals they value – as a means of contributing to family functioning, and to achieve beneficial outcomes for children. Prevailing ideologies about motherhood, fatherhood and parenting are therefore acted out through leisure practice (Shaw and Dawson, 2001, p. 229).

It is hoped therefore that this volume will bring leisure to the attention of some fatherhood and family researchers who may not have considered leisure in much depth before. It is a source of some frustration to leisure studies scholars that our field has such a variable external profile! For leisure is a major social and economic force: leisure forms, activities and organisations have long played a pivotal role in the construction of social life in the private and public spheres. Today there are few social policy agendas with which leisure does not connect. The arts, sport and cultural activities are all regularly deployed to engage the disaffected, divert the criminally intended, enhance the well-being of the inactive and build social capital and citizenship among the isolated. At home parents and families are urged to contain the demands of paid work, reject the long-hours work culture, and spend time in recuperative and relaxing activities. Internationally both sport and cultural activities are being used to build social networks in impoverished countries and rebuild them in post-conflict areas. But there is a dark side too. Leisure can be destructive for individuals, as the impacts of substance and alcohol abuse testify; it can damage social relations as much as repair them, as we witness when leisure sites – sport especially – provide arenas for the reinforcement of sexism, homophobia and racism; and outdoor leisure and tourist activity can have undesirable social and environmental impacts. For an area that some might dismiss as frivolous, leisure has some serious implications.

We are now beginning to appreciate that leisure is particularly central to fathering – creating what Liz Such has termed 'leisure-based' parenting (2006 and this volume). Leisure features more prominently in fathering than mothering, and sport, with which this volume is also concerned, has a special significance as a form of activity in which fathers have traditionally nurtured relationships with their children. But fathering is changing, families are changing – and leisure forms are changing. In this book we set out to explore exactly what role sport and leisure are playing in the ideologies and practice of fathering today.

Structure of the book

The book presents research and analysis that has been undertaken into fathering, sport and leisure in Australia, Canada, the United Kingdom and the United States of America. It consists of 13 chapters contributed by 14 authors. The themes are so closely interwoven that it is artificial to place chapters in separate sections, but there is a broad pattern to their sequence.

- Chapters 1–3 establish the broad landscape of contemporary fathering and the position of sport and leisure within it. They sketch out the parameters of fathering and discuss the historical and current connections between fathering, sport and leisure.
- Chapters 4–6 report on substantial empirical studies that establish the centrality of sport and leisure in contemporary fathering, both for fathers who live with their children and fathers who do not.
- Chapters 7–11 present five further, more specific empirical studies of fathering, sport and leisure, each of which lets us add depth to the picture established so far.
- Chapters 12 and 13 look at how we can build on the current knowledge base to ensure that research into fathering, sport and leisure can progress and diversify in future.

In Chapter 1, I provide some contextual information for the analyses of fathering, sport and leisure that follow. The chapter provides a profile of the family and employment status of fathers in Australia, Canada, the United Kingdom and the United States of America and considers some of the main themes in current debates about fathers and fathering, especially the tension between fathers' traditional roles as providers and their emergent roles as 'involved', nurturing parents.

In Chapter 2 Ralph LaRossa documents the historical link between the game of baseball ('America's national pastime') and fathering, exploring how 'in certain segments of the population, the game of playing catch not only is indispensable to learning the fundamentals of baseball, but is also instrumental to being defined as a caring dad'. LaRossa gives an intriguing account of earlier eras. By dispelling any notion that fathering through sport and leisure is a recent phenomenon he encourages us to think more critically about how we conceptualise fathering in the current time.

This is what Jay Coakley does in Chapter 3, where he examines how men's parental behaviour is underpinned by prevailing ideologies of fathering and parenting. Coakley explores this in the North American context, situating changing expectations of fathers within wider, dramatic transformations in parenting over the past two generations. Mothers and fathers are today held responsible for the whereabouts and actions of their children 24-hours a day, 7-days a week – an unprecedented standard. Leisure is clearly a major site for this to occur, and Coakley considers how youth sports provide parenting contexts that fulfil expectations of involved fathering.

In Chapter 4, Maureen Harrington's study of leisure as a site for fathering in Australian families considers how the relationships that fathers have with their family in leisure contexts reflect the construction of their own identities as fathers. Harrington applies the concept of 'generative parenting' to examine how some fathers attempt to conduct their family lives in ways that foster the next generation, drawing links with Shaw and Dawson's (2001) work on purposive leisure. She concludes that being with and doing leisure activities with their children, and using these occasions to bond, communicate and instil values is central to the generative notion of fathering.

In Chapter 5, Liz Such further develops her analysis of leisure in the lifestyles of dual-earner parents in order to explore the relationship between fatherhood, personal time and leisure-based parenting. Taking a life-history perspective, she examines how the structure, nature and meaning of men's leisure is crucially altered by the onset of parenthood: although leisure still retains meanings of autonomy and personal pursuit in fathers' lives, it also becomes a context for parenting. Fathers' and mothers' accounts uncover activities, opinions, experiences and dynamics that contribute to a construction of 'good' fathering built around moral understandings of the legitimacy of autonomous, personal leisure, and the discourse of 'being with' children.

In Chapter 6 John Jenkins provides us with a new, empirically based analysis of the issues he and Kevin Lyons put firmly on the agenda in 2006 – the role of leisure in non-resident fathers' relationships with their children. High quality interviews reveal the importance non-resident fathers attach to leisure as a means of being good fathers. Leisure time, however it is constructed by fathers in the presence of their children, is not trivial: it is an aspect of life which parents and children can share, through which they can develop skills, bond, strengthen resolve and learn about each other and aspects of life. It is an especially important avenue for non-resident fathers who only have limited, highly regulated contact to make a valuable contribution, as parents, to the lives of their children.

Chapter 7 reports on my own study of fathers' involvement in soccer with young sons playing at a local sports club in England. We had expected, as has been suggested, that sport would be a familiar site for men in which they could play out 'new' fatherhood in an established area of competence. In this particular case we found the opposite. The fathers in this study were not 'sporty dads' and had had no prior direct involvement with soccer: they had become involved in support of their sons' interest through their desire to be good parents. They had a strong consciousness of ideologies of involved fathering and were explicit about these being strong influences on their involvement in their children's leisure.

In Chapter 8 Nicole Willms' study of fathers and daughters brings a valuable additional perspective to this collection. Willms draws on the sociology of sport to locate father–daughter within a gender relations framework. Her study is the only chapter in this book to view fathering through the eyes of children (albeit adult ones) – an issue over which Ruth Jeanes rightly takes us to task in Chapter 12! Willms introduces a note of caution to our analyses, reminding us not to be blinded to the darker side of father–child relationships, especially in areas of competitive achievement. Sport exemplifies this as a 'hyper-masculine' domain in which dominating and abusive behaviours can become normalised. In this environment it may seem acceptable for a father who is trying to encourage his daughter to achieve in sport to use various forms of control, dominance and coercion.

In Chapter 9 we return to non-resident fathers, this time with a specific focus on leisure satisfaction. Alisha Swinton, Patti Freeman and Ramon Zabriskie investigate the leisure satisfaction of non-resident fathers while spending time with their child(ren). Their quantitative approach is a very good complement to the qualitative research elsewhere in the volume. They find that the leisure satisfaction of non-resident fathers increases as their level of involvement in leisure activities with their children increases, and that even very infrequent participation in activities is beneficial compared to non-participation. Because leisure satisfaction is related to life satisfaction, increased leisure satisfaction during parenting time has the potential to bring wider benefit to non-resident fathers and their children.

In Chapter 10 Patti Freeman, Birgitta Baker and Ramon Zabriskie introduce a new dimension: the relationship between culture, religion, fathering and leisure. They focus on leisure and fathering among fathers who are members of the Church of Jesus Christ of Latter-Day Saints (LDS) living in the state of Utah. They explore the role of religion in shaping sub-cultural norms regarding fathering and leisure, and the ways in which these norms elicit experiences that differ from those of the larger culture in which the Utah LDS subculture is embedded. Freeman, Baker and Zabriskie's findings are thought-provoking because they show how religious teachings on men's family and fatherhood responsibilities directly influence their fathering practice and their approach to leisure, in this case leading them to give importance to shared family leisure.

Chapter 11 offers an interesting departure from addressing father–child relations. The preceding chapters have focused on the relationship that men have with their children, especially when they directly interact with them. But 'fathering' has a wider scope and Vera Dyck and Kerry Daly turn the spotlight away from parent–child leisure and examine how 'couple time' is negotiated in the context of family demands. Like Coakley, Daly and Dyck highlight the significance of a cultural context in which parents feel obligated to put their children first, 'always and in every way'. They remind us that 'supporting couplehood [is] one way to meet the deep needs of children' and suggest that couples 'may need to have their conscientious stance of always-putting-the-kids'-needs-first' explicitly countered.

The final two chapters are a bit of a departure from those that precede them. Their purpose is to build on the rich array of studies gathered here and to ask how we might now move forward in our research.

In Chapter 12 Ruth Jeanes hits us with a telling question – where are the kids? Where are the voices of children in our research into fathers? Jeanes draws on several years of experience of conducting research with children and young people, from pre-school to adult age and in a variety of environments, to make the case for including the voices of children in our research into fathers, parenting and families. She reassures sceptics by providing examples from social policy and youth sport studies in which children's voices have been heard, sometimes to devastating effect. She leaves us in little doubt about what can be gained by developing sport and leisure research in the same way.

In Chapter 13, I consider how we move this area of research forward. I am conscious how, in this book and elsewhere, research into fathering, sport and leisure has covered a wide geographical scope but a narrow cultural one. What we have done so far provides us with an excellent launch pad. The evidence assembled here leaves us in no doubt about the importance of sport and leisure to fathering and justifies moving to a more ambitious phase of work. Chapter 13 therefore advocates diversifying our knowledge base by conducting research across a much wider social and cultural spectrum and starts the ball rolling by illustrating a number of under-represented contexts and their associated fathering practices.

The book concludes with a brief Endnote that reviews the key themes emerging from the preceding chapters and advocates more diverse and nuanced analyses of how sport and leisure sit within ideologies of parenting and fathering. Such work is required, because from their different perspectives the authors of this volume converge upon one core theme: the centrality of sport and leisure to fathering. To date this prominence is not reflected in the increasingly voluble debates surrounding contemporary fatherhood. This is a rich opportunity.

1 The landscape of fathering

Tess Kay

Fathering is changing. High levels of maternal employment are eroding men's position as breadwinners; increased breakdown and reconstitution of families means that growing numbers of fathers are living separately from their biological children; and concomitant rises in remarriage and co-habitation are seeing an increasing proportion of men joining new households as step-parents. Higher levels of childbirth outside marriage have reduced fathers' automatic rights to involvement with their children unless asserted through legal process, and it is now less certain than in previous generations that fathers will live with their children and remain in their household. Yet at the same time as fatherhood appears to becoming more precarious, expectations about the fathering role are rising. A growing social consensus suggests that today's fathers should be, and want to be, more actively engaged with their children than previous generations have been (e.g. Brannen, Lewis, Nilsen and Smithson, 2002; Lamb, 2004; Fletcher, 2008; Palkovitz, 2002).

Fathers themselves are expressing their entitlement to greater involvement in their children's lives, most conspicuously through the emergence of pressure groups advocating greater legal and social recognition of this role. There is also evidence that men are responding to the changing expectations of what a father might be by parenting differently, becoming more emotionally connected to their children, more directly engaged in their children's lives and more egalitarian in their gender role expectations. But underlying these trends, diversity among fathers – in cultural identity, social class, family arrangements and sexuality – points not to one model of fatherhood but many (Flouri, 2005). The circumstances surrounding fatherhood are therefore complex and contradictory: it is increasingly unclear what the role of a father is, and perhaps even less clear what it 'should' be.

Messages about new forms of fatherhood do not arrive in a vacuum: 'The gender order does not blow away at a breath' (Connell, 2000: p.14) and nor do the structures that sustain and reproduce it. Labour markets across the globe continue to be based primarily on the model of the male full-time worker and welfare policies construct fathers first and foremost as financial providers for their families rather than carers and nurturers. In the UK men who are fathers have been working the longest hours of any of their European counterparts, earning on average two-thirds of family income (Lewis, 2000), while striving to respond to expectations of father involvement. They are more likely than childless men to report stress and general dissatisfaction. When Warin, Solomon, Lewis and Langford (1999) asked fathers what was expected of them today, answers included 'Too bloody much', 'An awful lot', 'All singing, all dancing'.

This is the context within which our understanding of the role of sport and leisure in contemporary fathering must sit. The changing conditions of fatherhood have made fathers a prominent social policy issue and a growing focus for social science research. Diversity and change in fatherhood are central to changing masculinities, changing family forms, and changing gender relations, and contribute to the patterns and ideology of family life that are defining features of cultural identity in increasingly multicultural societies. Individually, men face strong tensions between the traditional roles of provider and the modern role of carer that, as fathers, they are expected to embrace and combine. By retaining their function as main income earners while also facing expectations to be more involved in their children's lives, fathers – like mothers – appear to be assuming significant new responsibilities without shedding much of their old ones. This chapter therefore sets the scene for the book's examination of these aspects of fathering by first sketching out the broader landscape. It draws on a once scant but now burgeoning range of research to consider how the practice and ideologies of contemporary parenting are being negotiated by fathers.

Defining terms: fathers, fatherhood and fathering

Three interrelated terms are usually encountered in discussions of contemporary fathering: fathers, fatherhood and fathering (Dermott, 2008; Hobson, 2002; Morgan, 2004).

- The term 'father' is used to define the identity of a father, i.e. the connection between a particular child and a particular man. There can be complexities in this usage, as the term encompasses social as well as biological fathers, and varies in its application in different cultural contexts.
- The term 'fatherhood' refers to understandings of the role associated with being a father – in Hobson's (2002) terms, the 'cultural coding of men as fathers. This includes the rights, duties responsibilities and statuses that are attached to fathers, as well as the discursive terrain around good and bad fathers' (Hobson, 2002: 11). Morgan (2004: 378) talks similarly about 'the public meanings associated with being a father'.
- The third term, 'fathering', is the dimension with which this book is most concerned – the 'actual practices of men "doing" parenting' (Dermott, 2008: 7).

The three terms above are inextricably interwoven: when men carry out fathering, they do so in the context of the specific father-relationship they have to their child/children (e.g. biological/non-biological; resident/non-resident), and of societal expectations of fatherhood. The next sections sketch out the landscape within which they do this.

Identifying the parameters of fatherhood

Most industrialised nations have been documenting trends in family life for many years. Fathers, however, have been relatively invisible. This partly reflects methodological complexity. Although the majority of fathers are married and living with their dependant biological children, many are not. Some fathers are non-married, no-longer married or re-married; they may be the biological father or 'social' father of the children with whom they cohabit; they may live with their children in an intact, lone or reconstituted family, or apart from them; and some men may deny, or be genuinely unaware, that they have fathered children. Defining fatherhood and identifying fathers is not straightforward.

However, the lack of attention paid to fathering does not just reflect research practicalities. It is also indicative of the low importance that has been attached to understanding the role of parenting in men's lives. During the 1980s and 1990s changes were clearly taking place within families, but they were most visible in women's employment behaviour. Policy makers were far more concerned with responding to the implications of mothers' increasing involvement in the labour market than to fathers' – possible – increased involvement in the home. Maternal employment rates were rising, but fathers' work patterns continued to be relatively unaffected by the arrival of children and although many men were no longer the sole breadwinner for their household, virtually all were its main earners. On the surface the fathering role therefore appeared stable and unproblematic. There were obvious ramifications for the welfare state if more mothers went out to work, especially in relation to childcare provision, but no one was too concerned if fathers chose to spend more time with their kids outside work hours. There was also a certain blindness among family and child researchers about the significance of fathers and fathering:

> No attention was given to father–child interactions because there was no evidence that father involvement was important in explaining child well-being or development. We thought that the most important thing that the father could do was to support the mother and that mothers could provide whatever information we needed about that support . . . In addition, it was too difficult and too expensive to include fathers in research designs.
>
> (Evans, 2004: xi)

These views have changed. The role of fathers in child development has been increasingly recognised and a growing body of 'serious empirical research' has challenged early stereotypical views, revealing considerable diversity and complexity in men's parenting roles (Dex and Ward, 2007: 1). In the industrialised nations at least, we are now in a relatively strong position to sketch out the parameters of men's lives when they are fathers.

This chapter outlines the landscape of contemporary fatherhood within which men engage with their children through sport and leisure. It takes as its starting point its editor's location in the UK, draws a number of comparisons with the other three countries that feature in this collection, and makes occasional reference to a wider geographic range. The profile first addresses who fathers are as defined by their position in families, the labour market and the state, and then considers how they carry out fathering.

Fathers

Fathers in families

All men have been fathered and most men become fathers themselves. Fewer men become parents than women, reflecting the greater likelihood that a man will have children by multiple partners, but it is still far more common for an adult man to become a father than not. And although much has been heard in recent years about changing family structures, the majority of men still enter fatherhood living in a household shared with the mother of their joint co-resident biological child.

This is not to deny that fathers have experienced notable changes in patterns of family and household formation over the last three decades or so. In all four countries featured in this book the number of non-resident fathers has increased markedly, a consequence of rising levels of divorce and separation, and of the spread – and greater acceptability – of lone and single parenthood. None the less, in Australia, Canada, the United Kingdom and the United States, approximately three-quarters of fathers are resident fathers (69%–79%), and only a fifth non-resident (19%–24%) (Table 1.1). By far the majority of fathers live in a two-parent family household during their parenting years.

The four countries are therefore broadly similar in the continued statistical dominance of the traditional model of family. The persistence of this family

Table 1.1 Fathers in families

	AUS	CAN	UK	USA
Father and mother and in residence	79%	74%	76%	69%
Father not in residence	19%	21%	21%	24%
Father only in residence	3%	5%	2%	7%

Sources: Australian Bureau of Statistics, 2006; Statistics Canada, 2006; Office for National Statistics, 2008; US Census Bureau, 2007

form is one of the factors that makes it hard to shake off normative ideas about families, mothers and fathers. It is important to do so, however, because differences in fathering are not only created through change across time. Aggregate data indicates strong comparability across the four countries but obscures stark contrasts *within* the population of fathers in each.

One of the key discriminators in fathering status is the composite impact of class, education and wealth. In Australia, Canada, the United Kingdom and the United States family households in which fathers are resident are much wealthier than those in which they are not. Households with a resident father have higher income, are less likely to be in poverty, are less likely to receive state welfare benefits and are more likely to own their home than households with a non-resident father (Table 1.2). Comparisons of annual income show that in Canada, families with a resident father have more than twice the income of those with a non-resident father and in the United States more than three times as much. In Australia, where Linacre's (2007) comparison of the 'household net worth' of family households went beyond day-to-day income to a fuller assessment of assets, the net worth of households which did not have a resident father was found to be only 27 per cent of the net worth of those that did.

It is useful to look beyond these statistics to consider the processes that underlie them. Non-resident fatherhood does not occur in isolation: it is particularly common among parents with low levels of education and insecure employment, living in difficult social and economic situations, and is especially prevalent among certain minority ethnic groups. It is certainly true that non-resident fathers are more likely to be poor than resident fathers – but it is also true that fathers who are poor are more at risk of becoming non-resident.

These differences in fathering status become more complex when the relationship between race, ethnicity and family living arrangements is also considered. Australia, Canada, the United Kingdom and the United States all contain very sizeable non-white minority groups (Table 1.3), ranging from Indigenous Peoples who long predated white settlement, to current in-flows of economic migrants. In all four countries the highest levels of non-resident fatherhood occur among non-Whites, and among some of these groups more fathers are non-resident than resident (e.g. 50.7 per cent of Black Caribbean fathers in the UK (Table 1.4a), and 57 per cent of Blacks in the United States (Table 1.4b)). While the multifaceted deprivation with which non-resident fatherhood is associated does not appear conducive to fathering, some qualitative analyses suggest that these difficult situations can in fact foster it. Paschal's (2006) work on teenage African-American fathers (also referred to in Chapter 13) found that in depressed neighbourhoods with few employment opportunities, fatherhood could offer one of the very few routes through which young men could confirm masculinity. High levels of adolescent parenthood were therefore 'a cultural manifestation of various social and structural conditions, including the lack of jobs that pay a living

Table 1.2 Indicators of deprivation by family type in the UK, Australia, Canada and the USA

	Both parents resident	Mother non-resident	Father non-resident
Australia			
% low income households	16.4	32.8	41.7
% low economic resource households	11.0	39.6	49.9
% of households where main source of income is state pensions/allowances	8.2	47.1	63.3
% in owned accommodation	76.4	41.6	32.4
% rented accommodation	21.2	56.4	65.1
Mean household net worth ($AU)	471,000	171,000	123,000
Canada			
% of children living in households below poverty level	7.7	n/a	32.3
Average government transfers ($CAN)	3,300	3,900	7,400
% owning accommodation	76.4	41.6	32.4
% renting accommodation	21.2	56.4	65.1
Average total income, 2006 ($CAN)	93,500	67,100	40,900
United Kingdom			
% living on income less than 60% of the median after housing costs	21	n.a.	50
% distribution of all state benefit claimants with dependent children, between family types	18	n.a.	72
% of households in owned housing	48	n.a.	11
% risk of being in poverty	23	n.a.	52
Average weekly income 2004–05 (GBP)	427	n.a.	260
United States of America			
% of children living in households below poverty level	8.6	22	43.8
% of children living in households receiving welfare assistance	10	21.9	42.2
% of children in owned housing	78.2	53.8	38.1
% of children in rented housing	21.8	46.2	61.9
Median 12-month family income 2006 for families with own children ($US)	72,948	35,884	23,008

Sources: Linacre, 2007; Statistics Canada, 2006; Department of Work and Pensions, 2008; Office for National Statistics, 2002; Burrows, 2003; US Census Bureau, 2000, 2007

wage, the stigma of race, rampant drug use, and the alienation and lack of hope in the community' (Paschal, 2006: 19–20). Non-resident fatherhood may therefore be a consequence as well as a cause of exclusion, and may contribute to a self-perpetuating cycle of disadvantage.

Our four countries show considerable consistency in their internal diversity. In each, differences in men's material circumstances have fundamental implications for how fathers approach parenting and the resources on which

Table 1.3 Overview of ethnic composition of national populations in the four countries

Australia		Canada		United Kingdom		United States of America	
	%		%		%		%
White	92	White	85	White	92	White	74
Asian	7	Total Asian	10	Asian	4	Black/African-American	12
Aboriginal	1	Black	3	Black	2	Asian	4
		Latin American	1	Chinese	0.4	American Indian	1
				Mixed	1	Hispanic/Latino	15

Sources: Australian Bureau of Statistics 2007, 2008b; CIA, *World Fact Book,* 2008; Office for National Statistics, 2001; US Census Bureau, 2007.

Notes:

Australia	Above data are for ethnicity. Self-reported ancestry is much more diverse: 37.1% report Australian, 31.6% English, 29.8% other European.
Canada	Above data are based on 'visible minority' groups, defined as 'non-Caucasian in race or non-white in colour'.
United Kingdom	'Asian' includes Asian or Asian British; 'Black' includes Black or Black British
United States of America	Hispanic/Latino are also counted in figures for the other groups, as Hispanic/Latino are identified as White, Black, Asian, etc.

Table 1.4a Fathers' residential status and ethnicity: fathers' residential status v. mothers' ethnicity, child age 9–10 months, Great Britain

	White	Indian, Pakistani and Bangladeshi	Black Caribbean	Black African	All GB total
Resident	84	93	49	59	84
Non-resident	16	7	51	41	16

Source: Dex and Ward, 2007

Table 1.4b Fathers' residential status and ethnicity: fathers' residential status by race and Hispanic origin for children aged 0–17, United States of America, 2007

	White (non-Hispanic)	Hispanic	Black (non-Hispanic)	All US
Resident	83	72	43	74
Non-resident	17	28	57	26

Source: US Census Bureau 2007

they can draw to do so. The next two sections examine this in the context of fathers' position in the labour market and the state.

Fathers in the labour market

The provider role has been the essence of fatherhood since time immemorial. Although much research attention has recently been directed at mothers' employment patterns (O'Brien and Shemilt, 2003; Gray and Tudball, 2003), fathers are still by far the most entrenched in the labour market. They are more likely than mothers to be employed, more likely to be the main earners, and even in dual-earner households, are likely to have by far the highest number of hours in paid work (e.g. Lewis, 2000; Australian Bureau of Statistics (ABS), 2008a). Any understanding of how men practise contemporary fatherhood must address the relationship that fathers now have with the labour market.

At the aggregate level fathers have relatively high work volumes. Aligia's (2005) analysis of employment patterns in the 25 EU member states in 2003 showed that fatherhood 'increased' employment levels for men, from 86 per cent for men who were not fathers to 91 per cent for those who were. On average fathers worked longer hours than childless men, and they also had significantly higher employment levels than mothers, whose labour market participation drops when they have children (from 75 per cent to 60 per cent; Aligia, 2005). These differences in labour market participation mean that men approach parenthood on a very different basis from women.

The labour market not only frames mothering and fathering differently: it is also a source of differentiation between fathers. Employment rates vary according to educational level, ethnicity and lone parenthood and are universally lower among fathers from the groups vulnerable to marginalisation. In the UK the biggest gap in employment levels is between white (90 per cent) and Asian or Asian British (76 per cent) fathers. The highest paternal employment rates are found amongst the highest qualified: employment is virtually universal among fathers with higher education qualifications (95 per cent) and those with a degree-level qualification (96 per cent), but drops to 71 per cent for fathers with no qualifications (Office for National Statistics, 2002).

It is well known that the relationship between parenthood and employment is very different for men and women: motherhood decreases labour market attachment while fatherhood increases it. Differences in employment patterns *between* groups of fathers are however almost as strong and these are likely to have both practical and psychological impacts. These are significant given the persistence of the breadwinner role for fathers and the emphasis given by the state to fathers' capacity to provide financially for their families.

Fathers in the state

The priority men accord paid work does not just reflect the predilections of individual men. It also reflects the nature of capitalist democracies in which labour markets and welfare regimes continue to define fathers primarily as earner-providers for their families. While relational approaches to gender negotiations within the home correctly emphasise the significance of agency, it is necessary to also recognise structural influences that shape the context within which this occurs and from which men's ideologies of fatherhood emerge.

Hobson (2002) and her colleagues have demonstrated the significance of social policy in defining fatherhood. They emphasise that fathering does not only occur within the home and family, and that men are not only constructed as fathers within the private sphere. They illustrate the significance of welfare regimes as contexts for fathering, and as influential at both an ideological and practical level. The ideological and practical dimensions interact, are mutually reinforcing, and are influential in shaping the boundaries of the social institutions they affect:

> Through laws and policies, all states indirectly or directly shape the different borders of fatherhood, fathering and father identities, and this varies over time as well as across societies. These include legal parameters that define who the father is and on what basis (the biological or the social/household father). Policy frameworks shape the kinds of choices men make as fathers and foster certain kinds of identities and interests. Public discourse creates hegemonic ideologies around fatherhood, which can be enabling or constraining for fathers.
>
> (Hobson, 2002: 14)

Legislation that defines the rights and responsibilities of fathers provides particularly tangible expressions of the definition of contemporary fathers. In westernised states this definition has historically been almost wholly based on the view of fathers as economic providers for their children (Hobson, 2002). This has been strengthened by the growth of single-parent mother-headed households and the concern of policy makers that fathers should contribute to the cost of rearing their children. Legislation that increases the pressure on fathers to pay for their children shows the extent to which fathers' responsibilities are defined, legally, in terms of financial support. In Britain the establishment of the Child Support Agency in 1991 to pursue non-resident parents emphasised financial responsibility of fathers who are unmarried, separated or divorced, defining the responsibilities of absentee fathers towards their children solely in economic terms rather than the father–child relationship (Lewis, 2000). In the United States, Orloff and Monson (2002) highlighted the virtual absence of programs targeting men *as fathers* within a welfare regime in which men are treated almost wholly as workers and employees. 'To the extent that men have family

households, they must earn the means to support them in the market'
(Orloff and Monson, 2002: 90).

Fathers' broader contribution to family life is beginning to be recognised
in policy (e.g. Lewis and Campbell, 2007) – what O'Brien describes as 'the
beginning of a "caring" rather than "economic" father norm emerging'
(O'Brien, 2005:1). Recent reconfigurations of welfare policy and family law
therefore reflect a broader view of the role fathers play in their children's
upbringing. Legal recognition of men's greater involvement in family life
does not however dispel the engrained belief that the essential role of fathers
is to provide financially for their children. No one can quickly overturn a
culture in which for so long men's identities have been inextricably bound up
with their occupations.

Fathers: diverse and divided

There are multiple tensions surrounding men's roles as fathers. Expectations
of 'involved' fathers have emerged at a time when fewer men are becoming
fathers and more are living separately from their children; however, a high
proportion of non-resident fathers maintain contact and many form new
households in which they again assume a fathering role. In the workplace
fathers appear as driven as previous generations to father *through* paid work,
seeing providing for their family as their first responsibility; however the
fulfilment of this role limits their time with their children. Fathers' position
in the state straddles the two, being defined partly in terms of financial
provider whilst also being subject to an increasing array of 'family-friendly'
policies which, in practice, few seem to be able to take up. The identities of
fatherhood are therefore multiple and not obviously compatible – and the
differences between men positioned differently in the social structure are
immense. To gain more insight into how men are negotiating these uncertain-
ties in varied contexts we now turn to an examination of fathering practices.

Fathering

Negotiating the fatherhood dilemma

Entry into fatherhood signifies a fundamental change for men. In Marsiglio's
(2004a) study of step-fathers, Jackson described the intense emotions
invoked when his child first called him 'daddy'. With that word came a host
of images about parental roles and responsibilities that had not been a part
of Jackson's everyday life:

> [I felt] very glad and warm to hear it, but there was a surprising bit of
> fright to it because I was realizing the responsibility that was coming with
> that. If he was going to place that name into my world, then I needed to
> meet up to that. Which actually did help, because it helped me to realize

a little bit more what I was accepting in my life, that I was moving into the world of parenting.

(Marsiglio, 2004: 32)

But what does moving into the world of parenting now mean for men? There has been an ideological shift in men's orientation towards parenthood: the ideal of the involved caring father has become culturally embedded and is creating new benchmarks by which fathers are judged (Dermott, 2008; O'Brien, 2005). As we have seen, however, traditional demands also persist. Before they negotiate their fatherhood identity and their practice of fathering, fathers must work out what is required of them in the first place. And when they do, some are much less well placed to respond than others.

A number of writers have conceptualised the challenge fathers face as competing demands between their emotional and financial contribution to their children – deciding whether to be a 'good provider' or 'active father' (Kaufmann and Uhlenberg, 2000), 'caring' or 'economic' (O'Brien), 'nurturing'/ 'involved'/'engaged' or 'breadwinning' (various). Studies of how fathers actually conduct their lives suggest that dichotomous provider-carer categories do not describe modern fatherhood properly: most men work *and* care, but vary in how successful they are at doing so (Centre for Research for Families and Relationships (CRFR), 2007). At one extreme 'super-dads' may be successful in both arenas: they have higher hourly pay yet also manage to spend time with their children. At the other, 'struggling dads' have difficulty in fulfilling the same role, as lower earning power generates less income, requires them to work longer hours, and limits the time they have available for their family (CRFR, 2007). A broad spectrum lies between them.

Fathers do not appear to reduce their work involvement to accommodate caring – on the contrary, the data reviewed earlier in this chapter shows that fathers have higher work volumes than childless men, not lower. Men appear to respond to the expectation that they should spend time with their children by adding this to their activities rather than trading it off. To understand why fathers retain such a high level of involvement in paid work we need to look more closely at how this relates to their ideas of fathering.

Fathering through work?

The provider role has a lengthy historical tradition as an essential of fathering and its importance persists. Most fathers continue to be the main earners in family households and young people more readily associate 'being a man' with 'having a job' than with 'being a good father' (Gillies, Ribbens McCarthy and Holland, 2001).

An extensive array of research has pinpointed the pivotal significance of paid work in men's ideologies of parenting, emphasising the centrality of the provider role as the *raison d'être* for fathers. Lewis (2000) found that paid work defined the fathering role for men and that other parenting activities were seen as additions to the central task of earning (Lewis, 2000). Fathers interviewed by Hatter, Vinter and Williams (2002) explained how their attachment to work had increased with the onset of parenthood: 'You have responsibilities now . . . You have to feed and clothe all of them. The job becomes a lot more important. It is not just for yourself, the money, it is for your whole family' (Hatter *et al.* 2002: 31).

Fathers view income earned from work as evidence of their responsibility towards their family and mothers and children share this expectation (Gillies *et al.*, 2001; Lewis, 2000). Fathers also attribute emotional significance to providing financially for children: men on low income who are unable to 'just buy things' for their children can feel this means that they cannot show their love for them. This suggests that men not only see paid work as the critical practical contribution of fatherhood, but also as a constituent of the emotional work of family life.

Phrases such as 'work–life' balance and 'work–family' balance place work in opposition to family life. Even terms such as 'parental leave' suggests that mothers and fathers leave work to parent. But this is not how fathers see paid work. To most men, employment is a central component of being a father – the essence of the role, rather than an extraneous activity that detracts from it. Providing for their family lies at the heart of men's identity as fathers and their practice of fatherhood. But the priority accorded work stands as an obstacle to meeting expectations of engaging with their children: 'the terms, conditions and expectations of paid employment stand as the greatest barrier to men's involvement' (Lewis, 2000: 4).

Involved fathering?

Fathers *are* spending more time with their children. In Britain, time budget studies show an upward trend since the 1970s in the time spent by fathers with their children (O'Brien and Shemilt, 2003). Gershuny's (2000) analysis of international data showed increased time in childcare by British fathers since the mid-1970s, with especially sharp increases since 1985 and among fathers of pre-school children. In absolute terms, the time fathers of children under the age of 5 were devoting to child-related activities rose from 15 minutes per day in the mid-1970s to 2 hours per day by the late 1990s (Gershuny, 2000; in O'Brien and Shemilt, 2003: 21). Australian fathers' care of children has also risen substantially, with a particular increase in time spent by fathers in 'sole charge' of children at home (Fatherhood Institute, 2008). In Canada, the gender gap in time spent with children is reducing: in the 1970s, fathers' time allocation to childcare represented 40 per cent of mothers' time; by the 1990s fathers' time had increased to 67 per cent. The picture is also similar in the United States, where married fathers have more than doubled their time spent exclusively on childcare activities from 2.6 hours per week in 1965 to 6.5 hours in 2000 (Bianchi, Robinson and Milkie, 2006). Yeung, Sandberg, David-Kean and Hofferth (2001) found that

American fathers in intact families are spending increasing amounts of time interacting directly with their children, particularly at weekends.

While methodological differences make it infeasible to make exact comparisons of father–child contact time across the four countries, some approximate figures can be given. The amount of contact recorded for employed, resident fathers is an average of 2 hours/day (including weekend days) in the UK; 73 minutes on weekdays in Australia; 1.4 hours (c. 84 minutes) on weekdays in Canada; and 1.2 hours (c. 72 minutes) on weekdays in the United States. Increases in the amount of time fathers spend directly with their children have not however been accompanied by a decrease in mothers' time with their children. In the UK, research consistently finds that women continue to spend two to three times as much time with children as men do (Craig, 2006): in Australia, mothers spend 186 minutes a day with their child compared to fathers' 73 minutes (ABS, 2008b); in Canada, the time fathers spend is only two-thirds of the time mothers spend; and in the United States mothers spend 2.2 hours compared to men's 1.4. The increases in father–child time have therefore been one element of a general increase in parenting time spent with children, a theme that Jay Coakley picks up in Chapter 3.

These data suggest we should temper our assumptions that men and women are now expressing egalitarian attitudes toward parenting (Bittman and Pixley 1997; Casper and Bianchi 2002; Gerson 2002). Although Craig (2006) suggests we are 'moving toward a social ideal of father as coparent' (2006: 261), mothers everywhere spend more time with children than fathers do, and fathers continue to have higher time investment in paid work than mothers do. Evans offers an appropriately restrained and nuanced account of the mixture of change and continuity in fathers' expectations:

> It is probably a mistake to think that fathers want to be surrogate moms. Modern, well-educated fathers may well want to experience the rich interpersonal relationships with their children that mothers have traditionally enjoyed but they want these interactions on their own terms . . . Most men still aspire to traditional patterns, and this is especially true of low socioeconomic status minority fathers.
>
> (Evans, 2004: xii)

Evans is one of a number of writers who emphasise that men's attitudes to fathering are contingent on their socio-cultural and economic position. Day and Lamb similarly have observed that 'men's ability and/or motivations to become and remain involved in family life, especially when children are involved, are often a function of economic conditions and cultural expectations' (Day and Lamb, 2004: 3). It is important to keep this in mind when considering the amount of time different types of fathers spend with their children. In Britain the Millennium Cohort Study examined how social class and ethnicity correlated with fathers' involvement with their children and identified a number of differences across ethnic groups (Dex and Ward, 2007). Around the time of their child's birth, more than 80 per cent of Black Caribbean and White fathers took leave but the majority of Bangladeshi fathers did not (50.3 per cent). As their child aged, only a minority of fathers (38.8 per cent) felt that they were able to spend 'enough time' with their child, but most Pakistani and Bangladeshi fathers felt they did (70 per cent), although they were typically spending no more time with their children than fathers from other groups.

Similar variations are very evident in the United States, where black fathers have been recorded as spending around 70 minutes less time with their children at weekends than whites fathers do (and Latino fathers around 60 minutes more). Parke *et al.* (2004) have shown however that, contrary to stereotypes, *when family situations are similar and appropriate statistical controls employed*, African American and Latino fathers probably monitor their children more than Euro-American fathers do rather than less (Parke *et al.*, 2004; Day and Lamb, 2004). When financial stability is difficult to achieve, however, fathers' involvement is constrained by the need to work despite any orientation to be highly involved in family life. Craig simply notes (2006) the more time a father has to care for his children, the more likely he is to do so (Cabrera and Tamis-LeMonda, 1999; in Craig, 2006).

Hatter, Vinter and Williams (2002) suggested that men's varied approaches to fathering could be categorised into four broad 'types', defined according to men's time involvement with their children, the activities they engaged in with them, and the role they adopted in these interactions:

- *Enforcer dads*, who had a very 'hands-off' role, spent limited time with their children, but took an overview of their lives and were responsible for discipline. They could be conceptualised as the 'macro-manager' of the household while the mother was the 'micro-manager', with day-to-day responsibility for the running of the home and family.
- *Entertainer dads*, who defined their involvement with their children mostly in terms of play and leisure activities, and might 'distract' the children while their mother completed domestic tasks. Much of the 'entertainer' dad's time with his children took place at the weekend.
- *Useful dads*, who took more responsibility for household and childcare tasks, but tended to take their lead in this from the mother and defined their role as a 'helper' on the domestic front. These fathers' roles were 'supportive' rather than sharing, and involved less responsibility than mothers for day-to-day management of the home and family. These fathers, too, tended to spend most of their time with their children at weekends.
- *Fully involved dads*, who were equally involved as their partners in running the family and took the lead in childcare for substantial parts of the week. They tended to see fatherhood as a full-time commitment and when necessary arranged workplace commitments to accommodate this.

These tended to happen more irregularly and less frequently, however, than for working mothers (Hatter *et al.* 2002: 14–20).

Hatter *et al.*'s categorisation is by no means definitive but it serves as a useful device for alerting us to the different approaches that fathers may bring to their parenting. While on the one hand the range of tasks fathers undertake is growing and fathers have been found to be as capable as mothers of nurturing interactions with their children (Cabrera, Tamis-LeMonda, Lamb and Boller, 1999; Lamb, 1997; Yeung *et al.*, 2001), men vary in how much they wish to embrace this. These differences in how fathers parent are not just the outcome of structural factors, but are also the product of experiences and interactions at the micro-level.

Before they become fathers themselves, men's most direct and sustained experience of fatherhood has usually been with their own father. How men have been fathered is an important influence on how they in turn try to parent: some will seek to reproduce their fathers' style of parenting while others will actively strive to parent differently. In his reflective account *My Father Before Me*, psychoanalyst and clinical psychologist Michael Diamond (2007) examined how fathers and sons influence each other throughout their lives. He recalled his own experience as a teenager, when he felt too old to have his father attending his baseball games and asked him to stay away. His father felt otherwise and continued to come to matches – albeit in secrecy, watching the game hidden behind a hedge and peering through a gap. The deception was duly uncovered, and Diamond recalled being angered by his father's actions, yet also privately pleased by his attention and interest. It was only when he became a father himself however that he fully appreciated his father's skill in accommodating his contradictory adolescent needs by maintaining 'his fatherly presence'. This in turn inspired Diamond 'to provide the same sort of a model for my own son' (Diamond, 2007: 5).

The relationship which is most likely to be significant for men's parenting is, however, the one they have with their children's mother. Whether parents are in a relationship that is harmonious or hostile, whether they live together or apart, mothers exercise major influence on how men approach the parenting of their joint children. Marsiglio alludes to the importance of mothers in his description of the three trajectories of fathering as 'self-as-father, father-child, and *co-parental*' (Marsiglio, 2004b: 62; my italics). Mothers act as gatekeepers: they set the parameters of parenting, so that men's parenting is constructed in response to how women define the collective parenting enterprise and their own mothering. Pleck and Stueve (2004) have thrown light on this by investigating the degree of 'conjointness' in a mother's or father's parenting identity – i.e. 'the balance between self-as-solo-parent and self-as-coparent' (2004: 83). They found that fathers construct their parental identities within the context of coparental relationships much more than mothers do. When Andrea Doucet asked the question, 'Do men mother?' she too encountered the control that mothers had over the collective parenting enterprise. Her research identified a strong gender sensibility among men, of mothers occupying the primary territory of parenting into which fathers sometimes made incursions – 'oh wow, I get to try this' (2006: 128). Her description of parenting as a 'mother-led dance' captures the dynamics of the situation particularly well.

There is variation in the role fathers wish to take as parents, and also in the circumstances in which they do so. This translates into variation in the time fathers spend with their children and the activities they undertake when they are with them. Evidence such as Doucet's (2006) suggests that in comparison to mothers, many fathers perceive themselves as being secondary, in both importance and competence, where caring activities for their offspring are involved. Engagement through sport and leisure allows men to create their own area of activity with their children.

Fathering through sport and leisure?

How do sport and leisure sit within contemporary fathering? What role do they play? And while we have strong expectations of parents' responsibility for many aspects of their children's development, why should we extend our concerns to the playful, not-so-serious activities of sport and leisure? There are surely more important issues to address – whether parents safeguard their children's safety and physical well-being; whether they instil good practices such as active lifestyles and healthy eating habits; whether they foster their child's educational attainment and nurture their expectations and aspirations; whether they support and guide their children to good citizenship. Why be concerned with the frivolity of sport and leisure?

Leisure studies researchers have some very good answers to this question. Their lengthy tradition of research into families locates leisure at the centre of family relationships. At weekends, on holidays, through shared fun activities at other times, parents actively seek to spend time together 'as a family' precisely because this is what it means to 'be' a family. The idea that families (should) enjoy time together, and that in doing so (should) sustain productive family relationships, is compelling. The uninspiring jingle, 'the family that plays together stays together', retains its currency because it captures such a widely held aspiration.

The association of 'family' with shared 'leisure' is therefore a familiar message in everyday life and a consistent theme in leisure research. Sport and leisure research has not however thrown much light on fathering. Yet the evidence is that fathers who live with their children are expected to spend more time with them than ever before, and are doing this more through leisurely activities than caring ones; and fathers who live apart from their children are even more reliant on sharing leisure with their children to engender the positive experiences needed to sustain a potentially vulnerable relationship. A focus on fathers, sport and leisure addresses practices that lie at the heart of contemporary fathering.

2 'Until the ball glows in the twilight'

Fatherhood, baseball, and the game of playing catch

Ralph LaRossa

> Baseball is fathers and sons playing catch, lazy and murderous, wild and controlled, the profound archaic song of birth, growth, age, and death.
>
> Donald Hall (1985)

It has been said, 'Whoever wants to know the heart and mind of America had better learn baseball' (Barzun 1954). It may also be said that whoever wants to know the heart and mind of American fatherhood – the pattern of meanings associated with fatherhood – had best be familiar with the symbolism connected to a father teaching a child how to catch and throw a ball. In certain segments of the population, the game of playing catch not only is indispensable to learning the fundamentals of baseball, but also is instrumental to being defined as a caring dad (Rosenblatt 1998; McCormack 1999–2000).

How did baseball and the game of playing catch come to be associated with fatherhood? Drawing on a range of written and iconographic texts (e.g., newspaper and magazine articles, books, cartoons, films), I document the historical link between the institution of baseball (America's 'national pastime') and a fleeting but important component of father–child interaction. Focusing on the question of who, where, when, how, and why (as in, '*who* plays the game?' and '*where* does the game take place?'), I show how ecological contexts (backyards and sunsets) and gender-specific meanings (definitions of fatherhood and athleticism) have transposed a seemingly mundane activity into a sacred and memorable moment; and how the moment itself is constructed through a combination of talk (or silence) and geometry (distance between the players). Ultimately I aim to demonstrate, via the game of playing catch, how physical and social realities are intertwined.[1]

Baseball and fatherhood

As one observer put it, 'Chances are good that if you're a baseball fan, your dad had something to do with it – and your thoughts of the sport evoke thoughts of him' (Anonymous 2001). Baseball, however, was not always a part of America's social landscape; nor was it always central to fatherhood. How, then, did it become so?

Who invented baseball is open to debate, but lore has it that the sport was a variation of the English game of rounders and that it first became popular in the 1800s (Litsky 2004; Pennington 2004; Steele 1904). In its infancy, baseball was mainly the province of the upper middle class, but by the late 1800s, it had spread to the working class. Contributing to the diffusion was (1) the arrival of large urban parks or fields (rural havens in the city; Barth 1980); (2) the growing preoccupation with health and exercise (America went 'sports crazy'; Dubbert 1979, 175); and (3) the increasing belief that sport was an effective response to America's turn-of-the-century 'crisis of masculinity' (sport was a 'place where manhood was earned'; Adelman 1986, 286) (Kimmel 1990).[2]

Thirteen major league fields were built or reconstructed between 1909 and 1915 (Bluthardt 1987), and the presence of major league ballparks in populated areas helped make professional ballplayers objects of admiration and emulation. Children were afforded opportunities to see baseball skillfully played; and fathers, more often than not, were the ones who took their kids to their 'first game' – a phrase that, technically, can refer to any baseball contest seen for the first time, even if played on a sandlot, but that symbolically has come to be defined almost exclusively as a child's first visit to a major league venue.

Looking for early references to baseball and fatherhood, I examined over three hundred popular magazine articles published between 1900 and 1960, which were categorized under the heading of 'fatherhood,' 'fathers,' or 'father-child relationships' in the *Reader's Guide to Periodical Literature*.[3] If popular magazine articles are any indication, commercial media accounts of fathers taking their kids to a ballgame or teaching them how to play baseball were rare in the early twentieth century. The first article that I discovered was published in *The Outlook* in 1914. A father reported that he had escorted his eleven-year-old son to a baseball game every afternoon the previous summer, in an effort 'to take seriously the business of being a companion to the boy.' He said that he had bought a baseball glove for himself, so that he and his son could play. 'I mean to be closer to him in the next ten years than any other companion – to be a bigger influence in his life than any of the influences that are outside our control. He's going to be a better man than I am, if I can make him so' (Barton 1914). Eight years later, a father writing in *American Magazine* declared that if he did not help his ten-year-old son 'grow up right,' he would consider himself a 'failure,' no matter how much money he made or how big a reputation he achieved. So when his son asked him to play catch ('Dad, come on and peg me a few'), he immediately interrupted what he was doing and went outside. 'Is that the swiftest you can throw,' the boy asked. 'Do you want them faster?' the father replied. 'Sure, burn 'em in,' the boy answered.

Now I thought I knew that boy. I fancied I could tell anyone all about him. Yet it had been almost a year since I had tossed a baseball to him . . . To my surprise he could handle his mitt with ease and grace. He was not afraid of the ball and he caught what little speed I have left without flinching.

(Guest 1922)

And in 1923, in *Ladies Home Journal*, a father talked about how he and his two sons would drive into Boston to see the Red Sox or Braves play and that 'for a time baseball would absorb [them].' He also mentioned precisely how he played with his children. 'I used to lay down a glove to represent second base, station the boys on either side as shortstop and second baseman, and bat or throw . . . leaving it to them to make the instant decision who would go for the ball and who would cover . . . [the base]' (Merwin 1923).

The four-decade span of the 1920s to the 1950s generally is known as baseball's 'golden years.' Radio and later television began to broadcast the games, and arenas grew even larger. (Some 74,200 fans were in attendance when Yankee Stadium opened in 1923; Yankee Stadium History, n.d.) Prior to the 1920s, baseball was mainly a game of singles and doubles, batted balls that would advance base runners and add to a team's score. While this strategy continued to be important, the interwar years marked the glorification of the home run, wherein a ball would be hit over an outfield fence. The changing social meaning of the 'long ball' not only altered how kids viewed the physical world of baseball but also reconceptualized their own performances on and off the field. 'Swinging for the fences' became a prized strategy in the sport as well as an aphorism for striving for success in life.

From 1932 to 1937, *Parents* magazine ran a series of monthly articles under the banner 'For fathers only.' Curiously, only two articles mentioned baseball. The first, published in 1932, talked about the importance of positive reinforcement, using the game of catch to illustrate the point: 'A father who has been doing a little quiet research concludes that when parents adopt the "do" attitude, few "don'ts" are necessary . . . "Don't be afraid of the baseball" can be translated into "Do show me how well you can catch" ' (Motherwell 1932). The second, published in 1933, offered the observation, 'It is frequently only when a son becomes interested in baseball that a father begins to see a chance for companionship with his boy.' The article went on to offer advice on how to teach a child who was just learning the game.

If a father tries to get his son interested in baseball, he must be prepared to maintain poise and gentleness in the face of the boy's acting babyish, crying and complaining about a hurt finger, placing himself in a ridiculous position by making silly faces and gestures as he misses catch after catch, or slamming down his glove and sulking because of errors.

(Rademacher 1933)

After Pearl Harbor and America's entrance in World War II, the question arose as to whether baseball should be temporarily suspended. The commissioner of baseball wrote to President Roosevelt to seek his advice. The president 'responded the next day with what has become known as "the green light letter," offering . . . his personal opinion that baseball should continue.' Roosevelt felt that 'the benefits of the game would provide a much-needed morale boost to those on the home front and to American service personnel overseas' (Percoco 1992). As the war progressed, a number of professional baseball players were drafted into the armed forces but were replaced by others eager to play. It was during this time also that the All-American Girls Professional Baseball League was formed. The historical significance of the 'Girls' league is that it gave women the opportunity to play baseball professionally. Although fans initially seemed to enjoy the women's competitions, interest waned after the war ended. The league was disbanded in 1954 (Peterik 1995).

Little League Baseball, founded in 1939, expanded during the war, as well (Little League Online, n.d.). Although organized youth leagues existed in the 1920s and 1930s, none of them equaled Little League in popularity. (The leagues were thought to be an effective antidote to juvenile delinquency; Hurley 1935; Speaker 1939.) The growth of Little League put more pressure on children to learn the sport and more demands on fathers to instruct their kids in the intricacies of the game (Fine 1987).

Since the 1960s, baseball has become an even larger and more complex entertainment industry. Whereas before, professional teams were located mainly in the industrial North and the Midwest, major (and minor) league baseball now is played in cities and towns throughout the United States and Canada. Baseball also has taken hold in other areas of the world, especially in Japan and Latin America. Video games, sports television networks, and the further expansion and bureaucratization of youth baseball now encourage children to both learn and consume the game. (Profits on the sale of baseball paraphernalia are considerable.) Although baseball continues to be a game played by boys and men *for* boys and men, it is increasingly common for girls to play youth ball, and some women have played high school or college ball, on the same team as their male classmates.[4]

At the same time that baseball has grown, its share of the sports pie has shrunk. Over the past forty years, major league baseball has had to contend with the mounting popularity of other sports (Mandelbaum 2004). For example, fathers, who grew up in the 1950s and 1960s loving and playing baseball, have had children who enjoyed playing other sports more. Looking forward to the day they would play catch with their kids (as their own fathers did or did not do with them), men raised in the postwar era often have discovered that their sons and daughters would just as soon practice the deft footwork that soccer requires – a skill that the men may not have learned and thus cannot teach.[5]

The game of playing catch

A baseball enthusiast once remarked that although playing catch is called a game, 'there is really no game to it' because 'nobody wins or loses' (Rosenblatt 1998). The fact is, however, that while playing catch may not be a game in a conventional sense, it *is* a game, in a sociological sense, because the social institution of baseball penetrates the heart of the activity. So does the institution of fatherhood. Thus it can be said that the community of baseball and fatherhood 'exercises control over the conduct of its individual members' (Mead 1934, 155). To put it another way, 'America surfaces in a ball park' (Geertz 1973, 417) – and sometimes in a backyard.

What is the social nature of the game of catch? To answer this question, I initiated a series of bibliographic and Internet searches to find as many references to playing catch as I could. (I also had kept a file on the subject for several years.) Relying on these texts, I endeavored to dissect the game. I was interested in five basic questions: *Who* plays catch, and *where*, *when*, *how*, and *why* is the game played?

Who

Although nothing prevents several players from forming a circle and tossing around a ball, in the texts that I reviewed, playing catch almost always was described as a two-person game. What seems to make the game special – and memorable – is the opportunity the game affords to have private time, not just with 'any other,' but with a 'significant other.' Structurally and experientially, playing catch is a to-and-fro dance – a pas de deux, prized for its intimacy ('just you and me').

The fact that playing catch often involves two people who are at different skill levels is important, too. The game can be dangerous and does demand concentration. The adult must be careful not to throw too fast, so as not to hurt and/or embarrass the child. The child, especially if new to the game, must remember how to hold the glove to avoid getting hit in the face. As players get older, however, skill levels may reverse. One of my children, for example, is now a better fielder than I ever was, and the velocity of my 'fast ball' diminishes with each passing year.

Playing catch also is generally talked about as a game between fathers and sons. However, recent texts have included references to fathers and daughters, as well as to mothers and sons.[6] A daughter exclaimed, 'My dad is way, way cool . . . He taught me to believe in myself and be fair. He taught me how to throw a baseball' ('My dad is way, way cool,' 2003).[7] A son reported, 'I played catch with my father, of course, but also with my mother. She would borrow my father's big glove late on a summer's weekend afternoon' (Lichtenberg 1993). (Note the 'of course,' when the son talked about playing with his father.) A man spoke of the special relationship he had with his two girls, both of whom played softball: 'I've been doing it [playing catch] for over twenty-five years with my daughters. It binds us together, connects generations, widens our appreciation of some of the old-fashioned virtues of America just as much as boys with their fathers.' He also reminisced, 'Almost every day, when I would come home from work, one or the other, or both, would say "come on, Dad, let's play catch." It was our special time together. "We can do it," they seemed to be saying, "we can do it just like boys; we're no wimps" ' (Commins 2001).

Where

Not every recent reference to playing catch happened to mention where the activity took place. But of the cases in which location was identified, it was a yard or, more specifically, a *backyard* that was mentioned most of the time.

Notably, the yard as a location to toss a ball (or bat it) was not talked about much in the pre-World War II articles that I reviewed. I did find several postwar articles that included pictures of fathers and children playing ball, but the texts rarely specified where they were playing. One that did was a 1952 article in *Woman's Home Companion*. It had a photo of a father pitching a ball to his son in a yard in what appears to be the back of a house ('Today's Father,' 1952). A 1950 *Snookums* comic strip, published in the *Atlanta Journal and Constitution*, depicted a father taking his toddler son 'out in the yard' (far enough away not to 'break any windows'), hoping to 'get him interested in baseball.' And a *Sparks* strip, published in 1956 in the *Chicago Defender* (an African American newspaper) portrayed a father and son playing catch in an open, but indeterminate area. ('I wanna see how ya like this new fast ball I've developed . . . Daddy!' 'Okay! Let 'er fly!')

Recently published texts included more references to playing in a backyard. As some saw it, the game was something that *naturally* took place there: 'It's an American ritual for a father and son to grab a ball and glove and go out in the backyard to play catch' (Ward 2003). In one case, when both a yard and playground were mentioned, it was the backyard game that was the better remembered of the two: 'Many professional ballplayers . . . have come and gone since the days in the mid-1950s when my father and I played ball in our backyard or at Mohawk school across the street from our house . . . Dad is 82 and I just turned 56, so obviously it has been many, many years since we played pitch-and-catch *in our backyard*' (Hart 2002, emphasis added).

Where a game of catch happens to occur is significant. The availability of a backyard increases the likelihood that fathers will be engaged in the activity, since it does not take much effort to walk out the door to play. Playing catch in the backyard is, as one author put it, 'an easy thing to do – you don't need to have access to something like a basketball hoop and you don't have to strap on a ton of gear' (Codding 2002). A backyard also can make it more difficult for a father to deny a child's request. In the popular song about generational alienation, 'Cat's in the Cradle,' a son's appeal to his father

('Thanks for the ball, Dad, come on let's play'), is heart-rending because we assume that the boy simply is asking his father to step outside. The father's reply ('Not today, I got a lot to do') comes across as insensitive, because playing catch does not seem to be too much to ask. (After all, a few days earlier the son had been given a ball on his tenth birthday.) The father's refusal to make room for his son ultimately comes full circle when, later in life, his son refuses to make room for him ('I'd love to see you [son] if you don't mind.' He said, 'I'd love to, Dad, if I could find the time') (Chapin and Chapin 1974).

An ecological variable that may have contributed to the popularity of the game of catch was post-World War II suburbanization. The backyards of suburban homes were marketed as family-friendly areas, perfect for weekend barbecues and evenings of tossing a ball around. Suburban spaces also were designed to be safe places to play. In *Fathers Playing Catch with Sons*, the poet Donald Hall recalled playing catch with his father in the 1930s and 1940s, but he spoke about doing so near a busy street.

> [At first] I threw straight. Then I tried to put something on it; it flew twenty feet over his head. Or it banged into the sidewalk in front of him, breaking stitches [on the ball] and ricocheting off a pebble into the gutter of Greenway Street. Or it went wide to his right and lost itself in Mrs. Davis's bushes. Or it went wide to his left and rolled across the street while drivers swerved their cars.
>
> (Hall 1985, 28)[8]

Hall and his father were playing in traffic (literally), where a misthrown ball could put a child or father in serious danger. Suburban yards eliminated, or at least minimized, these risks.

Needless to say, not everyone can live in suburbia – or wants to. Fathers who reside in the city either by choice or circumstance, and who desire to play catch, may have to dodge cars, much like Hall's father was forced to do. Or they may invest more energy and time trying to find a safe place to play (e.g., walking or driving to a nearby park). Separated or divorced suburban dads, living in an apartment that does not have a yard, may discover that extemporaneous games of catch are not as easy to arrange as they once were.

Where family members engage in sports activities also is connected to spatial and temporal privacy. A backyard large enough to throw a baseball back and forth affords the players a space where they can interact without necessarily being observed. A child learning the intricacies of baseball thus may take solace in the fact that his or her mistakes are not open to scrutiny. Equally if not more important, the quality of a Little Leaguer's performance under the watchful eyes of his or her teammates may hinge on the opportunity he or she has to practice in what may be called a backstage region (Goffman 1959). A backyard also provides a measure of temporal privacy, because it reduces the likelihood that others will interrupt the game (Zerubavel 1981).

Locked in a temporal bubble, a parent and child can more easily manufacture 'quality time,' in which the sport itself becomes subordinate to the emotions engendered between the players.

When

Assuming a place to play can be found, throwing and catching a baseball can occur whenever people can get together. Two other factors, however, impinge on whether or not a game is played. The first is visibility. Without artificial illumination, playing catch is an activity that can happen only in daylight or lowlight (e.g., twilight). The second factor is the set of commitments that a parent and child might have. For a father, there is work; for a child, there may be school. These commitments often relegate playing catch to weeknights and weekends, but even this schedule assumes that the father is working from 9:00 in the morning to 5:00 in the late afternoon and has Saturday and Sunday off. (A father who works evenings and/or nights, and/or weekends, or is a stay-at-home dad, operates within different temporal constraints.)

Despite the number of possible permutations, playing catch typically was described in the texts that I reviewed as an activity that occurred not so much on the weekend as toward the end of the day, after the father had come home from work.

> It is almost evening, and I have just settled into my spot on the couch. I want nothing more than to slip off my shoes and be totally, blissfully idle.
>
> Suddenly my baseball mitt comes flying from behind and lands in my lap. 'Wanna play catch?' It's Dash, my ten-year-old son, the boy never seen without his baseball cap, the boy who sleeps with his mitt.
>
> 'It's almost dark,' I tell him. 'And I'm worn out.'
>
> He doesn't say anything, just gives me the look that says: SOMEDAY WHEN YOU ARE OLD AND I AM GROWN, YOU'RE GOING TO REGRET EACH DAY YOU DIDN'T PLAY CATCH WHEN I ASKED YOU.
>
> I put on my shoes. 'Grab a ball.'
>
> 'Already got one.' He grins and flips it to me.
>
> And the arc is renewed. The ball. The toss. Fathers playing catch with their sons.
>
> (Morris n.d.)

What is intriguing is the length of time referred to in the above excerpt. The father indicated that it was almost dark when his son asked him to play, which meant that they did not play for all that long. Later on in the article, the father talked about playing catch with his own father. He and his dad would go 'out back beyond the orange trees' and 'spend hours and hours just tossing the ball back and forth' (Morris n.d.). The fifty-six-year-old author (cited earlier), who reminisced about playing 'pitch-and-catch' with his father, also spoke of 'the hours' that they spent together 'after a long hard day at work' (Hart 2002). And another writer spoke affectionately of fathers and sons playing catch 'until the ball glows in the twilight' – a phrase that implied playing after the sun went down and suggested, too, a sacred quality to the act (Cozine 2003).

The chronological dynamics in playing-catch discourse is revealing of how the game is contemplated. The symbolism conveyed is that when fathers and children play catch, time becomes irrelevant. The moment is all there is.

How long fathers and children *actually* play catch is harder to decipher. If playing catch requires a certain degree of natural light, and if indeed the game can be played in twilight, how much time is there at the end of the day to play? The answer is a matter of both history and geography.

The father who recalled playing catch with his dad in the mid-1950s said that he grew up in Scotia, New York, which is just north of Schenectady. According to the U.S. Naval Observatory, sunset was at 7:38 and twilight ended at 8:13 on July 1, 1955, in Scotia. If we assume that the father worked from 9:00 to 5:00 and would get home by 5:45, that would leave approximately two hours of direct sunlight and about a half hour of twilight to engage in an outside game. The author spoke of 'the hours' that he and his father spent together playing ball at the end of the day. If indeed that were the case, the two would have had to begin playing as soon as the father got home and continue playing until just about dark. Dinner would have had to wait. This very well may have been the family's pattern. Then again, it may not. It could be that most games of catch in the 1950s lasted no more than forty-five minutes, maybe an hour, but that because the time devoted to playing was limited, the activity itself became more precious in the child's mind and also more memorable. It is possible, as well, that the wistfully recollected 'hours' of postwar fathers and sons playing catch is more emblematic of what baby boomers wanted, but rarely received.

The situation, however, is not the same today. In 1966, the Uniform Time Act was passed and signed into law. This act was an attempt to establish one pattern of Daylight Saving Time from April to October across the country. Up until then, daylight saving time was based on local laws and customs. (There are communities that, by state law, are exempt from DST, but they are few.) (Daylight Saving Time n.d.). On July 1, 1966, in Scotia, sunset and the 'end of civil twilight' were at 7:38 and 8:13, respectively, precisely when they were in 1955. But on July 1, 1967, both occurred *one hour later*, at 8:38 and 9:13. Thus after the Uniform Time Act was enacted, there was more daylight at the end of the day in the spring and summer and early fall (the baseball season) for families to play outdoors. Because of the implementation of daylight saving time, a father and child playing catch may have become more common in the *immediate* wake of the change.[9] As for comparisons between now and twenty or thirty years ago, the longer commutes between work and home and the overall 'frenzied temporal climate' (Daly 1996) may mean that contemporary fathers are playing catch less often with their children than their fathers played with them. In other words, the historical pattern, with regard to the frequency of the game, may be curvilinear (i.e., first a rise, then a decline).

Sunlight patterns also vary by latitude and longitude, creating different opportunities for playing outside in the evening. In midsummer, the sun sets in Boston at 8:25, in Atlanta at 8:52, in San Francisco at 8:36, and in Los Angeles, at 8:09 (USNO times for July 1, 2004). Thus, in general, fathers in Boston may play catch less often, and for shorter periods of time, than fathers in Atlanta; and fathers in Los Angeles may play less often, and for shorter periods of time, than fathers in San Francisco.

How

How to play catch is influenced, to some extent, by the amount of space available to the players and by the rules of baseball. A small yard or the presence of trees may limit 'pop-ups,' balls thrown high in the air by one player and caught on the way down by the other player, while a yard with shrubbery in the middle may limit 'grounders,' balls skipped across the grass or dirt. Needless to say, trees and shrubs, as well as other obstacles, may be cut down or eliminated to 'make room' for the game, which raises the question of how often fathers build or craft physical sanctuaries to facilitate play. In the tongue-in-cheek book, *How to Dad*, the point is made, 'Playing Catch with the Old Man involves more than merely tossing a ball back and forth . . . It is a ritual that connects one generation to the next and should make you feel compelled to build a lighted domed stadium in your backyard' (Boswell and Barrett 1990, 16). While building a baseball park is well beyond the reach of the average father, we certainly can envision the space around a home being modified to accommodate one sport or another. I recall cutting the grass in our backyard more frequently when our sons were young to make the terrain more suitable for our ball games.

It is not unusual, when playing catch, for fathers and children to pretend they are pitching to a batter, in which case they may mark off the official distance between the 'pitching rubber' (with which a pitcher's foot must always be in contact) and 'home plate' (behind which the catcher crouches). In Little League, the distance between the pitching rubber and home plate is 46 feet. In high school, college, and major league baseball, it is 60.5 feet. While a backyard may be available, it may not be large enough to accommodate throwing across these distances. If it is not, players may still 'pitch' to each other, but they will do so under artificial spatial conditions. (Imagine having a basketball hoop in one's driveway, but at lower than regulation height.)

The geometry of the game of playing catch is less contingent on institutional rules. The game can involve nothing more than repeatedly throwing and catching a baseball, with the players standing 20–30 feet apart. As the game ebbs and flows, the distance between the players will expand or contract, depending on how they feel at the moment (how much they are *in* the moment). In this scenario, it is the relationship between the players that determines the game's spatial parameters, rather than vice versa. For some who have played catch, this is the game they remember most and the game that captures best the game's aesthetics: 'We fell into the timeless pace of throw and catch and throw and catch: we found the timeless place of playing catch' (Littlefield 2002).

Clearly how people play is linked to the *meanings* they attach to the activity. Take, for example, whether players should talk to each other. According to one view, playing catch is optimal when quiet prevails.

> The best part of the game is the silence . . . Once I happened to be on the field of Yankee Stadium before game time when the players were warming up . . . Every easy toss was delivered at a speed greater than a good high school fastball pitcher could generate. *Thwack, thwack, thwack* in the leather. And the silence between the men on the field. It was interesting to note that even at their level, this was still a game of catch. We do what we can as parents, one child at a time . . . The trick, I think, is to recognize the moments when nothing needs to be said.
>
> (Rosenblatt 1998)

To others, however, talk is essential to the game. A writer who grew up playing catch with his father and his mother argued that conversation between a parent and child is crucial – *but not just any conversation.*

> My mother had nothing to teach me about the techniques of baseball. I threw the ball to her, she threw it back to me. Her chat was observation, not praise or prescription. My father called: 'Nice grab!' or 'Two hands!' or 'Keep your eye on it!' She'd say, 'That was a high one.' I had to ask her to throw me grounders and explain to her what they were. 'You know, grounders. On the ground. Like a ground ball. *Grounders.*' My mother smiled at me, half apologetic, half amused. I could hear as I talked baseball to her that, like her, I was new at this, not eloquent and authoritative like my father. I couldn't make every detail of skill and strategy seem like an absolute truth. As I explained to her a bit of what I'd recently learned from him, I could hear something a boy might otherwise miss: *baseball was strange.* Why would an intelligent person engaged in throwing a ball back and forth want the ball aimed at the ground? . . . What she threw me wasn't the official Dad stuff, but it was fine on its own terms . . . For boys and their fathers, baseball follows an established progression, from instructional games to catch to stickball or Little League, then school teams with fatherlike coaches, and finally employment, with 'team players' and 'hardball,' whether literal or figurative. But my mother and I had only a pickup game she offered to invent with me as we went along . . . Catch for me was preparation. My father was keeping in practice for the pickup softball games he loved. But

my mother never played softball. When my father threw with me it was as if to say, *This is how we do what we do.* Not with my mother. Our 'we' was not yet defined. She was not saying, *This is what we do.* She was saying: *Don't leave. We'll figure something out.*

(Lichtenberg 1993, 28–29)

Another man, recalling his relationship with his dad, said, 'As I grew older and more distant (the way sons too often become with their fathers), playing catch was sometimes the only way we could talk. Or try. The turf between us seemed wider than ever, our only connection the path of a ball' (Morris n.d.).

If every act of verbal and nonverbal interaction ultimately says, 'This is how I see myself . . . this is how I see you . . . this is how I see you seeing me,' and so forth (Watzlawick, Beavin, and Jackson 1967, 52), then the game of playing catch has as much to do with interpersonal relations as any other form of communication might have. The silence and the talk are ingredients in the mix, defining who we are, and would like to be.

Why

It is interesting that the game of catch is called 'catch,' when the game entails not only catching but also throwing. For many, in fact, learning how to throw the ball is the most difficult part of the game.

With arrival of youth baseball leagues, teaching children how to throw the 'right way' became a key reason to play catch. A boy who threw without the proper arm motion or, worse, 'threw like a girl' could be the object of ridicule, both on the field and off.[10] A father could be taken to task, as well. ('What kind of father would not teach his son how to throw?') A man who knew how to 'correct' his son's throwing, on the other hand, could be a hero. Said one author, recalling his youth:

> I'm 8 years old and I'm playing Little League Baseball for the first time and my dad's the coach! It's my first tryout/practice and it's an exciting, confusing, scary affair, with what seems like hundreds of boys . . . Later at home, my father informs me that there are two boys on the team who throw like girls, and that I, unfortunately, am one of them! By the next practice, he tells me, we will have corrected that problem. That evening, with glove and cap securely in place, I anxiously face my father on the front lawn. And we play catch. For quite a while, I am concentrating, working hard to throw correctly ('like a *man*'), pulling my arm back as far as I can and snapping the ball overhand, just past my ear. When I do this, it feels very strange – I really have very little control over the flight of the ball, and it hurts my shoulder a bit – but I am rewarded with the knowledge that *this is how men throw the ball.* If I learn this, I won't embarrass either myself or my father.

(Messner 1995, 46–47)

The professional baseball player Harmon Killebrew once talked about how he and his brother would play ball with their father and how his mother would admonish them for tearing up the lawn. Killebrew's dad reportedly would reply, 'We're not raising grass. We're raising boys' (cited in Kennedy 2003, 3D). In some people's minds, the whys and wherefores of playing catch have less to do with baseball than with gender and masculinity. Through the game, boys are shown 'how men throw' (i.e., how 'real' men *behave*).

Rationales for playing catch have not been constant, however. If we take a historical look at the texts, we can discern a shift. In the early twentieth century, a common justification for playing catch was that playing with a child would help a father to get to know that child. Playing catch thus was placed in the same category as playing marbles or playing hide-and-seek. ('To know a boy you must play with him'; Guest 1922.) Then, in the mid-twentieth century, as more children got involved in organized youth sports, playing catch became an instructional activity. Learning how to throw and catch 'correctly' grew in importance. (Recalling what it was like to grow up in the 1950s, a former Little Leaguer said, 'I was lucky to have a dad who cared enough to teach me the basics'; Hart 2002.) In the late twentieth century, the meaning of playing catch appears to have taken yet a different turn. The game is still about play and instruction, but also it has been transformed, at least for some, into a celebration of fatherhood (e.g., 'There's something about a father playing catch with his son that is just so pure, so iconic, so American'; Kennedy 2003). Playing catch, in addition, may now be perceived to be about *multiple* generations of fathers and sons, and through a process of temporal extension, the game has been reified; for example, 'I played catch in the backyard with my dad, as kids have done and dads have done *since baseball first arrived*' (Littlefield 2002, emphasis added); '*for 100 years and more now*, fathers have been playing catch with sons' (Codding 2002, emphasis added).

Hollywood also has embraced this theme. Perhaps the best example is the 1989 film, *Field of Dreams*. The film's story is about a man who lives with his family on an Iowa farm about to go bankrupt and who repeatedly hears a voice telling him, 'If you build it, he will come.' He interprets the message to mean that he should build a ballpark in his cornfield, which he does. (Anything is possible in fiction. By the way, few fatherhood and baseball films merge the physical and the social as well as *Field of Dreams* does.) Eventually the 1919 Chicago White Sox show up to play. This is an infamous team that included several members who were charged with deliberately losing that year's World Championship. Many baseball fans, however, feel that at least one of the players, 'Shoeless' Joe Jackson, was wrongly accused. The 'he' who 'will come,' however, turns out to be neither Jackson nor any other public figure, but the main character's dad. (An underlying premise is that the farmer and his dad were estranged.) When the father shows up on the 'field of dreams,' the son meekly asks, 'Hey, Dad, you wanna have a catch?' The film closes with the father and son lazily throwing a baseball back and forth to each other. The game is meant to symbolize paternal bonding. ('It is through baseball, America's game, that father and son are reconciled, that the pain of both father and son is finally healed'; Aronson and Kimmel 2001.) Men have confessed that they cried while watching this scene. I will admit that I have.

Field of Dreams was based on the novel *Shoeless Joe*, by W. P. Kinsella (1982). The film basically repeated the plotline of the book, but with one important exception. The final scene of the father and son playing catch was added. Apparently, the film's producers and writers felt that the new scene would resonate with fathers. Looking at films that have come out since 1950 and that have baseball and fatherhood as a theme, we see that films increasingly have used the connection between baseball and father-hood, and between fatherhood and playing catch, to tell a heartwarming story. *The Natural* (1984), *City Slickers* (1991), *Hook* (1991), *Free Willy* (1993), *The Sandlot* (1993), *Sleepless in Seattle* (1993), *Three Wishes* (1995), *Liar Liar* (1997), and *My Dog Skip* (2000) – among others – all rely on these connections.

Why did playing catch become more strongly associated with fatherhood in the late twentieth century? One can only speculate, but a combination of both the physical and social would seem to be involved. It could be that the growing popularity of Little League baseball, and other youth baseball leagues, in the postwar suburban (more available space) era created a gener-ation of kids who enjoyed playing ball. These kids then grew up to be fathers (and writers, artists, producers, etc.) in the late twentieth century, just when another wave of 'New Fatherhood' was encouraging men to 'be there' for their children. (An earlier wave of 'New Fatherhood' was evident in the early twentieth century; LaRossa 1997.) The spread of major and minor league baseball venues (imposing physical edifices) and the ubiquity of base-ball on television also may have increased children's desire to be baseball proficient and to emulate their sports heroes. Along with these factors, the passage of the Uniform Time Act in 1966, which created more daylight (temporal space) at the end of the day, afforded greater opportunities for fathers to play the game in the 1970s and 1980s. It appears that playing catch may occur less frequently today than twenty or thirty years ago, in part because of the growing physical distance between home and work in automobile-oriented America. But this turnabout actually may have elevated the game's nostalgic (remembrance of things past) value and further solidi-fied its sacralization in contemporary popular culture.

Future research

The game of playing catch clearly is central to the social meaning of father-hood in America. It is not an activity, however, that researchers have chosen to explore to any great degree. Relying on a variety of written and icono-graphic texts, I have pieced together a picture of how the symbolism attached to the game changed over the course of the twentieth century, but there is much that still remains unknown. Consider, for example, what we could learn from an interview study of men born in different decades. Such a study would be valuable in that it would allow us to uncover the subtleties of the game in the 1980s and 1990s (and beyond), relative to its subtleties in the 1940s and 1950s, and 1960s and 1970s. An important question would be whether the ecology and geometry of the game have changed over the years. What effect did suburbanization have? How exactly has the game been played under different physical and social contexts? Being retrospective accounts, the narratives also would shed light on how the game is remembered from one generation to the next. What do the stories – or, more specifically, the plotlines – suggest about children's feelings toward their fathers?

Comparisons between playing catch and other activities deserve scrutiny, as well. For some families, 'the game' they revere is centered not on throwing a baseball but on passing a football, or kicking a soccer ball. For others, it is playing one-on-one basketball ('shooting hoops'). Still others enjoy bowling or tennis, ice or street hockey. Studies that systematically examine the 'who, where, when, how, and why' of these games could be very revealing of family dynamics, particularly if they focus on the definitions that parents and children attach to the play and the physical realities that demarcate the interaction.

It is worth nothing, for instance, that the game of playing catch is enacted outside and is flexible enough to allow the players to move closer and farther apart, as they wish. Rarely, however, do they touch one another. Basketball can be played either outside or inside, with players staying in close proximity, moving vigorously, and often pushing off each other (if it is a competitive game). Physical contact also can be part of a one-on-one football game. I remember the times my sons and I would wrestle with each other on our living room floor while in the midst of watching a televised football game. Pretending to carry a ball toward an imaginary goal line, one or the other of us would be 'thrown for a loss' or 'break a tackle' to score. Times like these provided an opportunity for us to be close.

The game of playing catch also is generally a noncompetitive activity. If a parent and child pretend that they are playing in an actual event, they often will imagine themselves on the same team. ('It's a grounder to the shortstop [child], he flips to the second baseman [father] who then rifles it to the first baseman [child] for a double play.') One-on-one basketball, bowling, and tennis, however, generally develop into a competition. ('I finally beat you!') What difference does this make to families? What difference does it make to the flow of conversation during and after the game?

The role of talk in family sports indeed can be crucial. Bowling, for example, is played generally in a public setting with onlookers nearby (sometimes only a foot away). Marked lanes dictate where the players stand and deliver the ball. The same parameters are operative when fathers play tennis with their children at a public park. The chance to have a private chat is minimal. One could hypothesize that there are fewer heart-to-heart talks when parents and children bowl or play tennis than when they play catch. No one, to my knowledge, has done a study that examines whether there is a connection between the kinds of one-on-one sports activities that fathers and children have engaged in (and how often) and the perception of the quality of their relationships. This would be a worthwhile project.

Finally, it is imperative to explore how sport activities and the social construction of space are connected to socioeconomic status, race, ethnicity, and nationality. Whereas some groups perceive backyard baseball as a thing of beauty, others view cityscape basketball or open field soccer that way (Mandelbaum 2004). Our propensity to see an object 'glow in the twilight' depends on the 'thought community' to which we belong (Zerubavel 1997).[11]

Notes

I would like to thank Elizabeth Cavalier, Regina Davis-Sowers, Maureen Mulligan LaRossa, William Marsiglio, Kevin Roy, Cynthia Sinha, and Frank Whittington for their assistance with this chapter.

1 The texts tell us more about the culture of fatherhood than about conduct of fatherhood. By that I mean the texts reveal more about how fatherhood, baseball, and catch are *portrayed* rather than about how they are *performed*. Still, while the connection between culture and conduct should never be presumed, neither should it be denied. Thus there are times when, on the basis of cultural evidence, bits and pieces of conduct are inferred. (For a discussion of the distinction between the culture and conduct of fatherhood, and how the two may or may not be related, see LaRossa 1988, 1997, 2004.)

2 Commenting on the perceived crisis of masculinity, Kimmel (1996, 157) notes, 'By the beginning of the twentieth century, testing manhood had become increasingly difficult. The public arena was crowded and competitive, and heading west to start over was more the stuff of fiction than possibility. What was worse, many believed, a new generation of young boys was being raised entirely by women, who would turn America's future men into whiny little mama's boys. Men sought to rescue their sons from the feminizing clutches of mothers and teachers and create new ways to "manufacture manhood.

3 A more thorough survey would have included articles published in the nineteenth century, as well. My search was limited to articles indexed in *The Reader's Guide to Periodical Literature*, which begins in 1900.

4 Although men historically have dominated baseball, a number of women, over the years, have loved baseball, too. The All-American Girls Professional Baseball League of the 1940s and early 1950s is but one illustration. The historian Doris Kearns Goodwin wrote a memoir about her infatuation with the Brooklyn Dodgers in the 1940s and 1950s. She began, 'When I was six, my father gave me a bright red scorebook that opened my heart to the game of baseball. After dinner on long summer nights, he would sit beside me in our small enclosed porch to hear my account of that day's Brooklyn Dodger game. Night after night he taught me the odd collection of symbols, numbers, and letters that enable a baseball lover to record every action of the game' (Goodwin 1997, 13).

5 Youth soccer has become very popular in the United States (Youth Soccer n.d.).

A disjunction between fathers' and children's preferred sports also may have occurred in the 1940s and 1950s. Fathers who grew up in the 1920s and 1930s but did not play organized youth sports may not have been as adept as they would have liked at teaching their Little League sons how to throw, catch, and bat.

6 Mothers and daughters playing catch are rare but could become more common, given the number of single women raising girls who are interested in competitive sports.

7 A father whose six-year-old daughter is playing Little League baseball reported, 'She practices with me in the backyard too, but she can hit a lot better than her daddy. I hope she has the time of her life playing the great game of baseball and has lots of "Kid-type" memories, too!' (Piszek 2003).

8 Hall's 1985 book, *Fathers Playing Catch with Sons*, probably has done more to promote the *culture* of the game of catch than any other text. Other authors who have written about the game often reference (and revere) the book. The lead chapter, 'Fathers Playing Catch with Sons,' originally was a 1974 article (in *Playboy* magazine), but it is the 1985 book that has become synonymous with the game's sacralization.

9 The passage of the Uniform Time Act raises another interesting possibility. Fathers who had children in the 1970s and 1980s indeed may have played catch with their children more than their own fathers played with them. But they also may have forgotten that, prior to the act's passage in 1966, sunset came 'sooner' at the end of the day, leaving less time to play outdoors in the evening. That is, their fathers were operating under different ecological circumstances.

10 A skilled player's arm operates like a catapult to hurl the ball. A whip of the wrist can provide additional spin and speed. The connotation of 'throwing like a girl' is almost always negative. The denotation is harder to pin down. (What does 'throwing like a girl' look like?) The negative label often appears to be associated with an arm motion that *stops* just as the ball is released, as opposed to allowing the arm to *continue downward*, while finely timing the ball's release.

11 In a study of Korean and Vietnamese immigrant children, one son said, 'I love my dad but we never got to play catch. He didn't teach me how to play football. All the stuff a *normal* dad does for kids' (Pyke 2000). Baseball and football are integral to American culture. Some see understanding these games, and learning how to play them, as a benchmark of assimilation.

3 The good father

Parental expectations and youth sports

Jay Coakley

When I was successful in youth sports, people told my father that he was lucky to have a child like me. When my son and daughter were successful, people told me that I must be proud of them and their achievements. Today, when sons *and* daughters excel in sports, their success is directly attributed to parents, most often to fathers. In fact, the fathers of age group champions are now interviewed and questioned by others seeking the secrets to their success in 'creating' athletic prodigies.

These generational shifts in popular perceptions of a father's role in the sport participation of his sons and daughters are part of general cultural changes related to family, gender, and sports, especially in the United States. Fathers who don't actively advocate the interests of their children are seen by many people today as not meeting widely accepted standards for good parenting. In many communities fathers are expected to actively promote their children's success. In the case of youth sports this means that fathers are expected to support and guide children as they learn to play sports. Not surprisingly, some fathers take this expectation seriously and serve as teachers, coaches, managers, agents, mentors, and advocates for their child athletes.[1]

Fatherhood and the involvement of fathers in family life have not been given much attention by social scientists. Research does exist (LaRossa, 1988, 1997; Aldous, Mulligan and Biarnason, 1998; Dienhart, 1998; Lamb, 2004; Marsiglio, Roy and Fox, 2005), but it tells us much less than we should know about the concrete, practical implications of recent cultural changes in the meaning of fatherhood. I have found that youth sports provide a window for viewing and studying these implications in the everyday lives of fathers and families. But as I look through this window I confess that, like my colleagues in sociology and the sociology of sport, I have ignored fatherhood and fathers in my 35 years of studying sports in society. It was only when Tess Kay, the editor of the 2006 issue of *Leisure Studies*, called attention to this oversight that I focused on this topic.

Because I approach fatherhood though the window of youth sports I will begin with background on the growth of youth sports in wealthy, post-industrial societies, primarily the United States. Then I will discuss the connections between this growth and changing definitions of 'the good father'. Finally, I will attempt to theorize these changes drawing on the ideas of the French sociologist Pierre Bourdieu, and suggesting that parental commitment to their children's sport participation is grounded in an emerging family habitus centred in the middle- and upper-middle class of post-industrial societies.

The growth of youth sports

Since the 1950s, the leisure activities and sport participation of young people have increasingly occurred in organized programmes supervised by adults (Adler and Adler, 1998). This growth is the result of a combination of the following cultural and structural factors related to family, parenting, and childhood in many postindustrial societies:

1　An increase in the number of single parent families and families with both parents working outside the home.
2　An emerging neo-liberal view that parents are solely responsible for controlling and socialising their children and that child development is shaped primarily by parenting strategies.
3　A longstanding cultural belief that sport participation automatically involves positive character-building experiences.
4　A media-inspired belief among many parents that the world outside the home is a dangerous place for children.
5　A general fear that children, especially boys, are bound to get into trouble if they are not controlled and properly socialized by adults.
6　The increased visibility of high-performance sports represented as important cultural events and athletes represented as cultural heroes.

Taken together, these six factors, among others, have created a context in which parents actively seek adult-supervised activities for their children.[2] In this context, organized youth sports are seen by many parents as high priority activities because they occur under the control of adult coaches and teach important cultural lessons related to competition and working with others to achieve goals in rule-governed situations.

Additionally, youth sports are attractive because they have predictable schedules, provide parents with measurable indicators of their children's accomplishments, and enable children to gain status among peers and in the larger community. From a parent's point of view, organized youth sports keep their children off the street, out of trouble, and involved in a character-building activity that is enjoyable, popular with peers, and valued in society. In short, when children play sports, mothers and fathers feel that they are meeting their responsibilities as parents. For many fathers, organized sports also provide a setting in which they feel comfortable and competent as a parent. Their knowledge of sports and their past experiences serve as a basis for fathering and participating in child rearing in ways that are consistent with traditional ideas about masculinity and widely approved in society.

Fathers and fatherhood in contemporary society

For most of the twentieth century good fathers were good breadwinners. Although interpreted differently across cultures and social classes, this definition of fatherhood served in the United States and other industrialized societies to focus the attention of many fathers on work to the point that they spent little time on the quality of family relationships. As this occurred, fathers were gradually marginalized from family life. In the United States in particular, this led many families to be characterized by father–child and husband–wife alienation (Griswold, 1993).

Correspondingly, the power of fathers in the domestic sphere became increasingly tenuous and dependent on a combination of their income and an ideology of male supremacy. Despite romanticized, post-World War II depictions of families with breadwinning fathers and stay-at-home mothers, the social and economic realities of family life in the latter third of the twentieth century led an increasing number of women to seek full-time employment. As more mothers assumed part of the breadwinner role in many families, the foundation of fathers' power and authority eroded further. The pace and depth of erosion was accelerated after the mid-1960s as the ideological premises of the women's movement were accepted by many people. The feminisms that grew with the women's movement directly challenged the ideology of male supremacy and further undermined the traditional cultural foundation of fathers' power and authority.

These changes left fatherhood in a social and cultural limbo and forced people to confront a longstanding dilemma that first emerged when changes in the organization of work created a clear split between the private and public spheres of everyday life. After this split, the private sphere of family and home came to be organized around the values and experiences of women, whereas the public sphere of work and politics was organized around the values and experiences of men. Under these conditions meaningful fatherhood depended on dealing with the dilemma of how to simultaneously domesticate masculinity and masculinize domesticity (Gavanas, 2003).

According to feminists and other progressives, the strategy for resolving this dilemma required that fathers become co-parents, do their share of housework, and accept a definition of masculinity based on a commitment to gender equity and reformist, if not radical, changes in gender relations. According to conservatives and neo-liberals the dilemma could be resolved only if fathers asserted themselves as heads of their families and adopted a directive, hands-on style of leadership based on a commitment to traditional family values and individual responsibility.

In the face of these ideologically contradictory resolutions many men felt confused, threatened, or trapped. The strategy offered by feminists and other progressives required radical changes that made many men uncomfortable, if not desperately and aggressively defensive. The strategy offered by conservatives and neo-liberals was consistent with traditional and idealized conceptions of manhood and the family, but many men felt that it was out of touch with the realities of everyday life and the experiences of their wives and children. And both strategies required commitments inconsistent with jobs that provided little or no flex-time and had no father-friendly benefits (LaRossa, 1997). Therefore, fathers faced a difficult challenge: negotiate your job and/or career so that you can choose between entering and learning to participate in a feminized domestic sphere, or taking charge of the family and assertively change the domestic sphere to reflect an ideology supportive of hegemonic masculinity.

Of course, this explanation of fatherhood is oversimplified and it gives less credit to fathers than they deserve. The challenge described above did not catch most men by surprise. They already knew that it was difficult to negotiate the demands of work and family so that expectations could be met in each sphere. However, the stark contrast between the resolutions offered by feminists/progressives on the one hand and conservatives/neo-liberals on the other hand forced many men to revisit this challenge and consider the ideological approach and/or the strategic actions that might best resolve the fatherhood dilemma and guide their involvement in the family.

There is little research that helps us understand the diverse strategies employed by fathers as they have coped with the dilemma in family settings. We do know, however, that discourses describing a 'new fatherhood profile' now pervade some post-industrial cultures, and that many fathers perform household and childrearing tasks that their fathers never did. But at the same time we also know that the actual time that fathers spend with their children has increased only slightly over the past three decades (Pleck and Masciadrelli, 2004). This means that there is a need to understand more fully the structural and cultural constraints faced by fathers articulating a rhetoric of new fatherhood on the one hand but not making significant changes when it comes to spending time with their children.

In light of this background information, an analysis of the involvement of fathers in youth sports provides useful information about the dynamics of fathering in the context of the twenty-first century.

Fathers and youth sports

Sports in general and youth sports in particular have since the 1950s provided fathers with a context in which they can be involved with their children without accepting a need to resist or change dominant gender ideology. In fact, youth sports are unique in this respect because most activities related to the domestic sphere in post-industrial societies lack institutionalized support for the involvement of fathers. For example, the everyday operation of schools and churches has come to depend largely on the involvement and labour of women. And child care, when available, has been organized by women in response to the needs of mothers. In each of these feminized contexts many fathers continue to feel out of place even though there has been an emerging cultural consensus that they should be there. Not so with youth sports, a context that has been organized and controlled by men in ways that reaffirm traditional gender ideology at the same time that they meet expectations for father involvement.

In an insightful discussion of the politics of fatherhood in the United States, Anna Gavanas (2003) notes that sports, as largely homosocial arenas, serve as convenient sites for men to negotiate masculinity and be involved as fathers without being forced to make a choice between domesticating masculinity or masculinizing domesticity. She explains this in the following terms:

> by transposing the cultivation of masculinity and male parenting into sport arenas and framing fathering practices in terms of coaching and team sport, [men] . . . can differentiate between fatherhood and motherhood, and simultaneously make fathering seem manly, heroic and appealing.
>
> (Gavanas, 2003: 8)

Although this statement is accurate, especially in connection with the US-based Fatherhood Responsibility Movement that Gavanas was studying, it is an incomplete description of the way men have either resolved or skirted around the fatherhood dilemma described above.

In some cases, it is very clear that the men serving as coaches, league administrators, and officials in youth sports are committed to traditional gender ideology and use it on the playing field to help boys understand what it means to be a man. These are the men who chastise boys by referring to them as 'girls' or 'ladies' when they play poorly or incorrectly. Similarly, there are fathers who coach teams or simply encourage their son's involvement in sports with an eye toward making their boys into men tough enough and competitive enough to succeed in a 'man's world.' Even some fathers who coach girls' teams, and encourage their daughters to play sports, are strongly committed to traditional gender ideology and use their expertise with sports to reaffirm male superiority and teach girls that they are ladies as well as athletes.

Research by Janet Chafetz and Joseph Kotarba (1995) shows that mothers also reproduce traditional gender ideology and essentialize gender differences as they provide labour that makes youth sports possible. The upper-middle-class little league mothers observed in their study engaged in many gender-specific tasks that facilitated enjoyable sport experiences for their sons and husbands. The mothers laundered uniforms, bought and cooked meals, served as chauffeurs and social directors, and organized their daughters as cheerleaders (Chafetz & Kotarba, 1995; Thompson, 1999). At the same time, fathers consulted with coaches, scouted opponents, provided strategic advice to their sons, assessed the quality of playing fields and umpires, and critiqued the games that were played. In the end both mothers and fathers claimed moral worth as parents because each of them, in their highly gendered roles, enabled their sons to experience success in sports.

After studying youth sports for 35 years, mostly from the perspectives of the children who play them, I know that parental involvement in general and the involvement of fathers in particular may also be guided by progressive ideas about gender and fatherhood. Some fathers make concerted efforts to choose or organize for their children sports programmes that emphasize gender equity, cooperation, and the pleasure of movement in the place of male-centred, competitive, and performance-oriented ethos. These fathers integrate youth sport participation into family life in ways that clearly involve co-parenting, sharing household chores, and gender equity. But we know nothing about the conditions under which this occurs or the dynamics of how it occurs over time.

Other fathers use youth sports and a wide range of away-from-the-home recreational activities as experiences that they can enjoy as they spend 'quality parenting time' with their children. This often occurs at the same time that these fathers expect their wives to take care of in-and-around-the-home aspects of childrearing. As a result, this form of father involvement enables men to meet general expectations for spending time with their children while they also avoid choosing the feminist/progressive or the conservative/neo-liberal resolutions of the fatherhood dilemma. It appears that these fathers can use youth sports to incorporate masculinized activities into a realm of the domestic sphere, thereby avoiding the task of actually changing the culture and dynamics of lived everyday family life. This is the strategy used by fathers who buy moto-cross bikes, snowmobiles, ski boats, kayaks, camping gear, rock climbing equipment, and other recreational toys that can be enjoyed with children (see http://fatherhood.about.com/od/sportsandrecreation/index_r.htm). In these activities fathers are the teachers of instrumental skills outside the home, a role that involves a form of parenting without accepting the changes called for by feminists/progressives or altering predominantly feminized forms of everyday family life as called for by conservatives/neo-liberals.

Finally, in cases when a child is an exceptional athlete it often is the father who makes important decisions about training and competition. He may not drive his son or daughter to practice or launder their sports clothes, but he is likely to select the coach, the club, or the team on which his child will train and compete. He also supervises the selection of equipment and plans strategies for upcoming matches or games. And he often pays most of the bills related to training – sometimes amounting to as much as $10,000–$40,000 (USD) annually. To the extent that a father's child is successful, he is defined as a good parent.

With youth sports offering fathers a wide range of parenting opportunities it is not surprising that many fathers feel comfortable using them as sites to be involved with their children. This is one of the reasons that fathers and mothers are willing to invest so many family resources into organized sports participation for their children. Even as youth sports programmes have increasingly become privatized and expensive, parents have been willing to alter family budgets to support participation. For example, when my students and I interviewed the parents of elite youth ice hockey players who had travelled from near and far to play in a highly publicized tournament, we found that parents routinely spent between $5,000 and $20,000 per year to support their sons' participation in hockey alone.[3] Although they realized that such expenditures were excessive they explained that the benefits for their sons were worth the money and the time that the family spent travelling to and attending hockey games.

The general issue of parental commitment to youth sports has been the focus of limited research. Although data are scare, it is possible to use them to develop hypotheses related to contemporary parenting and fatherhood.

Parental commitment to youth sports

Parental commitment is a key factor in the sport participation of children because participation usually depends on parental expenditures of money, time, and energy (Chafetz and Kotarba, 1995; Hellstedt, 1995; Duncan, 1997). Prior to the 1980s in the United States, for example, the majority of youth sport programmes were publicly funded and neighbourhood-based, so children could manage their participation without extensive parental commitment and involvement. Fees in these programmes were minimal. Parental participation usually was limited to volunteer coaching and minor forms of administrative support. However, as youth sport programmes have become increasingly privatized, regionally located, expensive, performance-oriented, and highly structured in terms of participation schedules, children have become more and more dependent on their parents to make participation possible. At the same time, many parents have come to see participation in sports, especially performance-oriented, competitive sports, as an important part of their children's overall socialisation.

Research on youth sports gives us a glimpse into the origins and dynamics of parental commitment to the sport participation of children. Most researchers have raised social psychological questions and focused on how young people are socialized into sport participation and how parental support and beliefs are associated with the enjoyment, enthusiasm, self-esteem, beliefs, goal orientations, achievement, and continued participation of children (Power and Woogler, 1994; Averill and Power, 1995; Leff and Hoyle, 1995; Brustad, 1996; Kimiecek, Horn and Shurin, 1996; Hoyle and Leff, 1997). There have also been studies highlighting the outcomes that parents believe or hope to be associated with their children's sport participation (Jambor and Weekes, 1995). However, none of these studies helps us understand the social and cultural context in which parents make commitments to the sport participation of their children.

When Richard Dukes and I (Dukes and Coakley, 2002) studied parental commitment among the upper-middle-class white parents of swimmers in USA Swimming's competitive developmental programmes we were amazed at what parents did to support the sport participation of one or more of their children.[4] Parents explained their commitment in terms of the benefits they expected their children to gain from participation. But our data did not explain why, at this point in time in US culture, parents felt so totally responsible for the development of excellence among their sons and daughters.

Our explanation highlighted the prevalence of the conservative and neo-liberal view in the United States that parents are accountable for the behaviour and whereabouts of their children 24 hours a day, seven days a week, year round. In line with this view, if a child fails in a visible and measurable way, parents are held responsible for the failure. If a child succeeds, parents are deemed to be meeting expectations. If the child is a prodigy, parents are held in such high esteem that they are interviewed and even consulted by others interested in perfecting their own parenting. To the extent that parents internalize these expectations they blame themselves when their children do not meet or surpass relatively high developmental expectations; at the same time, when development surpasses expectations, parents often feel that they are morally worthy and deserve special credit.

Under these conditions, the achievements of children in an activity as visible and highly publicized as sports come to symbolize proof of one's moral worth as a parent. Talented child athletes, therefore, become valuable moral capital in neighbourhoods, communities, and the subcultures associated with high-performance youth sport programmes. This leads many parents to feel obligated to 'invest' in their child's sport participation. Not to make this investment would be taken by many people as a sign of a parent's moral failure. Of course, this also means that single parents, low income parents, and others who lack resources to support participation are, by definition, failures as parents, thereby reproducing the privilege of upper-middle-class people.

It is not surprising that in the United States, where competition and individualism are highly valued, some people become competitive when making their claims to moral worth as parents. They look for ways to document progressive skill development as their children play sports. Percentile ranks become important, as does moving up to higher levels of competition in a sport; in fact, many sport programmes are deliberately organized to make achievement explicit and visible. When children receive trophies and other external rewards, such as 'promotions' from the 'silver' to 'gold' level in a programme or receiving martial arts belts in colours representing 'advancement' in skills, these are used and often displayed as concrete proof of parental moral worth. This can be witnessed as parents describe the sport events in which the awards were earned by (them and) their talented children and the sacrifices that they have made to make possible the success of their children.

As Dukes and I theorized the relationships between parental commitment, parental moral worth, and youth sports we suggested that children's sport participation, especially in upper-middle-class families in the United States, occurs in connection with a particular family habitus that began to emerge during the 1980s. Our use of family habitus involves an extension and application of Bourdieu's concept of habitus (Bourdieu, 1978, 1984, 1985; Bourdieu and Wacquant, 1992). According to Bourdieu, habitus is an open, but relatively durable system of dispositions, perceptions, tastes, preferences, and activities learned through socialisation processes and regularly expressed by people as they make lifestyle choices and take action under particular social and material conditions.

As we used it to make sense of the data on parental commitment to youth sports, family habitus refers to a historically and socially situated system of dispositions and the family activities associated with them. It encompasses a combination of a belief system and lifestyle that is influenced by material conditions and historical practices that currently constitute family life in US culture. This concept is useful because it enables us to simultaneously consider cultural and structural factors as we try to understand the choices made within families.

Among the families we studied it seemed that family habitus involved a belief system and lifestyle that encompassed identifiable dispositions and practices related to social class, family life, parenting, child development, and sport participation. Family habitus incorporated developmental goals and identified the types of activities believed to be helpful in reaching these goals. By implication, family habitus subsumes activities that parents think will best facilitate the development of their children while also conforming to the current, widespread belief that parents are directly responsible and even legally accountable for the behaviours and achievements/failures of their children. As such, it entails the interrelated notions that child development is important, that development ultimately depends on the actions of parents, and that the type of development most valued among many middle- and upper-middle-income parents is achieved best through participation in adult-supervised, rationally organized programmes in which skills are built and manifested visibly and progressively through regular performances. Parents also see these programmes as sites where their children can gain or sustain social capital in the form of peer acceptance and cultural capital in the form of knowledge about how to succeed in organized, competitive reward structures in school and work.

Family habitus among middle and upper-middle-class households is also associated with norms that prescribe individualism and personal responsibility (Bellah *et al.*, 1985). In a society where individualism and personal responsibility are so highly valued, parental support and love can be 'narrowed to a reward for doing well. [Under this condition] moral standards give way to the aesthetic tastes and technical skills of the achievement-oriented middle class. "Being good" becomes a matter of *being good at things . . .*' (Bellah *et al.*, 1985: 60; italics in original). Organized, competitive, performance-based sports are among those 'things' because they are highly visible and involve progressive skill development that enables parents and others in the community to assess their children's achievement relative to age peers. These two factors have contributed heavily to the emerging positive status of organized youth sports in neo-liberal societies.

Do issues related to fatherhood contribute to the commitments that parents must make to support the participation of their children in youth sports? My guess is that these issues are very important. As fathers seek to become increasingly involved in their children's lives, youth sports provide parenting contexts that privilege men at the same time that they enable fathers to nurture relationships with sons and daughters and claim that they are sharing childrearing responsibilities with their wives, former wives, or partners. But the absence of research on this topic means that much of what is contained in this paper is best described as informed speculation. Hopefully, it will encourage future research on the dynamics of fatherhood and emerging ideas about the moral worth of parents today.

Notes

1 Research shows that fathers spend more time with sons than with daughters (Yeung *et al.*, 1999; Lundberg and Rose, 2002), and fathers are likely more often involved directly with their sons' sport participation than with their daughters' participation. However, men, including many fathers, play an active role in the sport participation of girls/daughters. I have no data on changes over time, but it is clear that fathers spend more time with their daughters in sports today because there are more sport opportunities available to girls. Fathers coach girls' youth team sports more often than do mothers, even though there have been significant increases in the number and proportion of women/mothers who coach teams and serve as administrators in leagues (fixtures). But the local and fragmented organization of youth sports in the United States makes it difficult to obtain reliable data on these issues. However, as I speak about fathers in this paper, my comments apply to their relationships with sons *and* daughters.

2 In many cases, fathers and mothers provide some or all of the (volunteer) labour needed to initiate and/or maintain the organized youth sports programmes in which one or more of their children participate (see Chafetz and Kotarba, 1995; Thompson, 1999).

3 These were informal interviews conducted every February from 1998 through 2004 as part of a course project. As parents sat in the stands, sociology of sport course students introduced themselves and asked if they could talk with them about the ways they integrated their son's hockey participation into their family lives. One of the last questions asked was how much money they estimated spending each year to support their son's participation in hockey. Their sons were unique in that they played on teams that travelled to tournaments regularly in addition to playing local games and being on the ice for practices and open hockey time. An estimated

300 interviews were done during the six years, and financial estimates were received from over half of the parents interviewed.

4 Data in this study were collected in 1996 in a questionnaire mailed to a random sample of 1100 households with USA Swimming membership. A total of 767 questionnaires were usable, and data on parents and family life were analysed using structural equation modelling.

4 Sport mad, good dads

Australian fathering through leisure and sport practices

Maureen Harrington

This chapter approaches fathering from the perspective of leisure studies to examine how the relationships that fathers have with their family in leisure contexts are reflected in their leisure and sport repertoires and identities. Family-based leisure relationships are one significant mode through which fathers express connectedness with their children. This chapter builds on feminist studies of gendered leisure relations in families, and rejects approaches that conflate mothers' and fathers' experiences and meanings of family leisure into that of 'parents'. In contrast it focuses on fathers' gendered experience of family leisure to further our understanding of what 'playing' with children means in relation to the identity construction of fatherhood. It considers the nexus between fathers' own leisure and sport repertoires, their understanding of their children's identities and leisure needs, and their involvement in shared family leisure and their children's leisure and sport activities.

Fathers have not featured prominently in leisure studies despite 25 years of feminist scholarship that has found that women living with male partners and children tend to neglect their own needs for personal leisure. Women who are wives and mothers fragment their leisure to fit around the demands on their time and energy for household tasks and meeting the needs of others, or they subordinate their own leisure to the leisure interests and activities of others in the family, particularly their children (Thompson, 1999). Feminist analyses have explained the subordination of women's lives including leisure as a result of male dominance and privilege in public and private life. For example, in Thompson's study of women and tennis, 'husbands' unnegotiable leisure interest was a major factor that organised their lives and was predicated on their unrecognized labor' (Thompson 1999: 121), irrespective of whether or not the women played tennis themselves. Thompson's research crystallised how women's leisure has been 'prescribed by domestic and caring roles and could not impact on others' (1999: 149) at the individual, collective and structural level.

This chapter poses the question that even if we assume men's leisure is privileged within the family, what does being a father mean for men's leisure lives? How do a father's leisure interests and pursuits bear on the leisure of other family members and their leisure interests relate to his? It takes as its starting point fathers' accounts of their own and their family's leisure lives, and argues from this evidence, that leisure is a site for fathers to connect to other family members, particularly children. It also raises the further question that father's leisure repertoires may become the basis for shared family leisure.

The chapter presents results of a qualitative analysis of textual data from interviews with 28 fathers living with wives and children in Brisbane, Australia to examine more closely the assumption that sport is a dominant cultural context for fathering in Australia (Thompson, 1999). This involves discussion of a number of themes that emerge from the interviews with fathers about their leisure, shared family leisure and their involvement in the leisure interests of other members of the family. The chapter argues that fathers' sporting knowledge and interests provide them with ways of communicating and bonding with their children. A father's leisure interests are also implicated in fathering in ways that he perceives to be similar or different from the ways he was fathered. In some families, the sporting interests of fathers have become the focus of shared family leisure. This chapter also presents evidence to suggest that sport may not be the only way fathers' leisure interests and repertoires can dominate family leisure, as cases of non-sport family leisure demonstrate.

Feminist contributions to understanding family leisure

Up until the 1980s a model of the male rational actor assumed in most leisure research rendered women's leisure experiences invisible (Glyptis and Chambers, 1982; Hantrais, 1983; Deem, 1986; Bella, 1989). Gender-blind research implicitly privileged male leisure both in families and public spheres of social life (Wearing and McArthur, 1988; Green, Hebron and Woodward, 1990). Thompson points out that this leads to 'overgeneralisations concerning males and undergeneralisations concerning females' (1999: 42; cf. Eichler, 1983: 20). Under an unexamined familist ideology, married women were seen to fulfil role expectations as wives and mothers and to put family first before their personal leisure interests. Family leisure was seen as a means of facilitating family interaction and bonding. An early review of family leisure literature by Orthner and Mancini (1991) confirmed that shared leisure experiences have positive benefits for the quality of family relationships, in terms of family stability, family interaction and family satisfaction (e.g. Orthner, 1975). This empirical work almost exclusively focused on the married couple rather than the family as a whole, and emphasised the relationship between leisure activity patterns and marital satisfaction.

Feminist researchers in leisure studies made women's leisure their problematic, and in so doing contributed to a more complex and nuanced understanding of family leisure as occasions of shared leisure activity reproduced by women for other family members, at the expense of women's personal leisure (see for example, Green *et al.*, 1990; Bella, 1989). The gendered nature of the work entailed in family leisure was most clearly evident in the reproduction of 'special events' such as birthday parties, picnics, family vacations and, in Bella's most extended example, Christmas (Bella, 1992; see also Thompson, 1999).

Largely influenced by feminist research, family leisure research since the 1990s acknowledges gender inequality in leisure entitlement and constraint but the literature on women's leisure could have been more fruitful for understanding family leisure. For example, in her early study of working class, middle class and 'feminist' mothers, Wearing reveals aspects of family life relevant to family leisure but does not make it part of her problematic:

> For the working class and middle class . . . mothers if the husband spends a reasonable amount of time before or after work and on weekends talking and playing with his children and taking an interest in their activities, especially their sporting activities, the mother expresses satisfaction. If, in addition, he will change nappies and/or get up at night when they are babies, bath or put them to bed when they are toddlers and take them out with him or let them be with him in the garden or workshop and encourage their sport when they are older, she feels she is very fortunate . . . On the other hand, if the husband has a sport or hobby or interest which takes up most of his spare time during evenings and weekends and which excludes the family, or if he goes to the pub most evenings after work, or if he does not make an effort to take some interest in his children's activities, the mother is not satisfied with the father's part in child-rearing.
>
> (Wearing 1984: 106–107)

Although what husbands did in their leisure time was not central to Wearing's research topic, it is interesting to know what the wives in her study valued about their husband's leisure: having family inclusive leisure and in particular spending time with children at all ages, showing an interest in their activities, including their sport, and caring for them.

Understanding women's experience of leisure and other aspects of family life was the main focus for feminist researchers, so their work did not extend to gaining an understanding of the family context of leisure and how that may differ in meaning and experience for the women, men and children. The leisure lives (or lack thereof) of wives and mothers was closely scrutinised but the same cannot be said for husbands and fathers. To paraphrase Hutchinson, Kardos, Scherphorn, Tung, Yang and Yarnal (2002), fathers have been the 'inaudible voice' in family leisure research, and this chapter among the others in this volume, is concerned with the experience of fatherhood in relation to family leisure, to which a subsequent section of the chapter will turn.

Parents and family leisure

While feminist researchers focused on women's leisure experience and regarded the family as both the main setting for and impediment to women's leisure, other researchers writing about family time or family leisure tended to refer to 'parents' rather than conceptualising different subject positions of 'mothers' and 'fathers'. For example, Kelly refers to family leisure as a 'social space for parenting'; ways for developing new facets of existing family relationships; and 'an opportunity for autonomy and independence' for both parents and children (1995: 48). In a study of family leisure involvement Zabriskie and McCormick (2003) found that having both core (i.e. everyday, home-based) and balance (i.e. less common and away from home) family leisure activities was positively related to family satisfaction. No gender differences were found, but the relationship between family leisure patterns and family satisfaction was stronger for parents than for children. These results should be considered tentatively however, since mothers constituted 77 per cent of their sample of parents.

Larson, Gillman and Richards (1997) designed a study to examine how mothers and fathers differ in their subjective experience of family leisure, although they also compare the experiences of 'parents' to young adolescents. Using the pager-activated Experience Sample Method, subjects were asked to rate family and home-based leisure activities for 'choice versus constraint', 'intrinsic motivation' and 'affect' (Larson *et al.*, 1997: 81–82). Pagers were set to trigger simultaneous self-reports, which revealed how different family members have divergent experiences of the same leisure activities. Among fathers, family and home-based leisure had a positive affect that was countered by below-average affect in other life spheres. In contrast, mothers reported positive experiences of family leisure but this was juxtaposed by negative experiences of 'obligatory family-based activities ... mainly housework and childcare' (Larson *et al.*, 1997: 89). A major finding in this study that bears on the current research is that family leisure was fathers' 'primary context' for leisure, a 'counterbalance' from work, and the main site for familial affiliation and attachment (1997: 92–93).

In recent work Shaw and Dawson discuss family leisure as 'purposive leisure ... planned, facilitated and executed by parents [who use] that time together to develop a sense of family and to teach children about values and a healthy lifestyle' (2001: 228). This concept of family leisure is useful for understanding parents' intentions, but begs the question about how mothers and fathers accomplish purposive leisure. Parents' gendered identities shape the acts they perform to bring about family leisure, the meanings they give to purposive leisure, negotiations over leisure choices that take place between a mother and a father, and between them and their children. Understanding purposive leisure from the subject positions of mothers and fathers attunes us to the complex gender and generational relationships that inform 'family leisure'. We need to ask, do mothers and fathers engage in creating a sense of family, passing on values, and building a healthy lifestyle for their children in ways born out of their own gendered upbringing, leisure repertoires and embodied experience?

Working with the concept of *family time* rather than specifically *family leisure*, Daly draws attention to the 'structural contradiction between' what parents ideally want and their 'experience of family time that is typically expressed through disillusionment and guilt' (Daly, 2001: 283). He describes what parents strive for in family time: togetherness, being a positive experience, occurring spontaneously and lacking a need for accountability to others. Typically, parents find their family time hindered by lacking enough time, having negative valence and being mainly in the service of children (Daly, 2001). In a later work, Daly (2004) sheds some light on the differences that fathers and mothers bring to 'co-parenting' in his discussion about parenting as performance, how parenting culture and practices are changing, and the recognition that children too are strategic actors. For Daly, shared parenting is more likely to be achieved through the expectation that mothers and fathers be complementary rather than interchangeable. While this formulation does not address discrepancies in power relations between men and women, it does 'recognize men and women as steeped in different gender traditions, having inherited different legacies in their own families, inhabiting different bodies and recognizing different strengths and contributions that they can make to co-parenting' (Daly 2004: 6). Just as purposive leisure needs to be sensitised to the gendered subjective identities of parents, Daly's point further rationalises examining fathers' experiences of family leisure, and how fathers use leisure and sport as contexts for fathering.

The following section reviews some of the fatherhood literature that discusses, however lightly, the topic of fathers and leisure, as a point of departure to an examination of fathering through sport and leisure in Australian families.

Fatherhood and leisure

Fatherhood is a contested area in the now burgeoning body of work on fathers in contemporary society and family studies is divided on how to capture fatherhood both as an ideal and a lived reality (see Marsiglio, Roy and Fox, 2005; Marsiglio, Amato, Day and Lamb, 2000). For example, fatherhood research by 'academic boosters' such as Popenoe (1996) has been interjected into discourses and family policy initiatives by hybrid political-religious organisations, particularly in the United States (Coltrane, 2001: 393). For present purposes the fatherhood literature was surveyed for reference to leisure with the unsurprising result that leisure activities and playing with children are identified as naturalised areas in which fathers show involvement with their children. The fatherhood literature tends not to examine the social and cultural processes entailed in shared father–child leisure activities, nor the subjective meanings these activities have for fathers.

In his social history of American fatherhood, LaRossa (1997) provides evidence of a 'culture of daddyhood' during the 1916–1929 Machine Age that cast the social and familial role of the father as a 'playmate' to his children (LaRossa, 1997: 17). Cultural expectations of middle class men included the primary role of economic provider, but in the 1920s an ideology of New Fatherhood also encouraged 'masculine domesticity', a norm that men should take on domestic responsibilities for child-rearing and spend some of their non-work time playing with their children (1997: 31). By the 1930s a norm of 'domestic masculinity' arose, without supplanting the earlier view. This new way of being a father entailed 'the maxim that men's manliness needed to be placed under house arrest (at least in the evenings), civilized, or tamed' (1997: 34). Now fathers were not only to play with their children but also be a 'male role model' to both sons and daughters, 'to counterbalance the presumably emotionally laden and potentially destructive influence of women' (LaRossa, 1997: 39). LaRossa argued that framing the ideal father as the 'pal' and a 'male role model' to his children effectively marginalised him from the more important position of the mother in the family. The father was the 'poet of parenthood': '[i]t meant having the "prerogative" to be the candy man and the bestower of toys; it meant holidays in the park. It also meant "irresponsible enjoyment," fun without any strings attached' (LaRossa, 1997: 140). By the 1940s white American middle class culture attributed more importance to fathers being a male role model rather than a pal; while this enhanced fathers' status within the family, it did not eclipse the higher status of mothers.

Some writers on contemporary fatherhood draw attention to fathers' predilection to play with their children as opposed to engaging in what is usually referred to separately as 'childcare'. A study of Australian fathers in the 1980s reports that they spent an average of 9 hours a week playing with their children, or 80 per cent of their interaction with children (Russell, 1987: 342). Fathers, in comparison to mothers, usually engaged their children in 'outdoor and amusement/fun play, and less frequently in indoor/conventional play and story reading' (Russell, 1987: 342). Russell concludes that mothers do more childcare while fathers participate in active play (1987: 343). Backett (1990) gives a rather pragmatic explanation for why fathers more readily engage in play rather than finding other ways of interacting with children:

> Playing with children and being a source of pleasure were thus highly meaningful ways of demonstrating father involvement. This was an area of activity which a father could carry out spontaneously and voluntarily with a minimum of specific knowledge or consultation with the mother being necessary. It could also be carried out regularly when little time is available ... the emotive salience attached to this area of paternal involvement also meant that it could be accomplished to the satisfaction of both spouses, even with a relatively small input of time.
>
> (Backett 1990: 6)

The generative fathering perspective that gained momentum in the 1990s (see Snarey, 1993; Hawkins and Dollahite, 1997a) adopted Erikson's original psychosocial concept of 'generativity,' which he had defined as 'establishing and guiding the next generation' (Erikson, 1965: 258) or as 'true care' (Erikson, 1971: 138) to emphasise the activities and work fathers undertake in order to meet their children's needs. This approach is self-described by its proponents as a move away from 'deficit' views of fatherhood (Hawkins and Dollahite, 1997a), and is seen as an improvement over framing fathers' activities as 'role' obligations (Marsiglio *et al.*, 2000: 1177). Noting the feminist critique that men opt for the 'fun' rather than the 'repetitive and mundane' aspects of childcare (e.g. Wearing, 1984; Gerson, 1997), Dienhart and Daly (1997: 161) counter by suggesting we view 'fun' activities as a parent's responsibility and 'important generative activities for many fathers'. By relegating them to the 'cultural domain of leisure, fathers are construed in a nongenerative manner' (Dienhart and Daly, 1997: 161), and the range of ways fathers are involved with and connected to their children is unrecognised.

The fatherhood writers discussed so far locate fathering in the context of playing with children, but Palkovitz is more concerned with how fatherhood encroaches on men's personal leisure and exercise regimes. In a qualitative study of American fathers, he notes that 'a significant proportion of the sample voiced parallel shifts from male-only sports-centred and leisure-time activities toward child- and family-centred activities' (Palkovitz, 2002: 200). This he argues has implications for men's health (2002: 158) and the quality and depth of their social relationships (2002: 198).

The fatherhood scholars do not give much attention to leisure, nor do they consider family leisure as a possible site of fathering. However, an edited volume on fatherhood that situates fathering in physical and social spaces (Marsiglio, Roy and Fox, 2005) holds promise for future scholarship on fathers and family leisure. They propose a theoretical problematic with two foci: how men behave as fathers, through interactions with children and others, as well as by themselves, and the meaning men give to fatherhood, 'the values; norms; and social, emotional, and cultural materials out of which men construct a fathering identity for themselves' (2005: 5). The invited authors cover a range of situated fathers, including stepfathers, non-residential fathers, long-distance trucking fathers, incarcerated fathers, farm fathers, and more. The editors of Marsiglio *et al.* (2005) claim to redress the 'acontextual and atemporal' studies typically done about involved fathers (Marsiglio *et al.*, 2005: 24).

In this chapter, the physical and social landscape of contemporary suburban Brisbane, with its large backyards, patios, barbeques, home swimming pools and numerous parks and sport ovals and clement weather is an ideal leisure-oriented place in which to locate a study of sport and leisure contexts for fathering (see LaRossa, 2005 and this volume on the importance of a backyard for a father to play catch with his child). The following sections of this chapter discuss Australian fathers' perceptions of family leisure and report my research in the area.

Fatherhood, sport and family leisure in Australia

Australian fathers have somewhat of a mixed cultural image. As Russell (1987) explains, one popular image and scholarly assumption is that Australian fathers are 'left out of family life, taking refuge in self-conscious masculinity around sport, ockerdom (defined as boorish, uncouth, chauvinistic Australianism) and alcohol as compensation' (Russell, 1987: 533). Other research (Russell and Radin, 1983) shows few differences in childcare participation from other Western fathers (Russell, 1987: 333).

In establishing her rationale for studying women's involvement in the game of tennis in Western Australia, Thompson (1999) compares the ways in which fathers and mothers are involved with their children's sport. Her preliminary survey showed that in addition to the time that mothers spent servicing their children's tennis, fathers tended to be involved for longer blocks of time, usually on weekends. She notes that while mothers performed home-based routine tasks associated with children's tennis, like laundering tennis clothes and washing drink bottles, fathers tended to do public 'special' tasks 'with the timing and degree of parental involvement more discretionary and under the control of the father, such as when he plays tennis with the child' (Thompson 1999: 50). Tasks fathers were most likely to do were sport specific (e.g. playing, techniques and sporting behaviour) rather than the more diffuse tasks usually done by mothers (e.g. providing transport, ironing shirts, making lunches) that shaded into more general childcare and support. Thompson (1999) recognises sport as a site of fathering in Australia, but her research challenges the perception that it is fathers rather than mothers who are predominately involved in their children's sport. The present research foregrounds what the Australian fathers studied endeavour to do with and for their children during self-defined leisure time, with particular focus on sport.

Methodology and study sample

The research reported here is part of a study of 28 two-parent heterosexual families in Brisbane, Australia undertaken during the period 1999–2004. Altogether there were 72 children ranging from 10 weeks old to 24 years old living in the family home. A total of 128 individuals were members of the families studied, but the focus in this chapter is the 28 fathers who participated in the study.

The research entailed parents (usually the mother) completing a seven-day diary of the leisure activities of all family members, followed by a one-on-one semi-structured interview with each parent separately, and with at least one of the children in the family, 10 years of age and older. The interview schedule asked adult respondents to talk about their favourite leisure activities, those they enjoyed the most and those they felt were most important to the family. They were also asked to describe the least enjoyable, to talk about when things did not work out, and to generally discuss their motivations for both individual and shared family leisure. The child interview schedule was designed to let children talk about what they enjoyed most and least about their leisure activities, and with whom they preferred to do leisure activities.

The first ten families were recruited among the parents of a boys' soccer team at a local soccer club. The remaining families responded to advertisements seeking study participants run in free neighbourhood newspapers that are delivered weekly to each household in the area. All families were selected using a purposive sampling technique with specific criteria, including living in a single detached dwelling, and having at least one child ten years or older. These criteria gave the sample some homogeneity in terms of the family's access to leisure space around the home and made it possible to interview children about their leisure likes and dislikes. However, it may be noted that families differed in terms of level of household income, with 11 of the families categorised as lower income (below $25,000) and 17 as middle income (above $30,000). At the time of the study, the median annual wage and salary income for couples aged 15–44 with dependent children in Australia was $32,698 (ABS, 2006). Data was collected during the school terms to minimise the possibility that families' leisure activities and everyday routines would be affected by family vacations and seasonal holidays.

Qualitative analysis of the interview transcripts was developed through the use of QSR NUD*IST software. In the earliest phase of the study two members of the research team open coded each transcript separately then jointly discussed and reached agreement on appropriate open codes. Through further iterations of the transcripts, axial codes for the interview material were identified and it was organised into analytic categories. Then selective coding was used for core categories which were further coded into themes. For a review of these analytic procedures used with qualitative data see Glaser and Strauss (1967), Strauss (1987); Miles and Huberman (1994); Strauss and Corbin (1998) and Neuman (2000). As with all interview data, the subjects were responding to questions posed by the interviewer on the day, and their interpretation of the question, and the subjective meanings they convey in their responses are not fixed. What is spoken about and how it is said, may be presumed to be fluid from one conversational context to another, and we should bear in mind that the semi-structured interview with a social science researcher is only one such context.

Fathers talking about leisure in the family

As discussed earlier, Shaw and Dawson (2001) conceptualise family leisure as 'purposive' to the achievement of parental goals. Their 1998 research on

31 Canadian families showed that parents put considerable effort into organising and facilitating family leisure activities to two short and long-term ends: to enhance the family's functioning as a cohesive, communicative and bonded unit, and to provide opportunities for children to learn what parents hope will become life-long values (see Shaw and Dawson, 1998). In the present research similar themes about the ways fathers relate to their children during leisure occasions have emerged. Most fathers in this study talk about sport being a context for *bonding with and showing interest in their children*, and *for inculcating values* but a few of them have leisure repertoires in non-sport areas that are contexts for these same processes. The themes explored in this chapter are *being with and doing with family*; *the family paradigm and generations of fathering*; *sport as a context for fathering* and *other leisure contexts for fathering*. These themes will be explored and illustrated in that order, as the first theme is the most prevalent, and in descending order to the last theme that appears least common among the fathers.

Being with and doing with family

During the one-on-one semi-structured interview with each parent, both parents were asked: 'Thinking specifically about the family activities listed in the diary (i.e., those done with your child or children) how important do you consider these activities to be?' In responding to this question, as well as at other intervals, fathers talked of being with their children and doing things with them as very important, often regardless of what they are doing together. In the excerpts below, two fathers say it is just 'being with' their children that matters, in order to know them, or just to be in their company:

> 'you know if I went down there and had sat down with them whether I sit down there with a cool drink or just sit down there talking that's just as beneficial. You learn as much off even just by looking at the children without even talking to them you learn how the, you know, how they behave and how they get on with other children.'
>
> (Father, family #26)

> 'I'm not a great TV person, there's so much soap on. TV doesn't interest me unless sport was on I'd watch any type of sport but the soaps like *Home and Away* like the girls like I am not interested in. I'll sit down and watch it with them probably because that's where they're at so I sit down as well but if the television was off it wouldn't worry me at all.'
>
> (Father, family #6)

Other fathers talked about 'doing things' with the children, but they make the point that what they do together is secondary to doing it together, as the following excerpt illustrates:

'Yeah any time you spend together I s'pose as a family is you know is always beneficial in regards whether you just give them a ball out the back yard or going a bit more elaborate and going down to theme parks or going to the beach or going somewhere else that is further afield.'

(Father, family #26)

Another father expresses why he thinks it is important to communicate and share thoughts with his children:

'I try to hear their sort of views on things and exchange views on what I think of things and how things have gone way ahead from what they used to be and that they should appreciate things more.'

(Father, family #2)

The same father, who ironically is a schoolteacher, goes on to clarify what he means by 'views':

'Yes and try to express the right sort of views on how you treat other people, and get on in life, is basically what I am trying to educate them on. The things that they don't learn about in school.'

(Father, family #2)

One father, a boiler maker by trade, not only feels being with his children is important whatever the activity, but also, as in the Larson *et al.* (1997) study where home based leisure was more enjoyable than work, this father likens being with his children to an escape from paid work:

'Generally during the week any time with the kids and whether that is watching TV or running them around to sport and I quite enjoy seeing them having fun. I watch them at karate or tennis whenever we can and that's a means of forgetting about work which is basically what I am hoping for . . .'

(Father, family #3)

The fathers discussed here clearly want to be a significant influence on their children's lives, to take advantage of the present time to do so. They want to spend time with their children, to be involved with them through shared leisure, to talk to them, to watch them grow and develop interests, skills and attitudes.

The family paradigm and generations of fathering

In his book *Families and Time*, Daly refers to 'the family paradigm' (1996b: 54) as a construction of ideals that family members create and maintain to sustain them through the 'frustrations and disappointments' (Daly, 1996b: 216) of everyday life. Family paradigms 'are composed of the family's persistent attitudes and assumptions about the social and physical world [and] shaped through individual member's memories of the family's history, myths, heroes, values and secrets' (1996b: 54). The concept of the family paradigm helps make sense of this father's explanation of what he meant by saying it is good *'to go out as a family unit'*:

> 'Yes because I'd hate to think that when the kids are 15 or 16 and the kids say oh yeah, Dad used to stay at home and be a real stick in the mud. My kids can't say that because I was there. We went to [a national park near] Monto and we abseiled down the rocks. A lot of the kids didn't do it but our kids did. I like to think that we do things as a family and when they grow up that same things rub off on them. So we like to think that they will be that way inclined. That might change but we don't know that at this stage. We like to think that when they marry that they will do things like we did and they can never say that our parents didn't take us anywhere. I think it is important.'
>
> (Father, family #9)

He (and his wife) deliberately gave their children leisure experiences they hope will be remembered and repeated in the next generation. As his comments attest, some parents go to great efforts to lay down positive memories of family life and instil their values in the hope that children will be guided by them in the future.

Another father evokes the family paradigm when he states explicitly what values he hopes to pass on to his children:

> 'Trying to teach some values to the kids. Values such as being together as a family unit and some of our values can be passed on to them. Such as sense of responsibility, sense of loyalty to the family unit, love and that sort of stuff.'
>
> (Father, family #7)

When fathers in this study talk about why spending time with family is important, it becomes apparent to the listener that when they refer to 'family' they mean children, and fathers realise that children are only within their sphere of influence for so long. Take for example, the following quotations in which fathers refer to the relatively short duration of childhood. The first rather wistfully explains why he thinks doing things with his children is important:

> 'Um very important any activity that you do with your children is always important because it won't be long before they are grown up and gone. So regardless whether you're driving the children around, picking them

up from activities, and that might seem to be a bit of a pain to start with, but when you think back at it you know . . . they're lucky as well as we're lucky.'

(Father, family #26)

The other echoes this view of the temporality of childhood:

'At the present moment it's actually . . . it is being with the kids and having fun and playing soccer and doing things like that. Umm, cause you don't get that much time in their lives so therefore it's good to be with and have . . . do activities with them.'

(Father, family #25)

As another father frames it, childhood is a critical time for parents to be a 'role model':

'To be a role model for the children. Children of that age are moulded by the way the parents act and speak to the kids and I think it is very important to be a role model at this age. When they get a bit older they probably won't want to know you anyway. They probably want to be out with their mates and at that time it is a bit late.'

(Father, family #1)

A fourth father also speaks in terms of role models when he sums up why he thinks family leisure is important, not just now, but for his children's future:

'The main reason is that the sharing is important in terms of what family life is about, the development of the children. It is critical that they have models in terms of their future life and so their development is critical, it is critical for time out for them and [my wife] from their working activities or student activities, so they are the three key reasons, the time out, the sharing and the development for the children.'

(Father, family #4)

These fathers have expressed why they feel it is important to share a range of activities with family members, which as suggested, signifies children. They are aware of the fleeting nature of childhood and that they must act now to have a lasting effect on their children's lives. But some fathers in the study also spoke of being a father in terms directly related to their own fathers, either to 'follow on' or 'do it differently' from their memories of growing up with their father (see also Dienhart, 1998). Sometimes this is expressed as forming leisure interests intergenerationally. For example, one respondent evokes the notion of the family paradigm when he speaks of his father passing on the 'family way' to him:

'He used to take me fishing and his parents started the Caloundra beach holidaying and [it] came down the family. His parents were very keen on that sort of thing, fishing and his interests. I guess he has followed on and I have followed on from him. Yes it has definitely passed on down the family way.'

(Father, family #1)

Another example comes from a migrant father of two daughters:

'We have a very close family which created an attitude for me about what was important and I am following that in my immediate family. Our family over in England was the same here. We used to do everything together like go for Sunday drives. So it has flowed on.'

(Father, family #6)

With some of the fathers who evoked the family paradigm the focus was on sport, such as this father who explains his love for baseball:

'When I was about five or six years old my father was already involved then and so I was raised that way and I started to play and [am] still playing.'

(Father, family #5)

Another father explains it more in terms of an Australian cultural mandate:

'Culturally mandated I'd say . . . it's just the things you think . . . the first thing you think of, 'oh, they'd better play sport' and 'they'd better play some music'. I mean, I was brought up in a family where there was a lot of music. That was the hub, the piano or what have you . . . so I guess I'm sort of driven that way a little. We all feel that sport . . . some sort of activity like that, a physical activity, is good for the kids and then you've got the benefits of particularly team sports . . .'

(Father, family #21)

For other respondents their identity as an involved father in their children's sport seemed to be formed in opposition to negative memories of parents' indifference, like this father who takes his son to football practice and games each week:

'Well, I've almost gone the opposite way [to my parents' attitude to sport] because my parents never really, they didn't in a way support me in sport. I did most of my sport alone, I actually took myself to sport . . . Umm, so I'm trying to play some sport myself. But it's been the opposite way.'

(Father, family #27)

Another father, who admitted in his interview that he was guilty of paying closer attention to his son's sport than to his daughter's, also invokes memories of his father in explaining to the interviewer why his wife complains about his lack of encouragement for his 15 year old daughter's sport:

> 'I think I might do it in a different way or I might not say it at the right time because when I was young my father was an extremely hard person and we never got too many pats on the back and had to strive for things because it was much tougher in those days. We never had the opportunity and if you wanted to play sport you had to get there on your own bat and bat for yourself and do the best you can. But here we actually go along as much as we can.'
>
> (Father, family #9)

These excerpts are a reminder that the family paradigm not only may be invoked to commemorate the warm sustaining feelings associated with living in a family, but painful memories of how it was 'when I was young' may also rationalise different choices for the procreated family in the present. Men are often particularly sensitive to missing out on sporting experiences as they are so valued within Australian formations of masculinity.

While sport has been featured in several of the quotations in this section, the next section will purposely focus on sport in order to show how it is a major context for fathering in the Australian families studied. As sport is one of Australian society's dominant cultural institutions, it is an area of discourse in which many Australian fathers feel at ease, are most animated about, show the most interest in, and in which they can claim some competence. Interestingly, Lareau (2000) makes a similar observation about the American fathers she studied in her research on child-rearing, but unlike the present study, she was not interested in hearing fathers' views on their leisure and sport! The following section explores the idea that sport is a predominant leisure context for fathering among the men in this Australian study.

Sport as a context for fathering

No other leisure topic or area of social and family life seems to warrant as much attention by these Australian fathers as does sport. All but three fathers (who will be introduced briefly in a later section) mentioned, or discussed at length, their own and their children's sporting activities during the course of the interview. For some, their only referent for leisure was sport. For example, when the interviewer asked one father 'Are there other family activities that you do that aren't in the diary?' he responded 'Sport?' While Lareau laments the relative lack of confidence with which her male subjects could discuss child-rearing compared to their own leisure and sport activities (2000: 408), in the current study, the cultural currency of sport talk meant that many of the fathers were within their comfort zone and expressed themselves at length about their own sport involvements and those of their children, and to a lesser extent those of their wife. In this section, the interview data is interrogated about two aspects in which fathering occurs within the context of sport: showing an interest and bonding with their children and inculcating values and life-long social skills. As has been noted earlier, these are the same two aspects of family leisure that Shaw and Dawson (2001) identify with purposive leisure.

Unlike the subjects in Palkovitz's (2002) study of involved fathers, who gave up individual exercise programs and organised sport once they had children, many of the Brisbane fathers reported sustained personal involvement in both organised team sport (e.g., cricket, softball, and swim team) and individual sport and recreation (e.g., golf, tennis, squash, surfing, and bushwalking). Sometimes a particular sport is the focal point of the family's leisure activities and social life, such as cricket for family #20 and tennis for family #4. Given the central place of sport in the social development of Australian society (Bloomfield, 2003), it is perhaps not surprising that masculine identities and fatherhood in Australia are bound up with interest in and practice of sport (see also Thompson, 1999).

It is not only fathers of Anglo-Celtic descent who parent through sport in Australia. Les Murray, head of sport for Australia's Special Broadcasting System was interviewed about Australian-Croatian football player, Mark Viduka, former Leeds United and Celtic forward, who at the time of writing this chapter was leaving Middlesbrough to join the Newcastle United team. Murray explains why so many Australians of central European ancestry have represented the country at the highest level of football (or soccer as it is called in Australia). In a quotation reminiscent of LaRossa (2005 and this volume), Murray says: 'that's what his father taught him – all those technical values that you see in players coming out of the former Yugoslavia. That's what he carries with him, what made [Viduka] the player he is. A Croatian father will show his son, when he takes him out into the backyard, how to juggle the ball until dark, to master the ball, that's the number one priority – it's not about running laps and doing weights, it's about having the technique. In that culture, if you don't have technique, nobody respects you' (*The Weekend Australian Magazine*, March 25–26, 2006). That is how his father taught him to play.

Showing interest and bonding through children's sport

Children's involvement in sport not only gives fathers interests in common with their children, and ways for fathers and children to bond together, but it also provides concrete ways of supporting children in their activities, and occasions for private and meaningful conversation. Several fathers made these observations. One father, an environmental consultant to local government, made the first point most clearly:

'Probably going to the kid's lessons or training for sports [is the most important activity]. I enjoy that. That is important because you are actually sharing something with the children and the opportunities for doing that are fairly limited and that is something that you can actually be involved in that they are doing and have some common areas of interest and conversation and something that you know about that they know about.'

(Father, family #10)

One father used the term 'bonding session' to describe backyard sport with his 13 year old son:

'with [my son] a couple of times, for a bonding session. Bonding is spending time with the child. A bit more closeness with a bit of competition between Dad and son.'

(Father, family #7)

Two fathers mentioned specific ways in which they show their support for their children at sport. A father of five living on a disability pension volunteers extensively at a local swim club:

Yes, [I am there] supporting the kids competing. Yes and I kept an eye on [my 6 year old son]. The kids like us being there. [My 6 year old son] always comes up to me and lets me know when he is going to swim in the race and I keep an eye on him. 'Dad I'm in lane 3.'

(Father, family #8)

The other, a self-employed housepainter, with a second home-based business as a sign-painter, tells of how he can support his children at swim club:

'It's important because it is part of being a parent to see your kids participate and it is good to be [there] when they hop out of the water as they may need a towel or something . . . Some parents may not be able to afford that time to be there as they have commitments elsewhere so they can't be there and I think that is sad that you don't see your kids. I'm not there every Friday night but I like to go down.'

(Father, family #9)

Fathers also show interest in their children's lives while transporting them to and from sport:

'Taking [my son] to sport . . . recently has been quite enjoyable because it gives me a chance to talk with him. It is important as it is one of the few times I get a chance to corner him in the car and so we can catch up and have a talk and that's always important but not always enjoyable.'

(Father, family #3)

Similarly, another father notes how it is easier to talk to his son when they are in the car alone, coming home from sport training:

'I take [my 11 year old son] to tennis on a Sunday night and the time I share when he comes off the court or just driving home in the car to share and encourage him and talk through something. So yes I think that it is important and less stressful than the four of the family together.'

(Father, family #4)

For fathers, the shared interest in sport can be the catalyst to communicate about other matters as well. Talking about sport facilitates other kinds of conversations about the child's emotional wellbeing, interests and everyday difficulties that fathers may find difficult to initiate given women's role in providing emotion work within families. One father expresses this notion well:

'Maybe that is what is valuable about some of the activities like playing sport with the kids you talk about things and it is a conduit to talk about other things. You don't just talk about the sport it lubricates your conversation until you get into the groove of talking.'

(Father, family #10)

These excerpts of fathers' talk about their children's sport show the ways in which they show interest in their children's sport activities, support their efforts, and use the time together to build their relationships. Fathers' engagement with their children through sport is arguably 'generative'; it is a social context in which many fathers are able to demonstrate their capacities for what Gerson calls 'nurturing attachments, ... ethically responsible choices and ... construct mutually fulfilling bonds with their children' (1997: 38). The next section of the data analysis focuses on fathers' talk about how they try to instil values through opportunities for children's sport. This can also be seen as generative fathering, bearing the original psychosocial meaning given to 'generativity', as 'establishing and guiding the next generation'. (Erikson, 1965: 258)

Fathers' talk on values from children's sport

For most of the fathers in this study, the notion that children's sport is a means of transmitting values seems unquestioned. In fact only the school-teaching father in family #2 felt that 'they don't seem to learn values out of sports'. The majority of both fathers (and mothers for that matter) believed that sport taught life lessons and prepared children for adulthood, as the following quotations illustrate:

> 'I like to take my son out and teach him how to fish. We touched on values and sportsmanship. Teaching your children how to handle themselves in the outside world later on.'
>
> (Father, family #1)

> 'Basically it gives them a discipline. She doesn't worry about losing a match and is confident in her own abilities and feels that she will get there one day.'
>
> (Father, family #3)

> 'The goal setting's important but I think they can get that in other areas, not just leisure and physical activities. I guess it's the team interaction. Learning to work with other people. Learning to appreciate their strengths and weaknesses and their opinions and learning to follow directions from a manager or a coach ... those are skills which they can carry on in any element of their life, whether working in an office, or working towards their own personal businesses or their own personal goals.'
>
> (Father, family #25)

While fathers in this study are not particularly articulate about their own values and what they want their children to value, this may be because the notion that sport is culturally valued is taken for granted. It is probably not surprising to the reader that many Australian fathers seem to have an abiding faith that sport is good for their children, given the prominence of sport and sporting figures in cultural and media discourses and as part of school curriculum in all states and territories. As Thompson remarked in her study of tennis, 'I suspect ideologies surrounding hegemonic masculinity in Australia are so strongly associated with sport that, when they translate into fatherhood, sport is perceived as a major site for fathering to occur and for the development of men's relationships with their children' (1999: 53). If, as Thompson found in her work, mothers and fathers have different relationships with their children through sport, a question for continuing research is whether mothers and fathers identify similar or different values being inculcated by children's sport.

Leisure contexts other than sport for fathering

As mentioned earlier, of the 28 families studied, only three stood out from the others for an absence of reference to sport activities either in the week-long diary or during the interviews. It is worth taking note of them here, if only to show the exceptional cases among these Australian families. For two of these families (families #14 and #16) religious observation, going to church, scripture reading and morning family prayer are routine and important parts of family life. Their leisure activities are centred on their church (e.g. in their interviews both fathers specifically mentioned as leisure painting a religious scene or an Australian bush backdrop for church pageants); they socialise with other members of their church and children's leisure activities are largely organised through their church. Both of these families have low incomes (under $25,000 per year, from manual and service jobs) and are close and loving families who spend most of their leisure time as a family. Wilcox and Bartkowski (2005) point out that compared to other fathers, lower-income fathers lack 'cultural, financial and institutional resources [to] draw on as they interact with their children', but for religious lower income fathers, these are compensated for by religious institutions which provide 'social sites that offer opportunities for social participation and leadership, a religious message that makes sense of everyday life, and a strong commitment to a moral code of decent family-centred living' (2005: 314). This explanation is apt for the families described here. For example, the father in family #14, a banquet worker, describes the values he passes on to their three children during family camping trips:

'I think they learn to be more responsible in these places because they have to look after their own welfare, their own safety. So, we teach them what they should be doing, what's right and wrong, not to light matches whenever they feel like it. That kind of thing. And there's always people there so you have to be careful not to upset the other campers. Not making too much noise.'

(Father, family #14)

Family #16 is an interesting case because the father's *'life service'* in the Salvation Army has a profound influence on both family leisure and the individual leisure pursuits of his children. A fitter by trade who was recently made redundant, he plays in the brass band as his ministry, Sunday mornings and evenings in their church, and Sunday afternoons in parks or shopping malls, and the family goes along to listen. His own father played in the Salvation Army brass band, and he recalls, 'when I was about nine or ten years old I used to go with him in the afternoon, to some of the parks and sit down and listen to the band or sit next to the guy that was playing the drums' (Father, family #16). His 15 year old son now also plays in the band with his father, another example of intergenerational leisure. The last family holiday they took was when the band toured Tasmania: 'I was one of the strange ones that took the family and the mother in law . . . staying in a cabin that's the size of about four metres by two metres wide and you've got five of you in there together. Somehow you've got to get on [laughs]' (Father, family #16). Like Thompson's (1999) study of tennis families whose leisure time is given over to servicing (on the part of the mother) and attending (the whole family) weekend tournaments, the same pattern also inheres in families where the father has a ministry.

A final case of a family where sport is not the context for family leisure and father's involvement with his children is Family #19, in which the father is a touring dancer and children's entertainer of Polynesian-Native American heritage, and one of the most talkative fathers in the study. With three sons, one aged 12 years who studies ballet, a 10 year old who does gymnastics, and a third only two years old ('he was like an afterthought'), the interview ranges through dancing together as a family, Monday night family meetings with song, dance and scripture lessons, his eldest son's ballet performances for the extended family and his own father's influence on him to play rugby rather than gymnastics or dance. In his words:

> 'See the thing is, when I was growing up my father put me into rugby which was great, I loved it. But I would have loved to have been put into gymnastics. Or even ballet. But rugby. Rugby [with a deep voice]. That's it. That's my father. And like when he takes [my 12 year old son] to ballet, he said to me one time, 'I can't believe I'm taking my grandson to ballet.' See and that was his mentality and if he had given me the opportunity [to do gymnastics or ballet] I would have taken it . . . And now I have the opportunity to give what didn't happen to me.'
>
> (Father, family #19)

These three cases illustrate the argument that fathers' leisure repertoires can shape the content and meaning of family leisure. They are also non-sport contexts for fathering, communicating with their children, sharing interests and instilling values that the parents hold dear, that hopefully will be lifelong values for their children.

Conclusion

Three concerns colour fathers' remarks about why it is important to do family leisure: communicating and sharing with their children; guiding them and inculcating values; and recognising that as parents, they only have limited opportunities to spend time with their children and guide their future development. Through their desire to be with their children, doing activities together, or merely watching their children play, fathers in this study show their emotional connection to them. These fathers are invested in their children's lives, and this is apparent when they talk about sharing leisure and sport experiences with their children.

The concept of purposive leisure attunes us to parents' intentions for their children, that is, their short and long term goals for their children, but it does not take into consideration the gendered identities and leisure repertoires that mothers and fathers bring to family leisure practices. The concept of generative fathering focuses attention on how some fathers conduct their family lives in ways that foster the next generation. They seem acutely aware they only have so much time afforded during their children's childhood to leave an enduring legacy. In this chapter I argue that leisure and sport are dominant contexts in which fathers do this. Being with and doing leisure activities with their children, supporting their sport, and using these occasions to bond, communicate and instil values is central to the generative notion of fathering.

Leisure and sport are major sites for doing fatherhood as a gendered practice, and a relationship between a father and child is not simply 'natural' but produces emotional connections in families. Thompson concluded that while women serviced children's sport through doing much of the invisible work, they did so through an 'agenda . . . largely set by the fathers of their children and generated by a commitment to their marriages, family relations, and the fostering of congenial relationships between men and their children' (1999: 57). When participating in sport became central to family life, and the nexus of relationships among its members, mothers 'were ensuring their children did things to which their fathers could relate, fostering for him his relationships with his children' (Thompson, 1999: 58).

As a final word, given this analysis of fatherhood and leisure, there is much to learn yet about what being a father means for men's leisure lives. It seems however, at least for the fathers studied here, that sport and leisure are major sites for connecting with their children, teaching them life-long values and creating a family paradigm, a sense of who they are *as a family.*

5 Fatherhood, the morality of personal time and leisure-based parenting

Liz Such

Gender, leisure and the family are established themes for leisure studies. As identified in this volume, a rich body of evidence has firmly situated the family as a critical site for leisure (Kelly, 1997; Rapoport and Rapoport, 1975; Roberts, 1970) and feminist critique has repeatedly demonstrated the family as a location for gendered leisure conflict (for example, Deem, 1986; Green, Hebron and Woodward, 1990; Henderson, Bialeschki, Shaw and Freysinger, 1996; Wimbush and Talbot, 1988). Despite this heritage, understanding fatherhood is a relatively new pursuit for leisure scholarship. Contrary to the state of knowledge on motherhood, substantial empirical and theoretical gaps exist in accounting for the relationships between men, their roles as fathers and their leisure lives. This is notwithstanding considerable contemporary emphasis on the role of the 'new man' in the home, debate about the value of fathers as role models for boys and young men and popular discussion about fathers as active 'involved' parents (Eichler, 1997; Forna, 1998; Gavanas, 2004). Fatherhood has become ever more scrutinised in the context of shifting socio-political values that place upon men the dilemma of aligning themselves with socially approved principles of gender equity and maintaining a sense of masculinity (Doherty, Kouneski and Erickson, 1998; Coakley, this volume). It is rarely noted that within this dilemma lies leisure. So dominant is the historical tie between fatherhood and 'breadwinning' that leisure as a site for constructing and reconstructing a fatherhood identity is frequently overlooked.

The balance is slowly being redressed. This volume adds to a growing body of work which seeks to explain the contribution of leisure to the construction of fatherhood (Craig, 2007; Kay, 2007; Shaw, 2008). Ways have been paved for such analysis in related fields. Fatherhood as a component of masculinity has been explored in a range of contexts (Lupton and Barclay, 1997; Hobson, 2002). The aim of this paper is to build on these initiatives and contribute to an improved understanding of fatherhood through leisure. This is attempted by exploring the lifestyles of individuals in a dominant contemporary family form: the dual-earner family. Fatherhood in this setting sits on the cutting edge of the dilemma expressed above: these fathers are co-earners in a world where mothers are both workers and carers. Mothers' engagement in the economic sphere could be seen as crucial to the legitimising of an 'entitlement to leisure' (Kay, 1996, 1998) as well as a platform from which to renegotiate the care of children. The discussion set out below uses the feminist techniques of critical gender analysis to explore the role of leisure in the lives of fathers in this challenging setting. After a brief outline of the location of dual-earner families in the UK, the paper identifies some of the key contributions to understanding fatherhood through leisure. The findings of a study that recorded the accounts of men and women in dual-earner families are then used to reveal how leisure and fatherhood interact in the everyday.

Fatherhood, dual-earning and leisure

The dual-earner family has superseded the male-breadwinner family as the dominant configuration of households with dependent children in the UK over the past twenty years (Harrop and Moss, 1995; Equal Opportunities Commission [EOC], 2007). Around half of all families with dependent children were dual-earner in 2003 (EOC, 2007: 2). These changes have sat alongside numerous other structural alterations in the configuration of households over recent decades. Increasing numbers of lone parent and non-resident fathers have been contributors to the decline in the male-breadwinner structure (see Kay, this volume). One of the few consistent features of this seemingly dynamic socio-demographic picture is, however, the nature of male employment itself. Men's engagement in the labour market has remained remarkably stable throughout the period. At a macro level, men have maintained almost continuous employment regardless of the presence or absence of children. Evidence also shows that men are unlikely to change their working hours to accommodate the demands of family life and are in fact more likely to *increase* their hours spent working at the onset of fatherhood (Lewis, 2000; O'Brien and Shemilt, 2003; in Kay, 2006). This act of 'propulsion' (Daly, 1996) contrasts sharply with women's experience of motherhood where the pattern of labour market participation is one of retreat at the birth of children and gradual reengagement as children age.

Academic work has been more successful at initiating enquiry about the changing face of women's family–employment relationship than it has been in its exploration of the continued stability of men's. Feminist commentary in particular has made great strides in unlocking the impact of the shift to dual-earning on the lives of women. Repeated empirical studies have revealed how mothers' domestic position as primary carers and homemakers has remained extremely resilient to changes in the structure and nature of their involvement in the labour market (Gittins, 1993; Hochschild, 1989). Women have been shown to work more hours than men when both paid and unpaid work are taken into account (Coltrane and Adams, 2001). This, according to many feminists, has resulted in a 'dual-burden' or 'second shift' of employment and domestic work for women in dual-earner families

(Hochschild, 1989). Women have assumed a 'dual-role' as workers and carers (Brannen and Moss, 1991; Bagilhole, 1994). A body of work has emerged on how economic participation has been (often problematically) incorporated into definitions of contemporary motherhood (Silva, 1996) and how assuming this dual role has affected women's sense of being a good mother.

In this early work in the late 1980s and 1990s, men and fathers often only emerged in analysis as agents in the formation and maintenance of unequal gender relations structured around ideologies of family life. Such ideologies were revealed as reinforcing the notion of motherhood as primarily nurturant, giving and expressive (Finch, 1983) or 'intensive' (Shaw, 2008) and fatherhood as detached and based on providing for dependents. More recent scholarship has pointed to some of the complexities of the relationships and tensions between contemporary understandings of motherhood and fatherhood. This has been part-informed by popular social discussions about 'involved fatherhood' which promote the value of fathers directly engaging with their children on a one-to-one level. Studies have demonstrated fathers' alignment to discourses of close emotional attachment with their children and the desire to be more engaged in practices of care (Barclay and Lupton, 1999). Other work has pointed to the difficulties some fathers have in communicating what this enhanced 'involvement' in their children's lives means in practice (Warin, Solomon, Lewis and Langford, 1999). Contemporary emphases of involved fatherhood can be seen as part of a broader social shift towards the values of gender equity as well as a response to a complex of factors such as changing family forms and contemporary definitions of masculinity.

At this juncture, the potential for the contribution of leisure studies to an understanding of fatherhood becomes apparent. Central to the discourse of involved fatherhood is the notion of 'quality time' spent with children (Snyder, 2007). This time could quite plausibly be defined as leisure time. The sense that there are distinct qualities to that time also urges us to explore the nature of those qualities: are they leisure-like? Despite this potential, the growth in social scientific exploration of fatherhood has only just begun to engage the leisure field. Leisure-specific research has rarely isolated fatherhood as a site of investigation (Henderson and Shaw, 2003). Leisure studies has largely studied fatherhood by proxy, for example, through the conduit of the work–leisure relationship or via exploration of family leisure (for example, Shaw, 1992; Zabriskie and McCormick, 2003). Rarely has fatherhood been placed at the centre of the research problematic.

Whilst indirect in nature, feminist critiques of the work–leisure dichotomy and shifts in the socio-economic profile have played an important part in formulating questions about leisure and fatherhood. Bodies of theory and evidence in the sphere of women's leisure (for example, Deem, 1986; Green *et al.*, 1990; Kay, 1996, 1998, 2001; Wimbush and Talbot, 1988) are particularly helpful even though such investigations provide insights into fatherhood through the eyes of women. Research reveals how imbalanced gender relations constrain women's access to leisure relative to their male partners. Women respondents reported that their male partners were better able to access autonomous leisure even after the onset of parenthood, arising out of an enhanced sense of entitlement to leisure (Kay 1996, 1998). In addition, men's lack of participation in domestic work acted to widen the 'leisure gap' between men and women in couples (Hochschild 1989; Willming and Gibson, 2000). These findings told us that leisure assumed different forms, meanings and levels of importance for mothers and fathers. Leisure as a constituent of motherhood and fatherhood is understood quite differently and interacts with the role and status of the two in distinct ways. Hearing fathers' own accounts of how these factors translated into practice was often beyond the scope of this work which was, quite understandably, attempting to redress gender imbalances in leisure studies itself.

North American research, particularly in the fields of social psychology, feminist symbolic interactionism and post-structuralist feminism, has best managed to incorporate men's experience of leisure in family contexts (Orthner and Mancini, 1990; Goff, Fick and Oppliger, 1997; Larson et al., 1997; Shaw and Dawson, 2001). Such research has not only shown that men experience greater access to leisure than women (for example, Larson, Gillman and Richards, 1997; Moen and Sweet, 2003; Thrane, 2000) but that this is magnified if women adhere to traditional gender norms (Firestone and Shelton, 1994). In addition, fathers find it easier to use leisure as a time for self expression and diversion whereas mothers find it harder to enjoy family leisure because of their role as family caretaker (Larson et al., 1997). Fathers' employment also has a greater effect on time spent with the children than does mothers' (Nock and Kingston, 1988) and employment can have a nega-tive effect on father–child interactions. Crouter, Bumpus, Head and McHale (2001) found that fathers' long hours directly predicted less positive father–adolescent relationships, and workplace stressors have been found to be associated with lower levels of father parenting quality (Goodman, Crouter, Lanza and Cox, 2008). Further, mothers are significantly more likely than fathers to experience family time as work and are less likely to report family time as leisure time (Shaw, 1992; Maume, 2006). Therefore despite fathers' reduced time for leisure during childrearing, a decline in free time amongst parents is often sharper for mothers than for fathers (Sayer, 2005; Craig, 2007) and 'free' time retains more of the qualities of leisure for fathers than it does for mothers (Larson et al., 1997). The type of leisure engaged in is also variable; there is a suggested movement from individual to child/family centred leisure activities for men moving into fatherhood (Palkovitz, 2002).

This body of work points to some of the many ways leisure interacts with fathers' broader behaviour. Other research with a leisure component expands this picture. For example, evidence supports the notion that men and fathers are participating more in domestic work (for example, Coltrane and Adams, 2001; Kiernan, 1992; EOC, 2006, 2007). It is possible that this is freeing up mothers' time for leisure and redistributing time resource and power relations in the home (Sayer, 2005). Some time-budget research from the US, for example, indicates a smaller than expected 'leisure gap' between men and women (Robinson and Godbey, 1997). Time budget research in the UK also does not indicate grossly unequal domestic and leisure activity (Gershuny, 2000). Evidence from Australia that adopts more complex time budget analyses, however, supports the notion that the domestic revolution has in fact 'stalled' with women continuing to 'double shift' at home and in the workplace (Craig, 2007).

The extent to which gender convergence characterises the reality of contemporary family life forms part of the question of modern fatherhood: is modern fatherhood becoming feminised or are men 'doing' fatherhood in different ways? Coakley (this volume) suggests that feminising (or traditional) discourses do not sit altogether comfortably with fathers' practices and understandings and that sport provides one route through which men can define and differentiate their role as a parent. Research shows some convergence of mothers' and fathers' discourse of family leisure. It is considered a duty that is purposive in terms of promoting family togetherness and bonding (Shaw and Dawson, 2001); leisure has been found to be positively related to family satisfaction (Zabriskie and McCormick, 2003); and planned family activities are considered by parents as 'quality time' with their children (Snyder, 2007). However, these attitudinal and discursive similarities are unlikely to translate into behavioural and experiential convergence, as papers in this volume show. What is not under contention is that leisure can provide an important space for fathers to interact with their children, both in resident (Harrington, this volume) and non-resident fathers (Jenkins, this volume; Swinton, Freeman and Zabriskie, this volume). The challenge is to reveal how these interactions are played out, what meanings are attributed to them and how they construct a sense of fatherhood.

Methods and study group

The following presents analysis of in-depth interviews with 14 dual-earner couples with dependent children. The couples interviewed were a self-selected sample of dual-earner couples defined as couples where both partners were actively involved in paid employment. The study group is skewed towards higher socio-economic groups. Most of the subjects were tertiary-level educated and had non-manual skilled jobs. The analysis that emerges from the fieldwork therefore refers to the experiences of dual-earners in the higher socio-economic groups, although generalisations across large groups of people are not possible or desirable given the small size of the study group. To summarise, the study group characteristics are:

- Age range 31–49.
- Seven couples worked a part-time/full-time mix.

- There were six couples where both partners worked full time.
- One couple ran a family business and worked variable hours.
- Most of the study were from majority ethnic groups (only one of the couples were of an ethnic/religious minority).
- Three couples had one child; six had two children; four had three children and one had four children.
- All couples had at least one dependent child aged under 16 in the household.
- Thirteen of the 14 couples were married.
- Five individuals had experienced divorce; four had experienced remarriage.

Both members of the couple were interviewed for the study. Partners were, however, interviewed separately and in direct succession so that they could not communicate the content of the questions/discussion between interviews and introduce the potential for bias in their responses.

The interview covered a rough mapping of the lifecourse from the end of compulsory schooling to the present day and depth questions about work (paid and unpaid), family life and leisure. The lifecourse map was used as an aid to questioning and is used in analysis as a context in which to understand life domains and their crossovers in the context of couple/family life.

The following presents the findings of research by first unpicking the patterns of the lifecourse and by examining leisure in the pre-children phase of the lifecourse. Hierarchies of work, family and leisure are explored and the strategies adopted by men in dual-earner families to access leisure are compared and contrasted with their female partners. Leisure in the post-children phase is then presented and the concept of 'leisure-based fatherhood' is unravelled. A broad definition of leisure is adopted throughout the analysis. This reflects subjects' varied and rich meanings attached to their experiences across the lifecourse.

The framework for analysis emanates from a gender constructivist perspective (see Such, 2006). This allows an exploration of gender in the context of relational environments (the couple and the family), recognising the agency of actors and the negotiations in which couples engage in their everyday lives (Brannen and Moss, 1991; Potuchek, 1997).

The patterns of the lifecourse

The lifecourse patterns of men and women in the study group are characterised in Figure 5.1. This is a simplification of the life trajectories of the men and women in the study group but it serves to demonstrate some of the typical similarities and differences in the activities of men and women in the employment, family and leisure spheres.

Figure 5.1 highlights two broad distinctive trajectories that can be divided

		TIME				
		➤				
FAMILY	**Men**	single	partner/ married	parent of infant	pre-school parent	school-age parent
	Women					
WORK	**Men**	full-time ➤				
	Women	full-time		inactive	part-time	full-time
LEISURE	**Men**	autonomy		personal leisure reduced and may be negotiated	**Leisure-based fathering** **Timetabled individual leisure**	
	Women	autonomy		personal leisure very constrained and effective negotiation limited	**Family-based leisure** **Flexible individual leisure**	

Figure 5.1 Traditional family, employment and leisure life trajectories and transitions

by gender. Men generally had a continuous attachment to the labour market and generally worked full time throughout the lifecourse. The women in the study, without exception, had less continuous patterns of employment and had periods of economic inactivity. More detailed analysis of employment histories revealed the almost universal complexity of women's employment patterns compared to men's. Male partners rarely dipped in and out of different types and forms of employment and tended to have largely continuous patterns of permanent employment (although some men experienced spells of unemployment).

Patterns of employment also appear to be less influenced by the birth and age of children for the men in the study. The leisure sphere was, however, strongly influenced by the birth of children for both men and women. Yet the onset of fatherhood brought with it different leisure experiences compared with the onset of motherhood.

Leisure and the pre-children phase of the lifecourse

As Figure 5.1 shows, full-time engagement in the labour market by both partners was the most common working arrangement in the pre-children years of the lifecourse. The child-free family was therefore employment-rich. The financial, physical and emotional independence of the two adult members of the household also influenced the form, nature and experience of leisure.

At this stage leisure activity and meaning converged for the men and women in the study group. Both groups made a clear distinction between work in the employment sphere and 'leisure'. Many suggested that the pre-children stage of the family life cycle was characterised by a strong orientation towards and engagement in paid employment and/or a 'career': 'pre children it was work, work, work, work' (Kelly, 42, library assistant); 'when I was younger I would work like crazy' (Suzanne, 41, secretary). Non-work time was largely time for leisure and there was a distinct work/leisure division.

In addition, non-work in the pre-children phase of the lifecourse was generally characterised by active leisure that was financially enabled by activities in paid employment. Nigel reflected this in his comments that:

> When I was younger my idea of leisure was to go to the pub with my friends and drink huge amounts of beer and that was really the leisure of the time . . . I used to do a bit of motor sport which I could afford to do when I was a young single man on a good income, er, but again, all that is really of no relevance to my current lifestyle.
>
> (Nigel, 44, town planner)

Others, such as Trevor commented that 'leisure' before children tended to be active, based outside the home and social:

> Obviously before we had children we went out a lot more . . . a lot of the things revolve around how much money you've got available to spend on leisure. And time. So before we had the children we used to go out perhaps three or four times a week, do various things, but, you know, for a long time now leisure has become much more home-based or going out as a family at the weekends.
>
> (Trevor, 44, landscape architect)

This theme of leisure as active, social, out-of-home and financially enabled by relatively high levels of independent income was common for both men and women. Other characteristics of leisure in the pre-children years upon which men and women converged was its autonomy and spontaneity: 'I could literally do what I wanted to, you know, I could enjoy myself, or if I felt like going out . . . you can just do it' (Claire, 44, photographer).

A final characteristic of leisure was couple interdependence (cf. Dyck and Daly, 2006). For many of the couples in the study, 'leisure' meant doing things together. Trevor spoke of this when reflecting on the leisure time he and his partner enjoyed together:

> It's quite a rare occasion for the two of us to go out now . . . I'm happy with it, you know, it's just one of those things . . . It's something that came as a – really I'll be honest and say – a terrible shock in the first few weeks being a parent, you know, it's a terrible shock. But . . . we've lived with it for 11 years now and it's just a different way of life and you just adapt to it.
>
> (Trevor, 44, landscape architect)

The interrelation between men and women in couples before children were born was, therefore, often characterised by co-dependency in leisure, although individual, active pursuits were also commonly reported. Clearly, not all couples represented this trend of dual full-time employment and active co-dependent leisure that was distinct from 'work', but relative to the post-children phase, these intra-couple relationships between work and leisure were commonly cited.

Parenting and the curtailment of autonomous leisure

For both men and women, the onset of parenthood symbolised a significant shift in the form, structure, meaning and experience of leisure. For the men in the study group the freedom associated with leisure in the pre-children phase of the lifecourse was largely reported to have declined since children entered the family. Charlie (44, computer manager), for example, commented that his commitments to active sport had reduced over the years: '[Sport] used to take up just about every evening at one time. So, when I was single and that used to be every evening and weekends as well. [But now] obviously you can't be out every evening, you can't do all those things and stay with a family.' Geoff felt that established patterns of leisure behaviour were unsustainable after his children were born:

LS: Have you ever sacrificed other things so that you can have your own personal leisure?

GEOFF (40, SELF-EMPLOYED): I did to start off with, but that soon stopped. Well, the cricket for instance, I would sacrifice being at home with Suzanne [his wife] and the boys to go and be out with a group of blokes hitting a ball around. You can't, if you sit back and look at that, you can't make it right . . . It wasn't appreciated, being away [but] it wasn't stopped. Suzanne wasn't going to stop me but she wasn't happy about it, and, of course, the boys would want to spend time with me and I wasn't there for them. So . . . it had to come to a halt.

In this example, Geoff expresses the feeling that a regular and formal commitment to a specific leisure activity was not reconcilable with the demands of home life and, after a time, had to end. Many of the men in the study felt that 'prioritising' and 'compromising' were invaluable when balancing work, family and leisure: 'You've got to prioritise whether it be for work or spending time here [at home]. A compromise, yeah' (Tom, 41, insurance broker).

'Moral' fatherhood as contested terrain

The discourse of compromise, mutuality and balance points to a moral fatherhood built around the notion of the involved, flexible father. Some of the men in the study group, however, developed strategies during the child-rearing phase of the lifecourse in order to maintain high levels of autonomous leisure after children were born. Many of the men in the study group used a 'timetabling' strategy in order to access personal leisure. For example, David (42, researcher) had established a pattern over a period of around 20 years of going running 'at least two times a week', and said that he would be 'prepared to go to long lengths to make sure I could manage to get it in'; Charlie (44, computer manager) worked as a volunteer for around 15 years 'maybe once or twice a week'; Chris (40, fitter) played snooker with his dad once a week and had done so for a number of years; and Barry (45, consultant engineer) belonged to an organisation that met twice a month on a weekday evening. This formalisation process seemed to reinforce the male partner's entitlement to leisure and 'fixed' it in a way that was similar to the non-negotiable timetable of paid work.

This strategy was not, however, unproblematic and unquestioned within the household. Structuring leisure time in a formalised way by some of the male partners caused some disagreement. Debbie (35, environmental health officer) and Tom (41, insurance broker) demonstrate the conflict of different behaviours within a couple and the pivotal role of leisure in the construction and maintenance of gender relations in the home.

DEBBIE (35, ENVIRONMENTAL HEALTH OFFICER): He plays golf . . . It's the one bug-bear of mine. He's been playing golf for a long time, well ten years now, might be even longer than that . . . it's every Saturday and occasionally mid-week as well . . . It just makes me annoyed that he gets time in the day to do his own thing and I don't. So if I want to do something on a Saturday I have to get in and book it before he books any golf or arranges that. It's not something I can do at the last minute because he's already arranged to play golf . . . So I can't sort of do anything on-spec . . . I think he's quite selfish about it to be honest.

LS: Have you ever tried to change anything about it?

DEBBIE: Oh, on several occasions, yeah. I get a stone wall. It's his thing, it's what he does.

The conflicts outlined by Debbie were also articulated by Tom:

TOM (41, INSURANCE BROKER): Sometimes I play golf, but the amount of time I spend on that . . . has reduced . . . Debbie would have been out on her horse, so we'd both go away, do our thing and come back again, carry on. With Charlotte [his daughter] on the scene that doesn't happen. The horse went, so a major part of her leisure activity disappeared. I also had a responsibility to look after Charlotte and spend time with Debbie as well so that had to reduce, I mean, the number of hours you actually spend doing other stuff . . . There are times that I've gone and spent time by myself, playing golf or whatever it might be when Debbie didn't want me to . . . There is a sacrifice there, you're spending time away from the family rather than with them.

LS: So how do you think Debbie's leisure, her ideas about leisure, differ from your own?

TOM: From a self-leisure thing I think change is probably fairly significant in that . . . if we talk about the horse for example, she would want to spend more time by herself with the horse but doesn't feel that she's got the time to do it. And it often comes out in a way that, I'm not giving [her] any time to do it either because I'm going out doing what I want to do, and there's often conflict. She sees me going out and not giving her the time to do it.

Tom's comments indicate that there are slightly different perceptions of his level of engagement in his chosen leisure activity since the couple's daughter was born. Tom perceived his involvement to be less timetabled and time-consuming than Debbie. Both partners, however, accept that behaviours and orientations towards leisure within the couple unit are a source of conflict, and from Debbie's perspective in particular, Tom's regular and fixed leisure pursuit is 'selfish' and irreconcilable with the demands of living in a dual-earner family with dependent children (although she did not directly comment on whether she saw this as incompatible with being a father). The perceived selfishness of Tom works counter to the seemingly important principle of 'fairness' within the couple unit and thereby resulted in conflict.

The strategy of timetabling not only highlights gender conflict but it also brings into question how leisure behaviour relates to fatherhood. Men who dismissed the potential for autonomous leisure after children were born intimated that this was based on their moral understandings of 'good fatherhood':

My brother is a sportsman and he has always spent Saturday doing sport . . . I've never had that degree of fanaticism about any particular interest . . . it's just a mind set of getting used to, or accepting that there are constraints and therefore this can wait for another day.

(Nigel, 44 town planner)

Andrew (39, self-employed) also reflected on this in terms of 'emotional responsibility': 'Like me not going for a swim; it's not because there's nobody here to care for Claire [his daughter], it's because I feel an emotional responsibility to be here as well'. Andrew also referred to behaviour change in emotional terms when discussing his pre-family visits to the pub: 'Going to the pub – I can't recreate and wouldn't want to in some respects now . . . Sarah [Andrew's wife] . . . when Claire was younger [would say] "well you're not going to work so why are you leaving me?" Emotionally, I just couldn't do it.'

Autonomous leisure after children was therefore a site of contestation.

Some fathers did not see the maintenance of personal pursuits as wholly incompatible with 'good' fatherhood. Many men who maintained personal leisure activities experienced conflict as a consequence but this was often referred to in terms of the *gender* conflict that arose rather than any parent–child or internal moral conflict. Others were less convinced and reflected on their moral responsibilities in ways resonant with mothers.

Leisure-based fatherhood?

Fatherhood not only brought about a contest between autonomous leisure, couple-conflict and moral 'rights and wrongs' but brought about substantial changes in the meaning of the leisure domain. At the onset of parenthood, leisure became closely tied to the needs and activities of children so that 'time spent with the children' was, for the most part, time that resembled leisure. This contrasted sharply with the experiences of many of the women in the study group who were generally engaged in more of the 'work-like' day-to-day childcare and domestic tasks.

The boundaries between family and leisure, therefore, became somewhat blurred for many men in the childrearing phase of the lifecourse. Leisure became child-centred and while this was often referred to in ambiguous terms as being 'leisure-like' rather than 'pure' leisure (i.e. something which was personal, chosen and relatively 'free'), it was often highly valued and positively experienced: 'I like us having a meal together. There are some TV programmes we all sit and watch together . . . I guess I do feel it's important' (Andrew, 39, self-employed). An example of the way in which men's 'time with the children' maintained its leisure-like qualities includes the adoption of activities with the children that reflected their own leisure interests. Geoff reflected this in his comments about his children's leisure activities:

> The youngest one plays cricket, so I take him to cricket club, that gets me out again onto the cricket field, although it's only coaching, helping the kids play, it's a leisure opportunity. He plays rugby, I used to play a lot of rugby, and I haven't done that, I stopped when I was 20 so it's a long, long time ago. There again that's another opportunity.
>
> (Geoff, 40, self-employed)

This notion of harmonising the leisure interests of male partners and children was not, however, universal and supporting the leisure activities of children was not always viewed as leisure-like. Peter (49, teacher), for example, viewed the leisure activities of his children as bestowing 'work-like' responsibilities on him: 'I think everybody goes through watching children on touchlines, tennis courts and all that sort of thing. But that's just being taxi driver and chief supporter. That's their opportunity really rather than mine.'

The orientation of fathers towards this time can be best described as a desire to 'be with' the children. This was revealed as a vital component of fathers' understandings of fatherhood and the role of leisure within it. 'Being with' children was frequently highlighted as a priority for fathers and leisure often provided the context for this: 'Work out how many days your kids have. Ten thousand days or whatever they have before they're 18 and I just think that that really isn't a lot. There will come a time that they will be gone and I do find that it is a very high priority to spend time with them' (Nigel, 44, town planner).

This was similarly reflected on by Richard (44, self-employed):

> I think it's very important to spend time with them [the children] because when you're working you're away from them . . . I've always tried to do things with them and I think it's shown in the fact that we *do* go away together with the Scouts camping and they're quite happy for me to go . . . so they're growing up knowing that I'm always there and I'll always do what they want to do and join in with them. It's taken me back to my childhood so I can carry on doing the things I used to enjoy when I was a child.

In these comments, Richard is communicating a multifaceted fatherhood-through-leisure. This can be described as a type of 'leisure-based parenting' (Wilkinson, personal communication) the qualities of which are being together out of work time, concentrating on the more leisure-like aspects of life and the less care-like. The discourse of 'being with' children is qualitatively different from the discourses of care and emotional responsibility described as 'being there' for the children by the female partners in the study group. 'Being there' was more removed from the context of leisure than was fathers' manifestations of 'being with' the children. For example, Nigel (44, town planner) commented: 'part of my relaxation is being with my family so . . . I wouldn't necessarily isolate particular things and call them leisure'. Women's references to time with the family did not highlight their relaxing qualities.

Discussion and conclusion

Research into leisure and fatherhood has great potential at both empirical and theoretical levels. The work presented here has begun to unravel some of the key issues that help explain the relationship between leisure and fatherhood. Reflecting the findings of other research (Willming and Gibson, 2000), the onset of parenthood has been shown to crucially alter both men's and women's leisure. Analysis of men's leisure throughout the lifecourse revealed that transitions to the fatherhood role were accompanied with a loss of the amount of autonomy and freedom fathers could exercise over their leisure time and leisure choices. Many fathers reduced or completely curtailed previous regular commitments. This was underscored by the view that self-determined, independent leisure was irreconcilable with their role as fathers and partners. Definitions of leisure as 'serious' leisure (Stebbins, 1999) whereby commitment is intense and time-consuming is considered inappropriate. This reflects notions of 'companionate' understandings of marriage and/or partnership (Orthner and Mancini, 1990) and contemporary definitions of fatherhood as active and 'involved'. This was evident in Shaw and Dawson's (2001) analysis of mothers' and fathers' view of family leisure. In this and Shaw and Dawson's study, parental talk about the importance of paternal time with children and family time in general was remarkably similar among men and women and highlighted the centrality of leisure to perceived family cohesion.

This 'morality talk' of fatherhood was not unproblematically translated into practice. Some of the couples in the study were, for example, in open conflict about unequal distributions of leisure in the household and the implications this had on some of the core principles of partnerships: fairness and equity. For some this manifested itself in altered behaviours (relinquishing autonomous leisure). For others behaviour was highly resilient to change despite more equitable intentions. In Scott's words: 'I think when we first had the children generally I thought I shall be a new man . . . we will do things in this particular way, and it just didn't happen like that. And it hasn't happened like that' (Scott, 41, lecturer).

These conflicts were in the most part gender-based between partners but some men articulated this as forming a broader conflict with their own sense of being a 'good father'. It is the connection between fathers' gender identity (masculinity), parental identity (a father) and moral identity (being a 'good' or 'bad' person) that requires further exploration in a 'lifestyle' or leisure context. While earning or 'breadwinning' may sit at the crossroads of these negotiations so too, it appears, does leisure. It is central to the space men carve out to express themselves as fathers.

A further moral component of modern fatherhood is a kind of leisure-based parenting. This centres on the notion that 'good' fathering means 'being with' the children. Togetherness in this respect was time that resembled leisure spent in each other's company outside of the responsibilities of employment and other obligations. This was a crucial difference between the men and women in the study that reflects previous findings (Shaw, 1992). Whereas mothers participated in leisure-like activities with children and the family, this was experienced more as work than leisure than for fathers. The notion of 'being with' the children in the context of leisure therefore is crucially different from the notion of 'being there' for children that is closely allied with theories of an 'ethic of care' (Larrabee, 1993).

'Being with' children is consistent with more traditional notions of masculinity that are tied to 'providing for' children as breadwinner or protector. Reflecting this traditional discourse, men more than women in families are more closely tied to understandings of family leisure that emphasise teaching values and providing role models (Shaw, 2008). This perhaps points us again to exploring further the tension between the morality talk of being a modern, good father and the traditional model of 'doing fatherhood'. Relinquishing traditional modes of fatherhood (masculine domesticity) requires behavioural change; maintaining it would demand defensive action in a hostile, changing world (resisting domestication of masculinity) (Gavanas, 2004). It seems feasible that leisure-based parenting may represent *part-change* and *part-resistance*. In the practice of leisure-based parenting, fathers are both embracing and resisting domestication. They are self-defining what modern fatherhood looks like against a backdrop of a rhetoric that is slightly mis-aligned with behaviour. Being with children in leisure-like time and space settings is a way of being 'involved' but not in the day-to-day, 'nitty gritty' sense of motherhood. It is at once 'providing' and 'engaging' through leisure. In this, fathers are retaining a masculine identity consistent with traditional (albeit financial) definitions whilst establishing a more modern, involved fatherhood. Findings from other work (Coakley and Harrington, this volume and Kay, 2007) suggest sport in a family, fathering context could be one such setting that balances competing social definitions of fatherhood. Further research would need to place broad definitions of leisure at the centre of the problematic to further meet the potential of understanding modern fatherhood.

6 With one eye on the clock

Non-resident dads' time use, work and leisure with their children

John Jenkins

Most fathers, regardless of their personal circumstances, want to be a good father (Dudley and Stone, 2001; Lamb, 1986; Smyth, 2005). However, separation and divorce are among several factors that have led to more and more fathers not sharing the same home address as their children. Despite increasing evidence that fathers can contribute significantly to their children's education, health and well-being, and that for many non-resident fathers contact with their children is important and highly desirable but inadequate, research on non-resident fathers, fatherhood and family as aspects of contemporary western society and family life is lacking (Fletcher, Fairbairn and Pascoe, 2004; Smyth, 2004a, 2004b).

What dads actually do when they are with their children is vitally important, but father absence rather than father presence has been emphasised in media coverage and research on separation and divorce. This focus tends to direct attention away from the benefits to families that can arise from father involvement. This situation is being redressed with a growing body of international research that directs attention away from father absence or deficit related matters and highlights instead how fathers can cope with separation and divorce, lead fulfilling lives and make major positive contributions to their children's health, education, well-being and happiness (Dudley and Stone, 2001). The amount of time fathers and children spend together or precisely when and where that time is spent is perhaps secondary to what they do together and how they engage (Amato and Gilbreth, 1999; Green, 1998; Jenkins and Lyons, 2006; Smyth, 2004a), but few investigators have explored the qualitative dimensions of non-resident parent–child contact.

A good deal of the time non-resident fathers spend with their children is likely leisure-oriented and shaped by commitments such as work or constraints such as low income (Sorenson, 1997; Smyth, 2004a, 2004b). How non-resident fathers and children use their time during contact and the extent and nature of leisure interactions between them have yet to be critically examined in Australia and also in almost all other countries (Sorenson, 1997; Amato and Gilbreth, 1999; Smyth, 2004b; Hawthorne 2005). Exploring the relationships between leisure, fathering and fatherhood and the changing roles of fathers in the context of non-resident dads could, as Rojek (2005) argues more generally, unearth social relationships and phenomena that might otherwise go unnoticed. Rojek's perspectives on the importance of leisure and what leisure can reveal about society are closely aligned to influential studies such as Veblen's (1994) critique of materialistic (conspicuous consumption) culture and Wearing's (1998) focus on leisure and feminist theory and account of women's leisure encounters, experiences and meanings in their everyday lives.

Following in this tradition, this chapter critically examines leisure within non-resident fathers' interactions and relationships with their children, reporting on a qualitative study involving in-depth interviews with eighteen non-resident fathers residing in the Hunter region of New South Wales, Australia. The chapter first sets the scene by discussing widely applied models of parent–child contact and reviews the research available on fathers' time use. Attention then focuses on the role of leisure in non-resident fathers' time use and contact with their children.

Non-residential fathers

In Australia, there are approximately 400,000 non-resident fathers. The ABS Survey of Family Characteristics (2004b) showed that in 2003 there were 1.1 million children aged 0–17 years (23 per cent of all children in this age group) who had a natural parent (in 84 per cent of cases their father) living elsewhere. Of these children, 50 per cent (or 543,500) saw their non-resident natural parent frequently (at least once per fortnight), while 31 per cent (339,000) only saw their non-resident natural parent either rarely (once per year, or less often) or never. Of the 283,000 children who saw their non-resident natural parent less than once a year or never, 64,300 (23 per cent) had some indirect contact.

Non-resident parent–child contact therefore varies greatly. Several models of contact have emerged and are used by parents or applied through courts of law. The more frequently applied models in Australia were studied and summarised in Smyth (2004b) (Table 6.1).

With great constraints to contact, many non-resident fathers find it difficult to maintain a 'normal' parent–child relationship. Specifically, this may be attributed to fathers' inability to spend time with their children on a daily basis, their lack of involvement in day-to-day decision-making and children's activities and progress at school, and the fact that they may no longer be regarded as a family member (Bailey, 2002). Other reasons for fathers losing or failing to maintain levels of contact with their children include being marginalised if their worth to the children's lives appears to be undermined by courts, counsellors or the children's mother; being unable to afford to support their children and subsequently withdrawing; feeling rejected by the children or others; giving up if they feel incompetent or find contact difficult; finding the geographical distance between fathers and their children too great; and becoming uninvolved if either of the parents re-partners.

Table 6.1 Models of non-resident parent–child contact

Fifty-fifty care: Care equally shared among parents (seven days and nights with each parent in a fortnight period). This model has benefits in that children can be close to both parents, but it is criticised because of the lack of stability (children move between two homes) and possibilities for children to be exposed to conflicts between parents, neglect and mental health problems.

Little or no contact: Very common. The most detailed studies of paternal disengagement have been conducted overseas, particularly in the US and Canada. This research in the 1990s indicates that a large range of variables influence disengagement, including fathers not wanting to see their children because they feel the children have turned against them, strained relationships with the mother, work engagements, substance abuse, distance, children growing older, feelings of inadequacy, role ambiguity, and fathers failing to cope emotionally and psychologically with divorce.

Holiday-only contact: Often arises when one parent relocates a considerable distance from the other parent and his/her child(ren). There is a gravity-model effect in that as distance increases, contact decreases. Problems arise in that contact becomes less and less frequent and may eventually cease. Or the nature of contact becomes such that children are often, if not always, in a 'school-free zone' when the father may in fact be taking time off work.

Daytime-only contact: Experienced by about 30% of Australia's non-resident parents. Children do not stay overnight. They and their non-resident parent may have limited opportunities to experience some important family activities such as cuddles and reading before bed-time; night-time and morning meals; transport to school; showering, dressing and cleaning the house together. Prominent features of this model are: 'child-age related factors (most notably the presence of a young or teenage child); relationship issues (perceived obstruction or disinterest by a parent, or the presence of a new partner or new children in the non-resident parent's household); and/or structural issues (unsuitable accommodation, geographical distance, or work schedules)' (Smyth, 2004b, 84).

Standard contact: Non-resident parents see their children every alternate weekend and half the school holidays. It is a common model, perhaps the most common in Australia and overseas (Ferro, 2004). There are a number of possible explanations for the evolution and widespread application of this model. These reasons concern 'traditional sex roles and work patterns' (Smyth, 2004b, 88). Non-resident fathers may continue in their 'traditional roles', working during the week and seeing children on weekends. While some fathers would like to see their children on every weekend, in an increasingly widespread situation where mothers are working, mothers too reserve a right to see their children on weekends (Ferro, 2004).

Source: Smyth, B. (ed.) 2004b. 'Parent–Child Contact and Post-Separation Parenting Arrangements'. Research Report No. 9. Melbourne: Australian Institute of Family Studies (AIFS).

There are also of course some fathers who simply do not care and refuse to support or be involved with their children (Green, 1998: 66).

International research on fathers and fatherhood shows that fathers have important influences on their children (Amato and Keith, 1991; Amato and Gilbreth, 1999; Commonwealth of Australia, 2006). Demographic and family circumstances, socioeconomic resources, and the nature and quality of father–child interaction have consequences for children's well-being, cognitive development, social competence and academic achievement, and their educational and occupational attainments as adults (Hernandez and Brandon, 2002). Research has also highlighted the importance of fathers in the lives of children and adolescents (Dunn, Cheng, O'Connor and Bridges, 2004; Jackson, 1999). While there are clearly cases in which children who grow up without fathers do well, and also instances where contact places children at risk of harm rather than benefits them, on average children who grow up without a committed and involved father are more likely to suffer disadvantage and lower levels of well-being (Horn and Sylvester, 2002). We need to uncover conceptual frameworks and models which might better capture the emotional, cognitive and contextual aspects of fathers' time use and involvement with their children. How fathers use their time as a whole will directly affect their levels of contact with their children and the extent of involvement they can sustain.

Studying fathers' time use, work and leisure

Our understanding of non-resident fathers' time with their children needs to be placed in the context of their broader pattern of time use but there are problems surrounding the data available for this purpose. Although considerable attention has been given to time use in Australia, most analysis focuses mainly on working couples with dependent children and generally captures an unrepresentative and limited cohort of non-resident fathers. The Australian Bureau of Statistics (ABS, 1998) Time Use data, for example, currently provides an inadequate basis for studying non-resident fathers' time use because the household survey conducted by ABS does not include identifiable cohorts of non-resident fathers; in addition the time use diaries used to collect data from survey respondents over two days are kept irregularly and there is no guarantee the records will coincide with days when non-resident fathers have contact with their children. The ABS most recently conducted its time use survey in 2006 and data became available from early 2008. Researchers who wish to identify and extract a non-resident fathers sample will need to explore its size and the extent to which it is sufficiently representative for robust conclusions to be drawn to inform further research directions. This may be aided by improved family related data in the Labour Force Survey released in late 2008.

Researchers in Australia also have access to longitudinal data derived from the Household Income and Labor Dynamics in Australia (HILDA) Survey, a dataset that involves the collection of annual data from 10,770 respondents. It allows researchers to unpack more reliable quantitative measures of non-resident fathers' time use than the ABS time use survey but still has limitations. Responses to the Wave 1 of HILDA for example were generally given five years after parents separated, by which time 'the initial grief, anger and resentment associated with relationship breakdown has subsided'

(Parkinson and Smyth, 2003: 17). The implications of this are that we know little about the early years of separation when parents negotiate child-contact arrangements, resolve asset disputes, relocate and re-partner, and when contact is very likely to be unsettled.

The HILDA Survey is none the less the most substantial resource as the sixth wave of data became available in 2008, and the Survey has collected detailed information on a wide range of factors impacting on fathers' time use (e.g., paid employment, housework, playing with children). Among Wave 1 participants, for example, 1,990 fathers had children living with them for more than 50 per cent of the time (resident fathers), while 367 had children living with them less than 50 per cent of the time (non-resident fathers). The non-resident participants' numbers are only small but HILDA provides the best data on the number of hours and minutes per week spent on nine activity-based time use categories: (1) paid employment; (2) travel to/from work; (3) household errands; (4) housework; (5) outdoor tasks; (6) playing with your children; (7) playing with other people's children; (8) volunteer and charity work; and (9) caring for disabled or elderly relative. HILDA also provides detailed demographic data for fathers; a suite of work-related data; information pertaining to the scope fathers have to balance work and family commitments; indices of socioeconomic advantage or disadvantage, economic resources, and education and occupation; a range of variables to measure financial pressure and debt; child support paid or received; a raft of income and wealth variables (by source); and information on health, well-being, living arrangements and access to social supports.

The Longitudinal Survey of Australian Children (LSAC) provides an additional database with more policy-related variables (for example, whether contact arrangements and child support payments are negotiated or court-ordered), but by 2009 there will only be two waves of LSAC data published. Moreover only Wave 2 will include data collected from non-resident parents, and this will be contingent on the resident parent (and so in most cases the children's mother) granting permission, thus introducing substantial sample bias. In addition, standard time use models often applied in leisure studies and other fields (ABS, 1998; Brown and Warner-Smith, 2005) are less definitive and accurate than the HILDA data set. The applied concepts of standard model used in the 1998 ABS survey (also see above) were: (1) necessary time: survival activities such as eating and sleeping; (2) contracted time: activities such as paid work and regular education; (3) committed time: commitments to social and community activities, housework and child care; (4) free time: the residual time use category.

Effective collection and analysis of time use data is fundamental to understanding parents' interaction with their children. 'Time' and 'free time' are problematic concepts with inconsistent meanings and questions arise about, for example, the significance of overlapping activities (e.g. child care and play and meal preparation) and the importance of knowing precisely who was present – and why – when particular activities take place. These issues become particularly significant in relation to non-resident fathers for whom contact with their children may be highly regulated, for example in instances where court rulings only permit fathers contact at stipulated times, and only when another adult is present. Existing surveys cannot detect these kinds of nuances in parent–child contact and relationships which may be central to the experiences of those affected by them. The capacity of widely applied classifications to recognise and address the consequences of structural changes caused by separation require greater recognition, for many reasons.

Time use and non-resident fathers' work

How people use their time and cope with life's demands may be significantly influenced by workplace arrangements, personal values and interests, physical and mental health, socioeconomic and demographic circumstances, attitudes to work and leisure, and place of residence and other factors (Duxbury and Higgins, 2003; Brown and Warner-Smith, 2005).

Participation in paid employment is an aspect of fathering that affects the economic and environmental circumstances of children's development (Tamis-LeMonda and Cabrera, 2002: xiii) but will also affect the time fathers have available for children and the quality of father–child relationships. Non-resident dads' work and contact arrangements will be influenced by recent policy development in Australia across several arenas. Social and economic changes in the last three decades have seen a new public policy focus on fathers and fatherhood in Australia. The Intergenerational Report (Australian Government, 2002) has raised concerns about the impact of population ageing and has seen priority accorded to measures that raise labour force participation rates. Second, recent amendments to the *Family Law Act 1975*, give priority to encouraging shared parental responsibility and the promotion of positive involvement by fathers in the lives of children.

Against this backdrop, there is concern that changes to the social constructs of fatherhood and fathering reveal 'extensive ambiguity and confusion' and that the practice of fathering has not kept pace with the rhetoric surrounding it, or with changes in policy settings (Hawthorne, 2005). The Human Rights and Equal Opportunity Commission (Goward, 2005) has warned that increasing labour force participation requires both a greater understanding of the pressures facing men and women in their efforts to combine paid work and family responsibilities, and an unpacking of the conundrum in which fathers are more willing to take on parenting responsibilities but are reluctant to adjust hours of work, use their full entitlements to annual leave and access family leave provisions, or take unpaid leave. To date little is known about the use of these arrangements by non-resident fathers, despite a substantial body of research on the use of family-friendly work arrangements by Australian mothers (Hughes and Gray, 2005). A small qualitative study by Smyth, Caruna and Ferro (2003) of separated parents with shared care (50:50) arrangements found that all of the men had reduced or relatively flexible work arrangements and all the women were in paid work. Non-resident fathers' work involvement, and the extent to which they can and/or are able to contain its demands, are therefore key parameters for the time they can spend with their children.

Non-resident fathers' leisure and contact with their children

Leisure-based interactions of non-resident fathers with their children take place within the context of arrangements for father–child contact, usually specified and reinforced by law and by fathers' work and other commitments. The interaction of 'leisure' and 'family' represents a significant gap in leisure studies (e.g. Kelly, 1997; Shaw and Dawson, 2001), but some attention has been directed to a number of dimensions including marital leisure patterns, joint leisure experiences, family bonding and strength (Hawks, 1991). Shaw and Dawson's (2001) work suggests that families sometimes see family recreation as a form of purposive leisure that can improve communication, bonding, health and fitness, and an opportunity for parents to express particular values, interests and world views. Zabriskie and McCormick (2001) used a family systems framework to develop the Core and Balance Model of Family Leisure Functioning. They argued that there are core leisure patterns which arise from low cost activities on an almost daily basis around the home. They also identified the need for families to be able to adapt to change and maintain balance, and suggested that adaptation skills are often needed and developed in leisure and recreational activities pursued away from home.

Family leisure with respect to men has received some attention in Australia. Morrison's research on househusbands (1994, cited in Veal and Lynch, 2001), for instance, revealed that some of these men expressed their individuality through leisure. In reporting on Morrison's work, Veal and Lynch (2001: 402) argued, 'In the case of men fulfilling the role of househusbands, leisure becomes a context for confronting traditional ideas of masculinity in Australian society, and for reconstructing a masculine gender identity.'

Overall, however, fathers have not been well represented in leisure studies family research (Kay, 2006). This is particularly evident in the dearth of research that explicitly examines leisure interactions between fathers and their children in the leisure studies literature. However, a parallel and relatively extensive body of literature in child development research highlights the unique and important role of fathers in the leisure of their children. Brown, Michelson, Halle and Moore (2001: 1–2) state that 'when parents are involved in activities with their children they are (often unconsciously) contributing to their children's cognitive social and emotional development . . .' and note that 'fathers' participation in play activities with their children has been found to be particularly important in forging a secure parent–child relationship'.

Parents make valuable contributions to their children's cognitive social and emotional development when they participate in activities with them. To date, however, examinations of father–child play interactions have failed to fully consider how the restricted and unique characteristics associated with being a non-resident father may impact activities, attitudes, perceptions and meanings for the parents involved.

Fathers in 'non-traditional' families, including non-resident fathers, have not been very fully accounted for in research into parent–child leisure interactions. Most focus has been on two-parent families although wider recognition is gradually being given to leisure in other family configurations including lone parent, blended and same sex couple households (Freysinger, 1997; Kelly, 1997; Shaw, 1992; Harrington, 2006). To date however, examination of non-resident parents' leisure with their children has been absent (Jenkins and Lyons, 2006). Despite this, leisure, recreation and entertainment appear to be important aspects of many non-resident parents' interactions with their children. Stewart's (1999) research in the United States indicates that most non-resident parents' primary interactions with their children actually take place in leisure contexts. These interactions were linked to a variety of factors affecting the role of the non-custodial parent. Woods' (1999) interviews with 252 non-resident parents revealed that 94 per cent of respondents provided recreation and entertainment activities involving a 'significant cost' during contact visits. Of those who provided recreation and entertainment activities, 55 per cent said that 'it helped to build the relationship with the children' (1999: 28).

Being a non-resident father also has implications for fathers' personal leisure, and this may affect their time with their children in a variety of ways. New found freedoms from daily parenting responsibilities allow some non-resident fathers to pursue new interests, develop new skills, develop social contacts and attain desired levels of fitness, health and well-being. These pursuits may help forge greater commonalities in non-resident fathers' leisure with their children or alternatively may act as diversions that detract from the time they spend together. At the other end of the spectrum, leisure may feature little in the lives of fathers who become depressed and may neglect their health and/or lose their motivation to play such that their leisure time with or without their children becomes a time of inactivity and sadness (e.g., Green, 1998). It has also been found that moments of guilt may drive some men to engage infrequently in leisure with their children (Pollack, 1999). Leisure therefore has the potential to impact fathers' time with their children directly and indirectly, in diverse ways.

Methodology

This study set out to gain greater insights into non-resident fathers' leisure with their children. It is difficult to recruit fathers for research projects, and this has been especially the case for non-resident fathers (Smyth, 2004a: 45). Further, despite the fact that women and men have different attitudes, perceptions and recollections of events and issues, 'Much of what we know about separated/divorced fathers in Australia comes from talking with mothers' (Smyth, 2004a: 21). There is therefore much to be gained from finding means of engaging non-resident fathers in research and talking to them in a variety of personal and family circumstances and this research aimed to contribute to this knowledge.

Semi-structured in-depth interviews were conducted with 18 non-resident fathers in the lower Hunter region. Respondents were recruited in a non-random manner (self-selection) which limits generalisations of the findings to the study's participants. Promotion of the study on the University of Newcastle's website and subsequent radio interviews, newspaper coverage and discussions on websites shortly after its posting encouraged many fathers to contact me as the Chief Investigator. Potential participants contacted me by telephone or email. Given this was a pilot project with resources available to conduct, tape and transcribe up to 20 interviews, the first 20 eligible respondents were recruited.

Interviews were conducted during September 2005 to February 2006 at locations and times convenient to participants. The questions in the interviews were directed to non-resident fathers' personal and social circumstances, their relationships with their children and other family members, their contact with their children and what activities they do with and without their children, particularly with respect to their leisure time.

All interviews were taped and lasted between 40 minutes and 90 minutes. Of those who were sent information statements and consent forms and who then indicated their willingness to participate, one father withdrew on the day of the interview and another moved out of town before the interview could be conducted and left no forwarding address. Despite testing of equipment and checking of digital taping performance during interviews, much of one interview was indecipherable because a component of the digital recorder broke down during the interview, but this was not evident to the interviewer or the interviewee until the interview was downloaded and replayed the following day.

The 18 interviews (including the remnants of the interview during which the recorder failed) were transcribed and the qualitative data from the interviews was analysed thematically. The use of an inductive approach, which incorporated the use of constant comparisons analysis, facilitated the construction of categories, themes and issues grounded in the data, rather than based on preconceived frameworks and ideas. Analysis of the interviews revealed four salient and interrelated themes: the effects of experiences of separation and divorce on fathers' life circumstances; lack of time and time pressure associated with contact; leisure meanings and activities; and aspirations for and experiences of leisure with their children. The narratives provide an avenue for fathers' voices to be heard. In addition to the interviews, several fathers provided other documentation including pictures, letters, emails, poems and cards. One father typed a summary of key issues and events and presented this to me at interview. In all cases pseudonyms are used and data is not aggregated in detailed profiles in order to protect fathers who participated in the project.

The respondents

The fathers interviewed ranged in age from 29 years to 57 years. The average age of fathers was 46 years and the median 45 years. Fathers had been separated for periods of between one year and 16 years and contact with their children at time of interview varied greatly from, for example, substantial shared care, to every second weekend with overnight stays, to daytime only contact two or three days a week, to no contact. One father had different contact arrangements for three different children, while several fathers' contact had changed substantially over time since separation. One father had one child; eleven had two children; five had three children; one had four children living with their mother. One child of a father of three had been institutionalised. Fathers maintained various forms of contact other than face-to-face contact – email, letters, cards, telephone calls and mobile phone text. Some attended school and sport-based activities outside of designated contact hours.

The ages of children ranged from 3 to 17 years at time of interview. Child support payments by non-resident fathers to CSA or directly to the mother varied from approximately $260 per year (the current legislated minimum child support assessment) to $36,000 per year. One father declined to indicate the amount of child support he paid. Two fathers declined to state their incomes, but incomes ranged from less than $10,000 per annum to around $200,000. Average weekly earnings in the December Quarter 2006 were AU$880 or approximately AU$45,760 per annum. All fathers, except one who was born in New Zealand, were born in Australia. Educational attainment ranged from completion of Year 10 (or equivalent) schooling to undergraduate university degrees. Twelve of the fathers had re-partnered. Eleven of the fathers' former partners had re-partnered. One father did not know whether the mother of his children had re-partnered. Some fathers had children who fell outside the specific scope of this project (i.e. children from previous or later relationships).

There was great diversity in fathers' life circumstances and experiences and contact arrangements. All fathers indicated the significant lifestyle changes that coincided with separation and divorce, their love and affection for their children, and their desire to be an active parent in their children's lives. There was a high prevalence of feelings of guilt at the impact of parents' separation and divorce on their children, alienation from family and community, a sense of emotional loss, feelings of helplessness or an inability to control events. The lack of institutional and personal support during emotional and financial crises were noted by several fathers, especially during lengthy and expensive legal battles over contact arrangements. As Justin explained:

'I don't see my children at all . . . As much as I desperately want to and I have court orders that say I should, my ex-wife has found ways around it . . . I don't know when or if I'll ever see them again . . . I'm very jaded, I'd write these letters and you put your heart and soul into it and you'd send it off but there is no guarantee it will reach its mark. That's why the telephone was good 'cause at least I could talk to them but I could always hear there was someone just in the background . . . So far it's been $90,000 just trying to see my children.'

(Justin)

Other problems noted by fathers included inadequate and poor professional advice (for example, one father was advised by a counsellor it was in the best interests of his children that he seek every second weekend and daytime only visits twice a week); financial problems and home re-establishment costs; powerlessness in determining contact arrangements and obstruction by the mother when either parent had re-partnered or when a fathers' level of contact had nearly reached a threshold that would have led to a pro rata reduction in child support payments; lack of say in children's well-being and upbringing; difficulties in establishing and maintaining contact with children; impacts of re-partnering where the wife of the father did not want substantial financial resources and time being given over by the father to keep contact with his children; and rejection by children without any explanation or understanding from the children or the mother.

There was evidence of good relations between some separated parents and fathers who coped reasonably well with separation, but the situation for most is a dynamic one and very prone to change. One mother moved into the home of her new partner and allowed the children's father and the children to stay in her second home during contact visits. That father travelled long distances to see his children. Scott was one of few fathers who described how the relationship between him and the children's mother had 'improved' or 'got better' over time'.

The work and parent–child-contact 'conundrum'

Some fathers made substantial changes to their workplace arrangements in order to see their children. One father described how he worked long hours between school holidays in order to make time to travel interstate to visit his children:

'I had between 12 and 14 weeks off a year with my work and all of every school holiday I'd go [interstate to see his children] . . . No normal person takes 14 weeks a year off. I couldn't care less about what normal people do. This is my relationship with my children and I'm trying to do the best that I can to maintain that and get it to a stage where they can ring me up any time they want whatever their need is and say hey dad I need to talk to you about this.'

(Joseph)

Other fathers described flexibility in their work arrangements that were vital to facilitating contact with their children:

'I'm very lucky that my hours of work are like 9.00 [a.m.] to 3.30 [p.m.]. . . . I've got a lot of flexibility in that compared to normal people's work hours . . .'

(Gareth)

'Flexibility and me being self employed is fairly important . . . I maintain approximately 20% to see my children; about 20% of the year . . . so that's about 75 days. So when I'm with my children I'm with them all the time. So that's a big commitment. And I can only do that if I work for myself. No one is going to give me a job where I have 75 days off a year. So I realised that pretty quick.'

(Callan)

'I had to work every second weekend; well I was supposed to work nearly all weekends, but I organized to have every second weekend.'

(Stanley)

Fathers exhibited a range of actions to facilitate contact with their children – changing from full-time paid employment to self-employment; limiting their hours of work; changing occupations; rearranging work/shift schedules sometimes at short notice. However, not all fathers were able to change their work patterns. For example, two fathers who worked in the hospitality field revealed significant constraints and barriers to making time to see their children. Casual employment, working nights, being on call and lack of predictable work arrangements made it very difficult for these fathers. One father living in another relationship often worked two to three casual jobs simultaneously while studying full time.

Two fathers spoke of the importance of their friendship with their work-place supervisor who allowed them to arrange their work hours to help them spend time with their children. As one of these fathers explained:

WILBUR: 'Well, my employer is [organisation]. And strictly speaking they don't have a system for father's type things. But my boss is a top bloke and we get on really well and I do over hours and he understands that. He says any time you need time to go and see your kids or do whatever it is you've got to do, just go.'

JJ (INTERVIEWER): 'So is there enough flexibility for you to be able to say something like "well I'll work a few extra hours this Monday to Thursday and then maybe get a Friday off"?'

WILBUR: 'Not really, no. it's only for dropping them off [to home or school] or doing things like that. I reckon he would, he's a top bloke. We all get along really well there. But there's nothing really set in concrete. I know they have it for mothers but no . . . not really. There is carer's leave. I could probably get that. I can get that. But no . . . no other thing that XXX offers.'

(Wilbur)

Flexible arrangements are vital to Wilbur, whose contact with his children operates on a three week cycle. Wilbur sees his children every week but each week the timing and length of contact varies.

Free time and time pressure: dads' leisure with their children

The interviews sought to obtain information about non-resident fathers' leisure with their children and without them. The following discussion focuses principally on fathers' leisure when they are with their children.

Fathers perceived leisure differently and did different things with their children, but it appeared not to be significantly more or less important to any of them in the context of their engagement with their children. Zac's view of leisure was closely related to conventional notions of leisure which encompass free (unconstrained or non-work) time and activity:

'Leisure according to the dictionary means an opportunity to do, or afforded by free time, time at one's own disposal. And I think it is the substance of what we're talking about, this free time; these opportunities we have with our kids that makes all the difference . . . This leisure is vital to the healthy interaction between parents and children. So, leisure to me was just going swimming and activities, and it's partly that but it's more than that. It's that opportunity to have that free time with each other that isn't constrained. Unconstrained time. And that's something that I believe the children and the dads, and the mums too, are entitled to have with each other.'

(Zac)

Conversely, for Terry, there was significant overlap between leisure (and pleasure) and work at his property

'I'm one of these people who'll often get accused of not getting any leisure because I find a lot of my work is my leisure and pleasure. You know the farm . . . so leisure is a bit of an odd thing for me. In its strictest form, going to the beach, going to the movies; you know, going to the gym, I would consider that's leisure . . . I consider that leisure. It's a bit of a hard thing for me. I don't have a particular leisure hobby that a lot of people have. My hobby is my farm.'

(Terry)

Both Terry and Zac went on to describe the range of activities they have enjoyed with their children, and Terry emphasised how he much prefers actively engaging in leisure rather than sitting back to observe children play. As Terry explained:

'I try to do everything with them that I can. I know a lot of people go to the Forum and mothers will take the kids to the pool, but they'll sit up in the stand and read a book while the kids play in the pool. I try to jump in the pool. I never ever take them somewhere to watch them play. And I think it's interesting that people have what they call engagement with their kids or contact with their kids, but they're only really having contact not doing things with their kids . . . I've often heard that separation can make good fathers. Some fathers take very little notice of them when they live at home. Normally you have two people focusing on the kids and that happens a lot in normal situations. But suddenly you are alone and you've got two of them full time and they are both really, really craving your attention. The whole thing changes dramatically.'

Among the fathers, leisure with their children took on the wide array of activities one might expect – skiing, surfing, swimming and other water sports; cycling; walking; camping; long drives; building sand castles and playing in the sand at the beach; kicking footballs; playing cricket. These are the typical active leisure pursuits frequently ascribed to fathers' engagement with their children in intact families (see Jenkins and Lyons, 2006). However, passive and educational leisure pursuits, less often associated with fathering, were also common – arts, crafts, drawing and reading; playing board and computer games – and everyday activities such as watching television and videos/DVDs were prevalent. Perhaps unsurprisingly, other activities such as home renovations and working on the property, mowing the lawn or even doing household chores with children sometimes appear to have taken on a leisure dimension for some fathers. Several fathers recounted the 'pleasures' of doing household renovations with their children, cleaning, washing up and the simplest of events involving child care around the home.

The timing, length, nature and quality of contact are all critical factors in fathers' leisure with their children. Regardless of the level of child support paid by the father, the financial costs of leisure were considered to be quite substantial, especially in providing for particular activities, maintaining diversity in activities, acquiring good equipment and catering to changing tastes that arise in and among children over time. Some fathers thought they perhaps made time and space for leisure during contact with their children to an extent they may not have done before separation.

Most fathers experienced a form of time stress or pressure, especially if more than one child was involved and especially where those children either varied by age or were of different sex. The problem was compounded by infrequent (e.g. daytime only or holiday only) contact. Stanley, for example, described his experiences of a weekend with four children as 'impossible' in terms of adequately accommodating their needs He went on to explain:

> 'That's what I miss, you know it's alright to have the weekend and you know you're a Disneyland dad, and all you do is muck around with the kids. Well, I'd rather have the kids during the week. What I miss with my kids is talking about how they went at school, helping with their homework, helping with school projects, discussing other kids in the class. And you lose all that. All you get is, you go to dad for fun time and it is . . . dad's try to jam 14 days of life with their kids into 2 days. You hear these women saying "he just spoils him rotten and takes him to McDonald's and does this and that". And I say, "well, who wouldn't? If you had someone, who, when they're born, you basically dedicate your life to them and then suddenly you can only see them a couple of days a fortnight, of course you're going to!" The couple of dollars a week you've got left you're going to spend it all on your kids.'
>
> (Stanley)

After deducting child support, reestablishment costs and maintaining contact with his children, it was apparent Stanley's intent in his expenditure on his children was not an effort to 'buy love' but an outcome of having little discretionary income and an acknowledgement of the significance of contact to him and his children.

In the course of discussions fathers were asked what aspirations they had in engaging in leisure with their children; what did they hope to gain from leisure activities with them? Many responses centred on developing a relationship with their children:

> 'Just a very loving relationship – a very loving relationship.'
>
> (Gareth)

> 'The only thing I hope for them is that they have a good connection with me as their father, so whatever they choose and what ever direction they go I just want to support them. I think that's important. Very, very important.'
>
> (Callan)

The interviews shed light on both the importance of leisure for fathers who want to develop relationships with their children and supported existing research that dads do want to be good fathers. Leisure with their children is an important means of them being good fathers. Leisure is an aspect of life which parents and children can share, through which they can develop skills, bond, strengthen resolve and learn about each other and aspects of life. It is salient to family life for intact *and* separated families, but it likely takes markedly different forms, and is especially noticeable in the ways in which non-resident fathers or fathers who experience long periods of absence from their children see any time as fulfilling, enjoyable and in some ways uncommitted time. Thus leisure (or free) time can even be experienced during what is normally considered necessary or committed time. Leisure time, however it is constructed by fathers in the presence of their children, is not trivial, and may very well be an especially important avenue for non-resident fathers who only have little and highly regulated contact to make a valuable contribution as parents to the lives of their children.

Discussion and conclusions

'Well, I didn't think I actually had much to contribute to this but it has actually brought to my mind how much I actually have done. I'm feeling really proud of what I've done with my kids.'

(Gareth)

'Good feeling of family . . . just a really nice bonding. Each time we go away and I do something with them it's just full on, "Dad! Dad!". They're very appreciative, they're beautiful children . . . They give a real lot back. It's always what you put in that you get back.'

(Wilbur)

'For me personally, I feel you should spend as much time with your kids as you can. They're not kids forever. Before long they're adults . . . I can see that coming and you got to be realistic about that . . . But I find if I spend as much time with them as I can now, when they do get to that age, hopefully, touch wood, they'll still want to come and see me.'

(Brett)

Given the prevalence of marital breakdowns and births outside marriage, frameworks to support non-resident fathers will remain a very important policy issue for the foreseeable future. International and Australian research (see Smyth, 2004a) has identified the need for research in the fields of fatherhood and non-resident parenting and a range of gaps in the current literature. This chapter offers a contribution to our knowledge of non-resident fathers, focusing on the role of leisure in their contact with their children and considering this in the broader context of non-resident fathers' time use.

Time is more than a quantitative construct; it is a 'container of meaning', and studies that critically examine how fathers comprehend time and manage different aspects of their lives are lacking (Thompson and Bunderson, 2001). A detailed understanding of time use patterns and activities will enable researchers to investigate why fathers make particular choices about the way they use their time; the key constraints on, and facilitators for, fathers' involvement with their children; whether there are significant differences between resident and non-resident fathers' time use; and whether framing alternative policy approaches to promote father involvement according to residential status is a valid and meaningful policy dichotomy in the overall context of fatherhood. Rojek (2005) is right: leisure, in this instance considered as a form of time use and the basis for building non-resident father–child relationships, is illuminating in unearthing social relationships and phenomena that might otherwise go unnoticed.

Policy measures to assist fathers and families must be based on a sound and dynamic understanding of what family members do and why they make particular choices. However, few investigators have explored the nature and determinants of contact between non-resident parents and children. We do not have a consistent or clear picture of either the quantity or quality of contact, and the role of work, leisure and other aspects of time use within this. We do not understand how the nature and benefits of involvement vary between day-only and overnight contact; and the extent to which telephone calls or letters can substitute for face-to-face contact when non-resident fathers are geographically distant from their children (Smyth, 2004a, 2004b). Interestingly, there are no studies that have directly compared, for example, the time use patterns of resident and non-resident parents to test the impact of separation on the nature of father involvement or whether non-resident fathers as a group are really spending much less time with their children as is commonly assumed. Some children in intact families attend boarding schools, while many resident fathers travel extensively for work, work more than one job, or are shift-workers. Perhaps, too, it might be hypothesised that the absence of children from non-resident fathers' homes means that some such dads actually look for opportunities to make their work arrangements flexible so as to spend time with their children. In some ways they are forced to do this.

To develop and refine policies that support the dual goals of promoting labour force participation and fathers' involvement in the lives of children, it is essential to understand the extent and nature of non-resident fathers' current participation and involvement and how this is linked to the social, economic and demographic characteristics of them and their families. In stark contrast to national policy objectives, almost one-third of children who had a natural father living elsewhere in 2003 saw them either rarely or never (ABS, 2004b).

This study of a small sample of non-resident fathers' revealed great diversity in their lives generally, and their work, leisure and engagement with their children specifically. The research makes no claims to having recruited a representative sample of non-resident fathers or to possessing the rigour required to make generalisations about qualitative aspects of non-resident fathers' time use and engagement with their children. However, its findings do suggest the need for research concerning non-resident fathers' time use and the potential impacts of recent legislation. There are indications that policy and legislation promoting fathers' roles in supporting and caring for their children is outpacing workplace arrangements that might better facilitate such roles. Widespread (traditional) family and societal models of fatherhood are out of step with the recent policy and legislative developments (how will separated families, which when intact were forged around traditional models of fatherhood and parenthood, negotiate 50–50 or shared care?). And, while non-resident fathers need support to develop and maintain strong relationships with their children, formal and flexible workplace arrangements that facilitate these outcomes are inadequate in many work environments.

A better picture of the extent of non-resident father–child contact is being unveiled, but examinations of non-resident father–child interactions have failed to fully consider how the restricted and unique characteristics associated with being a non-resident father may impact on activities, attitudes, perceptions and meanings for the parents involved. We know very little about how non-resident fathers juggle time. Many research gaps could be fruitfully explored. Some of these include: (1) the negotiation of occupation type and work hours by non-resident fathers to accommodate contact and caring for children after separation; (2) reasons for relocation of non-resident fathers; (3) the impact of public policy settings (including family law, child support and work practices) in determining children's living arrangements and father involvement; and (4) the supports and interventions required by fathers to enable participation in paid work, fulfilling leisure and positive involvement in the lives of children.

In conclusion, a move away from focusing on deficit assumptions associated with non-resident fatherhood was vital to studying leisure during non-resident father–child contact. Fathers who want to be good dads need adequate time with their children, and much of this time is likely to be arranged around leisure activities. This study reveals that leisure is a crucially important and positive aspect of non-resident fathers' engagement with their children, particularly as non-resident dads seek to reassert themselves as fathers. Indeed, leisure in the context of non-resident fatherhood is at the very fore of fathering for many non-resident dads.

7 Fathers and sons
Being 'Father Angel'

Tess Kay

' "Am I a good father?" represents one of the most widespread and important
acts of critical self-reflection among men.'

(Snarey, 1997; cited in Hawkins and Dollahite, 1997a: xi)

There is a long tradition of fathers engaging in sport with their children, as
LaRossa has shown; however, the meaning and significance of such actions
evolve with the social and cultural context in which they occur. This chapter
therefore examines the role of sport in fathering at a time when men are
negotiating a complex and often contradictory set of expectations about the
nature of fatherhood. Fathering 'through' sport offers one strategy for
involvement with their children by spending time with them, collaborating
in their activities, and experiencing emotional closeness through shared
experience and enjoyment. To what extent are men bringing the values of
these emerging ideologies of fathering to bear upon their engagement in
their children's sport?

Fathers and fathering

Most westernised states are witnessing changes in the expectations surrounding fatherhood. The concept of the father as the responsible provider,
authoritarian disciplinarian and – in comparison to mothers – remote and
detached guardian of 'manly' values is being replaced by notions of the
father who is caring, involved and nurturant, co-parents with his partner, and
is emotionally close to his children. However, cultural stereotypes concerning men as breadwinners also remain powerful. Lupton and Barclay (1997)
highlight the tension between discourses that argue that men should take a
more 'feminine' approach to their family interactions, and the continued
expectation that they engage in the workforce and provide for their households (1997: 19).

Fathers are therefore responding to societal cultural messages about their
role which may contain internal contradictions and can also be in conflict
with their own biographical experiences. The outcome is diversity in how

fathers perform fathering, prompting researchers to turn their attention to how men's construction of identity is affected by their experiences of fathering.

Palkovitz (2002) provides the most explicit investigation of the significance of fathering for men's construction of identity. His questioning included asking fathers to estimate in rough percentages what part of 'who they were today' was 'because of being a dad' (Palkovitz, 2002: 68). The responses showed that all fathers in his study considered fatherhood to 'account' for a proportion of their identity, but with enormous variations – from 20 per cent to 100 per cent. Palkovitz focuses mostly on those who were more affected, including some who were wholly centred in fathering to the extent that they felt literally incapable of separating their overall identity from that of being a father. Among the more involved fathers, 'change' was seen as a defining aspect of 'real fathering' – and there was strong criticism of men who had not changed when they became fathers and had thus 'remained' selfish. Palkovitz's overall conclusion was that where change occurred, it was long term and fundamental, suggesting that fathering 'catalyses men's growth into maturity and new levels of adult development' (2002: 3).

The notion that parenting 'matures' men has been elaborated by several writers (e.g. Cowan, 1991; Heath, 1991), with longitudinal studies showing that the changes brought by parenting differentiate fathers from non-fathers through later stages of their lives. Eggebeen and Knoester (2001) write about the 'involved father' role having benefits for men including encouraging a sense of responsibility, discouraging risky behaviours, pro-moting civic engagement, and initiating personal growth through the opportunity to care for others. Overall they suggest that fathers' level of involvement with their children, measured by the time spent with them, (Eggebeen and Knoester, 2001: 390), has wide-reaching consequences for them and can profoundly shape their lives as a whole.

These developmental perspectives emphasise that fathering must be conceptualised as reflexive, requiring men to look critically at their own practices, see how these compare to their understanding of a societal standard, and respond to current expectations of their role (Morgan, 2004). Lupton and Barclay (1997) emphasise that fathering is therefore culturally specific and (re)constructed on a continuing basis by fathers in their everyday lives. They describe it as a site of 'competing discourses and desires that can never be fully and neatly shaped into a single "iden-tity", and involve oscillation back and forth between various modes of subject positions even within the context of a single day' (1997: 16). Doherty, Kouneski and Erickson (1998) suggest that in westernised states at present, a central issue in this process concerns the extent to which fathers 'should' play a role in the everyday lives of their children that goes beyond that of the traditional breadwinner: 'To what extent should men emulate the traditional nurturing activities of mothers, and how much should they represent a masculine role model to their children?' (Doherty *et al.*, 1998: 277). Current discourses surrounding fatherhood are thus fraught with complexity.

While writers on men and masculinity have paid limited attention to the role of fatherhood in identity, those within fathering studies indicate a widespread influence, in some cases very strong. The purpose of the empirical study reported below is to see to what extent these values underpin the rationales, expectations and motivations that fathers bring to their involvement with children through sport. The next section sets the scene for this by overviewing what is known already about fathers' experiences of their involvement in their children's sport.

Fathering through sport

'Whoever wants to know the heart and mind of American fatherhood . . . had best be familiar with the symbolism connected to a father teaching a child how to catch and throw a ball.'

(LaRossa, 2005: 141)

In the last two decades the growth in social science writings on men and masculinities has been accompanied by a notable increase in analyses of contemporary fatherhood. In sports research the picture has been rather different. The burgeoning literature on masculinities has rarely touched on issues surrounding fatherhood and the private sphere of the family has had little visibility in analyses of men's experiences of sport. Outside gender analyses, although 'family' has been much studied by sports researchers, the emphasis has typically been on the socialising role of the family and its members, and the impact of this on children. Relatively little attention has been paid to parents' experiences of such involvement.

Work on the role that sport plays in parents' construction of parenthood is however accumulating. Marsiglio, Roy and Fox (2005) are among a number of researchers approaching from a family studies perspective who have identified sport as a prominent site for the reproduction and performance of fatherhood. Using the concept of 'situated fathering' to consider the physical spaces within which fathering occurs, they draw attention to shared sport and physical activity taking place in domestic areas ('a spacious yard . . . [offering] opportunities to play spontaneously with their children in specific ways') and outdoor spaces ('a snowy weekend . . . the ideal opportunity to bond with their child while sled riding') (Marsiglio *et al.*, 2005: 8). From a similar disciplinary perspective, LaRossa (2005 and this volume) chronicles more than a century of fathers and children playing catch in the backyard, laying down experiences and memories that for many come to embody their relationship. He cites Kennedy's (2003) description that 'There is something about playing catch which is just so pure, so iconic, so American', concluding that the game 'is central to the social meaning of fatherhood in America' (LaRossa, 2005: 154).

A small number of writers have probed more explicitly into the relationship between sport and ideologies of parenting. Shaw and Dawson (2001) used the concept of 'purposive leisure' to capture the way in which parents used free-time activities, including sport, to pursue goals that they valued for their children. This is in line with the 'generative fathering perspective' (Hawkins and Dollahite, 1997a; Harrington, 2006; Snarey, 1993), under which fathers' activities with their children are designed to 'establish and guide' the next generation. The concept of 'generativity' was developed by Erikson (1964, 1974, 1980) to describe what he designated as the primary developmental task of adulthood: caring for and contributing to the life of the next generation. Generative adults create, care for, and promote the development of others, from nurturing the growth of another person, to shepherding the development of a broader community (Hawkins and Dollahite, 1997a).

Coakley (2006 and this volume) suggests that fathers' increased involvement in youth sports reflects changing familial ideologies, including an 'unprecedented' standard of 'good parenting' that has come to be equated with parents being responsible for their children's whereabouts and activities '24-hours a day, 7 days a week' (Coakley, 2006). The character and achievements of children, supposedly instilled through these activities, are linked with the moral worth of the parents. Harrington's work highlights the qualities that fathers value in sports-based interactions. These include the opportunity to spend time with their children and do things with them, and also, like Shaw and Dawson, to encourage them to participate in activities which they believe promote appropriate values 'about what family life is about' (Harrington, 2006 and this volume).

These studies of fathers involved in sport with their children are consistent with the fatherhood literature that shows that contemporary fathers are spending more time actively engaged with their children, seeking greater emotional closeness with them, and engaging in 'generative' parenting. Sport and other free-time activities, especially 'worthwhile', 'constructive' ones, are important vehicles for this involvement. Sports researchers are already exploring how these fathering practices may be linked to ideology, although primarily in relation to parenting rather than to the more gender-nuanced notion of fatherhood. This study focuses more explicitly on the extent to which it is men's conscious and reflexive performance of *fatherhood* that underlies their involvement in their children's sport.

The study

The purpose of the study was to examine 'fathering through sport' in relation to three dimensions of contemporary fatherhood:

1   *Involvement and connectedness:* the extent to which fathers attach importance to being actively involved in their children's lives, regard

sport as a vehicle for doing so, and achieve emotional closeness to their children through this.

2   *Generativity:* the extent to which fathers view sport as a vehicle for 'generative parenting', i.e. for preparing their children for adult life.

3   *Ideology and reflexivity:* the extent to which fathers were reflective about fathering and referenced to societal expectations of fatherhood.

The study was conducted in winter 2004–05 in a medium sized (population 55,000) English town. The research was an exploratory investigation to examine the role which sport played in the way in which men fathered their children, and the extent to which this reflected their ideologies of fatherhood. The participants were fathers contacted through a local community soccer[1] club, who took part in in-depth semi-structured interviews. The interview sought information in three areas: respondents' family composition and employment profile; the football involvement of fathers and children; and fathers' accounts of fatherhood, relating both to their personal responsibilities within their own family and their broader views on expectations of modern fathers.

The interview sample consisted of eight fathers who had at least one child (all sons) who played football in the junior teams of the soccer club; all but one also had other children. Interviews were conducted in the family home of each of the fathers. In most cases the interview space was adjacent to where other family members were present, and on a number of occasions the men's children and wives were drawn towards the discussion in its later stages, joining in to add their own observations.

The strategy for accessing research participants was effective in generating sufficient respondents, but raises issues about the self-selection of interviewees who were willing to discuss fatherhood. Men who are receptive to discussing the emotional aspects of fathering and the nature of their involvement with their children may be particularly likely to conform to 'progressive' models of fathering. In the commentary that follows, this issue is kept in focus, with appropriate consideration in the subsequent discussion.

Findings

Sample characteristics

All of the fathers were married and living with their wife and 1–4 dependent children as part of a two-parent, dual-earner household. All respondents were white, partly reflecting the low proportion of minority groups in the local population, but also indicative of the tendency for different ethnic groups to organise voluntary sport separately. There was considerable variation in the apparent affluence of the families: in addition to information about employment status and occupation, the researchers' visits to each house to conduct the interview allowed us to observe the neighbourhood and living style of each family. The eight locations represented a spread of housing types that ranged from a low value, former council house (i.e. previously publicly owned by local government), to a substantial detached dwelling in one the most affluent local villages. The remaining six properties represented a broad spread of property types and values between these two extremes.

Involvement and connectedness through football

The fathers who were interviewed had become involved in their child(ren)'s football through a variety of mechanisms. Given the cultural significance and extreme popularity of football in the UK (it is the sport with the highest participation among males and the one with the fastest growing participation for girls and women), it had been anticipated that children's participation might reflect a pre-existing past or current involvement by the father, and that sons and daughters may even be junior players at their fathers' clubs. Among the interviewees, this was not the case: although all of the fathers had had some exposure to football (which for boys is almost universally taught and played in UK schools), most had never participated as adults and some were not only uninvolved in football, but described themselves as having no affinity for sport. With the exception of one father for whom football was 'a passion' and another who had a long-standing interest in it but was not a participant, the fathers in the study had become currently involved in football solely out of responsiveness to their children. A father who was wholly uninterested in sport, explained:

> 'I think I do it as a father's duty . . . I mean, with this interview coming up I've been analysing it myself more, what I do, and what I think, I'm sure my own dad never did anything like this with me, so perhaps that's why I do it, I think I see it as part of a father's duty. It's my job to try and be there for him encourage him.'

With one exception, all fathers stressed the importance of being involved in their children's football. They mainly described it in terms of 'being there' for them:

> 'We just like to be there to support them whatever they're doing. You know, if it wasn't football, if it was something else, then we'd be there to support them in that, to me that's what children are all about.'

> 'I suppose myself and my wife have always had the view that we were gonna be involved with the children and support them in any way that we can. The children come first, and other things that used to happen, stop. I can't imagine myself being any other way. That's what you have children for, isn't it?'

'Not being there is not an option.'

A number of fathers had, through their child's participation, become involved in actively assisting at the club. The father with the strongest interest in football had become manager for the team his son played in, moving up the age-groups with him in successive years. At the time of the interview, he and his wife were discussing whether he should continue to coach his son's team, or return to the youngest age-group and start again with a new intake that he could develop. He had a general enjoyment of working with young children:

> 'It is the kids, that is what it is all about, it's about the kids that's it. Some of the dads that run the teams do it to say they run a football team "I'm in charge", well that's not for me. I find it odd that some dads like to say they are the manager of a football club and the kids start to come secondary and to me that is not right.'

He particularly enjoyed seeing the progression from the early years to the later more skilled ones. His first priority was however his son, and although he hoped to return to the younger group at some stage in the future, this would not be until his son was significantly older.

The sample included one father whose interview responses distinguished him from the others in the study. He had had an interest in watching local football but no personal playing experience. He too had become actively involved in the club through his sons, initially when the regular team manger was unavailable. He had subsequently become a manager for a different age-group, and in his case, and uniquely among the sample, this role had become his primary focus. The father of four children, including twin girls aged three, his involvement with youth football appeared to separate him from his family rather than connect him to it. It prevented him from watching his own children who now played in older teams, and from spending time with his younger children at home. While he thought he 'might' later regret 'missing' his children in this way, he regarded his role as manager as 'a job' and throughout the interview, he repeatedly re-oriented questions about his fathering role to focus on his role as a manager in the club. His responses contrasted strongly with those of the other fathers and were a valuable reminder of the diversity fathers could bring to objectively similar roles.

Fathers were asked to consider whether and how their involvement in football contributed to their relationship with their child(ren).

> 'Definitely, certainly from a relationship point of view, having something to bond over, having that extra interest, and friendship . . .'

One of the ways in which football contributed to their relationship with their children was through shared understanding of sports experiences. Fathers described a real affinity with their child:

> 'It's a shared interest, a shared passion really. Sunday he scored the only goal of the game, so he sticks the ball in the back of the net, and the first person he looks round to see is me.'

> 'We can identify with each other, because if he's experiencing the good, and the not so good, I can see that. When he scored a couple of penalties, I could identify with him, and I said, you enjoy that, it was good being in that situation wasn't it? [He said] "Yeah really good, a thrill, wasn't it, a real good thrill". And I thought, hold onto that, grab that, you can cherish those moments, you know.'

A father with no background in football, who was helpful but quiet in demeanour during interview and described himself as being generally reserved in character, found himself becoming enthused and involved:

> 'Like I say, the sense of pride it does give on occasion is wonderful, you know, and I've been shouting and cheering with the rest of them, which is something – that sort of comes out of the blue at first, yeah, stirred a bit of emotion in me, excitement! It's good, yeah, yeah, feelings.'

Several referred to their children being aware of their presence and seeking them out for affirmation of what they had achieved:

> 'He just used to love the fact that you were there, after the end of a training session, if he'd scored a goal or done something he was pleased with, a good pass, or scored a goal, or saved a goal, you'd always see that little turn around, "Oh, did my dad see that?" you know, and I think the fact that they look round, did my dad see, or say at the end "Did you see that dad?" you know, you're sort of sharing in it and encouraging, I think it's important.'

However, involvement in football was also valued as a basis for developing broader shared interests and mutual understanding. Even the father with no affinity with sport found that the knowledge he was gradually accumulating could be used in this way, which he appreciated for allowing him to share his son's life. His commentary showed his desire to truly connect with, and be responsive to, his son's interests:

> 'When there's something like an England game on the television, you can sit down together and you can have a really good chat, about why is he playing there, and what does he think about this player, and didn't he do well or didn't he not do well, you know, and its nice to communicate on that level. To sort of, I suppose just be there for them, to be interested

in it, and live it with them a little bit, if you like. I suppose you get some pleasure about the fact that you're being involved, you know, that you can relate to them in some way I suppose, you can be there for them, you can talk to them about what they want to talk about, yeah.'

Another father also found that through watching his two sons playing football, his own understanding of their characters became fuller.

'I've learnt a lot about their strengths and their weaknesses, not just physically but mentally. There were a lot of incidents, too many to think of over the years, where the situations arise where I've been surprised by one [of them], [that he could] actually do that.'

A recurrent theme was the emphasis on shared interests as a basis for friendship, both in their current relationships with their children, and in their future adult ones.

'I think there's a bit of sharing interests, so you build a friendship with your children . . . I'd like to think that as he gets older and as I get older that we would have common interests, and a friendship. So eventually when he does move away from home, that we'll have things to talk about, and we'll be friends rather than father and son. And I think that's how, really, a relationship should be.'

All of the fathers in the study had football-playing sons rather than daughters, and some commented on the particular significance of shared time arranged around football for male bonding. Fathers referred both to the particular bonding associated with male sport, and to a wider sense of male space:

'I think it's very important for a male, a man, a young man, boy, to identify the bonding, the success, it's very much a man's area, that, I think. It might be a bit sexist, but it's something they, we need really. To feel good, confidence, it's a confidence booster.'

'On a Saturday we have six or seven hours together, it gives you a good time together to talk with no women about, man's things you know. It is nice to have time on your own to talk about different things, it's not just football it is other things in the conversation, school, music, and girls and things like that . . .'

As a final dimension of 'connectedness', one father commented on the broader contribution of football to family life. His family appeared particularly cohesive: his wife, who had had no prior interest in football, had become very involved in the club through their two sons' participation, and during the later parts of the interview the whole family gradually gravitated to where it was taking place, with the mother joining in during the final stages. Both parents spoke about the central role which football had come to play in the family dynamic:

'It does become part of your life, take over. And we can come home from the match, and we can sit and talk about it for the afternoon, you know what I mean, sometimes you don't switch off . . . If you've had a really good game, or, they've won a tournament, and they come home and it's a nice day and you sit outside and get a drink, you know [laugh] . . . I don't know what we'd do without it really, I think we . . . oh well I can't imagine.'

(Mother)

'I feel it is quality time for the five of us, we can turn up do what we all enjoy then we can come back and, even if we are not agreeing with what each other are saying we have all got something in common for us to talk about for an hour, and we will spend the day together and not a lot of people can say that every week. When we are all stood on the touch line, enjoying ourselves I often think to myself, oh here we are again, but at least we *are* here and we are enjoying ourselves.'

(Father)

This analysis of football as a site for fathers' involvement and connectedness with their children identified the importance fathers attached to being involved in their children's lives through football; their responsiveness to their children's interests as the basis for this involvement; and the benefits they felt accrued to the father–child relationship. Almost all responses concurred with current debates that position fathers as involved and emotionally connected parents and there was considerable homogeneity among interviewees. The sample did however include one father who described very different experiences. This lone voice must be recognised as an expression of an alternative but equally valid account of fatherhood and its relationship with sport – and one which may well be much more widespread outside the sample in this study.

Generativity: the extent to which fathers view sport as a vehicle for 'generative parenting', i.e. for preparing their children for adult life

Fathers showed a keen sense of the broad 'generative' function of football in their children's lives. In relation to their own children, they felt that playing football with the club had beneficial outcomes at the individual level which had a long-term relevance to their adult development:

'It's not just going out there to kick a football, become a superstar footballer, to me it's about a bit of development, they're learning lots of other skills, you know, communicating, and being part of a team . . . I'm certain, yes, there are skills there that they learn for life, yes.'

Fathers also echoed some of Snarey's observations (cited in Hawkins and Dollahite, 1997a) about the community dimension of generativity. Fathers' wider contribution to youth development had already been illustrated by the two fathers who were currently either managing teams that their own children no longer played in, or planning to continue to work with younger children in the club when their own had moved into the senior age groups. Several other fathers described how they had developed a wider interest in the development of the young players in the team:

'When they're young you want to be there because your son's playing, obviously the initial thing is that your lad's involved, but you still want that team to do well because you've become a supporter if you like, you want to see that team do well, and it's a big change. My own kids could be [not playing] for some reason and I would still have the interest in the football team, as much as I would if they were.'

Fathers talked of the specific types of 'skills for life' that their children were developing through football. Several valued the fact that football exposed youngsters to winning and losing, and also to the effort and discipline required to succeed:

'When you win you feel brilliant when you lose you don't, it is part of growing up. Well he has got to learn about it, that you'll not be the best at everything you do, if you try you can't ask for more, if you try your best.'

'I think hopefully it'll give him a competitive edge, and you know, he'll have some experience of both winning and losing, and accepting both, and just enjoying something that he likes doing.'

'I believe that sport is a great way of disciplining a person for life, anyway . . . It's good to feel disappointment in your efforts if you haven't reached your goal, but it's even better to feel good, when you have. You can't reach the highs if you've not felt the lows, if you know what I mean. So I know that in life, you're gonna get highs, you're gonna get lows, you've got to be disciplined and you've got to work hard.'

Fathers also commented on the socialisation benefits that might accrue. They spoke both in terms of specific friendships and social networks being forged, and in relation of the more generic social skills their children could develop through this interaction with others:

'They've got to get out there with a bunch of nine other children that they come together as a team, they don't really know each other, they've got to learn about each other, they've got to start getting on, and communicating, and eventually you see them make friends.'

'He's got to relate with people, he's got to understand how other people have a different point of view, he's got to respect those points of view, he's got to see the benefits of two people doing something, could usually do something more than twice as successfully, by working with others. So football is a cracking, great sport for that. I'm sure when he gets a bit older, he can enjoy these lads' company, and their friends company, outside of football, and he's got these kids, these friends for life, potentially, so it's a great game, potentially, for getting on with people. It's good.'

Some were more specific about the special forms of camaraderie experienced through team sports:

'I think it's really important that he senses the enjoyment of a team, and the camaraderie, and sort of the thrill that goes with that, and I think that's so important for a child of that age to understand, what you get from a team, the way you rely on each other, how you can support each other, how you congratulate each other, how you console each other, all the sort of fun that will come, in time, if he stays in football.'

Fathers also referred to the ways in which they felt their children's experiences in football could encourage them to develop overarching values for their adult life.

'I think, somebody who appreciates having to work hard to achieve what you want to achieve, would be able to take that forward anyway, into other areas of their life . . . there are a lot of kids [at the club] that I know who are their own biggest critics. And I think to myself yeah, that's a good thing.'

'Football's not gonna lead somewhere for everybody, but, while you're doing it, you've got to take something from it, you've got to be positive. And I always try to instil that into my lads. I've still never told them yet that they're not gonna be [professional] footballers, I daren't, but I let them have their dream as long as they can. But along the way, just give them the positives, and instil into them that whatever they're doing, it's good.'

The concept of 'generativity' was productive in framing fathers' views of the developmental outcomes their children obtained from football. Fathers felt that by facilitating their children's involvement, they were giving them opportunities to extend their self-knowledge, enhance their social interaction skills, and lay down values that could underpin a successful adulthood.

Ideology and reflexivity

A key purpose of the research was to explore to what extent the role football played in fathers' relationships with their children was linked to their broader construction of the fatherhood role. Questioning centred on their accounts of what was expected of a contemporary father, whether this was distinct from previous generations, and what they would consider to be successful outcomes of their own fathering.

It became apparent during this phase of the interview that what the researchers had constructed as the separate (although closely related) issues of, first, defining contemporary fatherhood, and second, comparing it to fatherhood in previous generations, were one and the same thing for most of the fathers in the study. In describing their view of current fatherhood, most respondents instinctively contrasted it with fathering in previous times. In other words, they felt that the fathering they undertook was by definition different from that of their own fathers' generation. Their comparisons focused on both quantitative and qualitative dimensions. While much of our interest lay in the qualitative aspects of fathering, what was first and foremost reported most strongly was that fathers were simply expected to be and do *more* – much more – than previous generations had been:

> 'I think probably to an extent too much is expected of fathers now really.'

> 'You're expected to do all wide-ranging things, much wider than perhaps a father would have done years ago. I do think, the thing is wide, and it's how wide can you go, really.'

Descriptions of the additional tasks of fatherhood focused very much on men being expected to be more involved with their children, as well as contributing more equally to household chores:

> 'I think 20 or 30 years ago when I was growing up, the dads went to work and brought the money home, kind of thing, and ran the household, and they didn't really have a lot of time for the kids, I mean in generations before it was a lot worse than that. But I think you're expected to do now, modern man and all this thing, house chores, looking after the kids, you know, fair share of the work, and I agree with it.'

One father articulated how these new expectations sat alongside, rather than replaced, the traditional functions attributed to male partners:

> 'I think probably nowadays that role [fathering] has changed completely, I think it's been turned on its head. I think fathers, is still generally seen as a breadwinner, it's still the man, it's still the heavy things that have to be done, the cars, and that type of stereotyped thing I think is still there,

but it's not as it was, you know. Instead of men coming home and them expecting women to be in the kitchen, they accept that women can do more and be more, so I think the role of a father's got to change as well, that's got to expand. So I think what's expected of a father, from my kids, is the same as what they expect from the mother, but not so gentle, if you know what I mean [laugh]. So that's my idea of a father, what's expected of a father as far as I'm concerned is the same as the mother, but with the ability to mend the car, and mend the fence, you know what I mean, the old men jobs that were expected before.'

The significance of wider societal discourses were evident when a number of fathers referred explicitly to (external) 'expectations' about their role. The strength of these expectations, in both the private and public sphere, was in itself a change. One interviewee felt that fathers in previous generations had much more autonomy and were less under scrutiny in their own households:

'Oh, I think fathers have changed, it's certainly changed since my day, I mean a father, husband-father figure, he worked, and I think whatever else he did was never explored, especially by the children. I mean, when he went out, who knows, I mean they went to the pub, or the club, or whatever . . .'

Another who felt that fathers – and parents generally – were now under an unreasonable level of expectation and scrutiny, illustrated this by describing the pressures sometimes experienced in public places:

'At home part of the stress is taken away because you feel you don't have to act a certain way, you don't have to be polite in front of other people, so if I've got Bradley and Cameron punching the living daylights out of each other, and I'm talking literally, then I feel I can shout at them at home, and that's fine. If we're out in public, you almost feel you can't shout at them, because everybody stares at you, even tho they probably do exactly the same thing with their children. So people's expectations, it does make it stressful, it just makes it more difficult.'

At a much more fundamental level, this father felt that societal expectations now sought impossible perfection in a father:

'[In the past], a father was just a father, bringing in the money, and as long as the kid turned out sort of ok then they'd done their job, pretty much. Whereas now, there's kind of the model father, the perfect father – that seems to be the expectation. And with children, directly with children, I think in a way you're expected to be like a kind of father angel, you know – this perfect guy, who never shouts at his children, never smacks them, encourages absolutely everything they do, never gets cross when he's absolutely knackered and all he wants to do is collapse in front of the TV, and the children have got demands for whatever. And there is that expectation there, whether people admit that or not, there is that expectation there, and it's obviously an unrealistic one.'

The questioning about understandings of contemporary fatherhood indicated a strong awareness of broader ideologies of fathering. In conclusion, fathers were asked what they would consider 'success' in their own fathering. Although some made reference to 'good education', none of the fathers focused primarily on extrinsic achievements: instead, all spoke in terms of moral values and psycho-social developmental outcomes:

'I feel successes are, getting them involved in what they've been involved in, showing them the things that they've got, rather than letting them dwell on things they haven't got, I think its been important for me to let them see that the material things that you've got aren't always the important things, you know, it's feeling good about yourself, and again we go back to football, feeling good about yourself, and knowing that you've done everything [you could] is a good thing. So that's a success, cos I think that's gone on board now. To make sure they're happy, to be honest, and make sure they're educated . . . If I could get them to leave school with plenty of qualifications, take on board what they've learnt about teamwork, enjoying their highs, getting through the bad ones, I'd call that a success, then they'd be old enough to do with them what they wanted, their experiences and their qualifications. And that would be a success. To me.'

'I think, a success would be, he was balanced, he knows what he wants, he knows when he's wrong, and he can admit it, and he can love some-one, and if he was happy with himself, and he's able to make certain judgements.'

They saw their own role as providing the environment within which this could be achieved:

'I don't think you should give them necessarily what your father gave you, I think you start again, and I think, you've just got to be a secure home for them, to be there for them, to try and create an environment where they can be happy, and be themselves. I don't think they should derive, try and copy my personality, because I'm their father, I think peers are probably more important than parents actually, but I think we should be here, I should be here as a father to be with my wife, and to make a family, within which they can develop and grow from.'

Some felt that staying connected to their children through a continuing close relationship with them would be the ultimate affirmation of 'success':

'I suppose the acid test for me would be that if they did have some problems at whatever age, that they could come and talk to their mum and me about it, that they can come home and say, "dad, this is happening". If they feel that they can come back and talk to you about something, then that to me means that we can't have done much wrong.'

The exploration of the *ideology and reflexivity* illustrated that the fathers in this sample all subscribed to prevalent ideologies of involved fatherhood and related these to their own patterns of fathering behaviour. Their involvement in their children's sport was one vehicle for parenting in a way that accorded with these values, and might justifiably be termed 'fathering through sport'.

Discussion

This study indicated the significance of societal expectations in influencing fathers' reflexive practice about how they should 'perform' the fathering role. The participants fathered 'through' sport in accordance with the prevalent ideology that contemporary fathers should be more involved in and emotionally close to their children than previous generations, and should guide their development to adulthood in a facilitative way that nurtures individuality.

It was significant that fathers' desire to be more practically and emotionally involved in their children's lives did not equate to being more controlling or prescriptive. Their concern was to be responsive to their children. This accords with Lupton and Barclay's suggestion that 'the emphasis now is upon individuality and self-development, and hierarchical relationships between parents and children are no longer valued' (1997: 20). Fathers spoke about fatherhood in terms of shared interests and current and future friendships. They sought a form of emotional intimacy with their children that is in contrast to dominant forms of masculinity in sporting cultures.

It could be suggested that the ideologies that 'involved fathers' bring to bear on sport therefore have the potential to resist and transform existing gender hierarchies in and surrounding sport. There are however reasons to be cautious in this regard. Despite the near consensus among the study sample, there were indicators that diverse forms of fathering were in evidence at the club. The interviewees described other fathers at the club who were domineering and verbally aggressive, overly competitive, intimidated their own and other children, fulfilled the classic stereotype of living out their personal aspirations through their sons' sporting prowess, and focused on their own position of power within the club rather than on their children's fulfilment. These approaches to fathering contrasted with those of the interviewees and concurred more with the hegemonic masculinities traditionally associated with sport.

It is naive to suggest, therefore, that a unified model of fatherhood can be identified within which fathers practise involvement in their children's sport. On the contrary, Morgan (2004) claims that moving away from a single discourse of hegemonic masculinity is of particular importance in relation to the competing discourses surrounding fathering (Morgan, 2004: 280). In drawing attention to similarly diverse constructions of fatherhood surrounding men's involvement in children's sport, this study supports McKay, Messner and Sabo's call for sports studies scholars to move away from an over-emphasis on sport as a conservative institution (2002: 7) and to also recognise its potential for resistance and transformation. To some extent the fathers in this study could be considered to represent these progressive tendencies, through their 'feminised' mode of parenting. There is, however, a danger of over-simplifying and exaggerating the significance of this. Fathers in this study did not always find their fathering role easy: some queried it and considered it problematic. Messner (1993) has further warned that emotionally expressive manifestations of masculinity have limited implications for the transformation of sport's hegemonic masculinity, and warned that 'new, softer symbols of masculinity' are more likely to represent a 'modernization of hegemonic masculinity' rather than a real desire for transformation in the structure of power (1993: 730). A fuller understanding is needed of the range of fathering ideologies men bring to bear upon their children's sports involvement, and the extent to which these are accommodated within the gender order in sport.

Conclusion

Explicit recognition of 'fatherhood' as a component of masculine identities opens up a productive range of questions for sports scholars. In focusing on fathers of football-playing sons, this study examined what is possibly the most stereotypically masculine of British father-and-child sports experiences. This offered the opportunity to uncover how even this most traditional and conventional activity might be underpinned – at some times, in some contexts, for some men – by ideologies that sit in direct opposition to those associated with sport. Beyond this lie multiple other questions not explored here. Do fathers in these situations experience conflicts? If so, (how) do they reconcile them? Are the values of 'involved fathering' visible to others, and if so, what response do they elicit? Does involvement in an overtly masculine sport conceal these 'deviant', progressive ideologies? Are the issues experienced differently in relation to sons and to daughters, and do they vary according to the gender-appropriateness of the activity in which their child participates? Does fatherhood act as a catalyst for developmental change in some men, as family studies researchers tell us, and if so, how does that affect their experiences of sport? Do some men resist the changes of fatherhood – and do they use sport as a site for this resistance? Although the fathers in this study were able to accommodate their emotionally expressive forms of fathering within sport, there is potential for conflict between emerging ideologies of fathering and the traditional masculinities of sport. Sports researchers have a role to play in illuminating the individual and structural outcomes of such conflict.

Note

1 The sport under study is 'soccer'; however, interviewees refer to 'football' throughout and the commentary therefore uses the same term for consistency.

8 Fathers and daughters

Negotiating gendered relationships in sport

Nicole Willms

Felicity, 20, is a talented water polo athlete: a starter for an NCAA Division I university and training with the Junior National Team, hoping for a chance to compete for the United States at the 2008 Olympics. When she started water polo at age nine, the sport was still developing in the United States, with women's water polo trailing behind the men's. So, when Felicity, a young swimmer, noticed the sport and asked to play, her parents enrolled her on the only team available, a boys' club team ('boys' despite the fact that there were two other girls on the team). She spent a few years on this team until joining an all-girls team at 12. Today, things have changed and girls have their own teams starting at ages as young as five. To Felicity, she's part of a changing moment for women's water polo. 'I was kind of like the last generation that really played with boys.'

As Felicity blazed a trail in the burgeoning US sport of women's water polo, there was another important influence on her sporting experience – her father, who soon became her biggest fan. She loved being able to hear his booming voice at matches, and as a photographer him taking pictures of the team, and him making an effort to get to know her team-mates and their families. At some point, though, it got to be too much. He began nagging her to practice, critiquing her, arranging extra time with trainers without asking her first. He wanted to talk about water polo whenever he saw her. He travelled for work and was not home enough as it was – and now Felicity felt that the only thing the two shared was water polo. She confessed that, 'sometimes I went through stages where he wanted it more than I wanted it'.

Water polo follows many of the patterns seen in the development of other women's sports – they generally emerge or are recognized after the 'men's' versions have already been established. Before this, women's sports exist at the margins, with limited availability, poor funding, and as principally women-run organizations. As women's sports continue to grow in popularity and enjoy some gains in legitimacy in today's Western society, institutions and organizations that previously catered only to men's athletics are responding, often adopting women into the fold. Examples in the United States include the NCAA and NBA: both organizations have incorporated women's teams/leagues in recent years. Individual men's interest and involvement in women's sports appears to be concurrently increasing, especially when there are economic rewards for their participation. Regrettably, this involvement can sometimes be at the expense of women's autonomy and leadership. For example, since the Educational Amendment Title IX[1] in 1972 facilitated more funding for women's sports in the United States, men are still gradually displacing women as coaches and administrators of women's teams (Acosta and Carpenter, 2006).

Fathers, too, seem to be getting into the game. Just as Felicity's father became excited about, and perhaps overly involved in, her entry into elite level water polo, there are many other fathers who see the opportunities now available to their daughters and who are as eager as – or sometimes more eager than – their daughters to see them on the playing fields. But what happens when fathers and daughters interact in sport, a sphere imbued with masculine dominance? We need to know more about how female athletes and their fathers negotiate these encounters within sport – or how the masculinity of sport may become manifest in men's practice of fatherhood.

Fathers and daughters

We do not know much yet about father–daughter relationships in sport, but the truth is that not much is known about father–daughter relationships more generally. Despite the growth of studies of parenting and fathering, the father–daughter dyad has received relatively little scrutiny.

In a review of the developmental literature on parent–child relationships conducted in 1997, Russell and Saebel (1997) noted that the father–daughter relationship had usually been studied in relation to the importance of fathers for daughters' development (e.g. in relation to reciprocal role theory, according to which girls are assumed to learn feminine behaviour by interacting with their father and complementing his masculine behaviour) and in relation to issues such as the impact of father absence (e.g. following divorce). Belenky, Clinchy, Goldberger and Tarule (1986) and Sharpe (1994) (both in Russell and Saebel, 1997) considered father–daughter relationships to be distinctive in comparison to the other three parent–child dyads (i.e. mother–son, mother–daughter, father–son) with Sharpe also emphasizing that the father–daughter relationship was diverse and varied across families. There was however limited evidence of what made this relationship distinctive, or how this manifested itself.

Some light is cast on father–daughter relationships by research into parental patterns of time-use. These consistently show that fathers spend more time with sons than daughters. Lundberg, Pabilonia and Ward-Batt's (2006) study of American parents' time investment in their children found that fathers spent more time with sons, especially young sons and particularly when they had more than one son, than they did with daughters. This deficit was not compensated for by mothers, i.e. young (pre-teen) girls did not receive equivalent extra time from their same-sex parent. Lundberg *et al.* also showed that this gendered pattern persisted when children were in their teenage years, when fathers spend significantly more time with teenage sons than with teenage daughters. At this stage, however, teenage daughters now spent more time with their mothers, undertaking 'women's work' (typically housework, cooking) and social activities together. Fathers and sons engaged in 'men's work' together (typically home and vehicle maintenance). The researchers concluded that 'in general, the father/son and mother/daughter engagement in gender-stereotypical activities is consistent with parental enjoyment in doing "boy" and "girl" things with a same-sex child or with a desire to train children in gender-appropriate skills' (2006: 14).

Fathers are therefore more likely to play a prominent role in their sons' lives than in their daughters', and to engage in activities with sons which accord with gender norms. Father–daughter relationships within the sport context step outside this norm in two important respects. First, when daughters are talented at sport, many fathers become very heavily involved in their lives – a phenomenon personified in the popular mind by Richard Williams, father of tennis players Venus and Serena. Second, as women in a masculine domain in which the authoritative voices are usually male, daughters who play sport occupy a complex and potentially ambiguous position in relation to sport and in relation to their fathers. In this context, how is the father–daughter relationship played out?

Fathers and daughters in sport

This chapter examines the relatively under-explored area of father–daughter relationships in the context of sport. Fathers (and father-figures) are a common and intimate source of sports knowledge in the United States where a study of sports interest (Wann, Merrill, Melnick, Russell and Pease, 2001) revealed that sports fans of both sexes were most likely to cite their father as the 'single greatest influence' on their interest in sports. While the bond that fathers and sons share through sport is already well-recognized, both in research (e.g. Messner, 1992; Wedgwood, 2003) and as part of the popular imagination, there is growing recognition that sharing sports interests and activities can also establish an intense bond between fathers and their daughters.

Recent qualitative studies of women in sport report women's testimonies to their father's influence on their sport career (e.g. Kwiat-Kowski, 1998; Scraton, Fasting, Pfister and Bunuel, 1999; Wedgwood, 2004). Wedgwood's (2004) research of female Australian Rules footballers revealed powerful father–daughter bonding experiences for several athletes. Wedgwood identifies the sport context as being a key arena for interaction between the girls and their fathers, highlighting however how this contrasts with father–son interactions in sports settings: 'The difference is that football is defined as a masculine arena, and so, for sons, it is a matter of confirming masculine identity, whereas for daughters it means eschewing traditional femininity in order to meet on their father's social territory' (2004: 147).

The tension between femininity and sport suggests that father–child relationships in sport may require more sacrifice or effort on the part of the daughters than of sons and may make women particularly vulnerable in terms of trying to gain approval from their fathers. As Wedgwood noted of the girls, 'Wanting to play is directly linked with their desire to inspire love and admiration in their fathers the only way they know how' (Wedgwood, 2004: 147). It is almost assumed in our culture that many boys will seek to inspire love and admiration in their fathers through sports; that girls now regularly pursue these goals speaks to enormous transformations in society that we do not yet fully understand. What are the special sacrifices, efforts, and vulnerabilities that girls experience when they are in a position of gaining closeness and love from their fathers, but in a way that may feel conditional on their achievements and commitment to a sporting world that does not yet fully accept them?

When fathers and daughters interact in sport they are doing so in a domain that has a deep connection to the preservation and celebration of traditional masculine values (Sabo and Runfola, 1980; Theberge, 1981). Sport 'privileges particular expressions of masculinity above others, and above all types of femininity' (Brackenridge, 2001: 81) and embodies much of what might be described as hegemonic masculine doctrines (Connell, 2002). The rising popularity of sport in Western culture over the last century is due in part to the resonance it holds with its audience: men hoping to reclaim some foundation of masculinity that may have been threatened or dissipated through modern life (Graydon, 1983; Putney, 2001). Just as Connell (2002) speaks of the masculinization of the state as 'principally a relationship between state institutions and hegemonic masculinity' (2002: 105), sports can be seen as masculinized because of the link between its institutions and hegemonic masculinity and with the male dominated gender regimes of sport.

While girls and women are now exploring new frontiers in sport, the paradox is that they are often doing so under the control, guidance, and discourse of an ever-persistent male-dominated sporting world. Men may be incredibly influential on individual women's sports development, in both positive and negative ways. Scraton *et al.*'s (1999) research with female European football (soccer) players found that many had been encouraged by fathers, brothers or male friends to become involved with football indicating that 'opportunities for girls to choose their physical activities were largely dependent on male encouragement and approval (1999: 107)

On an individual level, sports can be empowering for women, but 'the contradictory positioning of girls and women within sporting and physically active institutions as well as the hegemonic discourses that maintain the status of women in these institutions can have quite the opposite effect' (Garrett, 2004: 141). When the institution itself is structured to maintain male dominance, it is not surprising to see this dominance enacted in everyday interactions between males and females. 'Gender and power relations, as they are lived out within daily sporting practice, have been forces for the preservation of the status quo in sport, and some of the hidden and injurious consequences of that status quo' (Tomlinson and Yorganci, 1997: 136). Women face constant reminders of their marginalized status within sport (Messner, 2002), and this is reinforced through the treatment they may receive from males in positions of authority.

Within the hyper-masculine domain of sport, dominating and abusive behavior can become normalized. Much of this behavior comes from male coaches who are 'prone to excessive and exaggerated forms of macho self-assertion that belittles and humiliates their athletes, male or female' (Tomlinson and Yorganci, 1997: 136). For a father trying to help his daughter achieve in sport, it may seem acceptable to use various forms of control, dominance and coercion to keep her focused on achieving in sports. Individual males in positions of authority have the power to enact the hegemonic discourses and exert control over female athletes (and other subordinates). The stakes are inevitably raised when such relationships are played out between a father and the daughter who fears disappointing him or losing his love.

Fathers who take an interest in their daughters' sports form relationships with their daughters that embody the precarious position of women's sports today – do they represent growth and change or reconstitute old systems of dominance in a new context? How daughters make sense of their fathers' involvement can begin to help us understand this paradoxical situation. For daughters who share sports with their fathers – whether they train, watch, or just talk about sports together – how do daughters experience this relationship? What are ways in which fathers influence their daughter's sporting experiences and how do the daughters interpret this influence?

The study

The study consisted of ethnographic interviews with 22 female student-athletes at a private institution of higher education[2] located on the west coast of the United States (referred to in this chapter as West Coast University[3] or 'WCU'). It is a large university, and the varsity athletic teams participate in NCAA Division I athletic competition.[4] To acquire a fairly diverse sample, all female athletes at the university were contacted by e-mail and additionally, in a few cases, by word of mouth or in person. Athletes self-selected by responding to interview solicitations. Twelve of the interviewees were scholarship athletes[5] and the other ten did not have an athletic scholarship. Because WCU is considered a prestigious university, athletes sometimes made a conscious choice to turn down scholarships at less prominent institutions to attend WCU (if they could afford to do so). Some interviewees indicated that WCU recruited them without a scholarship offer or that their athletic talents may have given them sway in admissions. Others 'walked on' – that is, they tried out and were selected for the team without any prior agreement or incentive. Because of the prestige of WCU, the university could often recruit talent through its reputation in addition to offering scholarships. This probably made the sample, on average, more privileged than might be reflected at other institutions. They were majority white[6] (17 of 22) and middle/upper middle class (half reported a family income during childhood of over $100,000 per year[7]). Even so, the proportion of white female athletes participating in my study at WCU turned out to be identical to the proportion of white, non-Hispanic, female athletes participating nationally within the NCAA (77.4 per cent in 2005–06), and close to the percentage of white, non-Hispanic female athletes participating at the Division I level in the same year (70.1 per cent) (National Collegiate Athletic Association, 2007). Women athletes were interviewed from nine of the ten sports offered for women at WCU (golf was the exclusion): soccer, basketball, volleyball, cross-country, track and field, rowing, water polo, swimming and diving, and tennis.

The larger purpose of the interviews was to examine factors influencing female athletes, with a focus on how the women experienced the influences of families and family relationships. Using an interview guide, I asked questions from several key areas: (1) early exposure and initiation to sports, (2) experiences in athletics in terms of obstacles, resources, and influential people, (3) sports culture within the family, (4) ways that the athlete understood and thought about her achievements, and (5) future goals. During the interviews, I also interjected follow up questions, building on subjects the athlete brought to the table and trying to understand her experiences through her eyes. The analytic process began with several readings of interview transcripts while coding for dominant themes. For this chapter, I paid particular attention to the father-related themes that emerged. My process was also aided by exploratory drafts and presentations, discussions with peers, colleagues, and mentors, and a constant revisiting and re-envisioning of scholarship in the ways of 'extended case method' (Burawoy *et al.*, 2000).

Fathers and daughters sharing sport

My interviews revealed that fathers consistently have an influence on daughters when it comes to sports. Three main themes emerged in the accounts that daughters gave of their shared experience of sport with their fathers: positive and negative aspects of father–daughter bonding through sport; improper imposition by fathers on their daughters' sports experiences; and daughters' responses to fathers' forms of engagement in sport.

Bonding through sport

The interviews in this study explored the role that fathers played in developing and supporting their daughters' sports careers. The accounts obtained lend credence to the conjecture that sports can act as a bonding mechanism between fathers and daughters. Although fathers differed in the ways and degrees to which they interacted with daughters through sport, all but one of the interviewees had a father who had at least attended a game or expressed an opinion on sport. Sports were often a comfortable realm for men to connect with their children and it was evident that in the post-Title IX world, fathers had few concerns about their daughters participating in sports and often enjoyed, encouraged, and/or helped to engineer their playing careers.

Seven of the athletes identified their fathers as their 'biggest fan':

'My dad's always cheering in the stands. There's a couple of dads on the team that have pretty booming voices so you know you can always tell when they're at the games. That makes it fun because then you know somebody's cheering for you.'

(Felicity, white, scholarship, water polo)

'My dad for sure. Oh yeah. He's still the only voice I hear in the crowd. My dad always tries to keep a secret of how often he talks about me. He has one of my national championship rings, and I swear he wears it.'

(Valerie, white, scholarship, volleyball)

'My dad would always have the video camera. Very supportive. Extremely supportive.'

(Kelly, white, non-scholarship, swimming)

Fathers attended games, even if it meant traveling great distances:

'He [Dad] was always there when I was at meets or if I had a game.'
(Fiona, white, scholarship, swimming)

'Some of the time it was like a two hour drive and my dad would know the schedule and he'd like plan everything around it so he could still go.'

(Lisa, white, non-scholarship, diving)

'It [my boarding school] was about an hour and 15 minutes away from where my family lived, and he [Dad] came up every single volleyball game, every single soccer game, every single track meet. And I looked forward to that.'

(Olivia, white, non-scholarship, cross-country)

Fathers played the role of trainer or coach for nine of the 22 women overall including half of the athletes on scholarship:

'We used [to go to my] old high school . . . and he made, like, shoeboxes and put them out and he would just stand there and go "One" and I would hit "one" and stuff like that. I mean, he was just always trying to like help me do better.'

(Renee, African American, scholarship, volleyball)

'I would go down there every Sunday and shoot three pointers for as long as I can remember and do these dribbling exercises that my dad would make me do as long as I can remember.'

(Valerie, white, scholarship, volleyball)

'After he got back from work he'd take me to the volleyball court, and we would serve for half an hour.'

(Olivia, white, non-scholarship, cross-country)

'He would be on the bike and I would be running, so he would like bike next to me around the block which we clocked out to be about a mile. So, we would just do that like as fast as I could. Like, "Let's run all the way around the block as fast as you can." '

(Marcia, Latina, non-scholarship, cross-country)

The relationship built around sport created a unique bond for many of the athletes. The energy fathers put into their daughters as fans, trainers, and coaches was oftentimes remarkable. When describing activities with their father, there was a lot of appreciation in many of the daughters' voices. That fathers would spend this time with daughters engaging in a traditionally male-dominated activity shows a clear departure from the literature on father–daughter relationships and evidence of an increasingly changing position of the role of women as athletes.

Notwithstanding this, the relationship could be subject to degrees of strain. As fathers are still often the less available parent, both emotionally and physically, daughters tended to put particularly high significance on any attention they receive from their dads and this could create tension in the sports bond. In some cases, sport was at the heart of an intense relationship that was mainly built around a single activity. Some of the athletes reported feeling a degree of emotional stress: while they felt loved when training together, they also feared hurting their father's feelings, letting him down, or losing his love if they did not follow his lead.

'I think it's that it [training with dad] equated to love because he was spending so much time with me. It just showed that he loved me because my dad was a very unemotional person. So, I thought, this is his way of telling me that he loves me.'

(Emily, Asian American, scholarship, tennis)

'I just liked it [training with dad] because he was like interested in trying to . . . help me.'

(Renee, African American, scholarship, volleyball)

'He would be like, "Why don't we run? Why don't we do a mile? I'll time you." And even if I didn't necessarily want to race it, I'd put my all into it because I didn't want to disappoint him.'

(Olivia, white, non-scholarship, cross-country)

Within the study sample, the greatest level of pressure came in the sport of tennis. All three interviewees who played tennis had fathers who were described by their daughters as at best pushy and at worst abusive. They also described the experiences of other tennis players whom they knew, emphasizing that girls' tennis is a space of great conflict and strain between parents and their children. Hoyle and Leff (1997) confirm that among tournament tennis players, female respondents indicated a greater level of pressure from parents than male respondents. My interviewees also reported that fathers were the most common source of pressure in this sport.

In some instances emotional strain arose when fathers (and, at times, mothers or parents in tandem) invoked economic considerations. It was clear from these interviews that aspiring athletes have little hope for a college scholarship if they are not participating in some form of 'club', traveling team, or other sport training organization. These opportunities are in addition to or in lieu of high school athletics and most often require a costly fee, not to mention traveling and other expenses. Every one of the scholarship athletes interviewed, and most of the non-scholarship athletes, had participated in some kind of outside training organization or team. The level of economic investment required to achieve success in the majority of college athletics also sheds light as to why many of my interviewees were from a high socioeconomic class.

Several athletes recalled being constantly reminded of their parents' investment in their athletic career. The economic costs and potential benefits – in the form of scholarships – were clearly significant issues, especially in less affluent households. Seven of the interviewees were very vocal on this topic. One example is Emily, a scholarship tennis player whose parents are immigrants from the Philippines, and who reported a family income of between $50,000 and $100,000. Emily said that her dad would say, 'Why are you losing? We're spending so much money on you!' He would make her feel guilty for causing the family economic troubles and use it as leverage to get her to work harder on her tennis. In retrospect, she thought that one of the main reasons that he encouraged her in tennis was in hopes of her acquiring a college scholarship. Sarah, a white non-scholarship crew athlete in the same income bracket as Emily, reported that her parents had put pressure on her sister to commit to softball fully, or let it go entirely, although she observed: 'They're not really forcing her. They're just saying, "If you don't really want to do this, stop us now because we're wasting a lot of money on club and traveling." '

Overall my interviewees reported diverse experiences of bonding with their fathers through sport. Father support was deeply appreciated and treasured by many. The interest of fathers in their daughters' sport careers can be seen as evidence of more progressive attitudes towards women in sport. At the same time, athletes expressed mixed feelings about training with their fathers: enjoying the time with them, but also feeling some pressure to continue sports (and sometimes pressure to continue doing them well) in order to retain their father's time and attention. Although the daughters enjoyed and benefited from the sports participation, they also experienced a situation where their practice of sport was, in part, guided by a highly influential male figure. When they felt that their father's love and approval were on the line according to their participation and/or performance in sports, this opened the door for fathers to assume a controlling role within the relationship. The next section explores in more detail the idea of 'improper imposition' by fathers on their daughters' sport.

Improper imposition

Women's sports have struggled to gain both respect and autonomy against a powerful and deeply entrenched masculine sports establishment. At the micro-level, the daughters in this study found that their fathers oftentimes represented a similar source of power and influence on their athletic participation. Much of this influence could be considered benign and inherent to parenthood. However, as male authority figures in sport, several of the fathers had ways of imposing various levels of control over their daughters' sport experiences. In order to better understand the different ways fathers exert control, I am using a concept developed by sport ethicists to describe inappropriate attention by parents and coaches toward athletes: 'improper imposition' (VonRoenn, Zhang and Bennett, 2004) or 'ethical misconducts' that are imposed by parents, coaches, and other adults who act improperly during competition and put abnormal pressure on athletes. These ethical misconducts are not limited to father–daughter interactions, as is well documented by other research (e.g. Fine, 1987; Messner, 1992), but may take on particular meanings and consequences when experienced by girls in this context. In the discussion that follows I consider several forms of this imposition including over-involvement, advice and instruction, making decisions, inappropriate behavior during competitions, and verbal and emotional abuse.

Over-involvement

It was fairly common within the study sample for daughters to feel that their fathers had been just too involved in their sports career. This might involve trying to manage their schedule, advising them on training and diet, giving constant critique about the quality of their play, or even just asking too many questions, leaving all other subjects of conversation behind. Eleven athletes mentioned their father's over-involvement. They experienced it ambivalently – enjoying some of the attention, but also feeling frustrated by not having autonomy.

Jessica, a white scholarship basketball player, said that she mainly remembers the good times with her father, but she also said that it was 'sometimes pretty hard for me' when her father would ask, 'Well, why aren't you shooting more? Why aren't you outside with your sister shooting free throws? Why aren't you working harder?' He imposed his expectations on his daughter rather than letting her define how and when she would practice.

Felicity, a white scholarship water polo player, clearly loved her father and appreciated his interest in her sport. However, his behavior became overbearing:

> 'I mean, the guy loves me so much he just gets too into it, you know? He'll do stuff like set up private lessons or be like critiquing me like every minute of the game. He just makes – sometimes he'll just like make comments or like want to talk about water polo over dinner and it's like, "No. Don't do this to me. I'm away from campus for an hour with you. I can't – I can't talk about this right now." '

Felicity understood that her father's intentions were probably good, but his constant involvement made her feel trapped. She was not able to find her own way in sport, but was instead constantly bombarded by her father's suggestions and efforts to direct her.

Advice and instruction

Offering advice and providing instruction are widespread forms of intervention in sport. They are not inherently negative but can become so if used as a mechanism for asserting undue authority and control. The tendency for this to occur is a prevalent concern surrounding the role and interventions of fathers and father-figures in girls' and women's experiences of sport.

In this study fatherly advice and instruction were reported by 12 athletes and were one of the most common forms of intervention identified. Athletes experienced the advice in different ways – some appreciated it and remembered it fondly whereas others expressed exasperation or annoyance. Olivia (white, non-scholarship, cross-country) was appreciative: 'He was the first person I went to after I finished a game of any type just to talk about what I did well, what I did wrong . . . my first priority after a game was to get his reaction.' Renee, African American, a scholarship volleyball player, was more ambivalent as she described the 'lectures' she had to sit through: 'I mean from my dad, just like probably after every game or something, I'd be like, "Oh, I'm going to get the lecture." I mean, good or bad, I had to like sit there and listen.' Elizabeth (white, non-scholarship distance runner) was critical, pointing out the absurdity of her step-father giving advice about a sport he did not play or know as well as she (and also her mother) did:

> 'My step-dad used to play a lot of sports, so he kind of gives advice and stuff, but I kind of just take it for what it is because he's not really running or anything or athletic anymore. It's funny, he gives my mom and me advice and we're like, "You don't run!" '

These sorts of interactions are indicative of a culture within sport in which men's knowledge is positioned as authoritative. Fathers gave advice and tutelage even when their daughter had superior knowledge and ability in the sport and appeared to feel a certain right to take on this role. In some cases their words became a discourse that diminished their daughter's expertise and many daughters were resistant to the intrusion. Their expression of this resistance is examined more fully in a later section.

Making decisions

Some fathers' involvement was more directive and potentially significant in shaping their daughter's sports career. Eight of my interviewees related how their fathers had influenced their decisions about which sport to pursue or about whether to pursue it exclusively.

For the most part, the college athletes I interviewed had focused their energy on a single sport. Many felt at some point during childhood, they had to decide which one. It was her father who suggested to Ann, a scholarship volleyball player, in her eighth grade year that 'If you want to play it in college . . . then you should probably focus on one [sport].' She took his suggestion and began playing solely volleyball. Destiny, an African American scholarship sprinter, said of her dad (who did not live with the family):

> 'He always supported me in track and field, glad that I did that. And he's more of a macho kind of guy, so he doesn't really care for me playing basketball . . . I was really good in basketball, but he would never say anything about it.'

Although she was most influenced by her mother towards track, she was also quite talented in basketball (her aunt played professionally and helped train Destiny). Her father did not think that basketball was an appropriate sport for girls and Destiny acknowledged that his opinion played a role in her decision to pursue track in college. Athletes did not always follow their father's suggestions. Valerie, a white scholarship volleyball player, decided to give up basketball, the sport she worked on with her dad, in order to concentrate on volleyball: 'When I quit basketball it was hard at first. It was like my dad felt like I didn't need him. But I didn't need him as a coach anymore; I needed him as a father.' She was able to make her own decision, but it took an emotional toll knowing her father did not want to lose the relationship they shared through basketball. According to Valerie, it was also she who brought up the idea of training for volleyball more intensely which involved moving in with family friends in another town at age 16.

Whether or not daughters followed their fathers' lead when making decisions, they weighed their decision against his wishes. Fathers' views were significant elements in the choices daughters made about their sports career. In those cases where fathers sought to direct aspects of their daughters' sports careers, their influence could constrain their daughter's autonomy.

Acting improperly during competitions

Another form of imposition by parents described by VonRoenn *et al.* (2004), was acting inappropriately at youth sport competitions. Fine (1987) labels this behavior as 'over involvement in games', describing it as 'when parents criticize rather than cheer, do not let offspring who have lost a game forget about the defeat, or argue with the umpire' (1987: 36).

Improper behavior at competitions was not commonly reported by my interviewees. Only four recalled instances of disruptive behavior by their fathers. Katie, white, a non-scholarship water polo player, remembered being embarrassed by her father's loud enthusiasm:

> 'He would get really excited during my games, and like I could hear him, like, yelling, "Shoot! Make the goal!" Like, he was the only parent I could hear in the pool, so I was kind of embarrassed, and like, of course all the other girls heard it too, so, that was kind of embarrassing, but he was just very into it.'

Maura, however, had experienced less acceptable behavior. A scholarship tennis player, she described her father's behavior at a tennis match: 'He like yelled and screamed, and came on to the tennis court.' She went on to describe this sort of behavior as relatively common in the club tennis scene, and explained that in girls' tennis it was mostly fathers who were involved. Her account is in line with the suggestion that such behavior may become normalized in some sports settings and be replicated in individual father–daughter relationships.

Verbal/emotional abuse

A third form of imposition reported by interviewees is verbal/emotional abuse which Sharron Close (2005) defines as 'comprised of the use of words or gestures intended to denigrate, humiliate, or threaten the safety of an individual.' Defining such behavior in the sporting arena is more problematic, however, where it is accepted by many as a form of motivation. This is part of the sports ethic that teaches that hurtful language is acceptable if the ends justify the means.

Three athletes provided examples of apparent verbal and/or emotional abuse. Jessica, a scholarship basketball player, described how she and her sister would sit submissively after a game, accepting their father's verbal abuse:

> 'My dad has a bit of a temper . . . and we'd be in the car, and I'd just dread it – I'd dread getting in the car after a bad game – after any game because I knew he was going to yell at me. And you know, you just sit, and you be quiet, and you know he – I can't even remember what he'd yell about. Probably the most – the stupidest things ever, like, but it was just . . . you just regretted it. You just hated it. My sister and I hated going in the car with my dad after a game because he'd yell, "What are you thinking – what were you doing this for?" La-la-la. You know, and then we'd start crying.'

The most intense descriptions came from Emily and Maura, two scholarship tennis players at WCU who were at the end of their collegiate career. Emily and Maura are both second generation immigrants and were the only athletes in the study who had two immigrant parents, Emily's coming from the Philippines and Maura's from southern Europe. Espiritu (2001), in her research with second generation Filipina immigrants, found that 'the process of parenting is gendered in that immigrant parents tend to restrict the autonomy, mobility, and personal decision making of their daughters more than that of their sons' and it may be that being an immigrant family exacerbated the gender-power dynamic between father and daughter. This may be a contributory factor to the greater control exerted by these fathers.

In Maura's case the abuse took the form of her father undermining her by claiming credit for her achievements. She described how her dad would diminish her successes by telling her: 'If it wasn't for me, you would have never gotten to where you were, if it was left up to you, you wouldn't have done anything.' Emily described the abusive relationships she and her roommate (also Filipina) both had with their parents:

> 'We had parents that pushed us a lot. We had a very, very rocky . . . it did some emotional damage to me. He never [used] physical abuse with me, but verbally it was just – I would be petrified, petrified if I lost a match because he'd call me stupid . . . Just kind of like, just verbally [sic] negativity and it cut me down so bad that like I really thought I was stupid. I really thought I was useless. It did nothing for my confidence. So, I would put so much pressure on myself . . . And like her parents were worse. Her parents hit her. Her dad hit her. Yeah. And it's . . . insane. Like we both had a very similar like . . . it came to an extreme. I don't mean to scare you, but like . . . we didn't want to live anymore. You know what I mean? Like, we didn't want to do this anymore.'

Emily and her roommate's experiences were clearly abusive and dramatic. The two both enjoyed huge successes as Division I scholarship athletes, but their successes were tempered by this extreme influence and dominance by their fathers.

In their excitement over their daughter's involvement and success, fathers sometimes became heavily involved in their daughter's sport careers. They commonly gave her advice, encouraged her to practice, and helped her with decision-making. Although helpful and benevolent in many respects, some of this behavior became overbearing. As male authority figures in a male-dominated activity, even harmless advice and instruction is oftentimes imbued with gendered meaning. Daughters felt both the benefits and burdens of their father's treatment. It was rare that this behavior reached an extreme – outbursts at matches, abusive comments, or even physical abuse – but extreme behavior can also be indicative of underlying issues of control and dominance that can permeate father–daughter sport relationships.

Responding to fathers' involvement

The young female athletes in this study reported complex interpretations of and reactions to their fathers' involvement. Their responses were of three types: reproductive agency, resistance and renegotiation.

Reproductive agency

Reproductive agency is a strategy by which individuals neutralize negative treatment that others display towards them by adopting or defending the values and behavior. Eight of the athletes' responses to their fathers can be characterized in this way. Many of the girls defended the idea that fathers and/or coaches who were controlling or verbally harsh were all part of the game, or at least a necessary evil. Even the athletes who experienced some of the harshest and most controlling behavior from their fathers had something good to say about the experience.

Jessica did not enjoy her father's yelling, but felt it may have prepared her for facing coaches in the future, who she describes as often being 'derogatory' at 'this level'. Although she expressed disdain at the behavior of her father and coach she did not really challenge that aspect of sports, and even suggested it may ultimately have been helpful to her. She gave an account of her father yelling at her in the car after losses that appeared to normalize this behavior as a necessary part of forming her as a player:

'My dad was more of a tough love and, you know, but I think that was very helpful for me because when you get to this level, you have to do it yourself. You'll get yelled at. The best players . . . sometimes they'll get just reamed in practice. Some of things that my coaches have said to players are just so derogatory . . . So, I think it's good because I think I learned to zone it out and how to handle it . . . and how to turn it around and be like, well, he's kind of right. I need to change it. If I change this, then maybe he won't yell as much. And it worked.'

Emily, the scholarship tennis player with a father who exhibited abusive behavior, also felt she had in some ways benefited from the situation: 'It made me into such a stronger person. I know how to be driven and how to push myself to the limit and I have great tolerance, you know?' Maura, the other scholarship tennis player, had suffered verbal abuse from her father but spoke of the necessity of a 'pushy parent':

'I don't know how it is in some other sports, but in tennis it's very common to have a pushy parent. And, I mean, I can't think of anyone who's successful who hasn't had a parent or at least a coach who pushed them. Like it or not. There were times when I hated it, but looking back, there's no way I think that myself or any other person would have done as well without having that push.'

Although she knows how painful the pressure from her father was, Maura is willing to accept it as part of the game; as a necessary element of success.

Resistance

Several players disagreed with their father's behavior or the nature of the sport relationship with their fathers and had strategies for asserting themselves and trying to improve it.

One strategy players implemented was resistance. In some cases this was done peacefully, while in others it entailed a period of rebellion. In line with Brackenridge's (2001) work on athletes experiencing sexual abuse, this usually occurred as the athletes aged and became more able to resist or remake the situation. Six athletes spoke directly about some type of overt resistance with their fathers.

Some rebellions were subtle and low-key. Valerie, the scholarship volleyball player, played basketball under her father as a child. She described the experience: 'I mean, there was always those times when we'd butt heads, like, rebel almost. Like he would say run and I would jog.' The two other volleyball players in my sample, Renee and Ann, hinted that they may have chosen (even subconsciously) volleyball rather than basketball, their father's sport, to avoid intense instruction and scrutiny.

At the other end of the spectrum, if tennis appeared to be a sport ripe for intense pressure on players, it was equally ripe for rebellion by them. All three tennis players in my study fought for independence and for new relations with their fathers. For Maura, coming to college was her escape and rebellion. Her father wanted her to play professionally right out of high school, but Maura insisted on going to college and negotiated the application and recruiting process on her own. At first, her father boycotted her college matches, but eventually he reconsidered. Ultimately, this helped improve their relationship, and now she is clearly the one in charge of her career:

> 'I think he realized he may have to come and support me or it was going to ruin our relationship. He started coming out to a few and he realized that I am happy. And I had to remind him that when I was 8 years old you put me into tennis not because I was going to enter the pros but because my parents wanted me to have something to do. Not waste my time. I think my Dad finally realized . . . at the time. He was so involved in Juniors, he could not see it as something to enjoy. Does he now like the idea of me being here? Not really. But you can't always please your parents. At some point you have to do what you want to do.'

After years of taking the verbal abuse from her father, Emily described an incident where she deliberately threw a match involving her father's friends. She was injured at the time and he was still expecting her to play. The scene in the car afterwards was a turning-point in their relationship:

> 'In the car he started yelling at me. He's like, "You embarrassed me in front of my friends." Blah, blah, blah. He's like, "You're so stupid." I snapped. I had just – I had reached the point where I couldn't do this anymore . . . I start yelling; I'm like, "Don't ever call me stupid again!" . . . He didn't talk to me for two weeks, and then he just let go. And then after that, like . . . after that it improved.'

These shifts in relationships show how daughters were able to resist and eventually change the nature of their relationship with their father. They also talked about ways that they were gradually rebuilding their self-esteem. Maura is beginning to give herself credit for her successes and even considering hitting the pro circuit after college on her own terms. Emily is seeking therapy and learning to play tennis for fun with old teammates.

Renegotiation

Sometimes, the athletes preferred communicating or renegotiating with their fathers to active resistance. Felicity continually tried to renegotiate the relationship with her father.

> 'It took me like four years to tell him he needed to back off. So, once I could communicate with him – which is like a fairer thing to do, I mean I shouldn't be getting mad at him if I can't tell him to stop – then things got a lot better and our relationship got a lot better . . . I figured out I have to be able to communicate with him and find other things that are

similar between us, so that we can have a real relationship, because once water polo's over, what are ya gonna talk about?'

Felicity used her own understanding of how relationships work and her own communication skills to bridge gaps with her father. Her father was willing to listen, their relationship improved, and now Felicity is helping smooth the relationship between her father and her younger sister who is also an athlete.

Valerie found assistance communicating with her father by using her mother as a mediator:

'My mom's kind of my saving grace in communicating with my dad, just because she's not the athlete, she understands what time off is . . . she understood what I was trying to do. The way she communicated was a little bit better. When my dad communicated, I don't know if he meant it, but he's like, you need to be doing stuff every day, you need to get better at this by that point. So the communication between the two, balanced each other out. Yeah, just talk to my mom, when my dad says something, my mom's the translator.'

She was able to take a badly needed week off that her father disagreed with because her mother was able to help negotiate the situation.

Interestingly, Maura tried communicating first with her dad, but was not able to make it work. When asked if she ever stood up to him, she replied:

'I would try. But he had the ability to turn the situation around and make me feel that I was in the wrong. If I came up with an argument, I could never get my point across. At times I would say, "You know Dad you are really hard on me." He would say, "I do this, this, and this for you and if it wasn't for me you wouldn't be here. And you should thank me for doing all this." '

In instances where fathers became too controlling or overbearing, athletes at least tried to remake their relationships, resisting or renegotiating with fathers. At times a mother, coach or friend would even step in to help. Sometimes their efforts did not produce the entire desired outcome, but it appears to have helped them find a voice. In most cases, fathers seemed to listen and at least reduce their negative behaviors.

Conclusions

Fathers are more likely to be involved in sons' lives than daughters' and to reproduce gender conventions in their activities with them. Fathers who are deeply involved in their daughters' activities, within the masculine domain of sport, are in less familiar territory. Studying how these relationships play out allows us to explore unchartered aspects of father and daughter relationships. In doing so, it also offers us an additional perspective to bring to bear on the gendered nature of sport.

It is understandable that daughters experience their relationship with their fathers in sport in a nuanced and complex way. They enjoy the attention and camaraderie, but often feel pressured to train, compete and achieve in ways that please their fathers (and not necessarily themselves). They tend to interpret their father's love and attention as conditional on their involvement and success in sport. This offers fathers an opening for a great deal of influence on their daughters' lives that can limit daughters' autonomy. The daughters may resist their fathers' influence, attempting to rebel against or renegotiate with them to improve the relationship. A combination of some level of benevolence on the part of fathers and the powerful agency of daughters means that at least part of the outcome is personal empowerment. We can say that the influence on the daughters is, in general, a positive influence. However, we can also see the ways that a father's influence can be negative and disempowering. Hegemonic masculine discourses are often upheld by fathers and coaches who perceive it as a necessary element of training athletes for elite competition.

> Humiliation plays an important part in obedience training and may be manifested through physical, sexual or psychological denigration Such controlling behavior is frequently legitimated within sport where the superior knowledge of the coach is deemed to give him license [sic] to require complete obedience from the athlete.
>
> (Brackenridge, 2001: 91)

My research suggests that the power dynamic between men and women in sports can manifest itself within father–daughter relationships. Although a father's attention to his daughter's sports career was often experienced as loving, appropriate, and empowering, it was also experienced as domineering, manipulative, and disempowering. Thus, the sport relationship served as a site for both the contestation of and the reproduction of male dominance and control already prevalent within the world of sport. In those instances when the relationship is largely respectful and non-intrusive, it might serve as a positive example of social change within gender relations. After all, some fathers still put forth little time or interest into their daughters' activities or find it inappropriate for girls to be athletic. However, for daughters who have reached the level of college athletics, I found that involved fathers often sit on a continuum between respectful encouragement and dominant coercion with their behavior and actions often fluctuating between the two extremes.

If we apply the daughters' mixed experiences to the greater world of sports, we may interpret the situation as equally complex. Sports institutions are still heavily male-dominated and immensely powerful. Women's athletic experiences are influenced by these institutions – and this influence will most likely grow the more that women's sports gain popularity and legitimacy.

When we praise women's involvement in sports, we tend to become less concerned about how sports' macho nature can impede enjoyment (Sabo and Runfola, 1980), the status of sport as a masculinized institution that reinforces patriarchy (Connell, 2002), and sport's tendency to encourage violence against others and against the athletes themselves (Messner, 2002).

As we tout the many positive lessons and benefits sport brings, we forget to question what sports can mean and how the relationships within its domain may be recreating exactly what we are trying to change. When women find themselves accepting, rationalizing, or repeating the dominating behavior of fathers and coaches and trusting that male figures inherently know more about the game, they are supporting the gender order within sports; or, at the very least, they are diminishing the strength of their challenge to male dominance. Conversely, women renegotiating and resisting these dominant values are attempting to remake their sports experiences and incorporate new values into sport.

As Dworkin and Messner (1999) say, 'today's advocates of women's sports must walk a tightrope: they must assert the positive value of vigorous physical activity and muscular strength for girls and women while simultaneously criticizing the unhealthy aspects of men's sports' (1997: 355). In a sense, fathers and daughters must also walk this tightrope, wanting to share the sport experience, but not always being aware of or not having the tools to negotiate the masculine-dominated sports world in a way that is fully empowering for the daughter. One hopes that, if their intentions are good, fathers will respect their daughter's autonomy and creativity in her athletic endeavors rather than controlling and dominating her experience. Even more, they can become cooperative forces with their daughters to actively fight for greater equality and respect for women in sports. Perhaps this could fit into what Messner calls the 'social justice model' (2002) where there is a 'simultaneous quest of simple fairness and equal opportunities for girls and women along with critical actions aimed at fundamentally transforming the center of men's sports' (2002: 153). Those fathers and daughters that do achieve a balance between these two goals may give us a model for how to do it on a larger playing field.

Notes

1 Title IX is an amendment to the Higher Education Act passed by the United States Congress in 1972. It reads 'No person in the United States shall, on the basis of sex, be excluded from participation in, or denied the benefits of, or subjected to discrimination under any educational program or activity receiving federal aid' (Title IX of the Education Amendments of 1972, vol. 20 U.S.C. sec. 1681).

2 The US has a mix of private and public institutions of higher education that admit students based on institution-specific criteria. Federal and state governments directly subsidize public education, making it generally more affordable than private.

3 Names of people and places in this chapter are pseudonyms.

4   The National Collegiate Athletic Association (NCAA) is an organization that governs the majority of athletics programs at colleges and universities in the US. There are three divisions of schools. Division I schools must sponsor at least seven sports each for men and women and meet other benchmarks, whereas the other divisions have lower level requirements. Additionally, Division I schools are able to offer full and partial scholarships to athletes, whereas Division II can only offer partial, and Division III cannot offer scholarships at all (see www.ncaa.org).

5   Scholarships pay for tuition, room, and board and offer a stipend for books and other expenses. Because the NCAA limits the number of scholarships for each team and school, some positions are filled by non-scholarship athletes. This means that these students pay the full tuition, room, and board or find aid through another source (e.g. government grants and loans, private scholarships, etc.).

6   Smith (1992) notes: 'Low socioeconomic conditions impact women of color disproportionately such that their children must participate in stereotypical, "popular" sports such as basketball and track (sponsored by the schools, recreation departments, and other nonprofit agencies) or not participate at all in organized sports' (1992: 236). At the college level, institutions commonly offer three of these stereotypical/popular sports for men (basketball, track, and football) and only two for women (basketball and track). The percentage of Black, non-Hispanic athletes in Division I (2005–06) was 24.6 per cent for male athletes and 15.1 per cent for women (National Collegiate Athletic Association, 2007). I also venture that resources (such as parental interest and income) may mean more for female athletes who are not as likely to have peer influences on their sport interests (Wann, Merrill, Melnick, Russell and Pease, 2001).

7   As a benchmark, in 2006 the median household income in the US was $48,451. Only 17.9 per cent of households had an income of $100,000 or above. (Source: US Census Bureau, 2007, 2006 American Community Survey.)

9 Divorce and recreation

Non-resident fathers' leisure during parenting time with their children

Alisha T. Swinton, Patti A. Freeman and Ramon B. Zabriskie

Over the past 30 years, research examining divorce and the effects of divorce has increased substantially. The majority of this research has focused on children in conjunction with divorce or the new family unit following divorce (which typically includes the mother and child(ren)). This focus has resulted in a dearth of research on the father, who is traditionally the non-resident parent.

As divorce has become more common, family law courts have begun to allocate equal parenting time between spouses; this can be seen through increased joint custody agreements and joint residency agreements. Although fathers of divorced families have not received a lot of research attention, it is imperative that we understand their role, as the number of non-resident fathers facing the challenges of being well-integrated into the family unit post-divorce are increasing.

Recent literature suggests that non-resident fathers primarily engage in leisure activities with their children during parenting time. Little research from the leisure field has examined non-resident fathers and this interaction. Therefore, the purpose of this study was to examine non-resident fathers' leisure patterns with their children during parenting time and to better understand their satisfaction with these experiences. Attention to family leisure activities with associated benefits, such as increased cohesion or flexibility during parenting time, was given particular attention in this study. After first examining the family leisure patterns, a comparison with dual parent families was made to identify any differences in family leisure following divorce. The study lastly examined non-resident fathers' leisure satisfaction.

Research into fathers, divorce and leisure

Divorce and fathers

Over the past 50 years, divorce rates have generally increased across the world (US Census Bureau, 2002; Australian Bureau of Statistics (ABS), 2007; UK National Statistics, 2006) Consequently, the number of non-resident fathers has also increased, as courts tend to favor the mother as the residential parent (De Vaus, 2004; Pasley and Braver, 2004).

The involvement of non-resident fathers with their children following divorce has been found to aid children academically, socially, and emotionally (Dunn, Cheng, O'Connor and Bridges, 2004; Menning, 2002). Although this involvement is important, very little is known regarding the context in which it occurs. Stewart (1999) determined that most non-resident parents engage in leisure activities with their child(ren) during parenting time. Nevertheless, non-resident fathers' leisure with their children has received very little attention in the research literature (Jenkins and Lyons, 2006; Menning, 2002; Pasley and Braver, 2004). Increased understanding about family leisure involvement among non-resident fathers and their children may provide insight into possible behavioral characteristics related to positive outcomes following divorce.

Today, non-resident fathers play a crucial role in the lives of their child(ren). Research has demonstrated that the absence of a father, due to divorce, is associated with child(ren) who experience juvenile delinquency, difficulty in the academic arena, and higher levels of social-emotional problems when compared to child(ren) who have a father in the home (Amato and Keith, 1991, 2001). Non-resident fathers' involvement in their child(ren)'s lives is often easiest during scheduled parenting time and this parenting time is typically established by the courts and/or by the parents (Smyth, 2005).

During parenting time, fathers have the opportunity to interact with their children. Research examining non-resident fathers' paternal involvement is typically conducted in social science fields such as family sciences, sociology and psychology. These fields have examined non-resident fathers' involvement in terms of quantity of time or frequency of visits, yet the experience of what occurs during these visits has not been fully explored. Recent literature suggests most interaction that takes place between non-resident fathers and their child(ren), occurs in a leisure setting (Jenkins and Lyons, 2006; Stewart, 1999). Therefore, by exploring the leisure patterns of non-resident fathers, a new perspective may aid researchers to better understand fathers' involvement with their child(ren) following divorce.

Non-resident father involvement

Research has seldom addressed what actually occurs during the parenting time of non-resident fathers with their child(ren). According to Menning (2002), most research has simply measured the amount of parent/child contact. He concluded,

> parent/child contact does not by itself indicate that any activity takes place between the parents and child . . . it says nothing about the denseness of the activity within the block of time that contact occurs.
>
> (Menning, 2002: 651)

One study that did examine what occurred during non-resident parenting time was conducted by Stewart (1999). She found that non-resident parents tended to engage in leisure activities with their child(ren) during parenting times. Stewart's examination of non-resident parents and their activity choices with their children is one of the few research articles examining the role of leisure and non-resident parental involvement. Stewart's classification of leisure activities, however, was limited to only a few choices (e.g., outings, play, and school-based activities).

Pasley and Braver (2004) examined instrumentation available to researchers to effectively measure fathering involvement. When examining non-resident fathers' involvement, Pasley and Braver suggested 'new measures must do more to tap the recreational dimension of divorced fathers who see their children' (2004: 236). Therefore, by examining leisure involvement between non-resident fathers and their child(ren), a better understanding of the 'recreational dimension' of parenting time patterns between non-resident fathers and their involvement may be achieved.

Family leisure patterns

The Core and Balance Model of family leisure functioning provides a framework for better understanding the leisure patterns of non-resident fathers. This model is grounded in family systems theory, particularly Olson's (2000) Circumplex Model of marital and family systems (Olson, 2000). Olson's model explains family functioning in terms of cohesion and flexibility. Because families are affected by their environments and by qualities within the family system itself, their cohesion and ability to adapt to new situations greatly affects their family dynamics. Olson's model has been used by family scholars for nearly 30 years and has become one of the more reliable models used to measure family functioning.

The Core and Balance Model of Family Leisure Functioning (Zabriskie, 2000) was informed by Olson's framework that indicates that both family cohesion and adaptability are necessary for healthy family functioning. This model indicates that there are two basic categories of family leisure activities (core and balance) directly related to the different aspects of family functioning. Core family leisure activities are primarily associated with family bonding or feelings of closeness, and usually take place at home. These activities are quite common, inexpensive, and often spontaneous, such as eating dinner together, playing games together, or having snowball fights. Balance activities are more associated with family adaptability because they enable family members to learn how to function in unusual circumstances and environments. These activities tend to be more novel and require more planning, time and money. Activities such as family vacations, camping trips, and visiting amusement parks are common balance family leisure activities (Zabriskie and McCormick, 2001). The model suggests that both categories are essential and that families who regularly participate in both core and

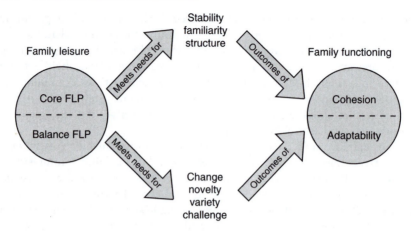

Figure 9.1 Core and Balance Model of Family Leisure Functioning

Note: FLP = Family Leisure Patterns

balance family leisure activities are likely to function higher and be more satisfied with family life than those who participate in extremely high or low amounts of either category (Figure 9.1).

It seems likely that both core and balance types of family activities are important for non-resident fathers to participate in with their child(ren) during visitation times. This leisure involvement may contribute to stronger relationships, increased feelings of closeness and bonding, and the ability to successfully adapt to challenges and changes. Such benefits are especially important within single-parent families who have likely experienced dysfunction related to divorce. Creating family leisure experiences may help ameliorate the effects of divorce in addition to creating healthier relationships between non-resident parents and their child(ren) (Smith, Taylor, Hill and Zabriskie, 2004). Satisfaction with leisure has been found to be associated with life satisfaction; therefore, the variable of leisure satisfaction during parenting time is important to consider.

Satisfaction with family leisure involvement

Satisfaction with leisure has been found to be highly indicative of life satisfaction (Russell, 1987, 1990). In 1990, Russell examined the interrelationships among leisure and other life circumstance variables, one of which was quality of life. She found that religiosity, sex, education, marital status and age were significantly related to income, health, leisure activity participation, and leisure satisfaction. These variables, however, were not found to influence quality of life directly. The only significant and direct predictor of quality of life was satisfaction with leisure involvement.

According to Zabriskie and McCormick (2003) '[if] leisure plays a substantial role in an individual's life satisfaction and quality of life . . . then it can be hypothesized that family leisure may also be a primary contributor to family satisfaction and quality of family life' (2003: 164). In order to test this hypothesis, Zabriskie and McCormick collected data from individual family members. Study participants completed a family leisure activity profile and family satisfaction scale. Findings indicated that family leisure involvement was positively associated with family satisfaction (Zabriskie and McCormick, 2003). Furthermore, Zabriskie and McCormick determined there was a negative relationship between families who had a history of divorce and satisfaction with family life.

> Both the youth and the parents reported having significantly lower levels of satisfaction with their family life if they had ever experienced divorce in their family, whether it was a current situation or if it had happened in the recent or even distant past.
>
> (2003: 183)

These findings suggest that non-resident fathers may be more susceptible to lower levels of leisure satisfaction and satisfaction with family life, due to divorce and the subsequent limited access to leisure time with their child(ren).

The study

As divorce has increased over the last 50 years, more non-resident fathers are in a situation where parenting time with their child(ren) occurs through pre-planned visits. Such parenting time tends to occur almost entirely in a leisure setting (Stewart, 1999). Research examining non-resident fathers' parenting time with their children is needed in order to fully understand the breadth of a fathers' role in his family following divorce. This research is specifically needed from the leisure science perspective.

By using the core and balance model of family leisure functioning as a framework, non-resident fathers' leisure patterns may be better understood. The core and balance model enables researchers to better understand what activities non-resident fathers are engaging in during parenting times, the frequency and duration of each activity, and any associated benefits, such as increased cohesion or flexibility, from the leisure activities they chose to share with their children.

Because family leisure is associated with family satisfaction, it is important to examine family leisure activities and non-resident fathers' satisfaction with these activities during the non-resident fathers' parenting time. Additional benefits to leisure satisfaction also include higher life satisfaction. Because divorce is related to lower levels of life satisfaction, much can be learned from gaining a better understanding of the role of leisure satisfaction in the lives of non-resident fathers during parenting time with their children.

The study discussed in this chapter was carried out from 2005–2006. Its three objectives were first to examine and describe the family leisure of non-resident fathers and their child(ren) during parenting time; second, to examine the differences between two parent families' and non-resident fathers' leisure patterns during parenting time; and third, to examine non-resident fathers' satisfaction with their family leisure involvement.

Methodology

Sample

The participants in this study were 170 non-resident fathers from 36 different states within the United States. Most fathers were Caucasian (81 percent) followed by Black (14 percent), Native American (3 percent), and Asian (2 percent). Their ages ranged from 23 to 64 years, with a mean of 43.7 (SD = 8.6) years. Seventy percent of the fathers were not remarried, and 28.8 percent were; 1.2 percent of the fathers did not answer the question. The length of divorce ranged from one month to 47 years, with an average divorce length of 3 years, not including the time separated prior to the divorce. Of the fathers who were separated, the length of separation ranged from three months to 14 years, with an average separation time of 4 years.

In order to participate in the study the men had to have at least one child between the ages of 5 and 18 years old with whom they spent parenting time (it was okay if the fathers had additional children who were younger or older). Children's ages ranged from less than 1 year to 32 with a mean of 11.68 (SD = 5.38) years. The number of children per father ranged from 1 to 5, with 38.8 percent of fathers having one child, 37.6 percent having two children, 15.3 percent having three children, 6.5 percent having four and 1.8 percent having five or more children. Household income ranged from less than $10,000 to over $150,000, the median income was $60,000–69,000 with 64.7 percent of fathers earning less than $80,000 per year. At about this same time in the United States (2005), the median quintile (middle fifth or 20 percent) household income was $34,738 (US Census Bureau, 2005).

Procedures

Non-resident fathers were recruited through the National Fatherhood Initiative (NFI) affiliate organizations, the Children's Rights Council (CRC) and the National Center for Fathers (NCF). Non-resident fathers who were willing to participate were given the option of completing the questionnaire online or by a paper/pencil version. Distribution of the questionnaire occurred through email or by mailing the paper/pencil version to the respondents. Participants were not compensated for participating in this study. The study was non-random; consequently, the results of this study are limited to those who responded to the questionnaire. In addition, participants in this study may have been subject to self-selection bias.

Instrumentation

The research questionnaire was comprised of three sections. In the first section, non-resident fathers' involvement in family leisure during parenting times with their child(ren) was measured using Zabriskie's (2001) Family Leisure Activity Profile (FLAP). In the second, non-resident fathers' satisfaction with family leisure involvement was measured using Zabriskie's (2000) Family Leisure Satisfaction Scale (FLSS). Finally, a series of sociodemographic questions were included in order to effectively describe the sample.

The Family Leisure Activity Profile (FLAP) (Zabriskie, 2001) is a 16-item scale that measures the frequency and duration of participation in core and balance family activities. The first eight items measure involvement in core family leisure activities and the next eight measure involvement in balance family leisure activities (Table 9.1).

The fathers indicated their average or typical frequency of participation in the 16 activity categories with their child(ren) by marking if they participated in them with their child(ren) 'at least daily', 'at least weekly', 'at least monthly', 'at least annually' and 'never'. Duration measured how long they tended to do both core and balance activities when they did participate in

Table 9.1 Categories of core and balance family leisure activities

Core family leisure activity categories	Balance family leisure activity categories
Dinners at home	**Community-based social activities** (going to restaurants, parties, shopping, visiting friends/neighbors, picnics)
Home-based activities (TV, movies, reading, music)	**Spectator activities** (movies, sporting events, concerts, plays or theatrical performances)
Games (board games, billiards, cards, video games)	**Community-based sporting activities** (bowling, golf, swimming, skating)
Crafts, cooking, hobbies (drawing, painting, model building, baking)	**Community-based special events** (museums, zoos, theme parks, fairs)
Home-based outdoor activities (gardening, playing with pets, walks)	**Outdoor activities** (camping, hiking, hunting, fishing)
Home-based sport/games (playing catch, shooting baskets, bike rides, fitness activities)	**Water-based activities** (water skiing, jet skiing, boating sailing, canoeing)
Attend other family members' activities (watching or leading their sporting events, musical performances, scouts)	**Outdoor adventure activities** (rock climbing, river rafting, off-roading, scuba diving)
Religious/spiritual activities (going to church, worshiping, scripture reading, Sunday school)	**Tourism activities** (traveling, visiting historic sites, visiting state or national parks)

them. For core activities, there were 13 duration categories ranging from less than 1 hour to more than 10 hours and ending with 'less than one day'. For core activities, frequency categories were coded 0–4 and duration categories were coded 0–12. For balance activities, frequency was categorized and coded the same as for core frequency. Duration of balance activities ranged from less than 1 hour to 3 or more weeks, included 33 categories of duration, and was coded from 0–32. To calculate leisure involvement scores from the FLAP, the coded values for frequency and duration of participation in each activity category were multiplied, creating an ordinal index. (For this chapter, duration was only used to create core and balance involvement scores in order to compare non-resident fathers' involvement in family leisure with family leisure involvement scores from two-parent families. It was not used in any other analyses.)

The eight core items were then summed to produce a core family leisure index with a lower score meaning less involvement (a combination of low frequency and low duration) and a higher score indicating more involvement. A balance family leisure index was computed following the same process. Total family leisure involvement was then calculated by summing the core and balance index scores (Freeman and Zabriskie, 2003). The FLAP has demonstrated acceptable psychometric properties in terms of construct validity, content validity, inter-rater reliability, and test retest reliability for core ($r = .74$), balance ($r = .78$), and total family leisure involvement ($r = .78$) (Freeman and Zabriskie, 2003, Zabriskie, 2001).

The fathers' satisfaction with their family leisure involvement was measured using the Family Leisure Satisfaction Scale (FLSS) (Zabriskie 2000). Following each of the 16 FLAP questions, a follow-up question asked: 'How satisfied are you with your participation, or lack of participation, during parenting time with your non-resident children in these activities?' This was modified from the original FLSS question of, 'How satisfied are you with your participation with family members in these activities?' Participants were asked to identify their satisfaction using a Likert scale from 1 indicating 'very dissatisfied' to 5 indicating 'very satisfied'. Even if a father did not participate in the given activity this question was important because a father may have been 'very satisfied' with his non-participation. Scoring for the FLSS was calculated by summing responses to the first eight items to indicate satisfaction with core family leisure involvement and the next eight items to indicate satisfaction with involvement in balance family leisure activities, with the maximum possible score for each being 40. Total satisfaction with family leisure was computed by summing core and balance satisfaction. The FLSS had acceptable internal consistency as indicated by the coefficients of $\alpha = .934$ for satisfaction with the eight core activity categories and $\alpha = .928$ for satisfaction with the eight balance activity categories. The total satisfaction scale also had acceptable internal consistency ($\alpha = .960$).

Demographic information collected included the age of the non-resident fathers and each of their child(ren), race of the non-resident fathers and each of their child(ren), household income, marital history, duration of time since divorce, and zip code (residential area code) of the fathers.

Data analysis

Descriptive statistics were used to examine the fathers' demographic information and to portray how the fathers spent leisure time with their child(ren) during parenting times. In order to more fully understand the non-resident fathers' family leisure experience, the reported frequency of participation ('never' to 'daily') in each of the 16 activity categories on the FLAP were examined more closely in relation to the fathers' satisfaction with their family leisure involvement using Analysis of Variance (ANOVA) and Tukey's *post hoc* tests. ANOVA determined if mean satisfaction with leisure involvement (core and balance) varied significantly by frequency of participation in family leisure activities. If there was a significant difference in level of satisfaction between frequency categories then the *post hoc* tests determined where the exact difference occurred.

A descriptive comparison of family leisure involvement between the non-resident father sample and traditional, two-parent family samples from four other studies was conducted to illustrate differences in family leisure patterns between the two types of family. Zero-order correlations were also computed to determine factors related to the fathers' satisfaction with family leisure. The correlation coefficient (r) was examined at an alpha level of .05.

Results

The first stage of the analysis was to identify non-resident fathers' broad levels of participation in leisure activities during parenting time with their children. First, non-resident fathers' participation in core leisure activities during parenting time was calculated from the responses recorded on the core family leisure index. Scores ranged from 0 to 132 with a mean score of 39.45 (SD = 25.28) (Table 9.2a). This score is slightly under the average score for the traditional, two-parent family leisure participation in core activities. In addition, the standard deviation (SD) is quite high, which means there is

Table 9.2a Family leisure involvement of non-resident father sample

Family leisure	Sample	N	Mean	SD
Core family leisure	Non-resident father families (2006)	170	39.45	25.28
Balance family leisure	Non-resident father families (2006)	170	38.61	26.51
Total family leisure	Non-resident father families (2006)	170	78.06	45.96

wide variation between one non-resident father's participation in core activities and another. Non-resident fathers' participation in balance family leisure involvement was then calculated in the same way, from data on the balance family leisure index. For balance family leisure, non-resident fathers' scores ranged from 0 to 122 with a mean score of 38.61 ($SD = 26.51$). Although this score was slightly lower than non-resident father's participation in core activities, the score was considerably less than those of traditional families. In addition, the standard deviation was again high, demonstrating a wide range of participation. Total family leisure ranged from 0 to 221 with a mean score of 78.06 ($SD = 45.96$), this score was also very low compared to non-divorced families. Obviously, the lower participation in balance activities by non-resident fathers impacted the total family leisure index score.

To put non-resident fathers' leisure involvement scores into perspective, comparison was made with equivalent data for two-parent families. To do this, family leisure involvement scores from four broad traditional, two-parent family samples, studied in 2000, 2005, 2006, and 2007, were set alongside the data obtained from the current non-resident fathers sample (Table 9.2b). The core family leisure index for traditional families ranged from 0 to 126 with mean scores for each study sample ranging from 42.21 to 43.2 (study $SDs = 13.22$ to 16.28). Traditional families, therefore, scored approximately 3 points higher than non-resident fathers on core leisure activities, and were more closely clustered around the mean. The differences were much greater

Table 9.2b Comparison of family leisure involvement of non-resident father sample (2006) and traditional family samples (2000, 2005, 2006, 2007)

Family leisure	Sample	N	Mean	SD
Core family leisure	Non-res. father families	170	39.45	25.28
	Traditional families (2000)	174	42.95	13.22
	Traditional families (2005)	898	44.21	15.90
	Traditional families (2006)	154	42.21	16.12
	Traditional families (2007)	495	43.26	16.28
Balance family leisure	Non-res. father families	170	38.61	26.51
	Traditional families (2000)	171	60.15	24.80
	Traditional families (2005)	898	51.30	25.68
	Traditional families (2006)	154	50.95	25.28
	Traditional families (2007)	495	49.30	24.01
Total family leisure	Non-res. father families	170	78.06	45.96
	Traditional families (2000)	167	102.51	33.37
	Traditional families (2005)	898	95.51	35.54
	Traditional families (2006)	154	93.17	36.91
	Traditional families (2007)	495	92.56	34.61

for balance activities: for traditional families, balance family leisure index scores ranged from 0 to 179 with mean scores from 49.30 to 60.15 (SD = 24.01 to 25.68). Traditional families, therefore, recorded much higher mean scores than the 38.61 recorded by the non-resident fathers' sample. This was also reflected in traditional families' scores for total family leisure which ranged from 0 to 252 with mean scores from 92.56 to 102.51 (SD = 33.37 to 36.91), all notably higher than the mean score of 78.06 for non-resident fathers.

The next stage in the analysis involved identifying non-resident fathers' frequency of participation in leisure activities during parenting time spent with their children. Analysis of the frequency of participation in the eight core family leisure activity categories (i.e. those that are primarily associated with family cohesion) indicated that the majority of non-resident fathers did participate in common, everyday, home-based core types of leisure with their children on a fairly regular basis (see Table 9.3). Fathers were sharing meals with their children, playing board games, or playing sports outside during their allocated parenting time. The frequency of participation in the eight balance family leisure activity categories (that are primarily associated with family flexibility) were much lower and indicated that many non-resident fathers did not participate in the less common, out of the ordinary, challenging or novel balance types of leisure activities with their children (see Table 9.4) such as camping trips, traveling/sightseeing, or participating in water-sports (waterskiing, surfing, kayaking etc. . . .).

The analysis next focused on the issue of leisure satisfaction. Using the Likert-type scale as described previously, non-resident fathers' leisure satisfaction ranged from 8 to 40 (M = 27.19, SD = 8.99) for core leisure activities (Table 9.3) and between 8 and 40 (M = 25.66, SD = 8.58) for balance leisure activities (Table 9.4). These scores indicate the fathers experienced the full range of satisfaction for both core and balance leisure activities. Furthermore, these results indicate that the fathers were slightly more satisfied with their core family leisure participation than their balance family leisure participation but that the differences between the two were relatively small. Both mean scores lie below the midpoint on the scale, indicating a slightly negative level of satisfaction. The two scores were then summed to give a score for total leisure satisfaction that ranged from 16–80 (M = 52.85, SD = 16.89).

To more fully investigate the differences in fathers' satisfaction with participating in core and balance family leisure, 16 ANOVAs were computed. The ANOVAs were used to determine if there were significant differences between satisfaction with core and balance family leisure involvement and how frequently the fathers participated in each of the 16 activity categories with their child(ren). This was done to assess if higher frequency of participation corresponded with higher levels of satisfaction.

The results confirmed there was a difference in satisfaction with leisure involvement based on frequency of participation. For the eight core family

Table 9.3 Comparison of frequency of participation in each core family leisure activity category with satisfaction with core family leisure involvement

Core family leisure activity category	Frequency of participation	N	%	Mean satisfaction core family leisure involvement	SD
Dinners at home	At least daily	11	6	24.64	10.86
	At least weekly	31	18	29.35	6.89
	At least monthly	48	28	30.44	5.74
	At least annually	48	28	29.92	7.80
	Never	32	18	17.03	8.60
Home-based activities	At least daily	7	4	33.00	4.83
(TV, movies, reading,	At least weekly	29	17	28.41	6.48
music)	At least monthly	52	30	28.92	6.65
	At least annually	51	30	31.47	6.66
	Never	31	18	14.81	7.68
Games	At least daily	6	4	29.33	7.58
(board games, billiards,	At least weekly	37	22	29.29	5.98
cards, video games)	At least monthly	54	32	30.72	7.28
	At least annually	29	17	29.65	7.95
	Never	44	26	19.18	9.22
Crafts, cooking, hobbies	At least daily	11	6	31.90	5.68
(drawing, painting, baking,	At least weekly	39	23	29.79	6.00
model building)	At least monthly	41	24	29.17	8.59
	At least annually	19	11	31.15	7.15
	Never	60	35	22.03	9.69
Home-based outdoor	At least daily	12	7	30.75	7.60
activities	At least weekly	43	25	28.88	5.45
(gardening, playing with	At least monthly	48	28	30.97	7.04
pets, walks)	At least annually	28	16	30.82	7.26
	Never	39	23	16.97	8.32
Home-based sport/games	At least daily	9	5	30.44	6.94
(playing catch, shooting	At least weekly	46	27	29.23	5.91
baskets, bike rides, fitness	At least monthly	42	25	31.19	7.01
activities)	At least annually	25	15	30.72	6.53
	Never	48	28	19.29	9.68
Attend other family,	At least daily	3	16	29.46	6.51
members' activities	At least weekly	37	34	29.38	6.39
(watching/leading sport	At least monthly	57	22	32.62	4.83
events, musical	At least annually	28	2	33.66	2.08
performances, scouts)	Never	45	26	18.11	9.58
Religious/spiritual,	At least daily	8	5	32.37	5.95
activities	At least weekly	33	19	30.12	6.42
(going to church,	At least monthly	34	20	29.97	6.93
worshiping scripture	At least annually	9	5	35.88	4.16
reading, Sunday school)	Never	86	51	23.58	9.59

Table 9.4 Comparison of frequency of participation in each balance family leisure activity with satisfaction with balance family leisure involvement

Balance family leisure activity category	Frequency of participation	N	%	Mean satisfaction with balance family leisure involvement	SD
Community-based social activities (going to restaurants, parties, shopping, visiting friends/neighbors)	At least daily	7	4	31.71	4.03
	At least weekly	54	32	29.15	5.81
	At least monthly	68	40	27.24	6.39
	At least annually	13	8	28.77	5.57
	Never	28	16	12.14	6.48
Spectator activities (movies, sporting events, concerts, plays or theatrical performances)	At least daily	3	2	28.00	3.46
	At least weekly	18	11	28.83	6.92
	At least monthly	78	46	28.73	5.42
	At least annually	31	18	29.10	5.24
	Never	40	24	15.40	8.77
Community-based sporting activities (bowling, golf, swimming, skating)	At least daily	3	2	20.66	11.01
	At least weekly	15	9	30.80	4.17
	At least monthly	57	34	28.84	5.63
	At least annually	24	14	30.33	5.38
	Never	71	42	20.64	9.37
Community-based special events (visiting museums, zoos, theme parks, fairs)	At least daily	1	1	26.00	—
	At least weekly	6	4	26.83	6.46
	At least monthly	40	24	29.02	6.09
	At least annually	77	45	29.09	5.54
	Never	46	27	16.82	8.80
Outdoor activities (camping, hiking, hunting, fishing)	At least daily	2	1	21.50	6.36
	At least weekly	8	5	26.00	7.83
	At least monthly	25	15	30.48	5.04
	At least annually	66	39	29.81	5.87
	Never	69	41	20.01	8.71
Water-based activities (water skiing, jet skiing, boating sailing, canoeing)	At least daily	1	1	40.00	—
	At least weekly	4	2	31.25	3.77
	At least monthly	13	8	30.38	4.66
	At least annually	44	26	31.38	5.37
	Never	108	64	22.41	8.48
Outdoor adventure activities (rock climbing, river rafting, off-roading, scuba diving)	At least daily	3	2	30.33	7.32
	At least weekly	4	2	29.75	2.21
	At least monthly	6	4	25.33	10.38
	At least annually	28	16	30.85	4.78
	Never	129	76	24.31	8.85
Tourism activities (traveling, visiting historic sites, visiting state or national parks)	At least daily	1	1	26.00	—
	At least weekly	1	1	27.00	—
	At least monthly	8	5	29.50	1.92
	At least annually	85	50	29.65	5.71
	Never	75	44	20.69	9.26

leisure activity categories, all eight ANOVAs indicated an overall significant difference in mean core satisfaction scores according to fathers' frequency of participation. Tukey's HSD *post hoc* tests were then used to investigate the relationship between satisfaction levels and the five specified frequencies of participation, i.e. at least daily, weekly, monthly, annually and never. Tukey's HSD *post hoc* tests revealed that satisfaction with core family leisure by fathers who 'never' participated in the activity was significantly lower than those who participated 'at least annually', 'at least monthly', 'at least weekly' or 'at least daily'. Doing an activity 'at least annually' resulted in a higher level of satisfaction than never doing the activity with their child(ren) during parenting times. There were, however, no other significant subgroup differences (i.e., weekly vs. monthly vs. annually) in satisfaction scores, showing that how frequently fathers participated did not matter to satisfaction levels: what mattered was whether or not fathers participated in the activity with their children at all. It is perhaps surprising that high levels of participation did not increase levels of satisfaction, and interesting that even infrequent participation – 'at least annually' – was sufficient to do so.

Equivalent analysis was applied to balance family leisure activities. For the eight balance family leisure activity categories, all eight ANOVAs indicated that there was a statistically significant difference between fathers' overall family leisure satisfaction score for each category of activity based on their frequency of participation in those activities. Tukey's *post hoc* test again found that non-resident fathers who participated at a minimal level (at least annually) demonstrated higher levels of satisfaction than those who never participated. For participation in community-based sporting activities (swimming, bowling, skating, etc.) and participation in outdoor activities (hiking, camping, fishing, etc.) satisfaction with balance activities was not significantly different for those who 'never' do them compared to those who do them 'at least annually'. These findings indicate that 'never' doing the activity and doing the activity 'at least annually' resulted in similar satisfaction scores for these non-resident fathers. These satisfaction scores, however, were significantly lower than for those fathers who participated in these activities at least daily, weekly, or monthly with their child(ren) during parenting times.

Zero order correlations were used to help examine the relationship between two variables while ignoring the influence of other variables. The zero order correlations among study variables indicated that non-resident fathers' family leisure satisfaction increased as participation in both core ($r = .534$) and balance ($r = .588$) activities increased (see Table 9.5). Together, core and balance activities (total family leisure) had a significant relationship to total satisfaction ($r = .639$). Income was another predictor of higher leisure satisfaction. Higher income resulted in higher satisfaction with both core ($r = .277$) and balance activities ($r = .308$). It appears income plays a significant role in determining the type and frequency of leisure activities that fathers are able to engage in with their children during parenting time. Because of the circumstances of divorce, money is a necessary facilitator

Table 9.5 Zero order correlations among study variables

	1	2	3	4	5	6	7	8	9	10	11
1. FLSS total	1	0.963**	0.959**	-0.015	0.002	0.081	0.119	0.277**	0.534**	0.588**	0.639**
2. FLSS Core		1	0.846**	-0.060	0.003	0.029	0.051	0.227**	0.559**	0.472**	0.586**
3. FLSS Balance			1	0.033	0.000	0.129	0.181*	0.308**	0.465**	0.663**	0.644**
4. No. children				1	-0.005	-0.097	-0.014	0.031	0.103	0.184**	0.167*
5. Remarried					1	0.073	0.107	0.254**	-0.010	0.056	0.025
6. Age						1	0.139	0.271**	0.041	0.182*	0.125
7. Ethnicity							1	0.426**	0.089	0.251**	0.190*
8. Annual income								1	0.124	0.343**	0.263**
9. Core									1	0.542**	0.875**
10. Balance										1	0.881**
11. Total leisure											1

Note: *p < 0.05 (2-tailed); **p < 0.01 (2-tailed); FLSS = family leisure satisfaction scale for fathers to engage in both core and balance activities (even if they are minimal, such as transportation for the child). If a father can afford to engage in leisure activities with his child(ren) then his satisfaction is significantly higher than a father who cannot engage at all.

Discussion

Non-resident fathers' leisure patterns

Contrary to popular belief or perception, the non-resident fathers' leisure patterns in this study were primarily home based, inexpensive activities done on a fairly regular basis (core activities). These activities included eating meals together, playing games, attending children's performances/sporting activities, attending church together, or playing outside around the house.

In the early 1970s terms such as 'Disneyland dad' became commonly used to characterize non-resident fathers' leisure patterns when they had time with their children. The term alludes to non-resident fathers spending large amounts of money on their children during parenting time, or treating their children to extravagant activities seemingly to replace daily, routine time at home with their children. According to this study, however, participation in balance activities (activities that require time, money and planning, such as family vacations or adventure activities) was much lower than participation in core activities. This finding is consistent with Stewart's (1999) examination of the types of activities non-resident parents engage in with their children. Stewart examined both non-resident mothers and fathers and found that non-resident fathers tended to not spend excess amounts of money or attend extraordinary events/activities while engaging in parenting time with their children. Her conclusion was that non-resident fathers did not deserve the 'Disneyland Dad' stereotype. Current findings support her claim.

Furthermore, when non-resident fathers' family leisure patterns were compared to those from traditional family samples, non-resident fathers' core scores were not much lower than the core scores from any of the traditional family samples. This may be an indicator of the essential nature of this type of family leisure involvement. Participation together in these common, everyday, home-based types of family activities are said to provide 'predictable family leisure experiences that foster personal relatedness and feelings of family closeness or cohesion' (Zabriskie and McCormick 2003: 169). Zabriskie and McCormick (2003) also found that children reported higher levels of satisfaction with family life when engaging in core activities with their family members versus balance activities. They explained that youth appeared 'to have a greater need for stability, consistency, and regularity in their preferences for family leisure involvement' and that they 'may simply desire to attain a stable sense of belongingness and closeness through family leisure' (2003: 182). Although data were not collected from children in this sample, the higher participation in core family leisure by non-resident fathers seems likely to reflect a similar and perhaps even greater need for stability and consistency as well as 'the desire to attain a stable sense of belongingness and closeness through family leisure' (2003: 182) from both children and non-resident fathers.

Although non-resident fathers engaged in high levels of core activities, their participation in balance activities with their children during parenting time was much lower when compared to traditional family samples. These findings are consistent with Smith, Taylor, Hill and Zabriskie (2004) who examined family leisure among young adults who were raised in single-parent homes. Smith stated, 'single-parent families participated in considerably less balance leisure, but not significantly less core leisure than dual-parent families' (2004: 54).

Because single-parent families and non-resident fathers are engaging in lower levels of balance activities when compared to other families, the associated leisure benefit of increased flexibility may be limited. Flexibility is an essential component of family functioning. Given the unique circumstances of divorce, it seems increasing family flexibility would be important for strengthening the family system following divorce for both the non-resident parent, and the child(ren). Likewise, the very nature and dynamics of divorced families are likely to demand the development of basic adaptive and flexible family skills. Perhaps when facing limited time together, however, the need to further develop these traits through balance types of family leisure falls second in priority to the need to redevelop and maintain the foundation of stable relationships and feelings of closeness related to core family leisure involvement. Either way, it appears that participation in both core and balance leisure activities with their children is desired among non-resident fathers.

Because divorce results in an array of parenting time agreements, opportunities to engage in both core and balance activities may not be possible for all non-resident parents. Many fathers indicated 'never' participating in each of the categories of family leisure activities. Non-resident fathers who do not have access to their children for longer periods of time are at a disadvantage when engaging in balance activities because traditional balance activities (e.g. camping, traveling, summer vacations) require longer periods of time for participation. There may be value for non-resident fathers in creating balance activities by planning with their child(ren), during their time together in their familiar environment, an extraordinary activity in the near future that can be anticipated and organized together. The additional planning for this activity should create a distinction between regular core activities that occur during parenting time, even if the balance activity must be completed in the same length of time as traditional parenting core activities, in order to comply with the parenting time arrangements. This necessary planning and preparation should help create flexibility between the non-resident father and child(ren) as their planning likely will include communication and compromise.

Another limitation fathers may experience to engaging in balance activities is a perceived constraint related to income. Although fathers in this sample reported an annual income that was higher than the US median, a negative correlation was found between income and perceived constraints to family leisure participation. The financial challenges of being a non-resident father may influence their perception of their ability to afford to participate in balance activities such as a summer holiday or a weekend at the lake. Although non-resident fathers may not be able to ameliorate their financial situation in lieu of their child support payment obligations, community programs may be able to facilitate more affordable 'balance type' activities such as community fun-runs, participating in a parade, or competing in a community cook-off.

Non-resident fathers' leisure satisfaction

Non-resident fathers who 'never' engaged in certain activities with their children indicated the lowest levels of leisure satisfaction. Non-resident fathers who were able to participate in certain activities 'at least annually' with their children demonstrated a much higher level of satisfaction. This suggests that if non-resident fathers can engage in some family leisure activities with their children during parenting time, even if it is infrequently, they will have a significantly increased level of leisure satisfaction.

Because leisure satisfaction is related to life satisfaction (Russell, 1987; 1990), increased leisure satisfaction during parenting time is likely to benefit life satisfaction among non-resident fathers. The ability to empirically identify a behavioral characteristic related to higher life satisfaction has considerable implications for non-resident fathers. Zabriskie and McCormick (2003) found a negative correlation between families who had a history of divorce and family satisfaction and reported that 'both the youth and the parents reported having significantly lower levels of satisfaction with their family life if they had ever experienced divorce in their family, whether it was a current situation or if it had happened in the recent or even distant past' (2003: 183). Similarly, the current findings suggest that non-resident fathers are likely to be more susceptible to lower levels of satisfaction with family life, due to divorce and limited access to leisure time with their family. Empirical evidence also suggests that simply increasing the amount of shared family leisure between non-resident fathers and their children is not only related to positive outcomes for the child (Dunn et al., 2004; Menning, 2002) but also contributes to higher satisfaction for the non-resident father. Therefore, court decisions and parenting time negotiations evidently should consider the amount of family leisure time needed when determining parenting time for non-resident fathers.

Further research

Findings from this study provide considerable insight into the family leisure involvement of non-resident fathers. Further research is needed, however, to further examine and understand other aspects and outcomes related to family leisure among non-resident parents and their children. Examining leisure constraints and leisure facilitators from a parent and child perspective for example, would likely add further insight into the dynamic of family leisure among this growing population. Not only would such research identify current constraints that need to be addressed but successful approaches to negotiation could be identified. Related variables such as life satisfaction, family satisfaction, and family functioning should also be included in future studies with this population. Further examination into the meaning and importance of family leisure for non-resident fathers and their children, particularly core family leisure involvement is also recommended. Such studies would also benefit from qualitative approaches.

Because divorce results in a vast array of parenting time schedules for the non-resident parent, it is also recommended that future research examine and compare the leisure patterns of fathers who are given different amounts of parenting time – for instance, non-resident fathers who have parenting time once a month compared to those who have it once a week or once a year. From this perspective, researchers could better understand parenting arrangements, given the circumstances of divorce, and the role of leisure involvement and satisfaction within that context. While this study was able to measure how often fathers engaged in certain activities it did not ask specific information about the parenting time arrangements agreed upon following divorce. This information would enable researchers to determine the percentage of non-resident parenting time that is generally spent in family leisure, and how it related to other outcome variables. Overall, it appears that family leisure plays an important role for non-resident fathers and their children, and is an area requiring further research.

10 Traditional marriages, non traditional leisure

Leisure and fathering in the Church of Jesus Christ of Latter-day Saints

Patti A. Freeman, Birgitta Baker and Ramon B. Zabriskie

The focus of this chapter is the relationships between culture, religion, fathering, and leisure. These concepts are examined using participants who are members of the Church of Jesus Christ of Latter-day Saints (LDS, or Mormon), living in the state of Utah. The role of religion in shaping subcultural norms regarding fathering and leisure and the ways in which these norms elicit experiences that differ from those of the larger culture in which the Utah LDS subculture is embedded are explored. Findings challenge the notion that patriarchal belief systems result in men having a strong sense of entitlement to personal leisure.

The research context

Defining culture

Culture consists of patterns of attitudes, knowledge, beliefs, behaviors, and customs that distinguish one group of individuals or society from another (Arab-Moghaddam, Henderson and Sheikholeslami, 2007; Chick, 2000). These learned characteristics are socially constructed (Sasidharan, 2002), learned and shared (Chick and Dong, 2005), and provide guidelines regarding acceptable norms for members of the culture (Chick, 2000).

Both religion (Goodale and Godbey, 1988) and leisure (Pieper, 1963) are fundamental components of, and expressions of, culture. As with all aspects of culture, religion and leisure are interrelated (Arab-Moghaddam *et al.*, 2007; Russell, 2005) and in fact, at times may be equivalent (Cohen and Hill, 2007; Goodale and Godbey, 1988). Both religion and leisure in turn also relate to other aspects of culture: parenting attitudes and behaviors (Freeman, Palmer, and Baker, 2006; Furrow, 1998). This section therefore reviews what is known of the characteristic of religion, fathering, and leisure in the cultural context of a particular United States subculture: members of the LDS Church living in Utah.

Religion

Religion is a key component of culture and religious affiliation may define a subculture (Cohen and Hill, 2007). In the case of members of the LDS church living in Utah, both religion and geography define their subculture (Hartman and Hartman, 1983). Residents of the Intermountain-West area are generally both economically and socially conservative (Fox, 2003). This regional tendency may be heightened by the numerical dominance of members of the socially conservative LDS church within Utah. LDS church affiliation by 75 per cent of Utah's residents results in the largest concentration of a single religious denomination in the United States (Merrill, Lyon and Jensen, 2003). Like the broader population of the area, LDS church members living in Utah are also found to be conservative socially and economically (Fox, 2003).

In addition to engendering socially conservative opinions, the LDS church espouses specific views on gender roles and parenting. Religious institutions have significant influence over many aspects of family life. In addition, the norms of a religious tradition and the degree to which parents are actively involved with their religion influence their interactions with their children (Wilcox, 2002). Culturally influenced attitudes, beliefs and behaviors include those focusing on acceptable parenting practices and the preferred roles of fathers and mothers (Hofferth, 2003). Many religious traditions contain cultural narratives that define the 'ideal father' and explicate the expectations that society holds for fathers (Furrow, 1998).

Fathering

Guidance from LDS church leaders supports a traditional division of labor for men and women and has a strong pro-family ideology (Hartman and Hartman, 1983; Iannaccone and Miles, 1990; Lehrer, 2004). The LDS church encourages child bearing and provides rewards of approval and social status to those who have large numbers of children (Lehrer, 2004). This has resulted in a trend of large families that diverges from norms in the larger US culture (Merrill, Lyon, and Jensen, 2003). For most members of the LDS church, the preferred family situation is one in which several children are raised by a man and a woman in a financial situation in which the father earns enough for the mother not to need to engage in paid employment (Iannaccone and Miles, 1990).

According to the teachings of the LDS church, a father's role goes beyond economic provision. In 2000, Gordon B. Hinckley, the President of the LDS Church declared:

'The father's responsibility does not, however, end with providing financially for the family. This is a subject which I take very seriously. It is a matter with which I am deeply concerned. I hope you will not take it lightly. It concerns the most precious asset you have. In terms of your happiness, in terms of the matters that make you proud or sad, nothing – I repeat, nothing – will have so profound an effect on you as the way your children turn out.'

(Faust, 2006: 3)

Another LDS Church leader went further in describing the varied responsibilities expected of fathers when he stated:

'We know that a father's role does not end with presiding, providing, and protecting family members. On a day-to-day basis, fathers can and should help with the essential nurturing and bonding associated with feeding, playing, storytelling, loving, and all the rest of the activities that make up family life.'

(Ballard, 2006: 29)

In summary, according to LDS church doctrine, the role of the ideal father includes providing financially for his family, providing spiritual leadership and counsel, and nurturing and bonding with his children. These varied roles combine aspects of traditional gender roles with the expectations associated with the 'new fatherhood' described by Henwood and Procter (2003) that involves wanting to and being actively involved in the children's lives through spending time at home, responding to the children's needs, and caring for and nurturing the children.

Leisure

In addition to influencing parenting expectations, culture and its subset of religion has a significant impact on leisure (Arab-Moghaddam *et al.*, 2007). Religion both prescribes and proscribes a variety of behaviors including those associated with leisure (Cohen and Hill, 2007). In addition, worship activities may constitute part of an individual's leisure repertoire (Goodale and Godbey, 1988) and religious organizations may facilitate leisure through the provision of facilities, organized programs, and a social network (Stodolska and Livengood, 2006). The LDS church discourages many leisure activities common to society in general including gambling, alcohol consumption, and premarital sex. Recreation of other types, however, has been encouraged by leaders since the early years of the LDS church's existence.

Brigham Young (1801–1877), the 2nd Prophet and President of the LDS church was explicit regarding the importance of wholesome recreation to human wellbeing:

I want it distinctly understood, that fiddling and dancing are no part of our worship [services]. The question may be asked: What are they for, then? I answer, that my body may keep pace with my mind. My mind labors like a man logging, all the time; and this is the reason why I am fond of these pastimes – they give me a privilege to throw everything off, and shake myself, that my body may exercise, and my mind rest. What for? To get strength, and be renewed and quickened, and enlivened, and animated, so that my mind may not wear out ... Recreation and diversion are as necessary to our well-being as the more serious pursuits of life.

(The Church of Jesus Christ of Latter-day Saints, 1997: 188–189)

More recently, Bruce R. McConkie (1966: 622), a noted leader within the LDS church stated,

Recreation is an essential and vital part of the gospel of salvation ... wholesome recreation may include parties, banquets, dinners, games, athletic endeavors and contests, dramas, dances, concerts, radio and television programs, picnics, outings, camping trips ... and vacations in general.

Leaders of the LDS church continue to extol the virtue of leisure for individuals and as a means for strengthening families. Hales (1999: 3) encouraged members to 'build family traditions, plan and carry out meaningful vacations together, considering our children's needs, talents, and abilities. Help them create happy memories, improve their talents, and build their feelings of self-worth.'

In summary, LDS church leaders, whose discourse is viewed by church members as direct revelation from God, have provided specific direction regarding appropriate leisure. Although certain activities are forbidden by LDS church leaders, they are also vocal in their support of leisure. They regularly explicate their beliefs regarding the importance of leisure to physical and mental health and the role of shared recreation in strengthening families. Given the importance of gender roles within the LDS faith and the importance of gender in determining leisure behaviors, it is important to also consider what is known about men's leisure.

Men's leisure

There has been a significant increase of research examining women's leisure in the last two decades (Henderson, Hodges and Kivel, 2002). There has been minimal recent research, however, exploring men's experiences of leisure and Henderson and Shaw (2003) have called for more research in this area. Men have often been a comparison group in research about women's leisure, yet variations among subgroups of men have not been explored. Evidence for gender differences in leisure has been found in studies in which gender was a secondary focus to the main variable (Hultsman, 1995; Witt and Goodale, 1981; Wright and Goodale, 1991) and in research initiated in the belief that gender inequities in other areas of life would be reflected in leisure patterns (Frederick and Shaw, 1995; Jackson and Henderson, 1995). In the context of literature which explicitly focuses on gender differences, gender is identified as transcending genetics to encompass the meanings and expectations assigned by society to biological sex (Jackson and Henderson, 1995). These culturally imposed meanings appear to result in differences between men's and women's leisure (Henderson, Bialeschki, Shaw and Freysinger, 1996; Shaw, 1994).

Support for gender differences in leisure preferences (Shinew, Floyd, McGuire and Noe, 1996), participation (Gibson, 1998; Shaw, Bonen and McCabe, 1991), and satisfaction/enjoyment (Bolla, Dawson and Harrington, 1991; Witt and Goodale, 1981) has been found. In the area of participation, men have been shown to be advantaged in comparison to women. Men participate more than women in sports (Henderson *et al.*, 1996; Robinson and Godbey, 1993), active sport tourism (Gibson, 1998), and total leisure time (Shaw, Bonen and McCabe, 1991).

Researchers have also suggested that men have more time for leisure than women, especially on the weekends (Henderson *et al.*, 1996; Thrane, 2000). Men report employment obligations as the primary limitation on leisure time, while women report both family and employment responsibilities as significant sources of time constraints (Henderson *et al.*, 1996). Although men work longer hours in paid employment, when both paid (employment) and unpaid (housework) are combined, women work more hours than men (Coltrane and Adams, 2001).The idea of the 'second shift' (Hochschild, 1989) reported among working mothers, is considered to be a significant leisure constraint for mothers and less existent among fathers. Thus, it makes sense that Larson, Gillman, and Richards (1997) found that fathers reported high levels of freedom, intrinsic motivation, and positive affect during family leisure in contrast to their wives who may have viewed family leisure as work.

Despite these trends, there are greater within-sex differences than between-sex differences on several leisure variables (Jackson and Henderson, 1995). This finding highlights the importance of recognizing the diversity in women and men's leisure experiences. Factors such as socioeconomic status (Raymore, Godbey and Crawford, 1994), personality (Henderson, Stalnaker and Taylor, 1988), employment status (Harrington and Dawson, 1995), stage of family life cycle (Witt and Goodale, 1981), level of education (Wright and Goodale, 1991) and race (Henderson and Ainsworth, 2001) have been correlated with variations in leisure participation.

While some gender differences have been consistently reported in leisure among mothers and fathers, the focus of most studies has been women. Researchers have identified a dearth of research regarding men's leisure (Henderson and Shaw, 2003) particularly among fathers. Furthermore, the influence of religion or a specific culture on father's leisure remains relatively unexamined. Given the specific expectations among LDS fathers and their concentration in the LDS subculture of Utah this population offered prime context to examine these variables. Therefore, the purpose of this chapter is to explore the relationships between fathering, leisure, and religion in the subculture of LDS church members living in the state of Utah.

Methods

Study setting

The study was conducted in 2003–2004 in Utah County which is located in the north central part of Utah, 50 miles south of Salt Lake City. Approximately, 55–60 per cent of the nearly 400,000 people living in Utah County are LDS (The Church of Jesus Christ of Latter-day Saints, Public Affairs Office, personal communication, June 30, 2004; United States Census Bureau, 2000).

Quantitative methods tend to ignore the social context and social meanings of leisure (Tirone and Shaw, 1997). Therefore, in order to explore central and meaningful life concepts as well as the role that leisure played in the lives of LDS fathers, a phenomenological approach based on in-depth interviews was used. Such an approach allowed for an examination of experiences through detailed descriptions provided by the study participants (Henderson, 1991).

Procedures and data analysis

The data were collected using in-depth semi-structured face-to-face interviews. Participating men were identified through a criteria-based snowball sampling technique. The criteria used in recruiting the men were: LDS religious affiliation; worked full-time in paid employment that was the primary source of income for the family; spouse did not work full-time outside of the home in paid market labor; at least two children lived with the couple; had lived for at least five years of their married life in Utah; and one or both of the spouses spent the majority of his/her years prior to college living in Utah. Men who met the criteria were contacted and invited to participate in the study.

To encourage the participants to respond honestly and accurately, rapport was established by providing background information on the study, time was given for the interviewee to ask questions before the interview began (Henderson, 1991; Lincoln and Guba, 1985), and standardized open-ended interview questions as well as probing questions were used (Babbie, 2002; Henderson, and Bialeschki, 2002; Henderson, 1991; Lincoln and Guba, 1985; Riddick and Russell, 1999). The researchers then conducted face-to-face semi-structured interviews with the men. At the end of the interview, the men were asked if they knew of any other men who met the study criteria. Each interview was transcribed in a timely manner by one of the researchers. Pseudonyms were given to the participants in order to ensure anonymity. The computer program QSR nVivo was utilized to organize the interviews and code the data.

The interview questions were divided into four sections. First, demographic information, such as age, number of children, and years married, was obtained. Second, following Tirone and Shaw's (1997) protocol the men were asked about what aspects of their life were important and meaningful, and provided them with satisfaction, enjoyment and relaxation. Third, the concept of leisure was explicitly discussed. The men were asked to define leisure, describe their current and ideal leisure, and discuss how their families did or did not support them in their leisure. Finally, how the men viewed their roles and responsibilities as father and husband was explored.

Rigor in data collection and the establishment of trustworthiness were achieved by meeting the criteria of credibility, applicability, consistency, and objectivity (Henderson, 1991; Lincoln and Guba, 1985; Riddick and Russell, 1999). Credibility was addressed through prolonged engagement, persistent observation, and member checking. Member checks were conducted by performing follow up interviews and allowing the participants to review their transcripts and the article manuscript. Member checks confirmed that the men felt their voices were being accurately represented. Applicability was addressed by developing a thorough narrative of the findings using both emic and etic statements (Henderson and Bialeschki, 2002). Consistency and objectivity were achieved by having an external auditor familiar with qualitative research verify the research process and the emerging themes (Lincoln and Guba, 1985).

Constant comparison was used to increase credibility of the study and guide the data analysis (Glaser and Holton, 2004; Glaser and Strauss, 1967; Henderson, 1991; Henderson and Bialeschki, 2002; Lincoln and Guba, 1985). Glaser and Holton stated, 'the constant comparative method enables the generation of theory through systematic and explicit coding and analytic procedures' (2004: 15). The constant comparison process followed four steps (Glaser and Strauss, 1967; Henderson, 1991; Strauss and Corbin, 1990). The first step was to reduce, code, and then display the themes that emerged from the data. We used descriptive open line-by-line coding. The data were then examined at a deeper level using interpretive and explanatory codes (Henderson, 1991). The second step was to organize the codes into concepts and categories (Glaser and Holton). We used axial coding that identified the possible relationships between the open codes and helped create concepts and categories. Memoing was also used throughout the coding process to help generate ideas about the codes, discover properties that existed within specific categories, and develop relationships that existed between certain codes. The third step was to delimit and refine the themes, identify disconfirming evidence, and find diversity in the data (Henderson). The fourth step was to provide examples from the data to explain how the themes were created (Glaser and Strauss, 1967; Henderson and Bialeschki, 2002; Lincoln and Guba, 1985; Strauss and Corbin, 1990).

Participants

The men (n = 13) in this study ranged in age from 29–52 years, with a median age of 40. They had been married from 7 to 27 years, with the median number of years married being 17. These men had between 3 and 7 children (median = 5). All of the men had earned a Bachelor's degree, three had Master's degrees, and six had received Ph.Ds. All men reported their household income to be between $40,000 and $100,000. The men were employed in professional occupations including: professor, attorney, engineer, airline pilot, business owner, accountant, counselor, and recreation administrator.

Results

During the interviews, the men shared what was enjoyable and meaningful to them, explained their beliefs about their role of 'father' and how their view of that role was shaped and supported by their religious beliefs, and described their perspectives on leisure, the value of personal leisure, and their commitment to family leisure. Six themes emerged from the data and support for the themes follows.

Paid employment, family and church provided satisfaction and meaning

Most of the men in this study stated that their paid employment was a primary source of personal satisfaction; they were also highly committed to their roles of husband and father and found great meaning in those roles. For example, Carl, a computer programmer, indicated that, 'doing good things with work' was very satisfying. 'It affects other people to make their lives better and more efficient.'

Similarly, Mike, a lawyer, indicated that it was his job that brought him great satisfaction. 'Most days I have pretty good fulfillment during the day in terms of feeling like I'm doing good things for my clients and they appreciate it.'

Although work was the most frequent source of satisfaction for these men, they reported time with family and serving others in their family, work, or church to be the most meaningful. Bob described the most meaningful aspects of his life as, 'The relationship I have with God and the knowledge that comes from that relationship ... My family is probably the most important next to God and everything else kind of just builds around that.' He explained further:

'I think it is the balance of everything that brings enjoyment. I also love hanging out with my family. One of the things we have tried to do but haven't been very successful on a regular basis is going on [outings] with my kids. Once a week I'll try to rotate through taking each of the kids out.'

Rick and Craig both simply stated what was most meaningful to them as, 'time spent with my family' and 'being with my family.' Mike talked about the meaning he finds in watching his children exemplify values taught to them by him and his wife. 'I tell them [his children] that nothing makes me happier than when I see one of them cheering for the other of them because they're building each other up and that builds the love and that makes me feel love for them.'

Beyond family, a variety of other activities or experiences brought about feelings of enjoyment and meaning. Craig indicated that he found enjoyment in being outdoors, reading religious scripture, keeping a personal journal, and serving in his church. Ryan found joy in seeing others succeed at his work. Rick found enjoyment from serving others. Mike stated, 'I enjoy the environment and am thankful for it and that does give me a lot of enjoyment.'

An ideal father provides for the physical, emotional and intellectual needs of his family

From the interviews with these men, it was clear that their beliefs regarding the role of father were tied to their religious ideology; which in turn undoubtedly shaped their beliefs regarding family time and about personal leisure versus family leisure time. Their views of the role of father included providing for the physical needs of their family through paid employment and household tasks as well as providing for emotional and intellectual needs of their family by spending time with their wife and children.

Without exception, all of the men when asked to describe what the role of father entailed believed they were to be the financial provider, family protector, and household 'leader'. Beyond these traditional perspectives, they also perceived that their role included nurturing, caretaking, and setting an example. Several quotes help illustrate this point:

> 'I think being able to provide for the emotional and spiritual needs of the family and being a leader. I don't think it's about quality time, it's simply time. It's being available and spending that necessary time with them.'
>
> (Scott)

> 'A caretaker. Someone who is responsible for the well being of the family; emotionally, spiritually, physically, and socially. I see a father as being a caretaker. I see a father also as providing opportunities for my children. I feel like it is my responsibility as a father to help my children to learn what behaviors are appropriate and what's not appropriate.'
>
> (Gary)

'We are supposed to be the providers and fix things around the house that break down. I need to set an example, for my wife and children. I need to take leadership in spiritual things at home.'

(Craig)

'I think it is part of the father's role to spend a lot of time with his kids. Not just quality time, but quantity time. You need quantity time. It's having a relationship with your kids. Being comfortable with them and knowing them really well. Talking to them a lot, but also feeling like you are setting the example . . . I think it is treating your wife like you are supposed to and showing the children that you love her and support her and that's a very important part about being a father. I guess traditionally, the father is the one who supports the family financially.'

(Nick)

'I would say the father is the patriarch of the home. That doesn't mean he is above or below the wife . . . we are side by side. But, I have the ultimate responsibility and am the ultimate decision maker and also the financial provider. I am supposed to provide her [his wife] the home and the financial means and hopefully emotional support.'

(Rick)

'I think that being a good father means being a good provider and also being there in a supportive role in the things your kids are doing. Being there as a teacher in the things they want to learn and being there emotionally. I think an important role for me is just being someone they can have fun with and someone they feel comfortable with and being a dad but also being a friend within the role of dad. It means to take the time to recognize and value all the changes that are going on in your kid's life and helping them see those changes and helping them rejoice in those changes in an effort to help them come to a sense of who they are and how they are important to the family and outside of the family. I think a father should nurture as well.'

(Bob)

From these statements, it is clear that the fathers felt a strong sense of obligation towards their family. They considered themselves responsible for not just the family's physical and emotional needs but also their spiritual needs. These feelings are likely tied directly to their membership in the LDS church.

Religion shaped fathering beliefs

Practicing members of the LDS church regard the President of the church to be a prophet who receives revelation directly from God, and thus consider the words from the prophet to come from God. Members of the LDS church regularly receive counsel and direction from church leaders. These addresses are often directed specifically to the mothers and fathers in the church (e.g. www.lds.org). Therefore, when LDS church leaders speak about the roles of husband and father the men in this study felt it was important to listen and follow the counsel of their church leaders regarding how best to fulfill their roles.

Male LDS church members are frequently counseled regarding their role to preside over as well as protect and provide for their families. According to LDS church leaders, the first priority for LDS married men should be to support, appreciate, and be considerate of their wives and to treat them as full and equal partners in marriage. Their second priority should be to be good fathers, teachers, and examples to their children (Benson, 1981; Hinckley, 2004; Perry, 1977). A recent President of the LDS church exemplified the general counsel given to men regarding their familial duties when he said to LDS men, 'Honor your wife's unique and divinely appointed role as a mother. You share, as a loving partner, the care of the children. Help her to manage and keep up your home. Help teach, train, and discipline your children' (Hunter, 1994: 50).

All of the men in this study not only identified with the words spoken by their church leaders but strived to follow the leaders' counsel. Bob appreciated that the church leaders spoke often about the duties of fathering:

> 'I think what the [leaders] are saying is great wisdom as far as keeping our focus. That it is important to be a good breadwinner but if being a good breadwinner [is] at the expense of being a good father or being a good spouse that is not good ... I think they (church leaders) are speaking very strongly to make sure you know where your priorities are and what it means to be with your children and to have a good relationship with your children and how important it is to the choices they are likely to make.'

Likewise, Gary enjoyed receiving counsel from his church leaders and took it as a time to reflect and self-assess:

> 'I like receiving that direction. I like the opportunity that it gives me to reflect and to assess what it is they're saying with what it is that I am doing. My relationship with my family is eternal. That's why those relationships and those roles are the most important to me. Everything else is a temporary thing. Everything else is temporary so I appreciate the apostles and prophets speaking to that because it is helping me in those eternal roles that are most important.'

Similar to Gary, Mike and Scott found the guidance to be motivating and inspiring:

'Their words are inspiring to me and uplifting to me. I feel, and in most cases I feel pretty good that I'm doing a pretty good job. But there's also a lot of times where I'll come out of there going "but I could sure do better in many ways" and I don't feel negative about it though. So I feel . . . I come home motivated to do some things differently and say "OK I can do that better and it will change the way I do things because I'm inspired to do some things better." '

(Mike)

'I think it gives me hope and encouragement to be better. I don't think any of us are perfect in that regard (of being a parent) and I think it just helps keep our focus on exactly what we should be doing and what we need to be doing.'

(Scott)

Nick stated that he feels guilty but also inspired. He had attended a recent conference where the LDS prophet and other top leaders had spoken specifically to the men of the church. He stated, 'They said really important things that I need to be reminded of like spend more time with your children. Almost everyone said your first responsibility is to your family.'

The men seemed to appreciate the value given to parenting by their church leaders. The counsel from the leaders was generally motivating and inspiring. The men's strong indoctrination towards feeling role obligated as fathers and spouses including all that comes with those roles may help explain how they tended to view personal leisure time.

Guilt and role obligations produced a mismatch between ideal and current leisure

Ideal leisure

Although the men listed activities they did for leisure they did not provide great detail about their current leisure. Many of their comments were prefaced by something like, 'I use to do . . .' or 'Before I was married . . .' or 'Before we had children . . .' On the other hand, when asked what their ideal leisure would be the men spoke with much greater detail and energy. Several talked about traveling more or spending more time outdoors. Three of the fathers explicitly stated that their ideal leisure would be either by themselves or with just their spouse doing something they enjoy; they would be without their children. In contrast, Carl, stated, 'I believe the greatest would be taking all the kids in an RV and just roaming for two weeks maybe and see places I've never seen.'

More generally speaking, Mike stated, 'I'd get tired of it (leisure) if I had too much of the same thing. So no one thing, but a combination of things and the freedom to not have to even work and choose from all those others (activities), would be great I guess.' It seemed that these men were less satisfied with their personal, current leisure and more energized by what they wished their leisure could be.

Current leisure

The men in this study defined leisure in traditional ways (i.e. unobligated time, activity, state of mind) and engaged in a variety of leisure activities. Given the heavy obligation these men experienced towards family time, it was not surprising that when the men were asked what they did for personal leisure most of their answers involved doing activities with their family (with wife and/or children). The men recounted participating in leisure activities such as camping, hiking, watching sports on TV, playing games, laying around and just relaxing, watching movies, doing yard projects, being away from work, remodeling projects, and being outside. Rick provided a different perspective, 'My work is my recreation time. It's a break from home. Work is where I relax.'

Many of the men indicated that personal leisure time was rare or not a top priority. Mike stated, 'There's not a ton of what you'd call pure vegging out, relaxation right now . . . You know if I go play tennis, I would say that is closer to leisure.' Carl likewise indicated, 'I love to study books, particularly about church history, but now I don't have that much leisure to read like I used to. It's much more rare.' Rick was more explicit with how he viewed the priorities in his life in relation to leisure, 'I take river trips or backpacking. But, it's rare because of my commitment to my spouse and children.'

An exception to the men taking little personal leisure time or indicating they had to schedule and plan for it was given by Scott, a recreation professional. He stated, 'It (leisure) pretty much revolves around personal interest, by myself or with my wife's brothers. I can't really think of anything that I want to do but I don't. I make time for my interests.'

Guilt and family obligations constrained personal leisure

Since most of the men indicated that they took little time for personal leisure in comparison to leisure time with family members they were asked to talk about whether they felt guilty about taking personal leisure time. Craig pointed out that he used to feel entitled to leisure prior to being married, but no longer did. Likewise, Bob clearly struggled with taking personal leisure:

'My biggest challenge is giving myself permission to do leisure. I think that's the biggest hindrance. Time becomes a real issue between church callings and job responsibilities. I think having set leisure times are important because I think it makes me more productive overall. But a lot of times I don't feel like I am deserving of it.'

When asked if he felt deserving of personal leisure, Rick stated, 'Rarely. It's pretty low on the spectrum. I have a stronger commitment and responsibility to be a husband and father.' Mike gave a similar perspective:

'There are times that we (he and his brothers) have gone and played basketball over the holidays, which takes me away from the family and I haven't felt guilty then, maybe because it's with extended family. We're going off to play together and the spouses are home together as well. But otherwise, I guess I do feel a little bit of guilt. I don't want to give the impression that I really want to do it (leisure) a bunch more, because that also wouldn't be true. I rarely go with a friend to go do something. It used to be that I played tennis and played with one particular friend that I had in Phoenix and we'd play quite a bit. But in the last eight to ten years, I can't think of, in fact, let's put it this way, in the last two years, I can only think of one time where I went on a hike with a group of guys.'

Nick made time for personal leisure, but it was less time than when he had no children and at an earlier hour than he preferred:

'I would want fewer restrictions on my time so I wouldn't just have to do them at 6:30 in the morning but I could do them at other times . . . Typically when I am playing tennis I play probably half hour or an hour less than I would like to because of time and constraints. Just thinking about my kids in the morning is hard because it is time when I like to do a lot of things and I like to be around when the kids get up and have breakfast with them.'

Carl implied that he subscribed to both feelings of guilt and an 'ethic of care' as the father of his family when he stated:

'Yeah I would say it (guilt) affects me in a lot of my decisions in my leisure time because I always feel like I have to be here and be available for them (his wife and children) for any problems. So, it takes quite a bit for me to get away.'

As with most of the other men, Craig believed it was more important to make time to be with his family than to engage in personal leisure:

'I'm away from them (family) enough at work, and if I take my discretionary time, and I'm choosing to get away from them, I don't think that's right. I think that's the source of my guilt, the perception that my free time away from home, away from work, should be spent with my family.'

Ryan and Scott were the only men who indicated they felt like they deserved leisure. Scott stated, 'I work hard and I feel like I deserve it (leisure). It's just relaxing. If I can get everything else done then I can clear my mind and be more refreshed.' Although he believed he deserved personal leisure, it wasn't without guilt. He described what he believed to be the source of his guilt.

> 'Just a realization that my family is more important than my self-interest. They need me more than I need to do whatever I was going to do. It's more important to stay here and help my wife with school or just be here to help out with the kids so my wife isn't alone.'

Like several of the other men, he also indicated that his leisure was fragmented. 'Probably the duration of leisure is not as long. So when I do get to go fishing it's when the girls are taking a nap.'

Interestingly, although almost all of the men indicated they felt guilty about taking personal leisure or believed time with their family to be more important, they all valued personal leisure. It appeared to be more a matter of feeling guilty about taking time away from their families or making time for it around their duties and responsibilities rather than a lack of valuing personal leisure.

Personal leisure is valued for individual benefits

Though feelings of guilt and lack of a sense of entitlement to personal leisure permeated these men's perspectives, they still valued personal leisure for the balance it provided as well as the many other benefits it afforded them personally and to their role of spouse and father.

According to Craig, 'recreation fills that need of variety in your life and getting away mentally and physically from what you do at work.' For Mike, stress reduction was the main benefit of personal leisure, 'it's a release from some of the pressures I'd say, that you deal with in life. I'd say that seems to me to be the main reason that I want leisure time.' Carl saw that it not only benefited him personally but helped in his fathering role, 'I think you need balance in all things. Your work turns out better. Your time with your kids works out better.' Likewise, Rick saw how personal leisure benefited his family relationships:

> 'It's a balance. Either extreme, having too much leisure or not enough leisure, is not healthy. Not having leisure decreases your performance and quality of life. There is a definite time and place to charge your individual batteries. It helps our relationship to have time apart. A time to ponder and meditate.'

Nick saw the psychological benefits of personal leisure but then questioned if maybe that is how he justified it:

'Well, for me it's a big psychological benefit. My day is just very different if I can go out and ride my bike for an hour and a half. I just feel more relaxed, patient, happier . . . Maybe it is how I justify it but I think it is true that those things do help me do the other commitments (work, family) better.'

In contrast to the contradiction between their expressed beliefs regarding the value of personal leisure and the reality that most of the men prioritized it below work and family obligations, their views and actions regarding family leisure were congruent.

Family leisure helped fulfil cultural ideals of fathering

It was clear from the interviews that these men truly valued time with their family. In fact, it appeared that either out of guilt or out of desire, the men spent considerably more time in family leisure than personal leisure. They were asked why they spent time with their children. Their responses indicated that in general they believed it was time to share values, communicate, have fun together, and instill in their children an importance of family.

Gary reflected his desire to build a close relationship and teach his children during leisure time:

'I like spending time with them and really I do it because I want them to have a strong relationship with me. I have consciously made the choice to be their soccer coach, to play with them, to read to them, to spend time with them because I want them to have a close relationship with me. I want them to be able to establish strong relationships with their spouses and I want them to know what it means to be secure and loved.'

Nick believed family leisure helped to build strong relationships with both his children and his spouse:

'We generally like each other and like doing things together. I think it is important for building ties with your children and establishing a relationship with them. So most of the time we do enjoy it but also we feel like it is important in terms of being a better parent. I feel like the leisure time with the children and with [my wife] is important because when you have time together things are better.'

Rick had similar reasons for making family leisure a priority and he also used it to teach his children:

'Doing these things together as a family deepens understanding for our children. It expands their minds intellectually and provides opportunity to draw closer as a family. Backpacking is the perfect way to introduce the "whole" world concept. Everything you need is on your back. You have to take care of transportation. You have to get from point A to point B safely and you have got to take care of your bedding, shelter, cooking, and personal hygiene. So that's one reason why I try to do backpacking with my children. It really shows them how to live at a minimal, simple existence.'

Scott believed family leisure was necessary and a way to build unity:

'I just think it is important that as parents we give our kids as much time as possible. So, that seems to be the basis for building family unity. You can sit around the house and do nothing and that's not going to build family unity.'

Bob indicated that his family enjoyed being together and had similar interests so leisure was an easy way for them to be together. He also saw it as a way to develop and strengthen family relationships:

'It's making sure that we have enough time as a couple and as a family. It is doing something that we all enjoy. So, we've tried to develop within our kids a love for the outdoors and a love for being together. We look for activities that are fun to do but we want to make sure that those activities fit within that relational recharging that needs to happen within our family.'

In summary, the men in this study derived satisfaction and meaning from their paid employment and their families. The role of father was important to them and they defined it according to the teaching of their religion as providing for the physical, emotional, intellectual, and spiritual needs of their families. They saw earning money through paid employment and spending time with their wife and children as the means to fulfilling this role. Their leisure activities reflected the emphasis they placed on this role. While they stated that personal leisure is important, this belief did not translate into ample guilt-free personal recreation. Instead, the value they placed on their role as a father was reflected in the primacy of paid employment and family recreation over personal time.

Discussion

The purpose of this chapter was to explore the relationships between fathering, leisure and religion in the subculture of LDS church members living in the state of Utah. The emergent themes provided considerable insight into leisure and fathering among this particular group of LDS fathers which appears to be quite different from what might be expected for fathers in traditionally patriarchal dual parent families. Fathers in this group found significant meaning in their lives through their families, employment, and their religious involvement and had a clear vision based primarily on their religious beliefs that ideal fathers have a duty to not only provide physically and financially for their families but also to meet intellectual and emotional needs as well. Although they also appeared to have an understanding and strong belief in the value of personal leisure in their lives their participation was limited, fragmented, and riddled with guilt and constraint. The majority of their leisure was spent with their families and they clearly had not only a religious expectation to do so but also an internal commitment and belief in the value of their family leisure involvement.

Given that these fathers were well educated, had relatively high socio-economic status, were the primary financial providers for their family, and belonged to a religion with strong patriarchical beliefs, we anticipated that they would have little guilt and would feel entitled to personal leisure. We were quite surprised, however, to discover that they had feelings of guilt when participating in personal leisure and found it difficult to justify time for personal leisure when considering their obligations to their work, family, and church. Social expectations of their cultural sub-group appeared to result in leisure experiences incongruent with previous research that would suggest that such men likely feel entitled to unconstrained guilt-free leisure involvement.

These findings highlight the importance of looking within larger categories such as subcultures to investigate variations in experience between individuals with stereotypical role expectations.

LDS fathers in this study are not only quite different from many other fathers but appear to have experiences more often seen in the study of women's leisure. Their dedication to both their paid work and their role of husband and father appear to have created an experience similar to the 'second shift' of working mothers described by Hochschild (1989). The concept of 'second shift' refers to what is often experienced by working mothers as they return home from working all day and resume the duties of household tasks and child care. The literature suggests that these women have little sense of entitlement to personal leisure time and when they do negotiate the numerous leisure constraints typically experience feelings of guilt because they should be with their families. More recent literature, however, suggests mothers find enjoyment and fulfillment in family leisure involvement (Freeman, Palmer and Baker, 2006; Shaw and Dawson, 2001; Willming and Gibson, 2000).

Although work played a critical role in meaning for the fathers in this study, their belief in the importance of family appeared to shape a majority of their personal, spousal and family leisure choices. These men felt a sense of personal responsibility to spend time with their families and they found enjoyment and relaxation within that context. They spent very little time engaging in non-family leisure. When they did take time for personal leisure, it was fragmented and often scheduled at non-optimal times to accommodate the needs of other family members. They described feeling guilty for engaging in individual leisure that would reduce the time spent with their wives and children. The men made an effort to strengthen relationships with their spouse through weekly couple's leisure that provided a context for communication and participation in shared positive experiences. They also saw family leisure as an opportunity to develop relationships with and among their children. The men in this study described their personal leisure in ways that appeared to parallel previous descriptions of women's leisure.

Based on the descriptions given by the men in this study regarding what they find satisfying and meaningful, their view of what it means to be a father, and their perspectives on personal and family leisure, it is evident their leisure values are likely shaped by ideology; in this case, religious ideology. Their religion values a father who is committed, responsible, loving, responsive, and involved. It is likely that they receive greater personal validation from being this kind of father than being one who puts more value on personal leisure. This type of focus on fatherhood reflects the recent concepts of 'new fatherhood' (Dermott, 2003), 'responsible fathering' (Doherty, Kouneski and Erickson, 1998), and 'generative fathering' (Dollahite and Hawkins, 1998) in which fathers have a much greater role in home and family life than seen in the stereotypical role of breadwinner and provider only. This recent cultural trend for fathers and society to focus more on family and family life is not a new concept among these LDS fathers and is clearly engrained within their religious beliefs and their personal identity of father (Roggman, Benson and Boyce, 1999). The fathers in this sample found great meaning and personal fulfillment through their leisure involvement with their wives and children.

Conclusion

The experiences of the men in this study provided a glimpse of a subculture, shaped by religious beliefs, in which the work of family involvement was expected and valued. Overall, these men were different from what would be expected, particularly when considering the stereotypical role of fathers in the patriarchal family-focused subculture of LDS fathers in Utah. Indeed, they shared many characteristics that are common in the literature among women's leisure including fragmented leisure, constraints, second shift, guilt, and lack of entitlement to personal leisure. On the other hand, they also had a clear vision and commitment to their role as husband and father and often fulfilled that commitment through intentional family leisure involvement. This difference in fathers' leisure was clearly related to the LDS ideology and highlights the importance of examining leisure functioning within cultural contexts.

11 Rising to the challenge

Fathers' roles in the negotiation of couple time

Vera Dyck and Kerry Daly

In order to understand the relationship between fatherhood and leisure, we believe that it is important to take a systemic perspective that examines the way in which relationships within the family affect leisure choices. Although the literature on gender and free time offers important insights into the different individual entitlements that women and men experience regarding time use, it puts less emphasis on the relationship negotiations that occur within families.

In this analysis, we were particularly interested in the way that men in families negotiate and experience couple time with their partners. For fathers, the roles of partner and parent are confounded as part of what has been referred to as the 'package deal' for men (Townsend, 2002). For example, the effort to find couple time as a partner inevitably involves negotiating the responsibilities of parenthood. Furthermore, couple time is pursued with dual purposes: enhancement of the couple relationship, and the personal rejuvenation that increases one's capacity to parent effectively.

Because dual earning couples with children are among the most time-stressed people in contemporary North America (Moen, 2003; Statistics Canada, 1999), an assumption that couples automatically have any time together at all is out-of-step with current realities. Little is known about the process by which this time together is negotiated when it does, in fact, occur. Using qualitative methods allowing participants to speak in their own words, this paper explored the ways that fathers negotiated and experienced leisure time with their partners.

Couple time, relationship issues and parenting

Very little research has been done which explores the relationship between couples' leisure time and parenting. However, parents interviewed about the dynamics of control over time in their families indicated that their children had a dominant claim on their time (Thorpe and Daly, 1999). One of the implications for how couples negotiate leisure time for themselves was that meeting children's needs was seen as a higher priority than couple time.

While some research has indicated that couples spending time together is important for marital satisfaction (Crawford, Houts, Huston and George, 2002; Russell-Chapin, Chapin and Sattler, 2001), exactly what this means is unclear. Presser (2000) reports that although certain scheduling arrangements negatively impacted couple stability, the actual amount of time couples had together did not appear to significantly mediate this relationship. Two leisure science studies looking for a long-term association between amount of shared leisure time and marital satisfaction (Berg, Trost, Schneider and Allison, 2001; Holland, 1995) found no significant relationships; a similar sociological study (Sullivan, 1996) had similar findings. However, adequate time together for sharing meaning and honouring dreams was found necessary for a sound marriage (Gottman and Silver, 1999), and increased time together was essential for couples who wished to improve their communication, intimacy, and/or sex life (Fraenkel and Wilson, 2000). Without enough time together for dealing with the normal challenges of life, couples' issues became problems and then crises (Nelson, 2001).

Little empirical research links couple time and parenting activities; however, the Cornell Couples and Careers study (Moen, 2003) found that spill-over flowed freely in just about every direction, and one could hypothesize that the normal challenges of couples' lives spill over into the parenting domain, and that the normal challenges of parenting spill over into the couple relationship. We were interested in the degree to which couple time was important for bolstering parenting roles, particularly fatherhood.

The process by which couple time is negotiated has received almost no attention in the literature. Fraenkel and Wilson (2000) found that although people sometimes felt that their partners had total control over the time patterns in their relationship, most couples unconsciously fell into patterns rather than intentionally creating them. Factors such as extended family system, health, ethnicity, work hours and schedules, and commuting time all contributed to couple time patterns, only some of which are within the control of individuals. In a context in which couple time is less likely than in former eras to happen without effort (Fraenkel and Wilson, 2000), this study was a preliminary exploration of such efforts. Our paper focuses on fathers' role in these efforts.

Gender and the construction of couple time

Studies in family and leisure sciences indicate that gender differences and power dynamics might account for some of the ambiguity in the literature relating marital satisfaction and couples' time together, such as findings indicating that husbands overall spent more time in leisure than wives (Dorfman and Heckert, 1988; Kulik, 2002; Moen and Sweet, 2003; Shaw, 1985), and that free time for mothers with grade-school children was especially scarce (Moen and Sweet, 2003). Crawford and Huston (1993) studied the impact of the transition to parenthood on marital leisure, and found that parenthood reduced both the amount of time husbands spent in independent leisure, and the amount of time couples spent in activities preferred by husbands, while it increased couple time spent in activities preferred by wives.

It has also been found that spending time together as a couple was more important for wives' marital satisfaction than for husbands' (Marks, Huston, Johnson, and MacDermid, 2001). The amount of time couples spent together did not significantly predict marital distress for husbands, yet it did for wives (Smith, Snyder, Trull, and Monsma, 1988). Gager and Sanchez (2003) found that the perception that a couple spends more time together increased the likelihood of divorce for men, but decreased it for women.

Other studies have found gendered patterns in time negotiation, but have not looked at the process of negotiating couples' joint leisure time. The Cornell Couples and Careers study (Moen, 2003) interviewed over 800 dual-earner couples; findings indicated that when couples have children at home, 'wives scale back [work hours] . . . to adapt to increased family demands' (Moen and Sweet, 2003: 24). Whether organizing 'couple time' is one such 'family demand' taken up by wives was not addressed. Friedlander stated that 'in most cases it is the woman who seeks help for the marriage' (1998: 520), but did not indicate whether women were more likely to take responsibility for maintaining relationships via couple time prior to initiating couple therapy. Daly (2002) found that among couples interviewed about their time choices, women consistently held the primary responsibility for family time schedules, but did not explore whether women took responsibility for scheduling couple time.

In this study, we examined gender differences in perceptions, preferences, and experiences relative to couples' time together. Looking for patterns of negotiation across couples, we inquired into dynamics of power, control and gender equality that take place in the construction of couple time. In particular we were interested in fathers' experiences regarding power and control in the negotiation of couple time.

Theoretical influences

Symbolic interactionism and feminism guided the formation of our questions, decisions about where to look for answers and what was relevant, and analysis of findings (Blumer, 1969). Assuming that individuals' subjective interpretations define, create, and change their subjective situations (Melzer, Petras and Reynolds, 1975), we looked for ways that participants' language shaped symbolic worlds, and these symbolic worlds in turn impacted behaviour and experience (LaRossa and Reitzes, 1993). A feminist interest in power and control relative to gender (Fox and Murray, 2000) influenced research and interview questions, and informed data analysis. Recognizing the role of the researcher's self in generating knowledge, we engaged in the feminist practice of 'reflexivity' (Fox and Murray, 2000: 1161) at every stage of analysis.

Method

Design

Given the almost completely uncharted territory ventured into, a qualitative research design was chosen to examine the processes associated with the construction of couple time that are difficult to capture numerically (Glaser and Strauss, 1967; Prus, 1994). Using the principles of emergent design, we were interested in understanding how couples talked about couple time, their perceptions of couple time as a priority in relation to other activities, how they negotiated the creation of couple time and how their decisions were shaped by their relationships to their children and broader reference groups. The first author conducted semi-structured, open-ended interviews for collection of textual data; both authors worked collaboratively to interpret data, develop theory, integrate reflexive insights from experiences with our respective spouses and children, and write this paper.

Sampling

Purposive sampling of 14 dual-earner couples (28 participants) was conducted through snowball methods. Flyers were posted in businesses, doctor's offices, and other community locations, and the first author extended a verbal invitation to participate in various social networks including an independent school and among graduate school colleagues. Excluded from participating were couples with only one wage earning partner, parents of toddlers and teenagers, and parents with partial or joint custody of children. Broad inclusion criteria for 'dual earner' status allowed variety in participants' conditions; couples qualified as dual earners if both partners were employed for pay – regardless of income level, hours spent working, and whether the work was home-based.

Participants

All couples were heterosexual and married – thirteen legally, one by common law. Participants had no toddlers or teenagers, and full custody of at least one child aged 3 to 12 years, therefore having 'around-the-clock' responsibility for children. This shared circumstance made them an especially appropriate sample (Charmez, 2002; Lincoln and Guba, 1985), since, for them, couple time had to be found, made, or otherwise negotiated if it was to happen. All participants were Canadian born and ethnically of European descent, with the exception of one couple from India. Couples ranged in age from 31 to 50 years, and in annual family income from $50,000 to over $151,000, with most couples in the $50,000–100,000 range; couples had an average of two children.

Data collection and analysis

The methods of data collection and analysis were based on the principles of grounded theory and constant comparison (Glaser and Strauss, 1967). Twenty-four semi-structured interviews with 28 participants lasting 60 to 90 minutes each were conducted in participants' homes or favourite coffee shop. An interview guide served as a template for conversations with participants, highlighting four general areas of questioning: (1) work–family background, (2) meanings of 'couple time', (3) process of achieving 'couple time', and (4) conditions affecting 'couple time'. Interviews were audio taped and transcribed verbatim; constant comparison of data within and between interviews began during the interviewing process and continued through every stage of analysis.

Interviews with the first ten couples were conducted with partners separately, and the remaining four couples were interviewed jointly. The choice to conduct initial interviews separately was based on a feminist interest in gaining access to the different experiences of women and men, and a symbolic interactionist interest in hearing about individual's unique realities (Prus, 1994). This was especially appropriate since Daly (2002) had found that in joint interviews about time negotiations partners were highly concerned with creating a shared narrative and unlikely to speak about different personal realities. However, after the first 20 interviews, categories tracking participants' individual 'couple time' experiences were reaching sufficient saturation (Glaser and Strauss, 1967), and conducting remaining interviews jointly provided an opportunity to refine ideas about joint constructions and negotiations within a now familiar landscape.

Field notes recording observations of participants during interviews, and of partner interactions in later interviews, were recorded in memos soon after data collection (Glaser and Strauss, 1967), as was reflexive commentary documenting evolving feelings, ideas, and relevant personal experiences (Fox and Murray, 2000). What emerged in the original analysis was a set of categories that reflected a series of underlying tensions associated with the construction of couple time. These tensions were expressed through conflict and ambivalent feelings associated with wanting to get things accomplished while at the same time wanting to escape tasks; wanting and not wanting to leave the children; and wanting to be spontaneous but feeling overscheduled. For the purposes of this paper, we were particularly interested in how these tensions were expressed and managed by these couples through a gender lens. Specifically, we were interested in how their role as mother or father shaped their perceptions and orchestration of couple time. To this end, continuing comparison within and between interviews facilitated the refinement of preliminary categories into themes specific to a focus on father's role.

Findings and discussion

Given the dearth of literature on couple time, our analysis begins with a discussion of the meanings that couple time had for participants. As part of this, we were particularly interested in the perceptions that these couples had of the cultural values and social support associated with couple time. They faced many challenges in creating couple time including dealing with uncertain social support, the stressful demands of daily living, unclear couple time preferences and meanings, and ambivalence regarding their desire for traditional courtship in the context of egalitarian parenting. We also examine the different roles that mothers and fathers have in the creation of couple time. In particular, the data indicate that fathers play an important role in *instigating* couple time whereas wives play a significant role in *implementing* couple time. The final section highlights various strategies that fathers with their partners have employed in rising to face these challenges.

The meanings of couple time

For couples interviewed, 'couple time' meant 'adult time', 'Mummy and Daddy time', 'our time', 'couple time like before we had kids', 'alone time for us', 'time without kids', 'quality time', 'one-on-one time', 'meaningful time as a couple', 'time for ourselves', 'prime time', 'grown-up time', and 'personal time together'. Couple time took many different forms; the common thread running through these varied forms was the 'couple focus', the intention of re-establishing a *sense of being a couple*.

We heard participant couples saying that they wanted to feel like couples. They wanted to enjoy each other's company, laugh, chill out, relax together, and work through deeper issues when necessary. Couple time was time for joint meaning making, and seemed to be a time when partners hoped to maintain or rebuild a couple identity as friends, lovers, and companions as well as co-parents and household/financial partners.

Participants who managed on occasion to orchestrate this kind of time for themselves said that it helped them tremendously as a couple, rejuvenated them personally, and re-inspired their parenting.

The context: cultural values and limited social support for couple time

The needs of children and the needs of the couple relationship seemed to be experienced as a constant tension for almost all participants, and for some, as a fierce competition. Many felt pressured by the wider culture to always place the needs of the children above the needs of the partnership, and for some couples this prioritization had become a way of life, chosen on principle. Their focus was on providing a foundation of love for their children by giving them time, and, as Larry said, 'couple time would probably suffer before we sacrificed the kid time' (5m 26).[1] Participants wanted to spend time with their partners, but the responsibility they felt towards their children, and the children's resistance to their leaving, very often overrode this desire.

At the same time, most also felt that couple time was important, even if not quite as important as meeting their children's many obvious needs. Those who had been through marital crisis and counseling articulated this most clearly. Andy explained, 'We have had difficulty in our marriage . . . And so we have been on a mend process. We know that we have to take the time and spend it and communicate' (13mf 1518).

Without exception, participant couples who regularly got out together had parents nearby who could take over running their homes and caring for their children in ways that maintained daily routines. But for those whose families were not close by, not interested in helping, or otherwise not felt to be trustworthy, finding childcare for a date night out or an overnight getaway presented a worrisome challenge requiring an enormous amount of energy to organize. Without good childcare, the couple outing was disruptive for the children. Kids were in such a state when parents came home that the 'break' created extra work, and the benefits of couple time were felt to be not as great as its costs. In most cases, mothers primarily organized childcare for couple time, and relied heavily on their personal social networks for help – particularly their mothers, sisters, and friends.

Most participant couples, even those who received practical childcare help for couple time, felt unsupported by the wider culture in creating this time. Some mentioned that friends made them feel a little guilty if they sometimes made couple time a higher priority than family time, one-on-one time with children, or children's many activities. They felt pressured to put the children first, always and in every way; their sense was that couple time was not seen as valuable for children.

Overall, women seemed to feel somewhat more support from their peers for having couple time than their husbands did. A few fathers spoke about male peers rolling their eyes when they declined invitations to go out with the guys in order to spend precious free time with their wives. Because they felt that couple time was not valued in their peer culture, they had become reluctant to be honest about their couple time choices with men that were not their closest friends. Both fathers and mothers gave examples of idealized media images that made them feel inadequate when they went through the messy, real-world process of leaving the children for a date night out. Creating couple time necessitated going against the cultural flow, particularly for fathers.

Given a context that didn't particularly support or value couple time, most participant couples said that in the midst of all of the stress and demands on them, just remembering that creating couple time was a possibility was a challenge in itself. If a couple had couple time once, it tended to build on itself – it helped partners forge enough couple identity that they remembered to make it happen again, and then again. But some couples rarely, if ever, managed to successfully rise to this challenge. They described themselves as being lost much or most of the time in the essentials of family survival. Although they thought couple time would be personally rejuvenating, they felt that they needed to rejuvenate themselves somewhat before the idea of couple time would even occur to them. Despite raving about past or fantasized couple getaways, in their current reality, they just couldn't rise above the challenges of daily living to think of such things. They needed couple time that was a break from family demands, but needed to escape family demands for a while to have the idea of couple time.

Negotiating couple time: fathers instigate, mothers implement

When couples did manage to negotiate couple time, it was almost always fathers who had the initial idea. Fathers and mothers generally agreed that it was most often the fathers who first got out of survival mode enough to have the idea of doing something as a couple, and who first thought of leaving the kids. Although few husbands courted their wives in a traditional fashion, it was common among many couples for the husband to initiate couple time by commenting on the lack of it, or expressing a wish to get out together, or get away from the children for a while.

Hugh explained to me how the idea of couple time occurred to him. 'Your interactions start to taper off; you look at the other person as a part of the furniture . . . The conversations are shorter; they become very business-like. "This is what we need to get done this week," click click click, and you go and get that done, and that's it' (3m 497). Hugh wanted to have an effective household/parenting relationship with Donna, but he wanted a sense of personal partnership too. Going out was his idea for restoring this. 'When you try to have dinner conversations, there's always somebody poking in . . . The personal side, I don't think we do a lot of that while we're home together, and that's probably something we end up doing on these dates' (3m 75).

Other husbands expressed a similar reason for going with their wives on trips, or overnight outings. Despite their own ambivalence about leaving the children, many fathers found it virtually impossible to have satisfying couple time, even a good conversation, unless they did. As Stan put it, 'The kids are always trying to interact with us at the same time. [While] having a conversation, we would be interrupted on a minute to minute basis' (4m 190). For any experience of being a couple together, they simply had to get away from the children. Apparently this was important enough to several fathers that even when life got busy, the idea of having couple time still occurred to them.

While fathers most commonly had the initial idea of couple time, typically, the wife then made arrangements for the children, and scheduled a couple outing on the family calendar. Several women told stories similar to Terry's: 'I think Mark might be more likely [than I] to say, "We haven't had any time alone in a while." ... He would acknowledge that that hadn't happened. I think I would be more likely to be the person to put the gears in motion' (1f 486). These wives said that they put their husbands' couple time ideas into action. But *is* this what was happening? Later in the interview, Terry said:

> 'I love to read before I go to bed ... and of course that's the time when Mark would like to cuddle, and be intimate. And I think, "You know honey, I'd love to, but, I just want 15 minutes." ... I think, and it's completely my perception, that Mark tends to get edgier and grumpier if we don't have good couple time ... and he's sort of going, "Hey, what's going on, how come we don't have any kind of chemistry going on at all?" '
>
> (1f 273)

When Mark said, 'We haven't had any alone time in a while', had he meant that he wanted to go out on a date – the action item that Terry implemented? Or did 'alone time' mean something else to him, such as spontaneous, unscheduled time, or time alone together that included physical and sexual intimacy? Several interviews indicated that partners sometimes held different views regarding couple time, although they did not always seem to realize this. Different and unclear meanings for couple time, perhaps hopes for sexual intimacy that were not communicated or not heard, might explain the resentment some fathers expressed about wives' scheduling of couple time.

Most husbands agreed that it was the wives' job to make sure that couple time fitted in with the other pieces of the family puzzle. Some men expressed appreciation for this; some seemed resigned to it; some seemed to resent it. Andy, who said that he generally accepted Penny's role as the family scheduler, still sometimes felt annoyed about it. He indicated that although in theory Penny tried to fit into the schedule everything that was important to family members, one thing that she did not schedule in was the kind of couple time that was important to him – unscheduled time at home together. Other men echoed the frustration that sometimes wives made social plans without consulting them first. These fathers were in a catch-22: they had the initial idea of couple time, but didn't do the scheduling, and the schedulers didn't always understand or incorporate their preferred ways of spending shared couple leisure time into the plan.

A closer look at the power dynamics of scheduling revealed that in almost every case, both partners agreed that the role of primary family scheduler was an aspect of the mother's identity. Mother was the one who kept in mind the larger picture of the family's activities. With a couple of exceptions, this was true whether she worked longer or shorter hours than father, worked one, two or three jobs, worked days or nights, worked from home or away from home, or worked mostly as a stay-at-home mum. It was true whether she had more or less traditional values regarding her gender identity.

Most participants gave the mother's role as family scheduler as one of the main reasons that she did most of the arranging and scheduling of couple time. While fathers more often had the idea of couple time, its implementation was usually picked up by mothers. The assumption here was that one role flowed naturally from the other: mother did most of the arranging and scheduling of family activities in general, so naturally she arranged couple time too. Arranging couple time meant arranging childcare; childcare often came from mother's family, and it was felt to be more appropriate for her to make arrangements with her own relatives. Hired sitters were generally girls, and it seemed more comfortable for everyone if the mother, not the father, interacted with them. Finding a sitter meant calling other parents, usually mothers, to get referrals, and this was felt to be naturally in mother's domain, not father's. Fathers arranging childcare, calling their friends for suggested sitters, or drawing on their families' for help, was uncommon.

In two negative cases this pattern didn't hold, and the interactions of these two couples were illustrative of a different type of couple time power dynamic. There were two women who consciously held more traditional values regarding their identity as mothers than the others in this study. These women said that they identified primarily as wives and mothers, worked only because they needed the money and not because they wanted careers, and wished they could be full-time mothers. And the scheduling and arranging of couple time childcare had a different pattern in their couple relationships.

Their more traditional values regarding their roles as mothers might lead one to assume that their sense of responsibility for making couple time childcare arrangements would be even stronger than the women who identified as being more egalitarian in their partnerships. Surprisingly, it was the women consciously holding more traditional values whose husbands consistently made the childcare arrangements for couple getaways. Both partners in these couples stated definitively that husbands not only had the idea of couple time getaways, but also made all other arrangements, including childcare plans. Interestingly, these couples did not assume, as most participants seemed to, that the role of central family scheduler – or mother – was naturally tied up in the role of arranging couple time childcare. The fathers in these relationships were more, not less, involved in making childcare arrangements for couple time, giving mothers a break from this job.

For example, Jack had the idea of a date and asked Mandy, who held the whole family's schedule in her head, what would be a good night to go out. Then he made the arrangements – even if this meant doing the things which other couples considered less natural for fathers to do: asking for recommendations from other parents, calling babysitters, or asking his wife's family members for help. He mentioned enlisting the services of neighbouring, male teens. Like Jack, Ravi organized childcare for the surprise couple getaways that he thought of, planned, and implemented. He was quite willing to risk double-booking Manju when he made plans to whisk her away. As family scheduler, she might have a plan, but that didn't stop him from planning too – at times his plan just took precedence.

Reconciling egalitarian parenting and traditional courtship: ambivalence in the planning of couple time

The negative cases explored above highlighted a subtle but notable tension expressed in various ways by several other female participants. These wives, who identified as having less traditional motherhood identities than the two above, seemed to have some interest in the experience of traditional courtship. Although they appeared to believe in and strive for egalitarian partnerships characterized by mutuality and self-responsibility, several women in separate interviews shared, almost by way of confession, a small wish to be courted by their husbands. They said that they knew this was old-fashioned, or didn't make any sense, or was funny. They said that they had really, honestly, stopped hoping for it, because it just wasn't fair. They didn't expect it.

But it occurred to them. Some remembered it fondly. Sometimes a court-ship dynamic had characterized the early relationship, but had gradually been replaced by the mutuality and self-responsibility of an egalitarian household/ parenting partnership. In some cases, this male-initiated courtship dynamic was reversed as children came along and the mother became the family scheduler. In some cases, male-initiated couple time had never existed, but now occurred to wives as an interesting idea – even if a silly one.

This subtle interest in traditional courtship appeared to be in sharp tension with wives' egalitarian values. They seemed to want more power over couple time plans than such a dynamic would have allowed them. They wished to be 'taken out' by fathers, or at least to have fathers arrange the childcare for couple time, yet they didn't seem to want the loss of control that they perceived would accompany such a shift. This tension in some mothers left their partners in a challenging, somewhat bewildering, position.

Many mothers freely admitted that they wished that they didn't always have to be the one to arrange couple time childcare, because they just didn't have the energy, and weren't usually the first to think of getting away from the kids in the first place. Yet it seemed that these mothers, who did not consciously identify themselves as primarily caregivers of their children, were none the less reluctant to give up their role as the primary arrangers of childcare. Several indicated that although they trusted their husbands to care for the children, they were less inclined to trust them with finding sitters. They said that they valued partnership in their parenting, but consistently took charge of arranging childcare for couple time.

It seemed that in the minds of the couples with mothers who identified with a more traditional role, although childcare in general was seen as women's domain, arranging childcare for couple time was considered to be an integral part of husband-initiated couple time, and therefore part of the male role. It was one of the ways that husbands laid the groundwork for taking their wives out – just like deciding where to go, or making a reservation. Father-arranged childcare was wrapped up in the traditional courtship package, and in the couples without this package, fathers taking full responsibility for arranging couple time childcare didn't seem to happen.

Women identifying as less-traditional-mothers expressed happiness about their more egalitarian partnerships, yet bemoaned the lack of father involvement in childcare arrangements for couple time. This dynamic was further complicated: although mothers sometimes wanted their husbands to arrange couple time childcare, they admitted that this longing, along with the even more privately and apologetically held wish to be 'taken out' occasionally, was almost never communicated out loud. Husbands faced the challenge of meeting wives' sometimes unspoken and often paradoxical wishes. These husbands were also fathers, interacting with wives who were also mothers – mothers who seemed invested in maintaining their position as family and childcare schedulers.

Strategies: rising to the challenge

In spite of what appeared to be a daunting series of challenges, almost all participant couples said that couple time did sometimes happen. Some couples rarely got out of survival mode and proactively made time for themselves as a couple, but did arrange it reactively, when a sense of urgency or imminent doom loomed, or when crisis struck. For several couples, some sort of marital crisis was seen as a turning point, a catalyst engaging one or both highly task-oriented partners in the challenging task of building a successful relationship. Other participants described a wide range of activities – exercising, reading, getting out with friends, and participating in church or other spiritually oriented activities – that recharged them individually, so that prior to crisis, couple time surfaced as an option, usually first to fathers.

When satisfactory childcare arrangements could be found, couple getaways happened. If good childcare supports were in place, couples often had regular dates. When childcare was too difficult to arrange, some couples created other solutions. One put the kids to bed early and had a quiet dinner together at home. One talked into the wee hours of the night. One met on the couch in the evening as soon as the kids were settled for the night. One developed the skill of maintaining focus on each other even in the midst of the children's clamouring. Peter described the way that he and Kim 'got away' into their partner roles without actually leaving their children: 'We do a pretty good job of ignoring the kids . . . At the dinner table, we will chitchat with the kids, but a lot of the time Kim and I will talk' (14mf 235).

Another strategy for getting away as a couple to some extent without actually leaving the kids or finding a babysitter was seizing the rare moment when partners' moods spontaneously coincided, and implementing an impromptu kid plan. Putting kids in front of a video, or bringing them along on an outing with incentives to occupy them and elicit their cooperation, enabled the couple to focus primarily on their own conversation and fun, even if they were not completely alone. Even without childcare help, many couples created some opportunities for time alone together.

The experience of getting away as a couple was often described as having its own challenges. One couple had a first date that dissolved in arguments and tears, and landed them in marital counseling. One wife said that on a trip with her husband she felt pressured by an unpleasant internal expectation that this time be extra special: 'It wasn't comfortable, because suddenly, "Oh, we're away together. Oh, now we're supposed to have sex, and we're supposed to be romantic, and have fun." And there's a lot of pressure to have all this fun. And it preys on the back of your mind' (2f 923). A husband explained his challenge in this way: 'as a man you have a hard time getting your head around' the idea that intimacy 'doesn't have to necessarily end up in bed' (5m 607).

Many couples described moving through initial discomfort as they learned to have joint leisure time away from the kids that satisfied needs for personal recreation as well as couple connection. Although one wife said that she would be more likely to go away alone or with a friend than with her husband, most participants said that after the initial anxiety, they genuinely enjoyed getting away from the children as a couple. They found themselves doing new things and getting out of mental and conversational ruts. They relaxed into enjoying each other's company, remembered or discussed their dreams and goals, or got back in touch with 'the spark'. Several couples combined work-related travel with couple getaways. Others planned recreational overnight trips. Some took turns with friends, taking care of each other's children, swapping houses for a weekend. Some couples facilitated couple time on family vacations by bringing along a relative or sitter.

Leaving the kids seemed to be easier for couples when they shared personal leisure preferences. Fathers seemed to feel particularly satisfied when couple time meant sharing an activity with their wives that was also personally rejuvenating. This kind of couple time worked well because it was less work – it was fun regardless of moods, energy levels, and feelings between partners. When each partner enjoyed the activity anyway, doing it together was a bonus. If they were too tired or grumpy to enjoy each other, they were still likely to enjoy the activity itself, and rejuvenate on a personal level, and experience some success in this.

But if the activity scheduled wasn't inherently enjoyable to both partners, there was a possibility that when the time came, the mood wouldn't be right, partners might feel an unrealistic pressure to have fun, and the date would be a bust. Different leisure preferences, difficulty transcending the artificiality of scheduled connection time, and an assumption that couple time should be fun, seemed to be the main reasons that some couples had very limited planned time alone together, particularly if good childcare was not readily available. But couple time that 'killed two birds with one stone' (14mf 200) was a way to increase the likelihood that couple time would be enjoyable, and therefore successful – something that seemed to be particularly important to participant fathers.

Developing research into fathers' and couple time

The couples in this study valued couple time. Despite the sense that the wider culture was not especially supportive of couple time and despite some of the challenges they encountered in making couple time happen within their relationships, almost every participant couple said that they sometimes, somehow, rose to the challenge, and created together time. Almost without exception, participants said that they felt that this special time as a couple made them better parents. It put them in touch with the preciousness of being a part of a family, and restored their sense of attachment to their children. Partners also used couple time for rekindling romance and/or sexual intimacy, for sharing emotional support and friendship, for experiencing laughter and fun together, for working through difficult issues, and for envisioning their futures. They used it to talk about 'us', and figure out who 'us', was going to be, now that the kids were finally moving out of babyhood and more attention could be given to 'us' again.

The study yielded several avenues for further research. In this chapter we focused on fathers and found that fathers saw couple time playing a functional role within the family in helping them and their partner to fulfil their roles as parents effectively. It helped them to feel less overwhelmed by drudgery, and infused their joint life at home with new energy. Fathers in particular said that it helped them to work with their partners more effectively as co-parents, increased their perspective on and enjoyment of the kids, and generally rejuvenated family life. Although these couples reported that couple time helped them to be better parents, we need to explore in future research how this occurs and the effects that it has on relationships. It was apparent that having time together away from children played an important role in helping them to be more available and connected with the children. Whether this dynamic is different for fathers and mothers also requires empirical study.

Other research issues raised by this study relate not to parenting but to the relations between partners. One of the key areas identified was the role of fathers in negotiating couple time. This research showed that amidst the swirling tornado of dual earner parents' lives, envisioning couple time as a possibility seemed to be a particularly important role for fathers. Perhaps this was because fathers were less likely than mothers to feel that children had a claim on their time (Thorpe and Daly, 1999), and were therefore better positioned to see the possibility of getting out of parent roles and into partner ones. Furthermore, since fathers typically have more personal leisure time than mothers (Dorfman and Heckert, 1988; Kulik, 2002; Moen and

Sweet, 2003; Shaw, 1985, 1992), they may have been in a better position to rejuvenate personally to the point where couple time surfaced as a value. We speculated too that since fathers are often perceived as holding the position of secondary parent or as being in some way deficient relative to mothers (Hawkins and Dollahite, 1997b), they may have been more aware than mothers of their own need for 'partner' attention, and as a result, initiated couple time to redirect wives' attention to themselves. Couple time research with a larger sample could help to determine if the pattern of father-initiated couple time is widespread. Further inquiry into the 'package deal' (Townsend, 2002) of parents/partners might enhance our understanding of how and why fathers initiate couple time.

The study also threw light on some of the tensions and complexities that fathers and mothers experienced in arranging couple time. Our finding that husbands usually initiated couple time and mothers usually implemented it is consistent with Daly's (2002) finding that mothers had primary control over family scheduling and did most of the planning and arranging for children in general. Paradoxically, however, the power gained through controlling the scheduling of couple time seemed to hold these wives in a somewhat unwanted traditional motherhood role. Their sense of being burdened with responsibility for children was exacerbated by their position of control relative to scheduling couple time. At the same time, fathers faced their own challenge. Either couple time was planned for them in accordance with mothers' overall family scheduling, or they had to try to take scheduling power away from mothers and have more input into how, when, and where couple time would be spent. In some cases frustration was expressed when fathers did not have, or did not feel they had, much control over the scheduling of couple time. This tension may help to explain the ambiguous relationship currently found in both the family and leisure science literatures between time couples spend together and marital satisfaction. Further exploration of the power dynamics of scheduling couple time, particularly as they relate to the meanings and preferences that partners have for this time, are needed.

The study gave further evidence of gendered differences in couples' expectations and aspirations for the time they spent together. Fathers preferred to spend time with their partners in a way that left space for spontaneity, while wives more typically wanted to get out of the parenting role by scheduling a non-parenting activity away from home. Research exploring the sexual dimension of couple time is needed. It was not thoroughly addressed by this study, yet seemed significant when it surfaced. To what extent does 'couple time' actually mean 'time for sexual intimacy?' To whom? Are there gender differences in this regard? How do unspoken assumptions or hopes regarding sexual intimacy affect and/or reflect the ambiguous power dynamics of scheduling couple time, and/or attitudes towards traditional courtship?

Although focusing on fathers, the study also illuminated some aspects of mothers' role in relation to negotiating couple time. While considering the pragmatics of achieving couple time, we noted that, curiously, it was only in couples where the women identified as having more traditional motherhood values that fathers consistently did this work. Given our sense of the dominant gender dynamics at play, these cases stand out as theoretically anomalous, and seem to defy the argument that mothers necessarily arrange childcare for couple time in order to streamline work. Were these mothers in actuality more bound by a traditional power dynamic, or less so? Possibly, this question is only partly useful, reflecting as it does an either-or assumption about couple power dynamics that blurs our vision of what is occurring within and between heterosexual partners. A better question might be, how do partners' personal perceptions about their power to negotiate satisfactory couple time relate to the behavioural expressions of power that researchers can observe?

These questions have broader implications for gender analyses of families within sport and leisure studies. This study was shaped from the outset by the theoretical perspectives of symbolic interaction and feminism. From a symbolic interactionist perspective, our analyses would indicate that while couples may have shared meanings about the importance of couple time in their lives, they often approach couple time with different expectations and may enact different roles in the process of making couple time occur. From a feminist perspective, it was apparent that for most of these couples, a traditional power dynamic was at play: notwithstanding fathers' contribution, mothers were more likely to be doing the (main) work behind the leisure (Shaw, 1992). Still, there appears to be an important complementarity in this dynamic that does bring it to fruition. As Barnett and Rivers (1996) have argued, both partners in dual earner families operate under high levels of work–family stress and as a result, it is important to consider the pragmatics of making something like couple time work, especially in the face of so many challenges.

Most participant couples, regardless of whether or not they had practical support from their families for getting out as a couple, did not feel supported by the wider culture in ever making their time as a couple a high priority. They seemed to feel pressured to put the children first, always and in every way. Most couples struggled with this pressure and, while not quite giving up on being a couple, still didn't feel like a couple in their children's presence, or get out of their presence to re-establish a sense of couplehood very often. As long as influential segments of culture such as the mass media give the impression that either good parents don't leave their children, or that good parents find it very easy to leave their children, many couples will likely feel unsupported in facing the real life challenges involved in taking time away together. They may need to have their conscientious stance of always-putting-the-kids'-needs-first explicitly countered by those who see supporting couplehood as one way to meet the deep needs of children.

The creation of couple time in these families serves as another illustration of the complexities of 'doing gender' (West and Zimmerman, 1987). For fathers in particular, there is evidence that they are invested in the emotional health of their relationship with mothers, and in turn, the overall well-being of their relationships with children. Although it is apparent from these data that women continue to play the central role in organizing time in the family, fathers are expressing their stake in ensuring the health of both their couple relationship and the well-being of their children. Fathers today are encouraged to spend more time with their children. At times they may find themselves in conflict – torn between initiating direct, active engagement with their kids, and initiating couple time. If indeed couple time is as valuable and beneficial to both partners and to parenting function as our study indicated, fathers together with mothers also need encouragement to spend time alone together – even when this means leaving the kids.

Note

1   Excerpted from interview with male partner of couple #5, segment starting on line 26. References to joint interviews list the gender of participant being quoted first; i.e. '11mf' indicates a reference to the male in a joint interview with couple #11.

12 Where are the kids?

Researching fathering, sport and leisure through children's voices

Ruth Jeanes

The rich and divergent collection of research presented in this book clearly signals the centrality of sport and leisure activities to father–child relationships. But there is a caveat: only the voice of the fathers – and occasionally mothers – have been heard making this claim. Where are the children, the supposed beneficiaries of 'involved fathering' and child-centred parenting?

Sport and leisure researchers are by no means the only ones to have underplayed the perspectives of children and young people in family-related research. Although children are known to have the capacity to be 'constructive and reflective commentators about the concept of family' (Morrow, 1998: 2), they have not been participants in the majority of research into fathers and families. Most of the knowledge in this area has instead been developed from the views of adults, either reflecting on their own childhood, giving their account of their own experiences of interacting with their children, or expressing their views of how their children respond. Although children are of course participants in research in which they are the specific focus of study, they are not routinely included as valid and necessary voices within generic studies. In consequence, we know relatively little about how children experience family.

Sport and leisure studies research fits this pattern. Very few studies of how family, sport and leisure interact have included the viewpoint of children. This is therefore a fertile and key area for development, with multiple questions to address: how do children experience family-based or family-facilitated sport and leisure activities? How do these fit into their interactions with their parents? What impact do they feel that being parented 'through' sport and leisure has on relationships within the family? Within this, examining how leisure contributes to relationships with fathers from the perspective of the child could contribute significantly to understanding the concept of fathering 'through' sport and leisure.

This chapter therefore advocates the involvement of children and young people in research into sport, leisure, fathering and family. Acknowledging the broader trend within the social sciences to participatory research with young people, it builds its case in three stages. It first outlines the growth of political and academic momentum for making children visible in the research process and the implications this has for social science enquiry. It considers second the relevance of children's and young people's participation in research specifically within the context of sport, leisure and family. An outline review of family and leisure research is given with specific attention paid to what is known about children's roles within family leisure. Third, the chapter draws on studies within the broader social policy field, including sport policy, that have successfully engaged young people in family-related research to identify lessons applicable to research into sport, leisure and family. The chapter concludes by assessing the contribution a child-centred approach can make to research into fathering and outlines some of the challenges researchers will need to address when undertaking this type of work.

Why listen to children? The broader UK policy context

The importance of listening to children and allowing them the opportunity to share their viewpoints has been an increasing political focus in the UK over the last 15 years (Alderson and Morrow, 2004). There has been a growing recognition, particularly within the children and family services sector, that children need to be engaged in decisions that affect them and, like their parents, need to be provided with support and information. Whereas early initiatives to support children in challenging family circumstances attempted to help them indirectly through parental support and education, attention now focuses on directly assisting children themselves (Wallerstein, 1991; Petersen and Steinman, 1994; Kelly, 2000).

In the UK this shift has been evident in welfare policy where a number of developments have successfully raised awareness of the importance of listening to children and consulting with them effectively. The 1989 Children's Act required social workers to take into account the views of young people whilst the 'Working Together' (1999) Department of Health document provided an illustrative guide to how this should be achieved. The Children and Family Court Advisory and Support Service, which looks after the interests of children involved in family proceedings, is also now required to work directly with children rather than relying on parents' views on what is best for their child (Buchanan, Hunt, Bretherton and Bream, 2001). In 1998 the Human Rights Act placed young people's participation centrally within the 'Quality Protects' programme (Department of Health, 2001). This policy focus subsequently gained further attention and momentum through the development of the 'Every Child Matters' government white paper produced in 2003 and the appointment of a Children's Commissioner through the Children's Act in 2004. The overarching aim of much of the policy in this area has been to change the status of the child's voice. Children and young people's views are no longer seen as either irrelevant or unreliable, but instead recognised as the source of legitimate views that must be listened to and should play a central role in shaping services that are provided to support them.

Alongside this policy shift, academics working in the area of childhood sociology have shown that children and young people can be articulate and informative commentators about their social lives and issues affecting them (Greene and Hill, 2005). Using a social constructionist position, recent research has emphasised the value and importance of the child's voice and of listening to their understanding and knowledge. This epistemological standpoint sees the child placed firmly at the centre of the research process and acknowledges that the child plays an active part in constructing their own world. The claim that children do not have sufficient knowledge or understanding to provide valuable information has not stood up to close scrutiny when they have been given appropriate tools through which to communicate their views (Kellett, 2005). The development of such tools has therefore been an important issue and a key focus of childhood sociology research.

It became evident at an early stage in the move to involve children and young people in research that whilst there was a desire and need to provide them with the opportunity to express their opinions, appropriate ways of facilitating this process needed to be developed. In particular it was necessary to shift away from assumptions that children were 'mini adults' and could communicate in the same way. The use of participatory techniques has been key to addressing this concern. Children, particularly younger ones, are often comfortable communicating in non-verbal mediums because they are more practised in these forms (Alderson, 1994; James, 1993). It can be useful to integrate mechanisms such as drawings, pictures and photographs into mainstream qualitative techniques such as focus groups and interviews to allow children to express their views through these tools. Making multiple participatory techniques available enables children and young people to communicate in a variety of ways, select methods which they are most happy using, and offer interpretations of the work they produce using different approaches. Asking children to explain why they attribute certain meanings to their paintings and stories allows them to engage more productively with researchers' questions but still use the talents which they possess (James, 1993).

Both politically and academically children have therefore come to be seen as having an important role to play in generating knowledge and influencing decisions about their lives. The development of methodological techniques within the sociology of childhood has improved the way in which data can be collected from children and helped ensure that the research process is engaging for them and offers an opportunity to share their views and ensure their voice is heard. Academics within sport and leisure have been slower to embrace these changes but a growing number are exploring the views and experiences of children, particularly within sport (Jeanes, 2005; MacPhail, Kinchin and Kirk 2003; Oliver, 2001; Fitzgerald, Jobling and Kirk, 2003). This work provides a starting point for fuller development within research into sport, leisure and families.

Hearing the child? The missing children in research into sport, leisure and family

Within leisure studies it has been recognised that children are key actors in family leisure experiences but relatively few studies have directly investigated their views and experiences (Freysinger, 1997; Jackson and Rucks, 1995; Robertson, 1999). In 1997, Shaw found that 'almost no data exists on the attitudes and reactions of children to family activities, nor the outcomes beneficial or otherwise for these family members' (1997:109). Although numerous studies have since explored a variety of dimensions of family leisure (e.g. spouses' impact on each others' leisure; the influence of husbands' and wives' leisure on marital satisfaction; the impact of parents on children's recreation and leisure interests and participation), the perspective of the husband, wife or parents have dominated throughout and children's voices have seldom been heard (Freysinger, 1997).

Research into leisure and family has focused on how life changes such as marriage and children impact on individual leisure preferences. Early studies found that marriage and parenthood results in a shift from individual and shared marital activity to child-centred collective family recreation (Horna, 1989; Kelly, 1982), with this continuing into early teenage years. As children age, all-family leisure reduces with a shift first to leisure shared by one parent with the child and later to more individualised leisure patterns (Horna, 1989). While the overall pattern is known, however, little attention has been given to analysing *why* children's leisure patterns and preferences shift through their early life course. Leisure research has also illustrated the impact of family and work commitments on leisure (Kelly and Kelly, 1994; Such, 2006), but the perspective of the child within this is missing.

As well as focusing on how families affect individuals' leisure opportunities, leisure research has also examined how family leisure can contribute to family development. The literature in this area generally suggests that family leisure leads to positive benefits for families, with the adage that 'the family that plays together stays together' (Orthner and Macini, 1991) reflected in much of the early writing on family and leisure (Carlson, 1979; Kelly, 1990). Research focusing on outcomes of family leisure suggests it leads to higher quality family relationships and enhanced family cohesion (Shaw, 1997; Fromberg and Bergen, 1998). Parents view family leisure as a useful mechanism for pursuing goals that contribute to good family relations and children's personal and social development, and often regard it as a way to develop relationships with children and provide children with positive role models (Freysinger, 1988). Shaw and Dawson (2001) suggest that parents view leisure as a duty and activities are usually goal-orientated rather than intrinsically motivated. Family leisure, they indicated, should be viewed as 'purposive leisure', shaped and facilitated by parents to achieve particular outcomes.

Some research is available that has examined in more detail how different family members experience family leisure. This too has primarily focused on adult experience but has been useful in revealing some of the complexities underlying collective 'all-family' leisure. Research that has differentiated between men and women's experience of family leisure has shown that whilst family leisure is viewed as generally positive, it is not always enjoyable for all family members, particularly mothers (Shaw and Dawson, 2001). Freysinger (1994) in a study examining parent satisfaction and family leisure interaction indicated that leisure time with children had a significant effect on men's satisfaction with the parental role but not women's. It has been suggested that women's experience reflects mothers' role as the 'family care-taker' and the need to (continue to) be 'responsible' during family leisure; in contrast fathers, whose family role is mainly defined as the breadwinner, regard family leisure as a diversion from 'work' and an opportunity for self expression (Larson and Gillman, 1997). For mothers, family leisure is often contained within caring for children and running the home which compromises their experience and enjoyment (Henderson, 1990; 1991; Shaw, 1992). Leisure can also be a further site for tension and conflict between parents and between parents and children during periods of family difficulties and stress (Larson and Gillman, 1997). The available literature therefore indicates that family leisure is contradictory (Shaw, 1997). The need to understand the subjective experience of all family members, including children, is evident.

In recent years, prompted by the health agenda and obesity/physical activity policy concerns, some work has been undertaken examining children's leisure time and the influence of parents on children's leisure experiences. A number of studies have examined how children spend their leisure time and particularly how physically active they are during this (Telford *et al.*, 2005; Aarron *et al.*, 1993; Harrell *et al.*, 1997). This research has generally involved children as research participants, taking part in quantitative surveys, and has not explored family context in depth. Qualitative research is also available that examines their leisure behaviour and parental influence. This shows that leisure activities have a central role in children's lives, particularly for adolescents (Marshland, 1982; Meeks and Maudlin, 1990; Raymore, Godbey and Crawford, 1994), but parents can substantially direct leisure choices and influence attitudes and beliefs. Parents have been shown to influence whether children believe leisure is important, promote ideas regarding the value of particular activities (Wood, Read and Mitchell, 2004), share stories about leisure experiences and communicate the importance of leisure to children (Shakib and Dunbar, 2004). Parents also shape children's leisure behaviour, attitudes and values through their own behaviour (Shannon, 2003).

Some parents have also been shown to make leisure decisions for children or set limits on activity participation (Hutchinson *et al.*, 2003) and there is evidence that parents holding negative attitudes towards activities or pursuits can be viewed by young people as a constraint to engaging in certain types of leisure (Shannon, 2006). Kay's (2006) study of Muslim young women participating in sport in England showed that parental approval/disapproval was particularly significant in certain cultural contexts. Although peer influence on young people's leisure activities becomes more significant during adolescence (Kleiber, 1999), parents' influence has been shown to be stronger with regard to children joining particular activities (Hultsman, 1993). Research in this area has illustrated the extent to which parents attempt to locate and initiate their children's involvement in leisure experiences they regard as 'worthwhile', often at the expense of unstructured, less organised leisure activities that young people choose for themselves but are not valued by parents (Kloep and Hendry, 2003). Parents of higher socio-economic status in particular have been found to intervene in the leisure activities children are undertaking, directing them towards structured and regulated leisure formats (Zinnecker, 1995).

Research that has examined how parents shape children's leisure has not usually elicited children's and young people's views on how this occurs or what outcomes it produces. Parents' roles in determining their children's leisure choices have been explored but there has been little investigation of children's agency within the process, e.g. how/whether children negotiate over their leisure experiences, what they gain from 'family' and/or parent-approved leisure, and whether participating in their own preferred leisure offers different experiences from those taking place with, or sanctioned by, parents and other family members. Whilst the family and home are the primary context of parents' leisure activities (Horna, 1989), children have a great deal of free time to take part in leisure opportunities outside the family, especially from adolescence (Larson and Richards, 1994). How they value this compared to family leisure is unclear.

Very little is known about younger children's experience of family leisure, but some research has addressed the experiences of adolescents. This suggests that leisure often has different functions for teenagers compared to their parents. Larson and Gillman (1997), for example, found that one of the key functions of leisure for adolescents is excitement, which is not always fulfilled through family leisure. Young people during the adolescent life phase also use leisure for development needs, such as social interaction, forming attachments with peers, and identity construction. Young people involved in Larson and Gillman's study felt all three were difficult to achieve through family leisure which was more constrained, less individually motivating and less enjoyable for adolescents than for their parents.

The research evidence on young people's experience of family leisure can be a bit dispiriting for parents of adolescents! One study has suggested however that family leisure can play a very important role for young people living in challenging family circumstances. Delinquent adolescent males interviewed in Robertson's (1999) work discussed having a lack of structure and stability within their family units and a lack of attachment to parents. They felt the lack of shared family leisure experiences beyond the age of ten had contributed to this, including a perceived lack of parental interest in sons' activities. The young people participating in the research expressed a desire for more shared leisure activities, particularly with fathers:

> Participants valued leisure experiences shared with family . . . although most participants felt close to their mothers they looked to their father for shared leisure experiences, mostly ones centred around outdoor pursuits and sports. Participants highly valued such experiences but there was little evidence in the data to indicate that fathers committed much time to shared activities with their sons.
>
> (Robertson 1999: 353)

Robertson's findings are particularly pertinent in the context of the underlying thesis of this volume – that leisure is an area in which men can be 'involved' fathers, creating shared experiences and establishing emotional closeness. Harrington gave some excellent examples of this in her account of Australian fathers in Chapter 4. One of her interviewees spoke about sports experiences providing 'a conduit to talk about other things' and explained how 'you don't just talk about sport, it lubricates your conversation until you get into the groove of talking'. However 'unexciting' adolescents may find family leisure, Robertson's work suggests that it can provide a solidity that contributes to family functioning. The converse of this is that the absence of such shared opportunities may be damaging, particularly for relationships between fathers and their children, especially sons. Mothers, through their caring activities, are likely to experience a certain amount of regular, extended contact with their children without necessarily engaging in much shared leisure with them; this is less automatic for fathers, with their lesser involvement in this area.

Robertson's study therefore emphasises the importance of understanding how family leisure is viewed by children and how they feel it can contribute to their family relationships. While family leisure can be perceived as a constraint by young people who want more independence from their parents, it appears of great potential value to those who may receive less attention from them. The limited research available in this area means however that there is currently a lack of detailed understanding of what leisure provides for children and young people in different family situations. To effectively analyse the impact of leisure on the family unit it is necessary to encourage children to express these views and examine them alongside those expressed by parents. It already appears from the studies referred to above that age impacts on how children and young people value and enjoy family leisure with a suggestion that as children move into adolescence, family activities may conflict with their desire to undertake independent and peer focused leisure. The experiences of children taking part in family leisure at different life stages would therefore benefit from further exploration.

The current research base is limited but provides sufficient evidence to indicate that leisure might play a central role in children's overall experience of being supported in their family unit. Parents certainly believe that family leisure brings families together in positive ways and the fathers who have spoken in this volume have been articulate and emphatic about the opportunities sport and leisure provide to develop emotional intimacy with their children. These adult voices need to be complemented – and in some cases may possibly be counterbalanced – by in-depth research with children themselves. This is required across all areas of research into fathers and families, including those with resident and non-resident fathers, and also the diverse range of cultural contexts discussed in Chapter 13. The father–child relationship is situated in very different situations within different family structures, including those with absent fathers, those with 'social' rather than biological fathers, and those in which fathers are gay rather than heterosexual. This is likely to impact the role leisure plays and how it is experienced by children and young people in their particular family settings.

In summary the available family and leisure research suggests that exploring how children influence family leisure, how they use leisure to develop family relationships, and how they experience family leisure within different family structures and circumstances would all be useful further research areas.

Undertaking research into children's experiences of sport, leisure, fathering and family: lessons from social policy and sport research

Whilst there is limited child-centred leisure and family research within the field of leisure studies, social policy research has been very successful at undertaking work with young people to illuminate the nature of family life. The section examines a small number of these studies. Most have adopted a participatory, qualitative methodological approach that allows children the opportunity to be engaged more fully within the research process and to express their views easily. Much of the research in this area has focused on how children deal with family change and illustrates both the importance of listening to children but also the significance of understanding their experiences to develop and improve policies for supporting them more effectively during family disruption.

Research in this area comprehensively illustrates how competently children from a young age can discuss their views and experiences of family life and other complex issues within this context (Morrow, 1998). Wade and Smart (2002) used a range of participatory methods focused around in-depth interviews with children aged 5–10 years to elicit their views on their preferred method of support during parental separation. The methods adopted allowed children to communicate about this potentially distressing topic in a non-threatening way. The researchers initially provided children with three vignettes describing 'typical dilemmas in reordering families'. From the generic discussions these generated, interviewers were able to guide young people to discuss more extensively their own personal circumstances.

Children were also encouraged to use drawings to visually illustrate particular family circumstances if they wished. Their research demonstrated that individually, children experienced family transition in very varied ways depending on previous family circumstances. For some children separation was perceived as a major disruption whilst for others it was only one thing amongst numerous changes occurring in their lives. By talking to children the researchers felt they gained an understanding of the 'ebb and flow' of family change. Rather than seeing broken families as dysfunctional, the children's views highlighted that the quality of relationships between parents and child was of greater importance than considering how the family was now structured. For some children who had been living in difficult family circumstances divorce was seen as a good thing. It signified the end of turbulent family relationships within the home and the opportunity to establish loving relationships with both parents without conflict between parents being a constant in their lives. The research highlighted that whilst divorce is commonly viewed as harmful, children sometimes considered it as positive and in some circumstances felt it had improved both their family life and their relationships with their parents.

Research in this area has highlighted the importance of communicating directly with children during periods of family change. Children generally were not included in communication by parents regarding separation (Bell and Wilson, 2006; Dunn and Deater-Deckard, 2001) and this led to them feeling confused and distressed by the situation. Grandparents and friends were often key confidantes during this period; in contrast, confiding in fathers was extremely rare. This particular research highlighted the need for continual involvement of children in discussions when family circumstances were changing. The research indicated that children particularly welcomed the opportunity to discuss the implications of having two households and how their time would be divided between them. Most wanted to play an active role in deciding how they would spend time with each parent.

Further research has highlighted the value children place on being involved in family discussions, particularly when decisions are being made that will directly affect their lives. Bell and Wilson (2006) examined the involvement of children in family group conferences. These have been developed in the UK in recent years in response to the shifting child policy context as a mechanism for involving extended family, professionals and children in decisions regarding the latter's welfare. Again through the use of in-depth interviews, supported by techniques such as mind mapping and drawing, children were able to provide their views on this support mechanism. In general they felt valued and empowered by being consulted within the conferences. They welcomed the opportunity these conferences gave them to be provided with information and ask questions about their circumstances. The conferences were also felt by children to have contributed to a more positive atmosphere at home and helped them develop better relationships with, and feel more supported by, extended family members.

Whilst the role children play in negotiating and influencing leisure decisions has not been explored, Butler, Robinson and Scanlan (2005) have examined at a more general level children's involvement in family decision making. This work has illustrated that young people often play an intricate role in decision making within the family. Most families were found to operate democratically but children accepted that parents held ultimate authority. Generally decisions were accepted if they felt they were fair and children welcomed being involved and having input into family issues. Children also identified that parents had differing roles within family decision making. Fathers were felt to be less engaged in making domestic decisions unless these concerned public rather than wholly domestic matters.

The research undertaken in this area illustrates that given the right tools children can contribute confidently to discussions regarding complicated family and social issues. A selection of quotes is provided in Box 12.1 from children across a range of ages. These demonstrate the capabilities of children to discuss complex, and sometimes emotionally difficult, topics easily and articulately.

The value of understanding how children perceive family life and their role within it is evident within all of these studies. They demonstrate that children may view situations differently from parents and have alternative notions of how they can best be supported. It is also evident that different children have different subjective experiences within similar family contexts and it is necessary to allow individuals the opportunity to describe how particular family circumstances impact on them personally within a given context. It is also notable from these studies how much children welcome the opportunity to express their views both within the research context and within family life more generally.

The studies illustrate the value of involving young people for researchers working in the area of family, sport and leisure. They demonstrate at a practical level how research methodology can be successfully adapted to include young people and offer clear examples of the capacity of children to contribute to debates within research. The studies also reveal the complexities of understanding family life as seen through the child's eyes. They are invaluable for establishing what has been hinted at in leisure research – that children may perceive things differently from their parents and that parents may not always reflect what is best for their offspring. Without direct communication and involvement of children in research it is however unlikely that we will be able to adequately understand their experiences.

Sports policy research also provides some examples of studies with young people. In sport, academics within the sociology of sport and pedagogy have sought children's views – although rarely in the family context. UK sports research involving young people has tended to focus on their experiences of particular sporting contexts, the role of sport within their lives, and the impact of sports policy on their engagement with sport. A substantial literature has developed on young people's experiences of PE with particular

Box 12.1 Young people's voices on family life

Sasha (age 10): My mum is always the first one on the dance floor. She's not old fashioned or anything, she is a really cool mum . . . There was a period of a couple of months last year when mum and dad, they were having a really hard time and mum went to a friend's. They were like fighting every night load and . . . we didn't like it, it was really horrible because there were problems with the family. My dad's side of the family were being rude to my mum's side . . . And they were fighting over that. So mum went to her friend's house for a couple of months . . . I was afraid she wouldn't ever come back and my dad was coping very well. And I mean I wasn't coping very well either . . . And then she came back they took a really long holiday together and it was okay.

Miriam (age 10): We used to have a little saying that we used to say to grandma when things got really horrible, we used to say 'Can I sleep at your house tonight?' and she used to go, 'Well go on then, fine' . . . [But sometimes she] used to slag off my dad. That was really horrible . . . She shouted at me if I said 'I hate mummy for messing up this family. I hate daddy for messing up this family', and all this. She'd start yelling and say it was all dad's fault.

(Wade and Smart, 2002: 8)

Boy (age 7): Everything I see and hear, it just goes inside my head, it's just like a prison in my head, it just shows me pictures and it's like a stereo going round and round, seeing all the things what they said when I was little, so I really know everything because I got a good brain in my head . . . They split up because he always used to be horrible to my Mum, chucking her down the stairs and on the bed, and they always used to have fights . . . After they split up I was happy because I didn't want to see him because of what he did to my Mum.

Boy (age 10): Once I thought those two were going to split up and it was over an argument about me . . . she [mother] was very upset because she didn't like it when he [stepfather] acts to me and [sibling] like we're not his real daughter and son . . . he gets all affectionate to [new half sibling, the stepfather's daughter] and he totally ignore us.

(Dunn and Deater-Deckard, 2001:17)

attention paid to girls and their disengagement from sport in their teenage years (Renold, 1997; Skelton, 2000; Swain, 2000; Williams and Bedward, 1999; Wright, 1997, 1999). Other studies within this area have considered how girls construct and negotiate sports participation within a feminine identity (Jeanes and Kay, 2007; Shakib, 2003; Oliver, 2001). All of these studies have consulted young people directly, with Jeanes and Kay and Oliver using a range of participatory methods, including story writing, disposable cameras and visual prompts to encourage communication. Fitzgerald (2005) developed an extensive range of participatory tools to provide young people who had a range of learning disabilities with the opportunity to communicate their experiences of PE and sport. Again this work illustrates the value of communicating directly with children and demonstrates practically how this can be achieved. Box 12.2 provides illustrative examples of the quality and detail of information that can be obtained in research into sport and leisure.

Box 12.2 Young people's voices on sport and leisure

Girls discussing the influence of gender on playing football (soccer):

> Girl (14): 'It's just the boys in this school are really bothered with sport. They like competing against each other. X [male PE Teacher] he's like a Nazi, seriously. It's like, Y [female PE teacher] she doesn't force you to do anything but she tells you what you'll achieve out of doing it whereas with [male PE teacher], you've *got* to do it and the boys pick up on that competitive culture.'
>
> (Fimusanmi, 2007: personal communication)

Teenagers discussing the family impact of having a sibling competing in elite sport

> Boy (14): 'It is the top priority without a doubt. Natalie, Mum and Dad would drop anything for her swimming. It has been like this now for a few years so I am getting used to it . . . I sometimes feel like I come behind her most of the time in terms of importance which, although I don't like it, does get me angry and jealous at times. She also gets much more money spent on her but she is really good so it is worthwhile and mum and dad always try to do everything they can for me in-between her swimming.'
>
> (Kay, 2000: 161)

Young people's views on gender relations in Zambia

> Boy (13): 'It is slowly becoming women are becoming more inde-
> pendent and they want to have an equal share and they want to get

more independent. Most of them want this and they want to live life the way they want to. I think the way people have lived they have concentrated so much on the men, the women have to do all the housework but it is slowly coming up. Most women now it is increasing what they can do and what influences they can have and they are getting jobs . . . she doesn't have to live her life through the man, she can live. But one thing she knows she must have respect for her man. But you should both have respect, you need to live up to one another and have respect and if you both have respect that is good, it must be mutual. That is what my mother and father have, that is a good way to be.'

(Kay, Jeanes and Lindsey, 2007:37)

The social outcomes of sports policy programmes for young people

Boy (14): 'We both play now on a Saturday and there's like all these people with really good jobs [at the cricket club]. It just makes you realise what you can do if you do well at school. And they are really nice to us, it is not like we are kids or we come from [public housing estate with bad reputation], they treat us with respect and I think that is what I want to be like.'

(Jeanes, Lindsey and Kay, 2007:19)

Developing child-centred research into sport, leisure, fathering and family

The case for involving children and young people in sport and leisure research that focuses on fathering, or more broadly on family, is compelling. In fact, omitting children and young people from a research area to which they are so central is a dubious venture. There is an obvious lack of leisure research that presents the views and experiences of children. However the value of designing and developing research that captures their experiences is evident when examining literature drawn from other areas. Allowing children the opportunity to share their experiences will provide many benefits to leisure and family research. In relation to fathering 'through' sport and leisure – Liz Such's 'leisure-based' parenting – it enables a greater understanding of the two-way dynamics of this process, the way children may use leisure to develop relationships with their fathers, and the process through which leisure experiences may in turn shape the bonds that develop between them. This is particularly important given that fathers throughout this book attribute such high importance to the role of sport and leisure in their relationships with their children.

The preceding chapters have revealed considerable complexity in how relationships between fathering, sport and leisure play out in different circumstances, and Chapter 13 further discusses a wider range of contexts that sport and leisure researchers might address. The voices of children and young people need to be heard within each of these areas. It has to be acknowledged however that involving children also creates additional challenges for the researcher. Ethical considerations are especially complex when working with children and young people. The ethical issues associated with involving children in research occur in three areas: informed consent, confidentiality and protection (Davis, 1998). All of these require careful consideration when attempting to undertake research work with children. Among them, Alderson and Morrow suggest that the biggest single ethical challenge for researchers working with children is how to address disparities in power and status (2004). There is always a potential element of coercion present because researchers are seen as authority figures, and this is further complicated with children because they have been socialised to fear declining adult requests (James, 1993). Adult/child power dynamics therefore need to be acknowledged and carefully managed (Roberts, 2000).

Researchers working with children also need to consider carefully how to develop appropriate methods to ensure young people are able to express their views and opinions in ways that they are comfortable with. Ideally researchers should endeavour to involve children and young people wholly in the research process, developing both the research focus and methods through a participatory approach. The effort, resources and expertise required to achieve this inevitably create demands and can greatly extend the research process. None the less, the value of understanding young people's experiences by allowing their voice to be heard far outweighs the challenges this type of research presents.

Among the issues that might take priority are children and young people's experience of leisure in different family structures, particularly when fathers are not resident within the family. Understanding how children may use leisure to connect with absent fathers would be a useful contribution to the growing literature in this field. There will also be value in differentiating between how fathering through sport and leisure are experienced by male and female children. The limited literature available suggests that sons look up to fathers as leisure role models and use leisure as an opportunity to develop relationships with them. It is not known if this is the case for girls. Willms in Chapter 8 has given an insight into the difficulties that can arise in father–daughter relationships in the sports context; how daughters view leisure with fathers more widely merits study.

Whilst this volume has focused on fathering, research exploring the perspectives of children will also contribute to sport, leisure and family research more broadly. The family is a subject of growing interest within both sport and leisure research but the omission of children's experiences could threaten the holistic understanding being sought. Research that actively involves young people encourages a consideration and acknowledgement of the importance, relevance and value of listening to young people's perspectives within sport and leisure research. The research practicalities may well create additional considerations and demands for researchers, but improving the understanding of children and young people's experiences of sport, leisure, family and fathering can only enhance research knowledge.

13 Reaching out

Widening research into fathering, sport and leisure

Tess Kay

The purpose of this chapter is to look forward – expansively! The research reported in this book has shown us how central sport and leisure can be to the fathering process. Through sport and leisure men can connect to their children, spend time with them and nurture them while fulfilling their own expectations of what is required of them as a father. Researchers who focus on sport and leisure home in on the micro-level of men's inter-actions with their children and begin to unpick further dimensions of their fathering ideology and practice. By making sport and leisure visible as a productive research focus, we therefore hope to have signalled the rele-vance of our work to the broader community of fatherhood and family researchers. But this is a two-way dialogue and the intention here is to consider how much there is to gain in the other direction – how sport and leisure research can be enriched by building on the extant body of father-hood research.

Drawing on this rich literature has one immediate advantage: it provides access to analyses that place fathering in very diverse contexts. This book managed to represent three continents, but although the geographical spread of the studies reported is wide, their socio-cultural base is narrow: all are western industrialised democracies in which the dominant language spoken is English and the power brokers have traditionally been white. There are certainly differences between them and diversity within them – but as Chapter 1 has shown, at the aggregate level the key parameters of fathering are remarkably consistent. In Australia, Canada, the United Kingdom and the United States of America, around 70 per cent of fathers live with their children in 'traditional' family households; around 25 per cent do not; and nearly all fathers – close to 90 per cent – are in full-time employment. At the ideological level, fathers in all four countries are exposed to the current emphasis on 'involved' fathering, with reinforcement of this in welfare pol-icies and legal systems. There are glimpses of diversity and disadvantage, but these too occur in broadly consistent patterns: in each country there are fathers who are multiply disadvantaged in terms of low education and low income, many of whom are members of minority ethnic groups, and these characteristics are individually and collectively often associated with high levels of non-resident fathering. Ultimately, notwithstanding this diversity, the dominant model of fatherhood remains a full-time working dad living with his children in a two-parent household – or a non-resident dad measured against this 'norm'.

This has been the context for the empirical studies that have featured in this volume, all of which were framed from a Eurocentric perspective. There are great opportunities to develop and diversify this knowledge base by conducting research into fathering through sport and leisure across a much wider social and cultural spectrum. One of the reasons for doing this is simply to address the greatly neglected gaps in our current knowledge base by identifying and making visible the missing populations. More fundamentally, extending research in this way enriches our current knowledge by encouraging deeper critical reflection on research findings and research processes that appear so familiar.

This chapter is intended to start the ball rolling by illustrating a number of alternative settings and contexts and their associated fathering practices. It continues the book's underlying concern with the interaction of underlying values and ideologies with fathering practice. Three areas in which we find different expectations of the fathering role, and different practices of it, are considered: fathering in the context of different cultures and ethnicities; fathering in the context of different religions; and fathering by gay men.

Cultural contexts of fathering

> Fatherhood is intertwined with the process by means of which men come to an understanding of who they are – their sense of identity and place – in society. Fatherhood does not occur in a vacuum; it is a socio-moral process informed by the dominant discourses of what it means to be man in one's society.
>
> (Mkhize, 2006: 8)

The chapters in this book are from countries which are multicultural societies and several of the empirical studies reported here have included participants of various ethnicities. Nonetheless, none of the studies here has focused solely on, or foregrounded, issues surrounding ethnicity and fathering, nor has the racial dimension of white identity been addressed. One of the most fruitful ways in which we can extend our understanding into fathering, sport and leisure is to step outside the current relatively narrow cultural contexts within which it is researched. Doing so means recognising explicitly how significant these contexts are to the lived experience of parenting.

There are strong reasons for attaching importance to this. Elliot (1996) places family very centrally at the heart of cultural identity and depicts different family arrangements and values as crucial distinguishing characteristics of different ethnic groups. Maintaining cultural traditions of family life is particularly important to minorities seeking to preserve and negotiate a distinctive identity within an alternative culture. Bhopal's (1999) research into women in east London found that a majority valued South Asian family traditions, including the practice of arranged marriages, precisely because they represented something distinctive about South Asian personal and collective cultural identity. Harvey's (2001) analyses of minority families in four different countries interacting with dominant cultures similarly emphasised the importance attached to 'maintaining our differences'. Berthoud too, in his analytical account of family formation in multicultural Britain, claims that 'it is diversity between minority groups which is their most striking characteristic' and that 'nowhere is this diversity more apparent than in family structures' (Berthoud, 2000: 2). Reflecting on similar findings, Beishon, Modood and Virdee (1998) have argued that because of the value attached to this variety of family forms, multiculturalism has to support a diversity in partnering and parenting.

In recent years there has been a shift in frameworks for researching issues relating to race and ethnicity. In the case of minority groups, assumptions about 'assimilation' have become outmoded in the face of growing evidence that populations preserve their traditions and draw on the cultural capital of their own communities of origin. In Britain, rather than experiencing a move to cultural homogeneity, we are witnessing cultural diversity both between the white majority population and non-white groups, and between different minority ethnic communities (Parekh, 2000). There is therefore potential for tensions to arise when minority groups interact with a majority culture with very different familial values. While minority ethnic groups do modify their traditional family arrangements as a result of interplay with the majority culture, they do so in ways that are consistent with their own traditions (Elliott, 1996: 41). This concurs with Pilkington's (2003) view that minorities draw on their own extensive cultural capital in establishing their identity in western contexts. Berthoud's analysis showed that in the UK, the three largest ethnic groupings in the population had quite distinct family patterns; he also showed, however, that the trend in all three was the same and all were in fact 'moving in the same direction', away from 'traditional' family values – albeit from very different starting points. With appropriate caveats, he described Caribbeans in Britain as being ahead of the trend in the white population and South Asians as being behind it (Berthoud, 2000). 'Family' is thus a central site for exploration of the significance of interaction between minority and majority groups in the construction of individual and collective identity.

The primacy of 'family' in defining ethnic identity is of particular significance in relation to gender relations within family settings. Many of the most visible distinguishing characteristics of the family arrangements of minorities lie in the roles ascribed to female members of the family. In

Britain today, the most conspicuous manifestation of this is among those Muslim families of South Asian origin observing a traditional interpretation of Islam (Elliot, 1996). Although many Muslims follow a more progressive interpretation, reflected for example in the presence of Muslim women in public life and in westernised dress, when Muslims in Britain do adhere to Islamic traditions gender roles are strongly distinguished and family arrangements are more different from the majority white population than those of any other minority ethnic group (Berthoud, 2000). Basit (1997) has highlighted how westernised family life appears repellent to many of South Asian heritage and encourages the maintenance of their traditions:

> English family life is perceived by many South Asian, particularly Muslim, families to be highly insecure and threatening. The stereotype that they hold is of remote relationships with little concept of family solidarity. Elders appear to command little love or respect and are sent into homes instead of being looked after by the younger generation. Sexual licence is thought to be rife and there is hardly any regard for the institution of marriage. Parents seemingly divorce and remarry without any consideration for their offspring, who may have to go into care. This kind of behaviour is viewed as outrageous by Asian standards; a culture not worthy of emulation.
>
> (Basit, 1997: 426)

The position of 'family' at the heart of cultural identity clearly has implications for how we approach research into fathers, sport and leisure. This section therefore considers key issues surrounding fathering in different contexts, and through this aims to highlight the cultural specificity of expectations surrounding fathers. It uses the rather blunt tool of case examples to illustrate the type of diversity with which it is concerned. Care needs to be taken with this approach to avoid essentialism and over-generalisation: Phoenix and Husain warn against portraying 'the assumed essence of the parenting of a [ethnic] group' in a manner which obscures internal differences (2007: 6). These risks are implicit even at the level of labelling – the national-religious label 'Pakistani' that is applied to South Asian families in Britain, for example, hides 'strong provincial, regional and kinship allegiances as well as distinct ideological and religious beliefs, the effect of rural/urban divide as well as class differences' (Husain and O'Brien, 2001: 15). Any study of parenting and ethnicity needs to acknowledge complexity within groups, address a plethora of contextual factors, and take account also of how gender and social class intersect with ethnicity (Phoenix and Husain, 2007: 21).

Examining culture, ethnicity and race as contexts for fathering is therefore challenging and requires an in-depth approach that cannot be attempted here. There are dangers however in not approaching diversity at all, and the illustrations that follow try to strike an appropriate balance. They offer descriptive accounts of three groups who are not members of white dominant cultures: a minority group within a western industrialised democracy, a majority population in a sub-Saharan developing country, and an Indigenous People. Within the limited pace allocated the accounts attempt to acknowledge fluidity, change and diversity within the cultural contexts outlined, but also aim to say something about any common characteristics of fathering that are distinctive.

African American fathers: an example of fathering and family contexts among a minority ethnic group in western industrialised states

The first example (Box 13.1) focuses on the African American minority in the United States of America who number more than 36 million, making up around 12 per cent of the population and forming the second-largest minority group behind white (73 per cent) and Hispanic/Latino (15 per cent) Americans. Although their situation has improved since the civil rights movement, African Americans remain at considerable social, political and economic disadvantage compared to European Americans and the analysis locates fathering within this broader socioeconomic context. It highlights divergence across class lines, with better-educated middle-class African Americans adopting a lifestyle, and associated family and fathering approaches, closely aligned with a white westernised model, while those with more limited resources and capital undertake fathering in much more constrained circumstances and approach it from a markedly different perspective.

Box 13.1 The context for fathering among African Americans[1]

Public portrayal of African Americans has often been very negative, with unfavourable representation of African American fathers a key component of this image. African American fathers have been variously, and frequently, described as 'absent', 'missing', 'non-residential', 'non-custodial', 'unavailable', 'non-married', 'irresponsible' and 'immature' (Connor and White, 2006: ix).

One reason why African American men have been so readily depicted as 'irresponsible' fathers is that these criticisms appear to be substantiated empirically. African American fathers as a whole have higher levels of non-resident fatherhood than any other group; teenage African American men are almost four times as likely as teenage whites to have 'gotten someone pregnant' (Paschal, 2006); and only 36 per cent of African American children are growing up in a home with a resident father, a dramatic decrease from 59 per cent a generation earlier (Hrabowski, Maton and Grief, 2006). But several writers argue that analysing African American fathering practices on the basis of normative assumptions about resident, biological fathers does not adequately capture 'the cultural nuances that surround the fathering role in the African American experience' (Connor and White, 2006: 6) and underplays the constructive side of African American men's parenting:

> We have wondered why it is/was so difficult to find literature, research, and comments regarding positive attributes of African American families in general and African American fathers in particular. Surely to have survived and have such a major impact on popular culture (i.e., language, music, style of dress, athletics, and so forth), there must have been some inherent and obvious strengths.
>
> (Connor and White, 2006: ix)

Connor and White ask the fundamental question 'What is the nature of "fathering" in African American communities?' and argue for more appropriate analyses that address this. They highlight the significance of 'social fatherhood' through which overlapping community, social and family networks have always provided fathering within the African American community. Collectively, uncles, godfathers, brothers and half brothers, cousins, grandfathers, ministers, stepfathers and biological fathers have assumed responsibility for children's upbringing. This concept of fatherhood implies that individually, men play a reduced role in their own biological children's lives, but fulfil a generic 'fathering' role towards other young people in their community. This approach echoes the ancient African proverb, 'It takes a village to raise a child'.

This focus on 'communal' fathering presents a critical challenge to certain Eurocentric orthodoxies but also needs to be critically assessed itself. First, social fatherhood is not universal to African American men: it is prevalent among poorer African Americans living in impoverished communities and markedly less common among the more educated, affluent and socially conservative African American middle class. Second, social fatherhood is not necessarily regarded as effective by African Americans: fathering 'roles' played by a range of men often do not provide mothers with day-by-day continuous support and may not be an adequate substitute for substantial involvement by a child's own father. Several studies record mothers' and children's dissatisfaction with the biological father's low level of involvement with, and responsibility to, his child and family (e.g. Paschal, 2006; Mkhize, 2006).

This less involved pattern of fathering must however be viewed in context. Angelia Paschal's exploratory (2006) study of African American teen fathers examined the high level of young fatherhood in poor African American urban communities. Her research highlighted the distinctive views African American young men held about several aspects of fathering, from attitudes to conception (relatively low levels of contraceptive use) and responses to pregnancy (strong opposition to abortion for unplanned pregnancies), to preferences for living/partnership arrangements (low expectation of cohabitating or marrying, and little social pressure to do so). Most of the African American young fathers in Paschal's study did intend to be involved in their children's lives, as a 'provider' or 'involved nurturer', or both. In practice however these intentions were seldom fulfilled: 'providers' had only low/unsteady/illegal income and could not provide, while 'nurturers' did not spend regular time with their children. (The consistent ones were 'independent' fathers – they did not intend to be involved, and were not). Young fathers who could not fulfil the role they described rationalised this by saying they were doing all that could be expected given their present personal and economic circumstances, and by referring to their intention to do more/better in future. None the less, 'they placed most, if not all, responsibility for raising and providing for their children on their children's mothers . . . in most instances, the fathers considered their roles as supplemental and "bonuses" ' (Pascal, 2006: 174).

Hrabowski, Maton and Grief's (2006) study of father–son relationships focused on a very different group with very different experiences – older fathers (age *c.* 50) of high-achieving African American men of college age. All held secure jobs, were much better educated than African American men as a whole, and most had always been resident fathers living with their child's mother. The research investigated how the fathers had parented their sons and reported fathers instilling a strong dedication to work, education and the church. Fathers had been closely involved in monitoring their son's educational progress throughout school years, including intervening directly to ensure sons stayed focused on academic goals. This was coupled with a drive to overcome hardship, including poverty, racism and limited access to employment and education. Fathers addressed issues of racism with their sons by preparing them to be treated differently, but exhorting them to respond by investing effort to rise above these barriers. All reported being constant and active presences throughout their sons upbringing (Hrabowski *et al.*, 2006).

The marked differences between these samples of low-income and more affluent African American men warn us against underestimating diversity. They also give a glimpse of the complicated process through which ethnicity and class may interact. While younger, poorer African American young men provide a strong contrast to a White American family 'norm', the older fathers are closer to it than to those of poorer members of their own ethnic group.

Fathering by African American men is therefore diverse and ranges across the spectrum of father involvement. Socioeconomic status and the life chances it brings are important influences on where on this spectrum individuals may lie. Significant barriers inhibit many African American men, whose lack of 'involvement' as fathers is not just the product of a cultural attachment to 'social' collective fathering. The absence of 'family sustaining jobs' and the corrosive economic and psychological effects of the loss of work is particularly significant in undermining these men's identities as provider-fathers, and influential in turning them to temptations of illegal street culture. 'Resolving the conflict between fathering aspirations and opportunities in a society with a strong residual from racism is not easily accomplished' (Allen and Connor, 1997).

1 'African American' is the term most frequently used by the writers referred to in this example. The term 'Black' is however also used here where this is the original author(s)' usage.

Black South African fathers: an example of fathering and family contexts in a southern hemisphere 'developing country'

The second example (Box 13.2) considers fathering among Black South Africans. Blacks make up the majority of the population in South Africa but through the legacy of race relations and apartheid much of this population is poor. Although the country has a growing Black middle class, outside the developed urban centres the majority live in rural poverty. It is among these sectors of the Black population that cultural traditions survive most strongly, and this includes the tradition of fluid notions of family and a focus on collective fathering.

The South African example has added weight because of the relevance of breakdown in family structures to the extreme social and economic problems being experienced in much of southern Africa. Large sectors of the black population have been devastated by the HIV-AIDS pandemic which has brought high mortality rates among women, high proportions of AIDS orphans, declining numbers of able-bodied workers and reduced average life expectancy to the 30s. Local economic structures and systems of social support have collapsed, removing traditional support systems for the care of the young and the elderly alike. The behaviour of men and fathers in this context is of special significance.

Box 13.2 The context for fathering among Black South Africans

> Attempts to understand fatherhood in South Africa will neither begin nor end with definitions created in distant, northern, industrial contexts.
>
> (Richter and Morrell, 2006: 1)

South Africa has a population of around 48 million and is known for its diversity. In addition to having the largest Caucasian, Indian, and racially mixed communities in Africa, the Black population which makes up 79.6 per cent of the total population is neither culturally nor linguistically homogenous and includes several major ethnic groups. Some of these are unique to South Africa and others also populate bordering countries, so there are some shared characteristics between South Africa and other groups in the wider region of 'southern Africa'. This is what is being referred to when commentators on South Africa sometimes also allude to 'southern Africa'.

By UN classification South Africa is a middle-income country but development and wealth is very geographically localised and socially stratified. Poverty is prevalent beyond the main economic centres and the vast majority of South Africans are poor. Although affirmative action policies have seen a rise in black economic wealth and an emerging black middle class, South Africa has one of the highest rates of income inequality in the world and in 2000 the average white household was earning six times more than the average black household. Among blacks who have become urbanised, aspects of traditional culture have declined as a westernised middle-class lifestyle has emerged. The South African black majority however still has a substantial number of impoverished rural inhabitants among whom cultural traditions survive most strongly. With its large income gaps and dual economy, South Africa is classified as a developing country and faces substantial economic and social problems including crime, corruption and HIV/AIDS.

Issues surrounding family and, more specifically, fatherhood have begun to emerge as public policy concerns. Fatherhood is seen as problematic in a number of southern African countries in which there is very low support of children and families by fathers and very high rates of child sexual abuse by men. Overarching this is the impact of the AIDS pandemic which has weakened family structures and led to a rise in 'AIDS orphans'. With rates of HIV/AIDS infection among young women 4–6 times higher than young men, many children becomes motherless making fathers increasingly important to children's well-being. However, although half of all South African men over age 15 are fathers, in general they 'do not seem especially interested in their children' and take little part in their lives (Richter and Morrell, 2006: 1). Many children therefore grow up without a father in their lives, and the absence of a senior, protective male adult is believed to contribute to childhood vulnerability e.g. risky behaviours that expose young people to HIV/AIDS.

This picture of neglectful fathering contrasts with traditional African conceptions of parenting which stress the needs of the child and the importance of adults meeting these. This is captured in the saying 'every child is my child', conveying that a child needs to be supported, loved and guided by adults, that s/he is a member of a community (and not just an isolated individual), and that adults have a collective responsibility for the upbringing of a child (Richter and Morrell, 2006). This collective mode of existence incorporates a fluid and extended notion of 'family' in which many people are treated as family members and addressed as e.g. father, mother and brother irrespective of the genetic relationship.

Within this broad concept of 'family', fatherhood is similarly conceptualised as a collective responsibility: for example, 'one's father's brother is also one's father, he is addressed as such, and is expected to behave in a manner deserving of a man' (Mkhize, 2006: 190). Defining fatherhood as a collective responsibility allows the role played by uncles, cousins and grandparents in raising their children to be acknowledged. It also offers a fatherhood role to all men, irrespective of whether they are biological fathers or not, on the understanding that children belong to everybody (2006: 190). The communal view of the self and the family that underpins this contrasts in fundamental ways with the individualised conceptualisations in western thought. Within communal life, 'psychological development is not an individual journey . . . a person realizes his or her place and responsibilities within a community of other people' (Mkhize, 2006: 192).

Much of this significant legacy of positive fathering has been lost:

> The respected father, the patriarch, is an image that no longer has even national resonance. Once respected in African culture(s) as a man of wisdom, good judgement, care and consideration, the father today is an object of suspicion. Indicted in cases of violence and sexual abuse of women and young children, his reputation is in tatters. And with the disruption of the family, both nuclear and extended, his authority has also declined.
>
> (Lesejane, 2006: 173)

Lesejane frames issues of uninvolved fatherhood in relation to the changing, or what he terms distorted, nature of patriarchy. Historically the broader African cultural system was a patriarchical system in which patriarchs' authority was balanced by their responsibilities and obligations. Lesejane views the current problems of uninvolved fathers as the consequence of men now being unconstrained and free of duties. He advocates a return to social fatherhood in the sense in which this extends the fatherhood duties of men to all children, rather than absolving them from responsibility for their own: 'If more men could become fathers beyond their biological and marital obligations, there would be fewer parentless children in our midst' (Lesejane, 2006: 180).

Mkhize attributes the emergence of alternative, very negative masculine identities to economic marginalisation, especially among township males and other poor groups:

> 'If you are not working, you are not a genuine father. You are a father because you work. My children do not love me as they used to, I have lost my dignity as a human being ... I am staying in someone's house because mine was taken away [repossessed]. My children are all over the place. I would like us to be together as a family. I cry a lot. Even today I was crying. I have lost my manhood. A man is a man because he can provide for his family.'
>
> (Mkhize, 2006: 185)

Despite the prevalence of at best social fathering, and at worst uninvolved fathering, there appears to be some latent desire for men to play a fuller family role. These are the aspirations that young men have for the type of father they would like to become in their own adult family life:

> 'I would like to walk into the house and the children yell daddy's here and they come and hug me. I would like to spend a lot of time with my family and know them inside out. I would like to play with them and cheer them on at every single sport game they play. I would be proud of them and take them on holidays. Watch movies with them and take them to parties and not let my wife pay one cent on fees and bills.'
>
> (Teenage boy; Richter and Smith 2006: 155; in Richter and Morrell, 2006)

Aboriginal fathers: an example of fathering and family contexts among Indigenous People

The third example (Box 13.3) introduces consideration of Indigenous Peoples. The lead in connecting leisure research with Indigenous Peoples has come from Karen Fox who has warned that 'Both the political and epistemological perspectives of Indigenous peoples challenge Eurocentric leisure practices, epistemologies, and scholarship' (Fox, 2006: 403). Fox illustrated the disjuncture of leisure research with the worldview of Indigenous Peoples with the example of the Haida Gwaii in Canada, 'who structured their governmental processes around food, storytelling, song and "gifting" rather than capitalistic and legalistic forms' (2006: 404). She sought to 'begin a conversation' about whether and how leisure studies could develop appropriate praxis:

> Indigenous people's worldviews are cognitive maps of particular eco-systems and are directed toward creating harmony in the world and cosmos. Leisure scholarship that has focused on linear, compartmental-ised, noun-related aspects of Indigenous peoples' worlds often mis-construes the dynamic, cyclical and verb-based world of Indigenous peoples. Tewa scholar Cajete (2005) argued that Indigenous contextual-isation is substantially different than the Eurocentric emphasis on delimited spaces and activities. Therefore, the extant research that documents and lists games, sports, and other activities without connect-ing them to spiritual, governmental, ecological, or community processes is an example of imposing Eurocentric categories upon Indigenous worldviews and in need of critical assessment.
>
> (Fox, 2006: 405)

The example of Aboriginal fathers presented here falls far short of the wholesale reorientation and reframing that is implicit in Fox's analysis. It provides a first step however: a descriptive account of a very different cultural context for fathering that demands study in its own right and may also help extend our own concepts further.

Box 13.3 The context for fathering for Aboriginal Australians[1]

The family arrangements of Aboriginal Australians are based on a kinship system. Kinship systems define the relations within the community and bind people together in relationships of sharing and obligation. Extended family relationships are the core of Indigenous kinship systems and are central to the way culture is passed on and society is organised. Kinship systems also define roles and responsi-bilities for raising and educating children, which are seen as the concern of the entire community. The raising, care, education and discipline of children are the responsibility of everyone – male, female, young and old.

Children are taught how they should behave through storytelling and modelling which are a part of everyday life in Aboriginal Australian society. Knowledge is passed on about everyday life, such as how and when to find certain foods, and stresses the relationship between the child and its social and natural environment. The storytell-ing arises from a long cultural history estimated at 50,000–65,000 years. Aboriginal culture is rooted in 'Tjukurrpa', the Dreamtime, when the

Ancestral Beings moved across the land and created life and significant geographic features. Aborigines have maintained a link with the Dreaming from ancient times to today through song, dance, painting and storytelling which express the dreaming stories. 'Elders' bridge the past and present, teaching important traditions and passing on their knowledge and experiences. Once a person becomes an adult they in turn pass on the information to younger people.

From the late 1800s until 1969 a devastating assault was inflicted on Indigenous Peoples through the forced separation or 'taking away' of children from their families. This occurred in every Australian state and involved as many as 100,000 children, later known as the Stolen Generation, being separated from their families and placed in state institutions or with white families. These policies destroyed communities and effectively halted the passing of cultural knowledge from one generation to another:

> In Aboriginal Society the family unit is very large and extended, often with ties to the community ... Having that family unit broken down has just opened the floodgates for a lot of problems, a lot of emotional problems, mental and physical turmoil. If you want to use a really hard term to describe the impact that removal of Aboriginal children has had on Aboriginal families, 'attempted cultural genocide' is a good phrase.
>
> (Kendal; in Cunneen and Libesman, 1995)

The policies illustrated the authorities' limited comprehension of Aboriginal family structures and values:

> 'Well there was nine of us in the family, old (Lambert) came along and said: "You can't look after these kids by yourself Mrs Clayton", but we were for months without welfare coming near us. We had the two grandmothers and all our uncles and aunties there and our father's brothers were there. We weren't short of an extended family by any means. We never went without anything. But they still took us away. What right did they have? I am still seeking answers to [my] family's removal.'
>
> (http://www.dreamtime.net.au/indigenous/family.cfm; accessed 20 November 2008)

The loss of land and traditional culture and forced removal of children has led to ongoing trauma within Aboriginal communities. Today the number of Aboriginal and Torres Strait Islander peoples are estimated at 517,174, 2.5 per cent of the total population (ABS, 2008c) and are among the most disadvantaged groups in Australia (ABS, 2003). Indigenous Peoples experience higher levels of poverty, overcrowding, poor sanitation, poor access to medical care and education, poor nutrition and almost 20 years lower life expectancy compared to national averages (ABS, 2003). Indigenous persons have low levels of formal education, high levels of unemployment and in 2001 the average household income for Indigenous persons was less than two-thirds (62 per cent) of the equivalent income for non-Indigenous persons (ABS, 2004a).

Research and census data provide a limited picture of contemporary Indigenous Australian family life. The 2006 census indicated that 28 per cent of Indigenous households are couples with dependent children, and 23 per cent are one-parent families (ABS 2008b). Western concepts applied in large-scale surveys however lack cross-cultural fit. Indigenous households are fluid, often with a core of residents but with additional members who may or may not be from the same family. Relations are decided not only by blood and marriage; people from the same language groups can also be referred to as family. Dwellings are often linked together with families spread across several and movement between households is common, especially for children, with the line between 'resident' and 'visitor' often unclear (Martin *et al.*, 2002). Under the kinship system families are divided into social categories or 'moieties', and members of each moiety take care of the welfare of their members. Within-moiety marriage is forbidden but in some communities the men may have more than one wife, often the wife's sisters, and in some cultures a couple may not be recognised as husband and wife until they have children.

This is the context within which 'fathering' occurs. Children are raised and educated within extended families in which many people share these functions. Elders, men or women, have the right to contribute to decision making in families; older siblings are responsible for the welfare of younger ones in the family, and aunts and uncles may take on the roles of mother and father. A basic principle of the kinship system is the equivalence of same-sex siblings, therefore a male child will call his biological father and his father's brother 'father'; his male cousins are also his brothers (Bourke and Edwards, 1998). Most childcare is however done by women who spend much of their time caring for the children within their household or community (Nevile, 2001). Men may spend limited time with children: over a two-week period; 40 per cent of Indigenous males took part in 'nil' domestic work compared to 28 per cent of non-Indigenous males (ABS, 2008a).

Recognition must also be given to the socioeconomic problems faced by Indigenous Australians. Their oppressed position within wider society contributes to problems within the family context where issues such as passive welfare, alcoholism, substance abuse and violence are evident (Saggers and Gray, 1998; Gordon *et al.*, 2002). The rate of family violence and child abuse is much higher in Aboriginal communities than non-Aboriginal communities, with Gordon *et al.* (2002) describing this as an 'epidemic'. High rates of alcohol consumption are said to contribute to domestic violence, child abuse and incest (Saggers and Gray, 1998; Higgins *et al.*, 2005).

Fathering in Indigenous cultures cannot be understood on the basis of Eurocentric frameworks: it is a fluid concept not necessarily represented by biological ties. In the case of Aboriginal Australians, historical relationships between the Indigenous People and later settlers have left a further legacy of complex social, economic and political damage that distinguishes the context in which fathering occurs.

1 The description in this box has been compiled from Australian Bureau of Statistics (2008c), culture.gov.au (no date), Department of Education and Training, Western Australia (2006), and Walker (1993).

Studying fathering, sport and leisure in diverse cultural contexts

The three cases represented here, and the further examples in the other sections in this chapter, are intended to serve two purposes. As well as encouraging us to extend the scope of our future research, they also encourage us to think more critically about our existing knowledge base.

Some quite fundamental 'rethinking' of families and fathering is needed to encompass issues of culture and ethnicity. Within western industrialised nations, demographic shifts have made populations more ethnically diverse in ways that challenge taken-for-granted assumptions. Scholarship is required which recognises diversity between ethnic groups and within them; responds to the different patterns as ethnicity and class intersect; and in societies in which 'mixed race' is the fastest growing category, is alert to the fluidity and complexities of any type of 'ethnic' identity.

More fundamental cultural differences also need to be addressed. While the nuclear family is the dominant family pattern in most western cultures, we have seen that elsewhere many societies tend towards collectivism. Millions of the world's children are therefore growing up with multiple caregiving figures to which the stereotypical model of the family in its nuclear two-parent form has little applicability (McHale, Khazan, *et al.*, 2002; McHale, Lauretti, Talbot, and Pouquette, 2002; both in Kurrien and Vo, 2004: 207). It is helpful for us to recognise that the western expectation that a father should live with his child is very much a product of a belief that prioritises – or in Morrell's terms, words, 'overestimates' – the influence of biological parents on their children, and underestimates other forces that shape a child (Morrell, 2006). It follows that treating non-resident fatherhood as some form of second-best deviation from the desirable norm is also culturally specific.

By acknowledging the existence and legitimacy of alternative forms we challenge the basis of analysis of fathering in any contexts, including western contexts. The examples given above show, for example, some commonalities between African American and South African fathering, reflecting a degree of shared legacy that is identified by both as 'African'. This legacy is one which emphasises collective fathering, places less value on biological relationships and more on social fathering, and describes fluidity in family relations and roles. This differs strongly from Eurocentric concepts of the family and parenting roles which frame, for example, fathering by white American men. Within these two perspectives, different meanings are attributed to father-absence and father-presence: being a non-resident father is seen as a normal form of family organisation in one setting, but evidence of family 'breakdown' in another.

Another strong feature to emerge from the examples given is the fluid and contested nature of ideologies and practices of fathering. Although ethnic groups protect their family practices as important elements of their cultural identity, these are subject to change. Contestation occurs within the group: African and African American men are criticised by mothers and children for their limited involvement as fathers; families of South Asian heritage are negotiating across genders and generations to establish appropriate levels of parental authority and child autonomy. Externally, idealised media portrayals of western nuclear families may play their part in fostering dissatisfaction with alternative models, especially if these family forms are perceived by some as 'progressive' and 'modern'. Consciously and subconsciously, there is continual reworking of the appropriate degree of accommodation and resistance to the cultural alternatives available. This is a further element of an already complex research challenge.

Fathers and faith

> 'Faith . . . is not a separate dimension of life, a compartmentalized speciality. Faith is an orientation of the total person, [that gives] purpose to one's hopes and strivings, thoughts and actions.'
>
> (Fowler, 1981: 14; in Batson and Marks, 2008: 406)

> 'Marriage is not an invention of individuals or even of societies. Rather it is an element of God's creation. It is God who created us male and female. It is God who joined man and woman so that they could be fruitful and multiply and fill the earth. Every civilization known to mankind has understood marriage as the union of a man and a woman for the procreation and rearing of children.'
>
> (Most Reverend Michael Sheridan, Roman Catholic Bishop, Colorado Springs)

In traditional societies participation in religious activity was simply a consequence of living in the community (Voas and Crockett 2005): in the modern world, patterns of religious involvement are disparate. The extent to which people find religion important in their lives varies between global regions, faiths, political regimes, cultural groups, generations and individuals. Historical patterns of religious affiliation have been displaced by the global movements of modernity: Islamic faith has reached further into the West and Christianity further into Asia; elements of Eastern faiths and cultures have been appropriated by modern industrialised societies; the process of secularisation has reduced adherence to organised religions while the rise of spirituality has increased involvement with alternative ones (Goh, 2004; Dawson, 2006).

In the early twenty-first century the world's principal faiths and spiritual traditions may be classified into a small number of major groups or world religions. The vast majority of adherents follow Christianity (33 per cent of world population), Islam (20 per cent), Hinduism (13 per cent), Chinese folk religion (6.3 per cent) or Buddhism (5.9 per cent). The irreligious and atheists make up about 14 per cent, and about 4 per cent follow indigenous tribal religions. The major spiritual traditions encompass multiple denominations, e.g. amongst others, Christianity includes Catholicism and Protestantism and Islam includes Sunni and Shia.

'Family' is a central focus for faith. Every religion seeks to regulate sexual behaviour and procreation through teachings and religious laws intended to promote approved forms of family life, and all religions contain rituals for key family events such as the sanctification of marriage and the naming and welcoming of children. Religious teachings and values emphasise and support the centrality of family life, the importance of positive family relationships (including spending time with children), and a focus on the concerns and needs of others over the self (Abbott, Berry and Meredith, 1990; Ellison, 1992; Pearce and Axinn, 1998; Wuthnow, 1991). Religious institutions promote pro-family messages during regular religious attendance, reinforced by private religious activities such as prayer and reading religious texts.

Religious teachings address a range of issues relating to the formation of intimate partnerships and families. These include issues of sexual behaviour and sexuality; marriage and monogamy; gender relations and the treatment and status of women; and issues surrounding pregnancy, fertilisation and abortion. There are differences not only between religions but within them, as followers position themselves differently on a spectrum of progress–conservative religious viewpoints within their faith.

In relation to sexual behaviour and sexuality, conservatives from all religions tend to agree that only opposite-gender sexual behaviour is moral, and then only between a man and a woman who are married to each other. At the other end of the spectrum, religious liberals broadly are accepting of a wider range of sexual behaviour as long as it is consensual, relatively safe and within a committed relationship. Those of no religious affiliation (e.g. Agnostics, Atheists, Humanists) tend to hold beliefs similar to those of religious liberals.

Religious teaching on marriage and gender relations provide a context for parenting. While all main worldwide religions condone chastity, monogamy and sexual constraint, historically polygamy has been practised in all and continues today with varying degrees of approval. In Islam, polygamy is allowed, and is fairly common in traditionalist cultures (but rare in others): in 2001 the president of Sudan, Omar Hassan al-Bashir, exhorted Sudanese men to take more than one wife to increase the population to aid the country's development (BBC News, 2001). Among Christians, the Church of Jesus Christ of Latter-day Saints historically practised polygamy but now excommunicates members who enter it; however splinter groups of fundamentalists continue to have 'plural marriage'. In Sub-Saharan Africa, there has often been a tension between the Christian churches' insistence on monogamy and traditional polygamy and African Independent Churches have sometimes referred to those parts of the Old Testament which describe polygamy in defending the practice. In India, marriage laws are dependent upon the religion of the subject: at present Muslims are allowed to have multiple wives while Hindus are not.

A number of attempts have been made to conceptualise how religions may in practise influence parenting (e.g. Clydesdale, 1997; King, 2003; Pearce and Axinn, 1998; Wilcox, 1998). This research has been primarily conducted in the United States and narrowly focused on Christianity, but includes some attempts to conceptualise the function of religion more broadly. Wilcox (2002) has suggested that religious participation influences parenting values in two broad ways: through specific religious rituals (e.g. baptisms) and discourses 'which dramatize the moral relations that bind parents to their children, often endowing them with a transcendent character'; and through the associated opportunities provided for parents to spend time with their children in worship services, educational programmes, and family-oriented social activities (Wilcox, 2002: 782). Mahoney, Pargament, Swank and Tarakeshwar (2001) similarly distinguish two broad forms of religious influence on behaviour in family and parenting roles – a religion's 'substantive elements', and its 'functional elements'. The substantive elements of a religion are the content of systems of beliefs and practices it promotes. These theological beliefs shape many individuals' core assumptions about good behaviour and may guide people's family interactions. The functional elements consist of 'the psychological or social purposes that religion may serve, largely independent of the content of religious myths, teachings, rituals, or practices'. These include activities such as involvement in a church, synagogue or mosque which provides families with opportunities to become integrated into their local community, obtain social support from people with similar attitudes, and take part in social activities. Participating in a religion can be an important way of accessing these benefits, but they are not directly dependant on the religion's specific teachings about family life (Mahoney et al., 2001: 565).

The relationship between religion and family life has been the focus of a number of research studies, especially in the United States of America where 95 per cent of parents report a religious affiliation and the majority of married women (60 per cent) and men (53 per cent) attend church at least once a month (Heaton Pratt, 1990; Mahoney, 2000; in Mahoney *et al.*, 2001). Religious institutions have been particularly influential carriers of family-related culture over the course of American history (Wilcox, 2002: 780) and although the influence of religion has lessened over time, Christian religiosity continues to be positively correlated with traditional family attitudes among Americans (King, 2003: 385). At a practical level religious organisations are significant sources of family-related social integration, offering family-related activities as well as informal networks that provide social support (Ellison, 1994; Stolzenberg, Blair-Loy, and Waite, 1995; in Wilcox, 2002).

Research into religion has not usually focused specifically on fathers; equally, research into fatherhood has seldom addressed religion as a context for fathering. There are however several reasons to hypothesise that religion might influence fathering behaviour. Christian religious culture potentially shapes fathers' values and behaviours by emphasising the importance of family relationships and encouraging men to be actively involved in the lives of their children (King, 2003: 384) and in the present ideological climate may reinforce notions of involved fatherhood. There is debate however about how the relationships between religiosity, beliefs about family and fathering behaviour actually play out in practice. One view is that religious fathers hold traditional beliefs about families and have a greater familial orientation and therefore may have a relatively high level of involvement with their children. However, traditional attitudes are also likely to support a gendered division of parental roles within the family and may encourage men to see their role primarily as the breadwinner and the care of children as primarily the responsibility of mothers (Wilcox, 2002; King, 2003; Mahoney *et al.*, 2001).

Empirical evidence of how parental behaviours are linked to religious participation has been mixed. Wilcox's analysis of data on residential fathers concluded that religious participation fosters an authoritative, active, and expressive style of parenting – e.g. parents who participate in church activities were more likely to value obedience in their children and be involved in their children's education than other parents, and fathers who attended church frequently were more likely to monitor their children, to praise and hug them, and to spend time with them (Bartkowski and Xu; in Wilcox 2002: 781). King (2003) however identified a very mixed literature: some studies reported higher father involvement (e.g. Bartkowski and Xu, 2000), some reported no significant relationship (e.g. Barnett and Baruch 1987), and others found lower involvement (e.g. Cooksey and Craig, 1998). She concluded that although there was some evidence that religiousness influences father involvement, it was not particularly strong (King, 2003: 383).

In attempting to resolve this, King (2003) undertook a more detailed analysis of fathering and child involvement and tested the hypothesis that religious fathers are more involved fathers and enjoy better quality relationships with their children, including providing them with more support and assistance. Controlling for an extensive range of mediating factors her findings were that religious fathers are more involved than non-religious fathers, and that this holds for both married and divorced men. She found that one of the mediating factors was marital quality and suggested that this played an important role in linking men to their children: 'Religious men enjoy higher quality marriages, and good marriages pull men into relationships with their children, suggesting that for men, marriage and childrearing might indeed be a "package deal"' (Furstenberg and Cherlin, 1991; in King, 2003). She concluded overall, however, that the influence of Christian religiousness on father involvement is generally modest and should not be overstated.

King is not alone in being tentative about drawing conclusions about the relationship between religion and parenting on the basis of existing research. Thornton (1985) emphasised the need to develop more fine-grained, conceptually based indexes of various aspects of religion to capture the substantive element of religious beliefs or practices and 'untangle the potentially beneficial and harmful functions that religion may play in the home' (Thornton, 1985: 387). King also suggested that more in-depth and conceptually based measurement tools are needed to undertake fuller analysis of the mechanisms that tie religion to family life. In addition to these methodological issues, a further very substantial concern is that the literature on the relationship between religion, family and fathering is currently almost wholly concerned with Christian religions.

To broaden this coverage, this section now considers two examples of family life in contrasting religious contexts – Christian and Islamic. As with the examples in the previous section of different cultural contexts, these are relatively short descriptive overviews. They are intended to give some indication of how different religions may influence the day-to-day conduct of family life and fathering.

Box 13.4a Family life and fathering in Islam

Around 21 per cent of the world population practise Islam; this is estimated at around 1.5 billion people (Adherents.com, 2005) making Islam the second largest religion. Islam is the state religion of all Middle Eastern countries, where legal citizens must be Muslim, and is also heavily concentrated in North Africa. Islam is not widely represented in the Western world despite recent growths and only small proportions of national populations are Muslims: 1.5 per cent in Australia (ABS, 2006), 2 per cent in Canada (SC, 2001), < 3 per cent in the UK (OFNS, 2001) and 0.5 per cent in the USA (US CB 2008). Islam translates to 'peace', and Muslims follow the original teachings of God,

Allah, in the Qur'an and the sunnah. Muslims belong to one of two major denominations, the Sunni (85 per cent) and Shia (15 per cent), which have different traditions.

The family is the base unit throughout Islam and is regarded as the cornerstone of a healthy and balanced society. The traditional Muslim family is extended, often spanning three or more generations, providing stability, coherence and support (Dhami and Sheikh, 2000). The obligations and legal rights of family members are defined by Islam and Islam provides specific teachings on family formation and relationships. Marriage is considered the union of two families and usually arranged by parents (Dhami and Sheikh, 2000) but cannot proceed without the consent of the two individuals who are to be married. Divorce is not uncommon, but can only be finalised by the man. Consanguinity (intermarriage) is particularly common in Muslims of south Asian and Arab origin although this arguably stems more from culture than religion: Dhami and Sheikh (2000) estimate that some 75 per cent of Pakistani Muslim couples are in a consanguineous relationship, and approximately 50 per cent are married to first cousins. Homosexuality is considered sinful and sex outside of heterosexual marriage is considered deviant, against the teachings of the Qur'an to maintain a wholesome society, and deserving of punishment in the hereafter (Dhami and Sheikh, 2000). Polygamy is permitted under restricted conditions, a practice allowed in some countries but not others. Where permitted, a man may have up to four wives if he believes he can treat them equally, but a woman may have only one husband (Glassé and Smith, 2001). Muslim opinion about contraception is divided.

The values of Islam are closely intertwined with cultural values and it can be infeasible, and not always appropriate, to try to separate one from the other. Certain ethnic groups who follow Islam also stress family relationships and obligations beyond the nuclear family in their cultural practice. Families of South Asian origin, for example, have traditionally been close-knit, cohesive units with very strong family loyalties and affectionate but hierarchical relationships within the family. They emphasise respect for elders, restraint in relations between the sexes, and the maintenance of family honour (Basit, 1997: 425). Families are traditionally ideologically focused on the family group with little regard for individual freedom or self-interest (Ballard, 1982). Verma and Darby (1994), writing about the British Bangladeshi community in the 1990s, described this as 'essentially collectivist': 'members perceive themselves not as individuals but also as members of a group – the family' (1994: 45). Bhopal captures this well in her description of marriage as 'an arrangement between two families, not two individuals' (Bhopal, 1999: 120).

In traditional Islam, relations between the sexes are governed by the principle of complementarity and women and men have contrasting roles (Obermeyer, 1992). This positions woman in the private sphere (i.e. the home) and men in the public sphere. The man is considered the head of the family and is obliged to support the family financially while women are responsible for bringing up children.

Islam does not however consider men and women to be unequal, but only to be different with different areas of expertise. Great status is however given to mothers: by nurturing her family a woman is seen as safeguarding the whole of society for society consists of family units. Many Muslim women may pursue a career, although family commitments still come first (Dhami and Sheikh, 2000; Watton, 2005). As with non-Muslim households, the amount and type of time Muslim fathers spend with their children both inside and outside of the home will be affected by mothers' activities.

Islam plays a very visible role in families' daily life especially through Salah, which forms one of the 'Five Pillars' of Islam. Salah is a form of worship – prayer – which is carried out five times a day. Salah 'not only helps us to remember Allah and that we are his servants. But it also keeps us on the right path, it helps us from not doing bad, from disobedience of Allah, makes us clean and healthy and also it gets us closer to Allah'. Salah takes place at dawn, noon, in the afternoon, at sunset and at night, and these are obligatory for all Muslim believers of sound mind and who have reached the age of Tammez (when a child can differentiate between right and wrong).

A stable and secure family environment is considered a child's right within Islam, and marriage is deemed to provide such an environment (Dhami and Sheikh, 2000). Children internalise the values of the parents at an early age and learn to behave in accordance with the ethos of the family (Basit, 1997: 426). This includes respecting and obeying the authority of their parents which are stressed in Islamic teachings (Joly, 1987). Many Muslim young people are therefore subject to more parental influence than their non-Muslim peers. Guiding the activities of young men and women – the next generation of Muslim adults – is seen as important in countering the excesses of western influence. Young people vary in their response to parental authority and for many it is a feature of family life which is expected by both generations and compared favourably to western lifestyles:

> 'I sometimes think that English parents give too much freedom
> to their children. Like the parents don't really care what happens
> to the children. My parents give me freedom, I am allowed to go
> out, but they like to know what time I am coming in, who I am
> going out with, stuff like that, and that sort of limits the freedom,
> but gives a nice sort of freedom where you know that they care
> about you.'
>
> (Teenage daughter)

'We should give them some freedom, so that they could get education. But they should know what is right and what is wrong. Of
course, they can go out and make friends and have a social life, but
they shouldn't stay out late: our culture doesn't allow that. I've
seen girls walking in the streets in the middle of the night. That
causes corruption and crime.'

(Father) (Basit 1997: 432)

Westernised lifestyles are perceived by many Muslims to be insecure
and threatening. The stereotype that they hold is of remote relationships with little concept of family solidarity, little love or respect for
elders, and minimal regard for the institution of marriage. Muslim
parents are therefore often concerned to instil their faith in their
children and can access an extensive range of parenting advice from
within their community, from Scholars, and from Islamic publications
and websites. The guidance shown below is available on the website of
'SoundVision', an organisation that produces 'Islamic Information and
Products'. The examples have been selected to show how young
people's leisure activities are seen as important sites for parents to
attend to reinforce faith, by encouraging activities which are compatible with Islam and discouraging those which are not.

Box 13.4b Keeping Muslim teens Muslim

22 Tips for Parents
http://www.soundvision.com/info/parenting/teens/22tips.asp

Tip #6: Take an interest in what they do
Does Noor play hockey in an all-girls' sports league? Attend Noor's
games as regularly as possible. Does Ihsan collect stamps? See if you
can find old letters from your parents in Malaysia or Lebanon and pass
the stamps on to her. Does Muhsin love building websites? Visit
his site, post a congratulatory e-mail on the message board and offer
some suggestions for the site. Give him a book on advanced web design
as Eid gift.

Tip #13: Take them out . . . to Islamic activities
Instead of a fancy dinner at a restaurant, save your money to take
everyone out to the next Muslim community dinner or activity. Make a
special effort to go to events where other Muslim teens will be present
and the speaker caters his/her message to this crowd.

**Tip #16: Establish a TV-free evening and monitor TV watching
in general**
Parents' biggest competitor for their children's attention is the TV

Monitoring what everyone watches simply means taking care to remind and help everyone avoid shows which depict sex, violence and encourage unIslamic activities. Put up a list of acceptable and unacceptable shows on the wall beside the TV.

Establishing TV-free evenings means having one evening of the week when no one, adult, teen or child is allowed to watch television. Hopefully, this is a first step towards general TV reduction in the home.

Tip #18: Have 'Halal Fun night' once a month

'Fun is Haram' is a joke sometimes heard amongst Muslim youth, mocking the attitude of some Muslims for whom virtually anything enjoyable is automatically labelled Haram (forbidden).

Islamic entertainment is a much neglected area of Muslim concern. Islamic songs, skits, etc. are a viable tool for the transmission of Islam. Maybe 16-year-old Jameel knows how to play the Duff, while his sister Amira, 14, can write and sing well. Let them present their own Islamic song to the whole family. Or have 12-year-old Ridwan recite some of his best poetry. Make one of the teens in charge of this event. Help them establish a criterion of acceptable and unacceptable Halal entertainment.

Box 13.5a Family life and fathering in Christianity

Christianity is the largest single religion globally, with 33 per cent of the world's population (around 2.1 billion people) practising some form of Christian faith (Adherents.com, 2005). It is most prevalent in the western world and is also the predominant religion the Americas and Southern Africa. In each of the countries featured in this book, around three quarters of the population classify themselves as Christian making Christianity a significant force in the developed world (67.9 per cent in Australia, 71 per cent in Canada, 72 per cent in the UK and 77 per cent in the United States (Australian Bureau of Statistics, 2006; Statistics Canada, 2001; ONS, 2001; US Census Bureau, 2008). The late twentieth century has however seen a rise in Christian adherence in the developing world and southern hemisphere in general. Central and Southern America, along with Southern Africa, have high proportions of Christians; countries including Bolivia, Paraguay and Ecuador all have over 95 per cent Christian representation (CIA, 2008).

There is diversity of doctrines and practices among groups calling themselves Christian. The five main denominations are Roman Catholicism, Eastern Orthodoxy, Oriental Orthodoxy, Protestantism and Restorationism. The Catholic Church is the world's largest

Christian church, representing over half of all Christians and one-sixth of the global population. In the USA the Christian faith is mostly Catholic (32 per cent of Christians) or Baptist (21 per cent of Christians), typically considered Protestant (US CB, 2008). Broadly speaking, Christians follow the teachings of Jesus as presented in the New Testament and notwithstanding variances between denominations, approaches to family and parenting are consistent with 'traditional' family values. Christianity generally supports monogamous heterosexual marriage, with different denominations varying in their acceptance of or opposition to homosexuality, sex outside marriage, contraception and abortion. There is diversity in approaches to parenting and some faiths are associated with authoritarian parenting (Woodberry and Smith, 1998).

It is difficult to generalise about the influence of Christian teachings on family lives and parenting approaches. In the face of secularisation, there is substantial debate about how actively those who identify themselves as Christians in social surveys practise their faith. In England church-going has been declining markedly for the last 4 decades (Brown, 2001) and there is uncertainty about what this signifies. Davie (1990; 1994) coined the phrase 'believing without belonging' (BWB), suggesting that decline in religious affiliation and attendance does not *per se* indicate a decline in faith. In its 'strong' version the BWB thesis argues that 'with the exception of a handful of atheists, [Europeans] continue to believe in God and to have religious (or at least "spiritual") sensibilities: the proportion of believers is high and has changed little in recent years' (Voas and Crockett, 2005: 12). Recent research in the UK does not support this empirically: data from the British Household Panel survey, a stratified longitudinal dataset obtained from over 5,000 households and 10,000 individuals, showed that young people were half as religious as their parents and that 'Religious belief has declined at the same rate as religious affiliation' (Voas and Crockett, 2005: 13). Voas and Crockett concluded that 'Between the extremes of full faith and noncommittal assent there is naturally a middle ground of more or less Christianised belief, but the passivity of so-called "believers" is itself a sign of religious decline' (2005: 24).

Academic research into the relationship between Christianity, family and fathering practices has tended to focus on those who practise faith most actively and tend to conservative ideology. Studies have been conducted with Catholics, Latter-day Saints and some groups of Protestants.

Conservative Protestantism accounts for <5 per cent of Christians in America but gives significant pastoral attention to family life and has been the focus of considerable research. Conservative Protestantism stresses traditional gender relations and strict discipline but also expressive parenting and parental involvement. Much of the discourse produced is aimed specifically at fathers and although it generally stresses men's traditional role as primary breadwinner/head of household, it also emphasises the roles of husband and father. Conservative Protestantism aims to orient fathers to their children in two ways: by modelling for their children the love that God has for persons by being an active expressive and strict parent (Bartkowski and Xu, 2000; Wilcox, 1998), and through an expressive ethos with a focus on relationships including paternal involvement (Wilcox, 2002).

Conservative Protestantism is associated with authoritarian parenting approaches to obedience, derived from the belief that human nature is sinful (Ellison and Sherkat, 1993). The research literature suggests that this produces a family culture with higher rates of corporal punishment and may restrict the child's autonomy. (Ellison and Sherkat) Strict discipline is however said to be balanced by a warm, expressive style of parent–child interaction in non-disciplinary situations (Wilcox, 1998). One study published on religion and fatherhood found that conservative Protestant fathers combine a strict approach to discipline with a warm, affective approach to non-disciplinary interactions (Bartkowski and Xu, 2000) and are more likely to hug and praise their children and be involved in their daily lives than other fathers (Woodberry and Smith, 1998). Conservative Protestant affiliation is therefore associated with both authoritarianism and high levels of father involvement.

Batson and Marks (2008) examined how Catholic families who actively practise their faith incorporate religion in family life. Parents alluded to the guidance that their faith provided for raising their children, the role of prayer in building family relationships and teaching life lessons, and the way in which they built their faith into everyday life:

'You also have all sorts of conflicting advice about how to raise your children. And a lot of it is garbage . . . I think having God's guidance and having a faith gives us [a] firm foundation, and a set of ideas that tells us how to do [parenting] well. We may not do it perfectly, but . . . [our faith] gives us a clear idea . . . [of] what we need to do.'

(Batson and Marks, 2008: 405)

'[During our] prayers that are said [with the children] every night, every one of them has the opportunity to pour out those things from the day. Inevitably, somebody's feelings got hurt, and we talk. Every moment is a life teaching lesson, and it becomes that at night . . . They learn to pray for that person [who hurt their feelings]. They learn to lift up those things that are [bothering them] . . . They believe that that [prayer to God] is where we derive . . . our help.'

(Batson and Marks 2008: 403)

'We'll do this thing sometimes before they leave for school, I'll bless them and they'll bless me and they'll say a little prayer. Our little daughter Jenny will put her arms around me and say, "Bless Mommy that she will have a very nice day." So our kids are getting that foundation and our family can feel that unity that's based on that foundation [of faith].'

(Batson and Marks, 2008: 404)

Like Muslim parents, Christians can access an extensive range of faith-based parenting advice. The example shown below is available on the website of 'ChristianAnswers.net'. It focuses on television and media use as a form of leisure which parents feel important to address to 'protect' their children's religious values.

Box 13.5b Violence in the media – How does it affect families?
http://www.christiananswers.net/q-eden/edn-f012.html

You may think that those sexy sitcoms or violent dramas are just entertainment and shouldn't really have serious effects. For any single show that's probably correct, but for too many people, we're not talking about a *single* show every so often, and it *is* a problem.

   Child psychologist, Dr. Debra Kowalski, explains, 'With children having so much exposure to the media, the messages that come across . . . are very important and they shape how a child sees the world and what a child sees as important . . . A lot of the messages related to violence and sexuality can negatively impact a child.'

   The repetition of violence causes children to become desensitized. The same thing happens to adults, but children are more vulnerable. It also holds true for explicit sexual content. In fact, relatively little exposure to pornographic material at an early age can significantly disturb a child and interact with their sleeping and other behaviors. It can also affect the way they interact socially with peers, as well as foster anxiety and fear in other situations.

   Michael Suman, coordinator of The Center for Communications Policy at the University of California at Los Angeles, is doing a three year analysis of the effects of violence on television. He makes the following observations: 'Violence on television, basically, has three types of negative effects on people.'

1   *Increases violence.* '. . . Many studies show that violence on TV actually leads to aggressive, violent behaviors in the world, most prominently through imitation. They see people being violent on TV and they copy them as models. They imitate them.'

2   *Desensitization and callousness.* 'People become desensitized. This includes being callous towards people who've been victims of

violence.' (Ted Baehr, movie and television specialist and publisher of the Christian 'Movie Guide', comments, 'We say "it's ok, we've seen it on television. That behavior is fine." We no longer object to behavior [and language] that a few years ago we would have been insulted by ... We've become very desensitized, and it's corrupting.')

3. **Fear.** 'It makes them more fearful.' Children may have the false notion that violence or abuse is around every corner and that there is no good in this world. While this may be partly true, it is mis-leading and can cause much damage during the developmental stages of life.

Do you allow your family to watch programming riddled with violence? Does your heart lead you down the path of worldliness, seeking violence? Or are you active in showing your family that true followers of Christ are known as peacemakers in this violence-scarred society? As the old proverb goes, your actions speak louder than your words. What do your actions say?

For more information, be sure to read this eye-opening discussion about the effects of media on the family, How much TV is too much TV?

Incorporating religious faith in research into fathering, sport and leisure

Religions vary in content; in their formal and informal status within different nation states, cultures and communities; and in how their adherents interpret their teachings and the intensity with which they follow them. Mahoney *et al.* (2001) suggest that the significance of religion to parenting lies in the central-ity of religion to parents' identities. It is therefore complex to assess the influence of religion, and also to distinguish between its explicit effects and its broader embedded cultural significance. There is also widespread recognition of the need to recognise that religion may have both positive and negative effects (Mahoney *et al.*, 2001; King, 2003). The situation is further complicated by the under-developed state of the research base.

Mahoney *et al.* (2001) have also raised the issue of disentangling *how* exactly religion may interact with parenting. They make the point that it may not be the explicitly religious content of religion that influences parenting, but the significance of a religious community as a source of psychosocial support:

Although the substance of religious beliefs about discipline may fully account for links between religion and punitive parenting, it is important to consider the 'nonreligious' psychosocial functions embedded in exposure to any given set of teachings about parenting. Religious institutions and their leaders offer recommendations from a position of authority about what parents should and should not do when raising children. Belonging to any social group that provides coherent, well-delineated guidelines about parenting could powerfully shape parents' attitudes and behaviours, whatever the content of those messages are. It could be argued that less religious parents often turn to the field of social science in a similar manner to obtain education and reinforce their childrearing attitudes or practices. Greater participation in religious activities in a religious community may provide parents with valuable psychological and practical resources independent of the content of religion.

(Mahoney et al., 2001: 590–1)

The purpose of this section has been to give recognition to the potential significance of religion as an influence on fathering, at both the ideological and practical level. Although it has been partly concerned with considering the 'substantive elements', i.e. the specific content, of different religions, its broader purpose has been to draw attention to how prominent religion may be in shaping fathering by some men. In the case of non-believers we might say that religion has no impact – although this may not stand up to scrutiny of how religious principles, such as fidelity in marriage, exert indirect influence through their assimilation into culture and secular institutions. Among those who class themselves as 'religious', the spectrum of belief is broad: there is a significant difference between a family who consider themselves broadly religious but undertake no religious participation beyond occasional events and festivals, and those who make daily acts of observance to celebrate a faith which is the foundation for all aspects of their life. Horwath, Lees, Sidebotham, Higgins and Imtiaz's (2008) detailed research with children and their parents in UK Christian and Muslim families found that regardless of specific faith, religion influenced family and social relationships, social presentation and education; parenting capacity in relation to guidance and boundaries, stability and emotional warmth; and additional dimensions including family history and functioning, wider family, and family's social integration. When religion is influential, its impact is broad, making it an important component to recognise in analysis of fathering.

Gay fathers

'A friend of mine recently said, "You are America's nightmare – this gay guy, with two kids, living in the city. It is so much of what this country doesn't want to see happening." '

(Mallon 2004: 21)

Gay fathers pose a unique set of challenges to how we conceptualise and understand fathers, fatherhood and fathering. The very existence of gay fathers stimulates us to think beyond taken-for-granted notions of natural conception and conventional parenting roles; to reconsider the nature of intimate partnerships and family life; and to question the roles of fathering and parenting in the multiple masculinities men perform. In the public sphere gay fathers place demands on legal and welfare systems that elicit complex and contradictory responses; in the public eye they can provoke intense, sometimes hostile, responses.

The literature on gay fathers is not extensive but it is informative. This section therefore provides an overview of the complex issues raised in the analyses of writers such as Barrett and Tasker (2002), Berkowitz and Marsiglio (2007), Mallon (2004), Stacey (2006) and Strah (2004). Readers wishing to learn more are guided especially to Mallon's excellent volume, *Gay men choosing parenthood* (2004), a detailed examination of the experiences of gay men in the United States who become fathers through fostering and/or adoption. In the course of examining the experiences of these men Mallon provides a far-reaching analysis of the emergence of fatherhood as a possibility for gay men, the individual and societal issues this invokes, and the experience of becoming a gay father.

The above sources are all of relatively recent origin. If fathers have been under-researched, gay fathers have been even more so. In the late twentieth century, academics and policy makers were paying increasing attention to fathers and also to homosexuality but it was some time before the two areas converged (Barrett and Tasker, 2002). This was not so much a case of research and policy lagging behind social practice, as a reflection of the fact that until the late twentieth century very few gay men had addressed the theoretical possibility of fatherhood, let alone embarked on its practical realities. There had certainly been gay fathers before the 1980s, and many gay men had in the past fathered within heterosexual relationships, but the deliberate pursuit of parenthood by men within pre-existing gay relationships and identities is a much more recent phenomenon (Patterson, 2000: 1058).

The relatively late emergence of the notion of gay fatherhood is indicative of the contradictions the role can contain and the controversy it can provoke. There is strong resistance to the idea of gay parenting, and to parenting by gay men especially. Some of the most virulent myths surrounding homosexuality are those that centre on gay men's relationship to children and young people and focus on 'the safety of children around gay men' (Barrett and Tasker, 2002: 3). Barrett and Tasker also list the 'huge variety' of fears and prejudices that prevail about parenting by gay men, including:

> that gay men will encourage peculiar dress habits, effeminate behaviour
> and all kinds of perverse sexual practices in their offspring or that they
> will challenge all the standard tenets of society and leave children
> uncontrolled, unsure about what is right and wrong, confused about

their own sexual orientation and vulnerable to 'predation' from peers as well as from adults.

(2004: 3–4)

No comprehensive data is available on how many gay fathers there are or about their individual and household characteristics. Our inability to construct a broad aggregate picture reflects many difficulties including the complexity of defining and identifying gay fathers, the practical difficulty of accessing gay fathers as a research sample, and the societal barriers which make some men unwilling to identify as gay while others are just as keen to be recognised as such. The very different treatment and status of homosexuals in different cultures and religions and under different welfare and legal systems also makes transnational comparisons infeasible. A number of high-quality narrative accounts have however been undertaken, mainly in the United States, and from these we can gain insights into qualitative dimensions of gay fathering.

In doing so we immediately confront one of the bias issues in research into fathering among gay men (Berkowitz and Marsiglio, 2007): most studies have been based on samples of higher-educated middle-class men, and often on predominantly white samples. This is in itself a reflection of the greater accessibility of certain routes to gay fatherhood to relatively well-resourced groups. In this respect we find ourselves yet again addressing an area of fatherhood where access to both social capital and material assets is a discriminating factor in fathering.

The possibility of fatherhood

Gay fatherhood is a relatively recent public phenomenon. Most gay men are not fathers and fatherhood did not feature in gay men's early public claims to visibility and entitlement. In Stacey's (2006) terms, the relationship between sexuality and paternity have previously been quite clearly delineated: 'Heterosexual "situations" lead most straight men to paternity, while homosexual "situations" lead a majority of gay men to childlessness' (2006: 377).

For some men, the expectation that being gay will mean being childless is very much to the fore:

> When it was clear to me that I was gay, there was a sadness I could not have children, and the coming out process for me was not [so much] about people knowing I am gay [as] it was more about losing the idea of having children.

(Mallon, 2004: 30)

This belief that gay men could not be fathers has been deeply internalised among many gay men and has been perhaps the major obstacle to gay fathering. The belief by others that gay men *should* not be fathers is however another barrier. Opposition has come partly from the wider social consensus which has resisted and often opposed the idea of same sex adults, especially men, parenting children (e.g. Barrett and Tasker, 2002; Mallon, 2004; Stacey, 2006). But there are also those within the gay community who are hostile to the idea of gay men 'acting like straights' and reproducing the family structures and ideologies of a society which can be so hostile to homosexuality. Since the 1980s, however, gay men have increasingly embraced the idea of fatherhood (Berkowitz and Marsiglio, 2007). Becoming a father has been the third of three phases in a trajectory of relationship and family building among gay men in America: 'In the seventies we expressed ourselves sexually, in the eighties we were coupling up, and in the nineties we are having families' (Mallon, 2004: 29).

Becoming a father

Gay men may take a number of routes to becoming fathers. Biological fatherhood is available through heterosexual intercourse or donor insemination of a surrogate mother. 'Social' fatherhood can be achieved through several routes including fostering, adoption, and co-parenting of a partner's biological child. Participants in a study of gay fathers by Berkowitz and Marsiglio (2007) had created their families in diverse ways, including various forms of adoption, traditional and gestational surrogacy arrangements, and co-parenting with a lesbian woman or women.

As routes to biological gay male parenthood are expensive and often socially and emotionally very difficult to negotiate (Stacey, 2006) most prospective gay male parents pursue social parenthood through fostering and/or adoption. These arrangements are psychologically and organisationally complex for any man and raise additional challenges for men who are gay. Formal procedures are not only bureaucratic and intrusive, but can place gay lifestyles under a particularly probing light. In the United States, variation in legislation across the Union has required gay men to adopt diverse positions in dealing with the authorities, ranging from full disclosure to full concealment of their status. Mallon's sample of gay fathers varied in the position they had to take to embark on fostering/adoption procedures. A number were advised against openly declaring their sexuality by the social services staff administering the process, who were themselves supportive of gay fathers but were working within a system which was not. One father recounted how in the very final hours of a process which had taken several months, he and his partner dare not tempt fate; rather than risking losing their child in the last moments of the transition, he hid upstairs in a neighbour's house, watching from a window while the child was formally handed over to his partner as the legal, and officially single, adoptive parent. It was only when he had seen the welfare officers leave the house that he raced to join the new family unit (Mallon, 2004).

Whether gay men become fathers through biological or social routes, the process requires a high level of deliberation and logistical planning. Berkowitz and Marsiglio observe that 'a gay man's journey to fatherhood is much more purposeful than the often spontaneous and even accidental process of fatherhood for heterosexual men' (Berkowitz and Marsiglio, 2007: 376). While the formalities required are demanding, Mallon found that some men pursuing fostering and/or adoption felt that the life-lessons they had obtained through living as a gay man had made them better equipped to deal with obstacles than heterosexual couples might be (Mallon, 2004: 57–8). The impact of planning and deliberation is not necessarily negative: the commitment required to negotiate logistical and discriminatory challenges might benefit families created by gay men:

> 'I think the biggest difference between us and straight dads is that there aren't any mistakes or unwanted children . . . it is really a conscious decision that you have to jump through hoops to accomplish, either financially or legally . . . we might not be able to trace exactly when we thought about it, but once you do decide, it is like a mission to get it done.'
>
> (Berkowitz and Marsiglio, 2007: 376)

The process through which gay men become fathers has implications for their own experience of fatherhood and for the family they create. Stacey (2006) noted the collision of class and race for gay men fostering and/or adopting in the United States, where prospective parents are disproportionately white and 'available' children are disproportionately not. Gay men who parent through fostering and adoption processes therefore have high rates of, often very visible, trans-racial parenthood. The multi-racial character of such families 'visually signals the predominantly social character of gay parenting' (Stacey, 2006: 30). In Strah's 'celebration' of gay dads, 'Derek' comments that as Filipino/black man, partnered by a Japanese-American, with three adopted children each of different racial origins, 'we are constantly outing ourselves. Stacked up, we look like a Benetton ad' (Strah, 2004: 109).

The practice of fathering

We currently have more evidence of why and how gay men choose to become fathers than evidence of how they practise fathering. Recent qualitative studies are helping to expand this picture. Mallon's account covers the many stages of family formation from the homecoming of the adopted/fostered child, the adaptation of the household from child-free to child-focused, and the changes and stresses – and enrichment – that ensue. He also steps outside the immediate workings of the family unit to examine how gay parents and their offspring connect to, and (re-)negotiate, their relationships with family, friends and community (Mallon, 2004). Strah's profile of 44 gay dads in 24 families similarly provides multiple cameos of the day-to-day realities of living as gay male parents with children.

Mallon and Strah emphasise how parenting requires a deep-rooted shift in the social positioning of gay men. Most prospective parents find that becoming a parent changes life but the change that fathering brings for gay men is of an order far beyond that commonly encountered by heterosexual parents. The journey into heterosexual parenthood may be an unimaginable adventure for individual men and women, but it is a normalised social expectation – a move into the next 'phase' of the 'life cycle' (however destabilised this may now be – Roberts, 1999) rather than a departure from the expected trajectory. Parenthood confirms and consolidates heterosexual identities, roles and relationships. It does the opposite for gay fathers. Fathering contradicts much of what is expected of gay men and means connecting with a world they had not been part of, may actively have rejected – and may indeed have been rejected by.

Fatherhood for gay men requires connecting with a world of parenting that is defined wholly on heterosexual terms. Fathering can therefore bring what Strah terms 'another' kind of isolation – 'this time from the gay community (Strah, 2004: 4). Already distanced from many elements of heterosexual society (including in some cases being temporarily or permanently alienated from their own biological families), gay fathers now find themselves more in tune with straight parents than childless gay men. While the new affinity they feel with heterosexual families is largely self-explanatory – 'After all, they have joined the Tribe of Parents' (Strah, 2004: 4) – the sense of distancing from the gay community can cause confusion and regret. 'Gay fathers sense that their gay friends are no longer interested in them, a recognition that becoming parents has so changed their lives and sensibilities that they no longer "fit" in that community – or at least, that the community doesn't seem to think they fit' (Strah, 2004: 5).

Encountering the world of parenting does not only mean entering a heterosexual sphere: it also means, first and foremost, encountering the world of mothering. The feminisation of parenting is almost universally evident: one of Mallon's interviewees referred to early childhood being 'just a female, mommy-driven culture' (2004: 69–70) and one of Strah's to the power and dominance of 'the mommy mafia' (2004: 97). Infant and pre-school community and public service provisions are dominated by mothers with little father presence. We are far more accustomed to seeing women taking on highly involved parenting than men.

Gay fathers encounter mothers and mothering more commonly than they encounter heterosexual fathers and fathering. Many are entering fatherhood as a primary parent, in a role more akin to that commonly taken by females. Qualitative accounts position gay men as highly engaged fathers, more comparable to heterosexual mothers than fathers in their levels of involvement with, and focus on, their children. Even in gay partnerships in which one man continues in employment while the other takes on a full-time, stay-at-home parenting role, the high level of deliberation and concerted effort required to bring a child into the family unit in the first place is associated with a continuing high level of involvement by the 'working' father.

Many gay men become very conscious of the lack of visibility of high paternal involvement. One way in which this manifests itself is by the reaction of others in public places. Several of Mallon's gay fathers reported interventions by women in areas such as parks, playgrounds and shopping centres who felt entitled to intervene – to help, advise or question – when they saw a man alone caring for a child. There was an underlying assumption that men did not usually perform such tasks and therefore could not be expected to be fully confident or competent about doing so. 'The whole experience really pointed out to me how unaccustomed we are as a society to seeing men in the role of caretakers for children' (Mallon, 2004: 69). While gay fathers reported responding courteously to such encounters, they often regarded them as presumptuous and also felt that their identity as a father was under scrutiny.

Many gay fathers seem to need to prove that they are indeed 'suitable' fathers – striving to be the best, the 'super parents' who are 'gooder than good' (Mallon, 2004; 72). This can manifest itself as very active parenting, in several ways and for several reasons. Partly it is driven by the sheer strength of commitment to a child that has been 'acquired' through lengthy and demanding processes, in the face of strong practical and cultural constraints, and has become the focal point of life. In an atmosphere of uncertain social acceptability, gay fathers might be expected to adopt a low profile – but there are multiple accounts within the literature of gay men not only joining, but leading, activities derived from their parenting roles e.g. in school contexts, in the community, in informal play arrangements and within their own homes. Mallon (2004) cites multiple examples of gay fathers assuming a high profile in local parenting activities – starting up a play network that endures throughout the pre-school years; being elected to lead their school's PTA; taking other community positions.

These developments consolidate gay fathers' position within the local (heterosexual) community and are one of the reasons that Strah suggests that gay fathering heralds not just a change for individuals but 'a sea change in our community'. The emergence and growth in gay parenting not only affects men who undertake it, but is impacting on the gay community as a whole through these new connections. By building a bridge to the heterosexual world, Strah suggests that parenting is connecting gay men to the community at large (2004: 5).

In negotiating this broadening of identity and connection, leisure emerges as a significant site. The link between leisure and the onset of parenthood is well-established within leisure studies research: it is commonplace for parents of both sexes to report on the loss of personal leisure through parenting, especially for the primary parent (usually the mother). With this loss of leisure goes a loss of identity – the sense of self that is achieved when we have the opportunity to express our preferences and individuality through freely chosen preferred activities. The care of children absorbs much of the time and energy previously invested in these activities. Gay fathers however appear to experience a more extreme challenge to identity through the loss of the leisure patterns of their child-free days. Stacey (2006) cites Dan Savage, 'gay sex columnist and comic', ruminating on the 'cultural stakes' when he and his partner embarked on parenthood through adoption: the point is more serious than the tone!:

> 'Terry and I would be giving up certain things that, for better or worse, define what it means to be gay. Good things, things we enjoyed and that had value and meaning for us. Like promiscuity.'
>
> (1999: 26; in Stacey, 2006)

Fadiman (1983) has referred to the 'double closet' affecting gay fathers: they are closeted not only from the heterosexual world but now also from a gay community which is often defined as overtly celebrating a culture of youthfulness and freedom from commitments (Bigner and Jacobsen, 1989; in Barrett and Tasker, 2002).

While all parents experience their leisure being re-oriented by children, for gay fathers this entails joining the patterns that have evolved around heterosexual parenting. Mallon reports a father describing how holidays have changed (family hotels instead of guest houses), eating out has changed (now taking place in family restaurants and fast-food outlets that welcome children – 'I didn't know these places existed'), and a whole array of new activities has been embarked on: going to play-parks, Disney, to Madison Square to see Sesame Street Live, visiting stores to see Santa (Mallon, 2004: 132). The challenges of developing child-focused leisure can also be experienced at home, as when one pair of fathers found their adopted son's sporting talent taking them into the very territory they had avoided in their own youth:

> 'As he grew, Mack's athletic abilities were in direct contrast to our own. We were always the last picked for sports and the dreaded gym class. Bill [other father] spent his childhood lip-syncing to Judy Garland records and now we are raising a jock . . .'
>
> (Mallon 2004: 125)

Berkowitz and Marsiglio report a parallel story:

> Marc, the proud single father of a 4-year-old girl explained, 'if I have a boy, will I be as good as a role model? You know, dads take their sons to ball games and things like that, which I am just not into . . . if I had a boy, it might be somewhat difficult to do that "macho" role model.' Because

Marc was never the stereotypical masculine athlete, he questioned whether he could participate with his imagined son in 'normal' male-bonding activities.

(Berkowitz and Marsiglio, 2007: 375)

Gay men broadening concepts of fathering

The accounts above emphasise the centrality of the parenting role to gay men who embark on it. By becoming very active parents many gay fathers appear to ideally model the contemporary expectation of involved fathering. In many respects their construction of fathering is a composite parenting role, undertaken by men and therefore labelled as fathering but more closely fulfilling the functions conventionally associated with mothering. This raises questions about whether the appropriation of parenting by 'the mommy culture' – and the institutionalisation of this in state policy that prioritises maternity over paternity – stand as an obstacle to (all) men's fuller involvement.

Schacher (in Strah, 2004: 5) has suggested that gay fathers are 'writing their own script' for parenting – partly because they have to, and partly because they are able to. In creating new family formations 'they blend the daddy and mommy roles into one totality, then split the totality of parenting roles and allocate those roles by inclination or talent or convenience'. Through this they remodel masculinities and remodel fathering. Stacey goes further, positioning gay men and lesbians at the forefront of contemporary trans-formations of families and intimate relationships, and seeing gay fathering as evidence of a 'creative if controversial' reconfiguration of male parent-hood (Stacey, 2006: 28). At an ideological level, however, the fathering practices that have been described above chime very closely with expressed expectations of more egalitarian, shared co-parenting by heterosexual parents. At the level of practice gay men appear closer than many fathers to *practising* involved fathering.

Conclusions: paths ahead for research into fathering, sport and leisure

This chapter has drawn attention to the potential to diversify our study of fathering, sport and leisure. Extending research to address some of the miss-ing populations will do more than extend the existing picture: it will also encourage deeper critical reflection on the processes through which more familiar patterns are reproduced. Recognising how differently the ideologies and practices of fathering are constructed in other settings, and the challenge this presents to our concepts, theories and methodological approaches, can liberate us from entrenched assumptions.

Endnote

Tess Kay

In westernised societies four-fifths of adult men become fathers: in countries where fertility is less regulated, the proportion is higher. Qualitatively, fatherhood can be a transforming and defining experience for men (Palkovitz, 2002). It is a role that sits at the interface of the labour market and the family domain, bridges the public and private sphere, and lies at the heart of gender relations. Analysts of fathers, fatherhood and fathering are therefore accustomed to situating 'fatherhood' in relation to men's work and their family responsibilities. But this volume has argued that we need to take a more critical look at the activities through which parenting is undertaken and to distinguish between those aspects of parental responsibility that encompass essential care activities and those that lie in the leisure domain. For fathers especially, it is within leisure that most interactions with children occur.

What have we learned from the studies reported here about fathering through sport and leisure? Many things, which include:

- That the parameters of fathering are changing and the contexts within which men parent are diverse.
- That the single biggest shift in the profile of fathering over three decades has been the sizeable increase in non-resident fathers.
- That patterns of multiple social and economic disadvantage mean that men who live within the same nation, region or even in close proximity within the same locality, may effectively be parenting in different worlds, especially when material divisions are associated with cultural and ethnic divides.
- That there has been a significant ideological shift towards 'involved' fathering and this is widely referred to by western commentators and also experienced acutely by fathers aware of the expectations surrounding their role. This concept of involved fathering is not however universally held within the industrialised nations and appears a poor match for the realities of many lower educated fathers, fathers from low income groups and fathers from some ethnic groups.
- That outside the industrialised nations the concept of involved fathering may have very little application indeed, especially among cultures where

social and collective fathering are practised. This heritage may also be a continuing influence on the fathering practice of some minority groups living in the west.

- That the expectation that fathers will be 'involved' parents sits alongside traditional expectations that they will be the main household earner. Fathers have shed little of their old provider responsibilities.

- That involved fathering through sport and leisure is not in fact a modern or contemporary phenomenon, but a long-standing component of father–child relationships; its lengthy tradition during times when fathers were expected to be less engaged with their children speaks to its innate suitability for father–child interactions.

- That in comparison with previous generations, contemporary fathers' involvement with their children through sport and leisure takes place within a much more demanding culture of child-centred family life, in which parents are expected to prioritise children continually, in every way – changed expectations that are especially pronounced for fathers.

- That in addition to the popular and policy discourse of involved fathering, fathers may be subject to other ideological influences (e.g. faith and/ or cultural) and will replicate these in their parenting. In some cases these will reflect quite different values and produce different practices.

- That fathers use sport and leisure to enact their fathering ideology. Sport and leisure are seen as areas that provide opportunities for shared activities and experience, build family relationships, and nurture development and skills among children.

- That the opportunities provided by sport and leisure are especially significant to non-resident fathers for whom positive experiences during contact time with their children are important to sustaining a relationship in difficult practical circumstances. Being able to participate in a range of leisure is a positive contributor to satisfaction levels.

- That the prominence of sport and leisure within fathering may justify describing some men's parenting as 'leisure-based'.

There has been considerable consistency across this volume in relation to the above issues. All authors have reinforced the message that leisure and sport are, indeed, central areas for fathering. At the same time it has been evident that much more diverse models of fatherhood lie beyond the scope of the current studies. Chapter 13 has already considered the need to address the very different cultural and religious settings of fatherhood, and the experience of fathering within gay partnerships. There are other omissions however, relating not to fathers' characteristics but to how they practise fathering.

While this book has not been intended as a celebration *per se* of fathering through sport and leisure, most of its commentary is pretty upbeat. Most chapters focus on the valuable, positive, life- and family-enhancing impacts of sport and leisure shared by children and their fathers. It has been acknowledged that some fathers are less involved, but these observations have usually been made in the context of sympathetic accounts of the multiply constrained circumstances in which these men live. But the problems surrounding fathering should not be denied: there are many very negative models of fathering to be found – fathers who are not involved with their children and fathers who do not want to be involved (and in the worst cases, fathers who may be abusive). It would seem important to investigate further the perspectives and practices of fathers who are resistant to the ideologies of involvement.

The changing conditions of fatherhood and the implications for social support are making fatherhood an increasingly prominent social policy issue and a growing focus for social science research. Diversity and change in fatherhood are central to changing masculinities, changing family forms and changing gender relations, and contribute to the patterns and ideologies of family life that are defining features of cultural identity in increasingly multicultural societies. Connell (2000) refers to the internal complexity and contradiction of masculinities as states of being: masculinities are often in tension, within and without. In fatherhood, men are increasingly confronting the collision of the traditional masculine provider with the traditional feminine nurturer. Engaging with their children through leisure is emerging as a prominent strategy.

References

Aaron, D., Kriska, A., Dearwater, S., Anderson, R., Olsen, T., Cauley, J. and Laporte, R. (1993) 'The epidemiology of leisure physical activity in an adolescent population', *Medicine & Science in Sports & Exercise*, 25, 7: 847–53.

Abbott, D.A., Berry, M., and Meredith, W. H. (1990) 'Religious belief and practice: a potential asset in helping families', *Family Relations*, 39: 443–8.

Acosta, R.V. and Carpenter, L.J. (2006) *Women in Intercolleogiate Sport: a Longitudinal National Study: Twenty-Nine Year Update, 1977–2002*. Smith College's Project on Women and Social Change and Brooklyn College of the City University of New York. Online. Available. HTTP: http://www.acostacarpenter.org/2008%20Summary%20Final.pdf (accessed 18 March 2008).

Adelman, M.L. (1986) *A Sporting Time: New York City and the Rise of Modern Athletics, 1820–1870*, Urbana, IL: University of Illinois Press.

Adler, P.A. and Adler, P. (1998) *Peer Power: Preadolescent Culture and Identity*, New Brunswick, NJ: Rutgers University Press.

Alderson, P. (1994) 'Researching children's rights to integrity', in B. Mayall (ed.), *Children's Childhoods, Observed and Experienced*, London and Washington: Falmer.

Alderson, P. and Morrow, V. (2004) *Ethics, Social Research and Consulting with Children and Young People*, London: Barnado's.

Aldous, J., Mulligan, G. and Biarnason, T. (1998) 'Fathering over time: what makes the difference?', *Journal of Marriage and the Family*, 60: 809–20.

Aligia, C. (2005) *Gender gaps in the reconciliation between work and family life, Statistics in Focus 2004/5*, Luxemburg: Eurostat.

Allen, W.D. and Connor, M. (1997) 'An African American perspective on generative fathering', in A. J. Hawkins and D.C. Dollahite (eds), *Generative Fathering Beyond Deficit Perspectives*, Thousand Oaks: Sage.

Amato, P.R. and Gilbreth, J.G. (1999) 'Nonresident fathers and children's well-being: a meta-analysis', *Journal of Marriage and the Family*, 61: 557–73.

Amato, P.R. and Keith, B. (1991) 'Parental divorce and the well-being of children: a meta-analysis', *Psychological Bulletin*, 110: 26–46.

Amato, P.R. and Keith, B. (2001) 'Children of divorce in the 1990s: an update of the Amato and Keith (1991) meta-analysis', *Journal of Family Psychology*, 15, 3: 355–70.

Anonymous (2001) Book description accompanying *The Final Season: Fathers, Sons, and One Last Season in a Classic American Ballpark* by T. Stanton. Retrieved November 6, 2003, from http://amazon.com.

Arab-Moghaddam, N., Henderson, K.A. and Sheikholeslami, R. (2007) 'Women's leisure and constraints to participation: Iranian perspectives', *Journal of Leisure Research*, 39: 109–27.

Aronson, A. and Kimmel, M. (2001) 'The saviors and the saved: masculine redemption in contemporary films', in P. Lehman (ed.), *Masculinity: Bodies, Movies, Culture*, New York: Routledge, pp. 43–50.

Australian Bureau of Statistics (1998) *How Australians Use Their Time*, Canberra: Australian Bureau of Statistics.

Australian Bureau of Statistics (2003) *Australian Social Trends 2003*, Canberra: Australian Bureau of Statistics.

Australian Bureau of Statistics (2004a) *Australian Social Trends 2004*, Canberra: Australian Bureau of Statistics.

Australian Bureau of Statistics (2004b) *Family Characteristics Australia 2003*, Canberra: Australian Bureau of Statistics.

Australian Bureau of Statistics (2006) *Australian Social Trends 2006*, Canberra: Australian Bureau of Statistics.

Australian Bureau of Statistics (2007) *Family formation: Trends in marriage and divorce 2005*, Canberra: Australian Bureau of Statistics.

Australian Bureau of Statistics (2008a) *Australian Social Trends 2008*, Canberra: Australian Bureau of Statistics.

Australian Bureau of Statistics (2008b) *How Australians Use Their Time 2006*, Canberra: Australian Bureau of Statistics.

Australian Bureau of Statistics (2008c) *2006 Population Characteristics, Aboriginal and Torres Strait Islander Australians, Cat no. 4713.0*, Canberra: Australian Bureau of Statistics.

Australian Government (2002) *Intergenerational Report 2002–03. Budget Paper No. 5*, Canberra: Commonwealth of Australia.

Averill, P.M. and Power, T.G. (1995) 'Parental attitudes and children's experiences in soccer: correlates of effort and enjoyment', *International Journal of Behavioral Development*, 18: 263–76.

Babbie, E. (2002) *The Basics of Social Research*, 2nd edn, Belmont, CA: Wadsworth/ Thomson.

Backett, K. (1990) 'The negotiation of fatherhood', in C. L. M. O'Brien (ed.), *Reassessing Fatherhood: New Observations on Fathers and the Modern Family*, London: Sage.

Bagilhole, B. (1994) *Women, Work and Equal Opportunity: Underachievement in the Civil Service*, Aldershot: Avebury.

Bailey, S. (2002) *Nonresidential Parenting after Divorce*, Montana: Montana State University Extension Service.

Ballard, M.R. (2006) 'The sacred responsibilities of parenthood', *Ensign*, March, 26–33.

Ballard, R. (1982) 'South Asian families', in R.N. Rapoport, M.P. Fogarty and R. Rapoport (eds), *Families in Britain*, London: Routledge and Kegan Paul.

Barclay, L.M. and Lupton, D. (1999) 'The experiences of new fathers: a socio-cultural analysis', *Journal of Advanced Nursing*, 29 (4): 1013–20.

Barnett, R.C. and Baruch, G.K. (1987) 'Determinants of fathers' participation in family work', *Journal of Marriage and the Family*, 49: 29–40.

Barnett, R.C. and Rivers, C. (1996) *She Works, He Works: How Two Income Families are Happy, Healthy and Thriving*, Cambridge, MA: Harvard University Press.

Barot, R., Bradley, H. and Fenton, S. (1999) *Ethnicity, Gender and Social Change*, London: Macmillan Press Ltd.

Barrett, H. and Tasker, F. (2002) 'Gay fathers and their children: what we know and what we need to know', *Lesbian & Gay Psychology Review*, 3, 1: 3–10.

Barth, G. (1980). *City people: the rise of modern city culture in nineteenth-century America*, New York: Oxford University Press.

Bartkowski, J.P. and Xu, X. (2000) 'Distant patriarchs or expressive dads? The discourse and practice of fathering in conservative Protestant families', *The Sociological Quarterly*, 41: 465–85.

Barton, B. (1914, May 2) 'When your son is a fool', *Outlook*, 107: 37–40.

Barzun, J. (1954) *God's Country and Mine: A Declaration of Love Spiced With A Few Harsh Words*, Boston: Little, Brown.

Basit, T. N. (1997) 'I want more freedom but not too much: British Muslim girls and the dynamism of family values', *Gender and Education*, 9: 425–39.

Batson, M. and Marks, L. (2008) 'Making the connection between prayer, faith, and forgiveness in Roman Catholic families', *The Qualitative Report*, 13: 394–415.

BBC News (2001) 'Sudan pushes polygamy', Wednesday, 15 August, 2001, 20:28 GMT 21:28 UK Online. Available http://news.bbc.co.uk/1/hi/world/africa/1493309.stm (accessed 15 October 2008).

Beishon, S., Modood, T. and Virdee, S. (1998) *Ethnic Minority Families*, London: Policy Studies Institute.

Belenky, M.F., Clinchy, B.M., Goldberger, N.R. and Tarule, J.M. (1986) *Women's ways of knowing: the development of self, voice, and mind*, New York: Basic Books.

Bell, M. and Wilson, K. (2006) 'Children's views of family group conferences', *British Journal of Social Work*, 36: 671–81.

Bella, L. (1989) 'Women and leisure: beyond androcentrism', in E.L. Jackson and T.L. Burton (eds), *Understanding Leisure and Recreation: Mapping the Past, Charting the Future*, State College, PA: Venture Publishing.

Bella, L. (1992) *The Christmas Imperative*, Halifax: Fernwood.

Bellah, R.N., Madsen, R., Sullivan, W.M., Swidler, A. and Tipton, S.M. (1985) *Habits of the Heart: Individualism and Commitment in American Life*, New York: Harper and Row.

Benson, E.T. (1981) 'Great things required of their fathers', *Ensign*, 11: 34–6.

Berg, E.C., Trost, M., Schneider, I.E. and Allison, M.T. (2001) 'Dyadic exploration of the relationship of leisure satisfaction, leisure time, and gender to relationship satisfaction', *Leisure Science*, 23: 35–46.

Berkowitz, D. and Marsiglio, W. (2007) 'Gay men: negotiating procreative, father, and family identities', *Journal of Marriage and Family* 69: 366–81.

Berthoud, R. (2000) *Family Formation in Multi-cultural Britain: three patterns of diversity*, Colchester: Institute for Social and Economic Research, University of Essex.

Bhopal, K. (1999) 'South Asian women and arranged marriages in East London', in R. Barot, H. Bradley and S. Fenton (eds), *Ethnicity, Gender and Social Change*, London: Macmillan Press Ltd.

Bianchi, S. M., Robinson, J. P. and Milkie, M.A. (2006) *Changing Rhythms of American Family Life*, New York: Russell Sage.

Bigner, J.J. and Jacobsen, R.B. (1989) 'The value of children to gay and heterosexual fathers', *Journal of Homosexuality*, 12, 1: 163–72.

Bittman, M. and Pixley, J. (1997) *The Double Life of the Family*, St. Leonards: Allen and Unwin.

Bloomfield, J. (2003) *Australia's Sporting Success: The Inside Story*, Sydney: The University of New South Wales Press.

Blumer, H. (1969) *Symbolic Interactionism: Perspective and Method*, Berkeley: Prentice-Hall.

Bluthardt, R.F. (1987) 'Fenway Park and the golden age of the baseball park, 1909–1915', *Journal of Popular Culture*, 21: 43–52.

Bolla, P., Dawson, D. and Harrington, M. (1991) 'The leisure experience of women in Ontario', *Journal of Applied Recreation Research*, 16, 4: 322–48.

Boswell, J., and Barrett, R. (1990) *How To Dad*, New York: Dell.

Bourdieu, P. (1978) 'Sport and social class', *Social Science Information*, 17, 6: 819–40.

Bourdieu, P. (1984) *Distinction: A Social Critique of the Judgement of Taste*, Cambridge, MA: Harvard University Press.

Bourdieu, P. (1985) 'The genesis of the concepts of "Habitus" and "Field" ', *Sociocriticism*, 2, 2: 11–24.

Bourdieu, P. and Wacquant, L. (1992) *An Invitation to Reflexive Sociology*, Chicago, IL: University of Chicago Press.

Bourke, C. and Edwards, B. (1998) 'Family and kinship', in C. Bourke, E. Bourke and W. Edwards (eds), *Aboriginal Australia*, Brisbane: University of Queensland Press.

Brackenridge, C. (2001) *Spoilsports: Understanding and Preventing Sexual Exploitation in Sport*, New York and London: Routledge.

Brannen, J. and Moss, P. (1991) *Managing Mothers: Dual-Earner Households After Maternity Leave*, London: Unwin Hyman.

Brannen, J., Lewis, S., Nilsen, A. and Smithson, J. (eds) (2002) *Young Europeans, Work and Family: Futures in Transition*, London: Routledge.

Brown, B.W., Michelson, E.A., Halle, T.G. and Moore, K.A. (2001) 'Child Trends: Research Brief', June. Online. Available. HTTP: http://12.109.133.224/Files/June_2001.pdf (accessed 30 December 2004).

Brown, C. (2001) *The Death of Christian Britain*, London: Routledge.

Brown, P. and Warner-Smith, P. (2005) 'The Taylorisation of family time: an effective strategy in the struggle to "manage" work and life?', *Annals of Leisure Research*, 8: 75–90.

Brown, S.L. and Bumpus, M.F. (1998) *Men in Families: Looking Back, Looking Forward*, Mahwah, NJ: Lawrence Erlbaum Associates.

Brustad, R.J. (1996) 'Parental and peer influence on children's psychological development through sport', in F.L. Smoll and R.E. Smith (eds), *Children and Youth in Sport: A Biopsychosocial Perspective*, Madison, WI: Brown & Benchmark.

Buchanan, A., Hunt, J., Bretherton, H. and Bream, V. (2001) *Families in Conflict: The Family Court Welfare Service: The Perspectives of Children and Parents*, Bristol: The Policy Press.

Burawoy, M. et al. (2000) *Global Ethnography: Forces, Connections, and Imaginations in a Postmodern World*, Berkeley and Los Angeles, CA: University of California Press.

Burrows, R. (2003) 'How the other half lives: An exploratory analysis of the relationship between poverty and home-ownership in Britain', *Urban Studies*, 40 (7): 1223–42.

Burwell, B. (2003, August 17) 'Dad knew best: You can't strike out when it comes to baseball', *St. Louis Post-Dispatch*. Online. Available. Retrieved October 20 2003, from http://web.lexis.nexis.com (accessed 20 October 2003).

Butler, I., Robinson, M. and Scanlan, L. (2005) *Children's Involvement in Family Decision-Making*, York: Joseph Rowntree Foundation.

Cabrera, N.J., Tamis-LeMonda, C.S., Lamb, M.E. and Boller, K. (1999) 'Measuring father involvement in the Early Head Start evaluation: a multidimensional conceptualisation', paper presented at the National Conference on Health Statistics, Washington, DC, 2–4 August.

Carlson, J.E. (1979) 'The family and recreation: toward a theoretical development', in W. Burr, R. Hill, F. Nye and I. Reeves (eds), *Contemporary Theories about the Family: Research-based theories*, New York: The Free Press, pp. 439–52.

Caruna, C. and Ferro, A. (2004). 'Points of convergence', in B. Smyth (ed.), *Parent–Child Contact and Post-Separation Parenting Arrangements*, Research Report No. 9, Melbourne: Australian Institute of Family Studies (AIFS).

Casper, L. and Bianchi, S. (2002) *Continuity and Change in the American Family*, Thousand Oaks, CA: Sage Publications.

Central Intelligence Agency (CIA) (2008) *World Fact Book*, Washington, DC: Central Intelligence Agency.

Centre for Research for Families and Relationships (CRFR) (2007) *Working fathers in Europe: earning and caring?*, Research Briefing 30, Edinburgh: CRFR.

Chafetz, J. and Kotarba, J. (1995) 'Son worshippers: the role of little league mothers in recreating gender', *Studies in Symbolic Interaction*, 18: 217–41.

Chapin, H. and Chapin, S. (1974) (Music and Lyrics) Cat's in the cradle. On Harry Chapin *Verities and Balderdash* CD, released 1974.

Charmez, K. (2002) 'Qualitative interviewing and ground theory analysis', in J.F. Bubrium and J. Holstein, *Handbook of interview research: context and method*, Newbury Park: Sage.

Chick, G. (2000) 'Opportunities for cross-cultural comparative research on leisure', *Leisure Sciences*, 22: 79–91.

Chick, G. and Dong, E. (2005) 'Cultural constraints on leisure', in E. Jackson (ed.), *Constraints on Leisure*, State College, PA: Venture Publishing, pp. 169–83.

Close, Sharron M. (2005) 'Dating violence prevention in middle school and high school youth', *Journal of Child and Adolescent Psychiatric Nursing*, 18, 1: 2–9.

Clydesdale, T.T. (1997) 'Family behaviors among early U.S. baby boomers: exploring the effects of religion and income change, 1965–1982', *Social Forces*, 76: 605–35.

Coakley, J. (2006) 'The good father: parental expectations and youth sports', *Leisure Studies*, 25, 2: 153–64.

Codding, I. (2002). 'Do I really need a reason? Bullz-eye.com: The Guys' Portal to the Web'. Online. Available http://www.bullz-eye.com/coddingI2002/041701.htm (accessed 23 October 2003).

Cohen, A.B. and Hill, P.C. (2007) 'Religion as culture: religious individualism and collectivism among American Catholics, Jews, and Protestants', *Journal of Personality*, 75, 4, 709–42.

Coltrane, S. (2001) 'Marketing the marriage "solution": misplaced simplicity in the politics of fatherhood', *Sociological Perspectives*, 44, 4: 387–418.

Coltrane, S. and Adams, M. (2001) 'Men's family work: child-centered fathering and the sharing of domestic labor', in R. Hertz and N.L. Marshall, *Working families: The transformation of the American home*, Berkeley: University of California Press.

Commonwealth of Australia (2006a) *Family Law Amendment (Shared Parental Responsibility) Bill 2006, Revised Explanatory Memorandum*, Canberra: Commonwealth of Australia.

Commonwealth of Australia (2006b) 'Every picture tells a story', *Report on the Inquiry into Child Custody Arrangements in the Event of Family Separation, House of Representatives Standing Committee on Family and Community Affairs*, December, Canberra: Commonwealth of Australia.

Connell, R.W. (1987) *Gender and Power: Society, the Person and Sexual Politics*, Cambridge: Polity in association with Blackwell.

Connell, R.W. (1995) *Masculinities*, Cambridge: Polity Press.

Connell, R.W. (2000) *The Men and The Boys*, Cambridge: Polity Press.

Connell, R.W. (2002) *Gender*, Malden, MA: Blackwell Publishing Ltd.

Connor, M.E. and White, J.L. (2006) *Black Fathers: An Invisible Presence in America*, Hillsdale, NJ: Erlbaum.

Cooksey, E.C. and Craig, P.H. (1998) 'Parenting from a distance: the effects of paternal characteristics on contact between nonresidential fathers and their children', *Demography*, 35: 187–200.

Cowan, P.A. (1991) 'Individual and family transitions: a proposal for a new definition', in P. A. Cowan and M. Hetherington (eds), *Family Transitions*, Hillsdale, NJ: Lawrence Erlbaum Associates.

Cozine, G. (2003) 'Pop fly in the son', *Elysian Fields Quarterly*. Online. Available http://www.efqreview.com/NewFiles/v20n2/mytumatbat.html (accessed 20 October 2003).

Craig, L. (2004) 'Time to care: a comparison of how couple and sole parent households allocate time to work and children', Social Policy Research Centre, Discussion Paper No. 133, Sydney: University of New South Wales.

Craig, L. (2006) 'Does father care mean fathers share?: a comparison of how mothers and fathers in intact families spend time with children', *Gender and Society*, 20: 259–81.

Craig, L. (2007) *Contemporary Motherhood: The Impact of Children On Adult Time*, Aldershot: Ashgate.

Crawford, D.W. and Huston, T.L. (1993) 'The impact of the transition to parenthood on marital leisure', *Personality and Social Psychology Bulletin*, 19: 39–46.

Crawford, D.W., Houts, R.M., Huston, T.L. and George, L.J. (2002) 'Compatibility, leisure, and satisfaction in marital relationships', *Journal of Marriage and Family*, 64, 433–49.

Crouter, A.C., Bumpus, M.F., Head, M.R. and McHale, S.M. (2001) 'Implications of overwork and overload for the quality of men's family relationships', *Journal of Marriage and Family*, 63, 2: 404–16.

Culture.gov.au *The Dreaming*. Online. Available http://www.acn.net.au/articles/indigenous/dreamtime/ (accessed 10 November 2008).

Cummins, P. (2001) 'Fathers playing catch with daughters', *Santa Monica Mirror*. Online. Available http://www.smmirror.com/volume3/issue12/fathers_playing_catch.asp (accessed 26 July 2003).

Cunneen, C. and Libesman, T. (1995) *Indigenous People and the Law in Australia*, Sydney: Butterworths.

Daly, K.J. (1996a) 'Spending time with kids: meanings of family time for fathers', *Family Relations* 45: 466–76.

Daly, K.J. (1996b) *Families and Time: Keeping Pace in a Hurried Culture*, Thousand Oaks, CA: Sage.

Daly, K.J. (2001) 'Deconstructing family time: from ideology to lived experience', *Journal of Marriage and Family*, 63, 2: 283–94.

Daly, K.J. (2002) 'Time, gender, and the negotiation of family schedules', *Symbolic Interaction*, 25: 323–42.

Daly, K.J. (2004) 'The Changing Culture of Parenting, Contemporary Family Trends'.

Online. Available www.vifamily.ca/library/cft/parenting.html on 10/09/2004 (accessed on 27 June 2007).

Davie, G. (1990) 'Believing without belonging: is this the future of religion in Britain?', *Social Compass* 37, 4: 455–69, cited in Voas, D. and Crockett, A. (2005) 'Religion in Britain: neither believing nor belonging', *Sociology*, 39, 1: 11–28.

Davie, G. (1994) *Religion in Britain Since 1945: Believing Without Belonging*, Oxford: Blackwell, cited in Voas, D. and Crockett, A. (2005) 'Religion in Britain: neither believing nor belonging', *Sociology*, 39, 1: 11–28.

Davies, B. (2003) *Frogs and Snails and Feminist Tales: Preschool Children and Gender*, revised edn, Cresskill, NJ: Hampton Press Inc.

Davis, J. (1998) 'Understanding the meaning of children: a reflexive process', *Children and Society*, 12: 325–35.

Dawson, A. (2006) 'East is East, Except When It's West: The Easternization Thesis and the Western Habitus', *Journal of Religion and Society*, Volume 8. Online. Available http://moses.creighton.edu/JRS/2006/2006-5.html (accessed 1 November 2008).

Day, R.D. and Lamb, M.E. (eds) (2004) *Conceptualizing and measuring father involvement*, Mahwah, NJ: Lawrence Erlbaum Associates.

Daylight saving time (n.d.). Online. Available http://webexhibits.org/daylightsaving/e.html (accessed 18 July 2004).

De Vaus, D. (2004) *Diversity and Change in Australian Families: Statistical Profiles*, Melbourne: Australian Institute of Family Studies.

Deem, R. (1986) *All Work and No Play? The Sociology of Women and Leisure*, Milton Keynes: Open University Press.

Department of Education and Training, Western Australia (2006) *Families 2: differences between Aboriginal and non-Aboriginal families*. Online. Available http://www.det.wa.gov.au/education/abled/apac/lessons/pdfs/apac029.pdf (accessed 10 November 2008).

Department of Health (1999) *Working Together to Safeguard Children: A Guide to Inter Agency Working to Safeguard and Promote the Welfare of the Child*, London: The Stationery Office.

Department of Health (2001) *The Quality Protects Programme: Transforming Children's Services*, London: Department of Health.

Department of Work and Pensions (2008) *Family Resources Survey*, London: Department of Work and Pensions.

Dermott, E. (2003) 'The "intimate father": Defining paternal involvement', *Sociological Research Online*, 8(4).

Dermott, E. (2008) *Intimate Fatherhood: A Sociological Analysis*, London: Routledge.

Dex, S. and Ward, K. (2007) 'Parental care and employment in early childhood', Working Paper Series 57, London: Equal Opportunities Commission.

Dhami, S. and Sheikh, A. (2000) 'The Muslim family: predicament and promise', *Western Journal of Medicine*, 173, 5: 352–6.

Diamond, M.J. (2007) *My Father Before Me: How Fathers and Sons Influence Each Other Throughout Their Lives*, New York: W.W. Norton and Company Inc.

Dienhart, A. (1998) *Reshaping Fatherhood: The Social Construction of Shared Parenting*, Thousand Oaks, CA: Sage.

Dienhart, A. and Daly, K. (1997) 'Men and women cocreating father involvement in a nongenerative culture', in A. Hawkins and D. Dollahite, *Generative Fathering Beyond Deficit Perspectives*, Thousand Oaks, CA: Sage.

Doherty, W.J., Kouneski, E.F. and Erickson, M.F. (1998) 'Responsible fathering: an overview and conceptual framework', *Journal of Marriage and the Family*, 60, 2: 277–92.

Dollahite, D.C. and Hawkins, A.J. (1998) 'A conceptual ethic of generative fathering', *Journal of Men's Studies*, 71(1), retrieved from Social Science Module database (Document ID: 506106331).

Dorfman, L.T. and Heckert, D.A. (1988) 'Egalitarianism in retired couples: household tasks, decision making, and leisure activities', *Family Relations: Journal of Applied Family and Child Studies*, 37: 73–8.

Doucet, A. (2006) *Do Men Mother?: Fathering, Care, and Domestic Responsibility*, Toronto, Canada: University of Toronto Press.

Dubbert, J.L. (1979) *A Man's Place: Masculinity in Transition*, Englewood Cliffs, NJ: Prentice Hall.

Dudley, J.R. and Stone, G. (2001) *Fathering at Risk: Helping Nonresidential Fathers*, New York: Springer.

Dukes, R.L. and Coakley, J. (2002) 'Parental commitment to competitive swimming', *Free Inquiry in Creative Sociology* 30, 2: 185–97.

Duncan, J. (1997) 'Focus group interviews with elite young athletes, coaches and parents', in J. Kremer, J.K. Trew and S. Ogle (eds), *Young People's Involvement in Sport*, London: Routledge.

Dunn, J. and Deater-Deckard, K. (2001) *Children's Views of their Changing Families*, York: Joseph Rowntree Foundation.

Dunn, J., Cheng, H., O'Connor, T.G. and Bridges, L. (2004) 'Children's perspectives on their relationships with their nonresident fathers: influences, outcomes and implications', *Journal of Child Psychology and Psychiatry*, 45, 3: 553–66.

Duxbury, L. and Higgins, C. (2003) *Work-Life Conflict in Canada in the New Millennium: Status Report*, Ottawa: Health Canada.

Dworkin, S. and Messner, M. (1999) 'Just Do. What?', in *Revisioning Gender*, M. M. Ferree, J. Lorberand and B.B. Hess, Thousand Oaks, CA: Sage Publications.

Dyck, V. and Daly, K. (2006) 'Rising to the challenge: fathers' role in the negotiations of couple time', *Leisure Studies*, 25 (2): 201–17.

Eggebeen, D.J. and Knoester, C. (2001) 'Does fatherhood matter for men?', *Journal of Marriage and the Family* 63, 2: 381–93.

Eichler, M. (1983) *Sexism in Research and Its Policy Implications*, CRIAW Papers/Les Documents de L'ICRAF, Ottawa: The Canadian Research Institute for the Advancement of Women.

Eichler, M. (1997) *Family Shifts: Families, Policies and Gender Equality*, Oxford: Oxford University Press.

Elliot, F.R. (1996) *Gender, Family and Society*, Basingstoke: Macmillan.

Ellison, C.G. (1992) 'Are religious people nice people? Evidence from the National Survey of black Americans', *Social Forces*, 71: 411–30.

Ellison, C.G. (1994) 'Religion, the life stress paradigm, and the study of depression', in J.S. Levin (ed.), *Religion in Aging and Health: Theoretical Foundations and Methodological Frontiers*, Newbury Park, CA: Sage.

Ellison, C.G. and Sherkat, G.E. (1993) 'Obedience and Autonomy: Religion and Parental Values Reconsidered', *Journal for the Scientific Study of Religion* 32/4: 313–29.

Equal Opportunities Commission (2006) *Facts about Women and Men in Great Britain*, Manchester: Equal Opportunities Commission.

Equal Opportunities Commission (2007) *The State of the Modern Family*, Manchester: Equal Opportunities Commission.

Erikson, E.H. (1964) *Insight and Responsibility*, New York: Norton.

Erikson, E.H. (1965) *Childhood and Society*, Middlesex: Penguin Books.

Erikson, E.H. (1971) *Identity Youth and Crisis*, London: Faber and Faber.

Erikson, E.H. (1974) *Dimensions of a New Identity*, New York: Norton.

Erikson, E.H. (1980) 'On the generational cycle', *International Journal of Psychoanalysis*, 61: 212–23.

Espiritu, Yen Le (2001) ' "We don't sleep around like white girls do": family, culture and gender in Filipino American lives', *Signs* 26: 415–40, p. 416.

Espiritu, Yen Le (2003) *Homebound: Filipino American Lives Across Cultures, Communities, and Countries*, Berkeley and Los Angeles, CA: University of California Press.

Evans, V. J. (2004) 'Foreword', in R.D. Day and M.E. Lamb (eds), *Conceptualizing and Measuring Father Involvement*, Hillsdale, NJ: Erlbaum.

'Every Child Matters' (2003) HM Government Green Paper presented by the Chief Secretary to the Treasury, September 2003.

Fadiman, A. (1983) 'The double closet', *Life*, May: 76.

Fatherhood Institute (2008) *Fatherhood Institute Research Summary: Fathers, Mothers, Work and Family*. Online. Available http://www.fatherhoodinstitute.org/index.php?id=10&cID=627 (accessed 25 November 2008).

Faust, J.E. (2006) 'The father who cares', *Liahona*, 30(9): 2–6.

Ferro, A. (2004) ' "Standard" Contact', in Parent–Child contact and Post-separation Parenting Arrangements, Research Report No. 9, ed. B. Smyth. Melbourne: Australian Institute of Family Studies (AIFS).

Finch, J. (1983) *Married to the Job: Wives' Incorporation in Men's Work*, London: George Allen and Unwin.

Fine, G.A. (1987) *With the Boys: Little League Baseball and Preadolescent Culture*, Chicago, IL: The University of Chicago Press.

Firestone, J. and Shelton, B. (1994) 'A comparison of women and men's leisure time: subtle effects of the double day', *Leisure Sciences*, 16: 45–60.

Fitzgerald, H. (2005) 'Still feeling like a spare piece of luggage? Embodied experiences of (dis)ability in physical education and school sport', *Physical Education and Sport Pedagogy*, 10, 1: 41–59.

Fitzgerald, H., Jobling, K. and Kirk, D. (2003) 'Listening to the "voices" of students with severe learning difficulties through a task-based approach to research and learning in physical education', *British Journal of Learning Support*, 19, 3: 123–9.

Fletcher, R. (2008) 'Father-inclusive practice and associated professional competencies', Australian Institute of Family Studies, Melbourne: Australian Family Relationships Clearinghouse.

Fletcher, R., Fairbairn, H. and Pascoe, S. (eds) (2004, March) 'Fatherhood research in Australia', Research Report, Callaghan: The Family Action Centre and The University of Newcastle.

Flouri, E. (2005) *Fathering and Child Outcomes*, Chichester: John Wiley & Sons.

Forna, A. (1998) *Mother of All Myths: How Society Moulds and Constrains Mothers*, London: Harper Collins.

Fowler, J. W. (1981) *Stages of Faith: The Psychology of Human Development and The Quest for Meaning*, New York: Harper Collins, cited in M. Batson and L. Marks

(2008) 'Making the connection between prayer, faith, and forgiveness in Roman Catholic families', *The Qualitative Report*, 13, 3: 394–415.

Fox, G.R. and Murray, V.M. (2000) 'Gender and families: feminist perspectives and family research', *Journal of Marriage and the Family*, 62: 1160–72.

Fox, J. C. (2003) 'A typology of LDS sociopolitical worldviews', *Journal for the Scientific Study of Religion*, 42, 2: 279–89.

Fox, K. (2006) 'Leisure and Indigenous Peoples', *Leisure Studies*, 25, 4: 403–09.

Fraenkel, P. and Wilson, S. (2000) 'Clocks, calendars, and couples: time and the rhythms of relationships', in P. Papp (ed.), *Couples On The Fault Line: New Directions for Therapists*, New York: Guilford Press.

Frederick, C.J. and Shaw, S.M. (1995) 'Body image as a leisure constraint: examining the experience of aerobic classes for young women', *Leisure Sciences*, 17, 2: 57–73.

Freeman, P.A. and Zabriskie, R.B. (2003) 'Leisure and family functioning in adoptive families: implications for therapeutic recreation', *Therapeutic Recreation Journal*, 37, 1: 73–93.

Freeman, P.A., Palmer, A.A. and Baker, B.L. (2006) 'A qualitative inquiry into the leisure of LDS women who are stay-at-home mothers', *Leisure Sciences*, 28: 203–11.

Freysinger, V. (1994) 'Leisure with children and parental satisfaction: further evidence of a sex difference in the experience of adult roles and leisure', *Journal of Leisure Research*, 26: 212–26.

Freysinger, V.J. (1988) 'The experience of leisure of middle adulthood: gender difference and charge since young adulthood', unpublished doctoral dissertation, University of Wisconsin, Madison, Wisconsin.

Freysinger, V.J. (1997) 'Redefining family, redefining leisure: progress made and challenges ahead in research on leisure and families', *Journal of Leisure Research*, 29, 1: 1–4.

Friedlander, M. (1998) 'Family research: science into practice, practice into science', in M.P. Nichols and R.C Schwartz, *Family Therapy: Concepts and Methods*, 4th edn, Boston: Allyn & Bacon.

Fromberg, D. and Bergen, D. (1998) *Play from Birth to Twelve and Beyond: Contexts, Perspectives, and Meanings*, New York: Garland Publishing Inc.

Fullager, S. (2002) 'Governing the healthy body: discourses of leisure and lifestyle within Australian health policy', *Health: An Interdisciplinary Journal for the Social Study of Health, Illness and Medicine*, 6, 1: 69–84.

Furrow, J. L. (1998) 'The ideal father: religious narratives and the role of fatherhood', *The Journal of Men's Studies*, March: 17–18.

Furstenberg, F. F., Jr. and Cherlin, A. J. (1991) *Divided families: what happens to children when parents part*, Cambridge, MA: Harvard University Press.

Gager, C.T. and Sanchez, L. (2003) 'Two as one? Couples' perceptions of time spent together, marital quality, and the risk of divorce', *Journal of Family Issues*, 24: 21–50.

Garrett, R. (2004) 'Gendered bodies and physical identities', in J. Evans, B. Davies and J. Wright, (eds), *Body Knowledge and Control: Studies in the Sociology of Physical Education and Health*, New York: Routledge.

Gauthier, A.H. and Monna, B. (2004) 'Parent's Time Investment into Children', Research Brief Series, Issue #3. Comparative Public Policy Research Laboratory, University of Calgary. Online. Available http://soci.ucalgary.ca/FYPP/images/DOCUMENTS/Brief%203%20parental%20time-%20NEW.pdf (accessed 25 November 2008).

Gavanas, A. (2003) 'Domesticating masculinity and masculinizing domesticity in contemporary U.S. fatherhood politics', paper presented at Gender and Power in the New Europe, the 5th European Feminist Research Conference, Lund University, Sweden, 20–24 August 2003. Online. Available www.5thfeminist.lu.se/filer/paper_424.pdf (accessed 1 March 2005).

Gavanas, A. (2004) 'Domesticating masculinity and masculinizing domesticity in contemporary U.S. fatherhood politics', *Social Politics: International Studies in Gender, State and Society*, 11, 2: 247–66.

Geertz, C. (1973) *The interpretation of cultures*, New York: Basic.

Gershuny, J. (2000) *Changing Times: work and leisure in post-industrial society*, Oxford: Oxford University Press.

Gerson, K. (1997) 'An institutional perspective on generative fathering creating social supports for parenting equality', in A. Hawkins and D. Dollahite, *Generative fathering beyond deficit perspectives*, Thousand Oaks, CA: Sage.

Gerson, K. (2002) 'Moral dilemmas, moral strategies, and the transformation of gender: lessons from two generations of work and family change', *Gender & Society*, 16: 8–28.

Gibson, H. J. (1998) 'Sport tourism: a critical analysis of research', *Sport Management Review*, 1, 1: 45–76.

Gillies, V., Ribbens McCarthy, J. and Holland, J. (2001) *Pulling Together, Pulling Apart: The Family Lives of Young People*, London: Family Policy Studies Unit, Joseph Rowntree Foundation.

Gittins, D. (1993) *The Family in Question: Changing Households and Familiar Ideologies*, 2nd edn, Basingstoke/London: Macmillan.

Glaser, B. and Strauss, A. (1967) *The discovery of grounded theory: Strategies for qualitative research*, Hawthorne, NY: Aldine Publishing Company.

Glaser, B.G. and Holton, J. (2004) 'Remodeling grounded theory', *The Grounded Theory Review: An International Journal*, 4: 11–24.

Glassé, C. and Smith, H. (2001) *The New Encyclopaedia of Islam*, Walnut Creek: Altamira Press.

Glyptis, S. and Chambers, D. (1982) 'No Place Like Home', *Leisure Studies*, 1, 3: 247–62.

Goff, J.G. Fick, D.S. and Oppliger, R.A. (1997) 'The moderating effect of spouse support on the relation between serious leisure and spouses' perceived leisure–family conflict', *Journal of Leisure Research*, 29: 47–60.

Goffman, E. (1959) *The presentation of self in everyday life*, Garden City, NY: Anchor/Doubleday.

Goh, R.B.H. (2004) 'Asian Christian networks: transnational structures and geopolitical mappings', *Journal of Religion and Society*, 6: (no page numbers). Online. Available http://moses.creighton.edu/JRS/2004/2004–15.html (accessed November 2008).

Goodale, T.L. and Godbey, G.C. (1988) *The Evolution of Leisure: Historical and Philosophical Perspectives*, State College, PA: Venture Publishing.

Goodman, W.B., Crouter, A.C., Lanza, S.T. and Cox, M.J. (2008) 'Paternal work characteristics and father–infant interactions in low-income, rural families', *Journal of Marriage and Family*, 70, 3: 640–53.

Goodwin, D.K. (1997) *Wait Till Next Year: A Memoir*, New York: Touchstone.

Goodwin, M. (1984, October 7) 'On common ground', *New York Times Magazine*, 79.

Gordon, S., Hallahan, K. and Henry, D. (2002) *Putting The Picture Together: Inquiry Into*

Response by Government Agencies to Complaints of Family Violence and Abuse in Aboriginal Communities, Perth, Western Australia, Department of Premier and Cabinet.

Gottman, J.M. and Silver, N. (1999) *The Marriage Clinic: A Scientifically Based Marital Therapy*, New York: W. W. Norton.

Goward, P. (2005) 'After the barbeque: women, men, work and family', speech by the Federal Sex Discrimination Commissioner to the 9th Australian Institute of Family Studies Conference, Melbourne, February 2005.

Gray, M. and Tudball, J. (2003) 'Family-friendly work practices: differences within and between workplaces', *The Journal of Industrial Relations*, 45, 3: 269–91.

Graydon, J. (1983) ' "But it's more than a game. It's an institution", Feminist Perspectives on Sport', *Feminist Review*, 13: 5–16.

Green, M. (1998) *Fathers After Divorce: Building a New Life and Becoming a Successful Seperated Parent*, Sydney: Finch Publishing.

Green, D., Hebron, S. and Woodward, E. (1990) *Women's Leisure: What Leisure?*, Basingstoke, Hampshire: Macmillan.

Greene, S. and Hill, M. (2005) 'Researching children's experience: methods and methodological issues', in S. Greene and D. Hogan (eds), *Researching Children's Experiences: Approaches and Methods*, London: Sage.

Griswold, R.L. (1993) *Fatherhood in America*, New York: Basic Books.

Guest, E.A. (1922, August) 'My job as a father', *American Magazine*, 94: 13–15, 124.

Hales, R. (1999, May) 'Strengthening families: our sacred duty', *Ensign*, 29: 32.

Hall, D. (1985) *Fathers Playing Catch With Sons*, New York: North Point.

Hantrais, L. (1983) 'Leisure and the family in contemporary France', Papers in Leisure Studies, No. 7, London: Polytechnic of North London.

Harrell, J., Gansky, S., Bradley, C. and McMurray, R. (1997) 'Leisure time activities of elementary school children', *Nursing Research*, 46, 5: 246–53.

Harrington, M. (2006) 'Leisure and sport as contexts for fathering in Australian families', *Leisure Studies*, 25, 2: 165–84.

Harrington, M. and Dawson, D. (1995) 'Who has it best? Women's labor force participation, perceptions of leisure and constraints to enjoyment of leisure', *Journal of Leisure Research*, 27, 1: 4–24.

Harrop, A. and Moss, P. (1995) 'Trends in parental employment', *Work, Employment and Society*, 9, 3: 421–44.

Hart, A. (2002, December 24) 'The man who made it Christmas one day in May', *Times Union*. Online. Available http://web.lexis-nexis.com (accessed 31 October 2002).

Hartman, M. and Hartman, H. (1983) 'Sex-role attitudes of Mormons vs. non-Mormons, in Utah', *Journal of Marriage and the Family*, 45, 4, 897–902.

Harvey, C. (ed.) (2001) *Maintaining Our Differences*, Aldershot: Ashgate.

Hatter, W., Vinter, L. and Williams, R. (2002) *Dads on Dads' Needs and Expectations at Home and Work*, London: Equal Opportunities Commission.

Hawkins, A.J and Dollahite, D.C. (1997a) *FatherWork: Understanding and Encouraging Generative Fathering*, Newbury Park, CA: Sage Publications.

Hawkins, A.J. and Dollahite, D.C. (1997b) *Generative Fathering Beyond Deficit Perspectives*, Thousand Oaks, CA: Sage.

Hawks, S.R. (1991) 'Recreation in the family', in S.J. Bahr (ed.), *Family Research: A Sixty Year Review 1930–1990*, New York: Lexington Books.

Hawthorne, B. (2005) 'Australian men's experiences of non-resident fathering', paper presented to the 9th Australian Institute of Family Studies Conference, Melbourne, February 2005.

Heath, D. (1991) *Fulfilling Lives*, San Francisco, CA: Jossey-Bass.

Heaton, T.B. and Pratt, E.L. (1990) 'The effects of religious homogamy on marital satisfaction and stability', *Journal of Family Issues*, 11: 191–207.

Hellstedt, J.C. (1995) 'Invisible players: a family systems model', in S. Murphy (ed.), *Sport Psychology Interventions*, Champaign, IL: Human Kinetics.

Henderson, K.A. (1990) 'The meaning of leisure for women: an integrative review of the research', *Journal of Leisure Research*, 22, 3: 228–43.

Henderson, K.A. (1991) *Dimensions of Choice: A Qualitative Approach To Recreation, Parks, and Leisure Research*, State College, PA: Venture Publishing Inc.

Henderson, K.A. and Ainsworth, B.E. (2001) 'Researching leisure and physical activity with women of color: issues and emerging questions', *Leisure Sciences*, 23: 21–34.

Henderson, K.A. and Bialeschki, M.D. (2002) *Evaluating Leisure Services: Making Enlightened Decisions*, 2nd edn, State College, PA: Venture Publishing Inc.

Henderson, K.A. and Shaw, S.M. (2003) 'Leisure research about gender and men: the weaker link', in S. Stewart and W. Borrie (Compilers), *Abstracts from the 2003, Symposium on Leisure Research*, Ashburn, VA: National Recreation and Parks Association.

Henderson, K.A., Hodges, S. and Kivel, B.D. (2002) 'Context and dialogue in research on women and leisure', *Journal of Leisure Research*, 34, 3: 253–71.

Henderson, K.A., Stalnaker, D. and Taylor, G. (1988) 'The relationship between barriers to recreation and gender-role personality traits for women', *Journal of Leisure Research*, 20: 69–80.

Henderson, K.A., Bialeschki, M.D., Shaw, S.M. and Freysinger, V.J. (1989) *A Leisure of One's Own: A Feminist Perspective on Women's Leisure*, College Park, PA: Venture Publishing.

Henderson, K.A., Bialeschki, M.D., Shaw, S.M., and Freysinger, V.J. (1996) *Both Gains and Gaps: Feminist Perspectives on Women's Leisure*, State College, PA: Venture Publishing.

Henwood, K. and Procter, J. (2003) 'The good father: reading men's accounts of paternal involvement during the transition to first-time fatherhood', *British Journal of Social Psychology*, 42, 3: 337–55.

Hernandez, D.H. and Brandon, P.D. (2002) 'Who are the fathers of the 1990s?', in C.S. Tamis-LeMonda and N. Cabrera (eds), *Handbook of Father Involvement*, New Jersey: Lawrence Erlbaum.

Higgins, D., Bromfield, L. and Richardson, N. (2005) *Enhancing Out-of-Home Care for Aboriginal and Torres Strait Islander Young People*, Melbourne: Australian Institute of Family Studies, National Child Protection Clearinghouse.

Hinckley, G.B. (2004 November) 'The women in our lives', *Ensign*, 34: 82–5.

Hobson, B. (ed.) (2002) *Making Men into Fathers: Men, Masculinities and The Social Politics of Fatherhood*, Cambridge: Cambridge University Press.

Hochschild, A. (1989) *The Second Shift: Working Parents and The Revolution at Home*, London: Piatkus.

Hofferth, L.S. (2003) 'Race/ethnic differences in father involvement in two-parent families: culture, context, or economy?', *Journal of Family Issues*, 24, 2: 185.

Holland, K.L. (1995) 'Marital satisfaction and leisure activity' doctoral thesis, University of Missouri. [Abstract] *Dissertation Abstracts International*, 55, 5556.

Retrieved October 24, 2002 from Cambridge Scientific Results (PsychInfo Database).

Horn, W.F. and Sylvester, T. (2002) *Father Facts*, 4th edn, Gaithersburg, MD: National Fatherhood Initiative.

Horna, J. (1989) 'The leisure component of the parental role', *Journal of Leisure Research*, 21: 228–41.

Horwath, J., Lees, J., Sidebotham, P., Higgins, J. and Imtiaz, A. (2008) *Religion, Beliefs and Parenting Practices: The Influence of Religious Beliefs on Parenting, From The Perspectives of Both Adolescents and Parents*, York: Joseph Rowntree Foundation.

Hoyle, R.H. and Leff, S.S. (1997) 'The role of parental involvement in youth sport participation and performance', *Adolescence*, 32, 125: 233–43.

Hrabowski, F.A., Maton, K.I. and Grief, G.L. (2006) 'Father–son relationships: the father's voice', in M.E. Connor and J.L. White, *Black fathers: an invisible presence in America*, Hillsdale, NJ: Erlbaum.

Hughes, J. and Gray, M. (2005) 'The use of family-friendly work arrangements by lone and couple mothers', *Family Matters*, 71: 18–23.

Hultsman, W. (1993) 'The influence of others as a barrier to recreation participation among early adolescents', *Journal of Leisure Research*, 25: 150–64.

Hultsman, W. (1995) 'Recognizing patterns of leisure constraints: an extension of the exploration of dimensionality', *Journal of Leisure Research*, 27, 3: 228–44.

Hunter, H.W. (1994 November) 'Being a righteous husband and father', *Ensign*, 24: 49–51.

Hurley, R. I. (1935, August) 'A city builds teams from gangs', *Recreation*, 29: 256–7.

Husain, F. and O'Brien, M. (2001) 'South Asian Muslims in Britain: faith, family and community', in C. Harvey (ed.), *Maintaining Our Differences*, Aldershot: Ashgate.

Hutchinson, S., Baldwin, C. and Caldwell, L. (2003) 'Differentiating parent practices related to adolescent behaviour in the free time context', *Journal of Leisure Research*, 36: 396–422.

Hutchinson, S.L.J., Kardos, P., Scherphorn, Y., Tung, H. Yang and Yarnal, C. (2002) 'A call for fathers: the absent voice in family leisure research', paper presented at the 10th Canadian Congress on Leisure Research, University of Alberta, May 2002.

Iannaccone, L.R. and Miles, C.A. (1990) 'Dealing with social change: the Mormon Church's response to change in women's roles', *Social Forces*, 68, 4: 1231–50.

Jackson, A. (1999) 'The effects of non-resident father involvement on single black mothers and their young children', *Social Work*, 44, 2: 156–66.

Jackson, E.L. and Henderson, K.A. (1995) 'Gender-based analysis of leisure constraints', *Leisure Sciences*, 17: 31–51.

Jackson, E.L. and Rucks, V.C. (1995) 'Negotiation of leisure constraints by junior-high and high school students: an exploratory study', *Journal of Leisure Research*, 27: 85–105.

Jambor, E.A. and Weekes, E.M. (1995) 'Benefits parents seek from children's sport participation', paper presented at the Annual Conference of the North American Society for the Psychology of Sport and Physical Activity, Monterey, CA, June 1995.

James, A. (1993) *Childhood Identities: Self and Social Relationships in the Experience of the Child*, Edinburgh: Edinburgh University Press.

James, A., Jenks, C. and Prout, A. (1998) *Theorizing Childhood*, New York: Teachers College Press.

Jeanes, R. (2005) 'Girls, football participation and gender identity', in P. Braham and J. Caudwell (eds), *Sport, Active Leisure and Youth Cultures*, LSA publication 86, Eastbourne: Anthony Rowe Ltd.

Jeanes, R. and Kay, T. (2007) 'Can football be a female game? An examination of girls' perceptions of football and gender identity', in J. Magee, J. Caudwell, K. Liston and S. Scraton (eds), *Women and Football in Europe: Histories, Equity and Experience*, International Football Institute Series Vol. 1, Oxford: Meyer and Meyer Sport.

Jeanes, R., Lindsey, I. and Kay, T. (2007) *Evaluation of the Chance to Shine Programme*, Year 1 Report, Loughborough: Institute of Youth Sport.

Jenkins, J.M. and Lyons, K.D. (2006) 'Non-resident fathers' leisure with their children', *Leisure Studies*, 25, 2: 219–32.

Joly, D. (1987) *Making a place for Islam in British Society: Muslims in Birmingham*, Research Paper in Ethnic Relations no. 4, Centre for Research in Ethnic Relations, University of Warwick.

Kaufmann, G. and Uhlenberg, P. (2000) 'The influence of parenthood on the work effort of married men and women', *Social Forces*, 78, 3: 931–49.

Kay, T.A. (1996) 'Women's work and women's worth: the leisure implications of women's changing employment patterns', *Leisure Studies*, 15: 49–64.

Kay, T.A. (1998) 'Having it all or doing it all? The construction of women's lifestyles in time-crunched households', *Society and Leisure*, 21, 2: 435–54.

Kay, T.A. (2000) 'Sporting excellence: the impact on family life', *European Physical Education Review*, 6, 2: 151–70.

Kay, T.A. (2001) 'New women, same old leisure: the upholding of gender stereotypes and leisure disadvantage in contemporary dual-earner families', in S. Clough and J. White (eds), *Women's Leisure Experiences: Ages, Stages and Roles*, Eastbourne: Leisure Studies Association.

Kay, T.A. (2006) 'Daughters of Islam: family influences on Muslim young women's participation in sport', *International Review for the Sociology of Sport*, 41: 339–55.

Kay, T.A. (2007) 'Fathering through sport', *World Leisure Journal*, 49, 2: 69–82.

Kay, T.A., Jeanes, R. and Lindsey, I. with Collins, S., Fimusamni, J., and Bancroft, J. (2007) *Young People, Sports Development and the HIV-AIDS Challenge: Research in Lusaka, Zambia*, Loughborough: Institute of Youth Sport.

Kellett, M. (2005) *How to Develop Children as Researchers*, London: Paul Chapman.

Kelly, J. (1982) 'Leisure subcultures', in J. Kelly (ed.), *Leisure*, Englewood Cliffs, NJ: Prentice Hall, pp.240–55.

Kelly, J.B. (2000) 'Legal and educational interventions for families in custody and access disputes', paper presented at the International Family Law Society Conference, Brisbane, Australia, July 2000.

Kelly, J.B. and Lamb, M.E. (2000) 'Using child development research to make appropriate custody and access decisions for children', *Family and Conciliation Courts Review*, 38: 297–311.

Kelly, J.R. (1990) *Leisure*, Englewood Cliffs, NJ: Prentice Hall.

Kelly, J.R. (1995) 'Leisure and the family', in C. Critcher, P. Bramham and A. Tomlinson (eds), *Sociology of Leisure: A Reader*, London: E & FN Spon.

Kelly, J.R. (1997) 'Changing leisure in leisure-family research – again', *Journal of Leisure Research*, 29: 132–4.

Kelly, J.R. and Kelly, J. (1994) 'Multiple dimensions of meaning in the domains of work, family and leisure', *Journal of Leisure Research*, 26, 3: 250–74.

Kendal, C. (1995) (no title specified), in C. Cunneen and T. Libesman (eds), 'Indigenous

People and the Law', Reed international Books, 1995. Online. Available http://www.dreamtime.net.au/indigenous/family.cfm 14th November 2008   (accessed on 14 October 2008).

Kennedy, L. (2003, June 12) 'Having a ball with dad', *Rocky Mountain News*, p. 3D. Online. Available http://web.lexis-nexis.com/universe/printdoc (accessed 31 October 2003).

Kiernan, K. (1992) 'Men and women at work and at home', in R. Jowell, L. Brook, G. Prior and B. Taylor (eds), *British Social Attitudes: The 9th Report*, Aldershot: Dartmouth Publishing.

Kimiecek, J. C., Horn, T. S. and Shurin, C. S. (1996) 'Relationships among children's beliefs, perceptions of their parents' beliefs, and their moderate-to-vigorous physical activity', *Research Quarterly for Exercise and Sport*, 67, 3: 324–36.

Kimmel, M.S. (1990) 'Baseball and the reconstitution of American masculinity 1880–1920', in M.A. Messner and D.F. Sabo (eds), *Sport, Men, and The Gender Order: Critical Feminist Perspectives*, Champaign, IL: Human Kinetics.

Kimmel, M.S. (1996) *Manhood in America: A Cultural History*, New York: Free Press.

Kimmel, M.S. and Messner, M.A. (2004) *Men's lives*, 6th edn, Boston: Pearson Education Inc.

King, V. (2003) 'The influence of religion on fathers' relationships with their children', *Journal of Marriage and Family*, 65, 2: 382–93.

Kinsella, W.P. (1982) *Shoeless Joe*, Boston: Houghton Mifflin.

Kleiber, D. (1999) *Leisure Experience and Human Development*, New York: Basic Books.

Kloep, M. and Hendry, L. (2003) 'Adult control and adolescent challenge? Dilemmas and paradoxes in young people's leisure', *World Leisure Journal*, 45, 3: 24–34.

Kulik, L. (2002) 'Marital equality and the quality of long-term marriage in later life', *Ageing and Society*, 22, 459–81.

Kurrien, R. and Vo, E.D. (2004) 'Who's in charge? coparenting in South and Southeast Asian families', *Journal of Adult Development*, 11, 3: 207–19.

Kwiat-Kowski, M. (1998) 'Sporting femininity: perceptions of femininity and homophobia with the sport and recreation experiences of women', unpublished thesis, University of Tennessee.

Lamb, M.E. (1986) 'The changing role of fathers', in M.E. Lamb (ed.), *The Father's Role: Applied Perspectives*, New York: Wiley.

Lamb, M.E. (ed.) (1997) *The Role of The Father in Child Development*, 3rd edn, New York: Wiley.

Lamb, M.E. (ed.) (2004) *The Role of the Father in Child Development*, Hoboken, NJ: Wiley.

Larabee, M.J. (ed.) (1993) *An Ethic of Care: feminist and interdisciplinary perspectives (Thinking Gender)*, London: Routledge.

Lareau, A. (2000) 'My wife can tell me who I know: methodological and conceptual problems in studying fathers', *Qualitative Sociology*, 23, 4: 407–33.

LaRossa, R. (1988) 'Fatherhood and social change', *Family Relations*, 37: 451–7.

LaRossa, R. (1997) *The Modernization of Fatherhood: A Social and Political History*, Chicago, IL: University of Chicago Press.

LaRossa, R. (2004) 'The culture of fatherhood in the fifties: a closer look', *Journal of Family History*, 29: 47–70.

LaRossa, R. (2005) 'Until the ball glows in the twilight: fatherhood, baseball and the game of playing catch, in W. Marsiglio, K. Roy and G. Fox (eds), *Situated Fathering: A Focus on Physical and Social Space*, Lanham, MD: Rowman and Littlefield.

LaRossa, R. and Reitzes, D.C. (1993) 'Symbolic interactionism and family studies', in P.G. Boss, W.J. Doherty, R. LaRossa, W.R. Schumm and S.K. Steinmetz (eds), *Sourcebook of Family Theories and Methods: A Contextual Approach*, New York: Plenum Press.

Larson, R.W., Gillman, A. and Richards, M. (1997) 'Divergent experiences of family leisure: fathers, mothers, and young adolescents', *Journal of Leisure Research*, 29, 1: 78–97.

Larson, R. and Richards, M. (1994) *Divergent Realities: The Emotional Lives of Mothers, Fathers and Adolescents*, New York: Basic Books.

Leff, S.S. and Hoyle, R.H. (1995) 'Young athletes' perceptions of parental support and pressure', *Journal of Youth and Adolescence*, 24: 187–203.

Lehrer, L.E. (2004) 'The role of religion in union formation: an economic perspective', *Population Research and Policy Review*, 23, 2: 161.

Lesejane, D. (2006) 'Fatherhood from an African cultural perspective', in L. Richter and R. Morrell, *Baba: Men and Fatherhood in South Africa*, Cape Town: HSRC Press.

Lewis, C. (2000) *A Man's Place is in the Home: Fathers and Families in the UK*, York: Joseph Rowntree Foundation.

Lewis, J. and Campbell, M. (2007) UK Work/Family Balance Policies and Gender Equality, 1997–2005, Social Politics: International Studies in Gender, State & Society, published online on April 19, 2007. Online. Available http://sp.oxford journals.org/cgi/content/abstract/jxm005v2 (accessed 19 September 2008).

Lichtenberg, G. (1993) 'About men: to catch a mother', *New York Times Magazine*, November 7: 28–9.

Linacre, S. (2007) 'One-parent families', *Australian Social Trends 2007*, Canberra: Australian Bureau of Statistics.

Lincoln, Y. and Guba, E. (1985) *Naturalistic Inquiry*, Beverly Hills, CA: Sage Publications.

Litsky, F. (2004, May 12). 'Now Pittsfield stakes claim to baseball's origins', *New York Times*.

Little League Online (n.d.) Little League Baseball historical timeline. Retrieved July 8, 2004, from http://www.littleleague.org/history.

Littlefield, B. (2002) 'The game of catch', *Only a Game* (from NPR and 90.9 WBUR Boston). Online. Available http://archives.onlyagame.org/archives/2001/06/0606comm.shtml (accessed 23 October 2003).

Lundberg, S. and Rose, E. (2002) 'Investments in sons and daughters: evidence from the Consumer Expenditure Survey', paper presented to the Joint Center for Poverty Research Institute, Family Investments in Children's Potential: Resources and Behaviors that Promote Children's Success, Chicago, 19–20 September 2002.

Lundberg, S., Pabilonia, S. and Ward-Batts, J. (2006) 'Time allocation of parents and investments in sons and daughters', Working paper, Department of Economics, University of Washington.

Lupton, D. and Barclay, L. (1997) *Constructing Fatherhood: Discourses and Experiences*, London: Sage.

Mac an Ghaill, M. (1996) *Understanding Masculinities: Social Relations and Cultural Arenas*, Buckingham: Open University Press.

Mahoney, A. (2000) 'U.S. norms on religious affiliation, self-reported importance, and church attendance of mothers and fathers of children and adolescents:

Secondary analyses of 1995 Gallup poll', unpublished manuscript, Ohio: Bowling Green State University.

Mahoney, A., Pargament, K., Swank, A. and Tarakeshwar, N. (2001) 'Religion in the home in the 1980's and 90's: a review and conceptual integration of empirical links between religion, marriage, and parenting', *Journal of Family Psychology*, 15: 559–96.

Mallon, G.P. (2004) *Gay men choosing parenthood*, New York: Columbia University Press.

Mandelbaum, M. (2004) *The Meaning of Sports: Why Americans Watch Baseball, Football, and Basketball and What They See When They Do*, New York: Public Affairs.

Marks, S.R., Huston, T.L., Johnson, E.M. and MacDermid, S.M. (2001) 'Role balance among white married couples', *Journal of Marriage and the Family*, 63: 1083–98.

Marshland, D. (1982). ' "Its my life": young people and leisure', *Leisure Studies*, 1: 305–22.

Marsiglio, W. (2004a) 'Studying fathering trajectories: in-depth interviewing and sensitizing concepts', in R.D. Day and M.E. Lamb (eds), *Conceptualizing and Measuring Father Involvement*, Hillsdale, NJ: Erlbaum.

Marsiglio, W. (2004b) 'When stepfathers claim stepchildren: a conceptual analysis', *Journal of Marriage and Family*, 66, 1: 22–39.

Marsiglio, W., Amato, P., Day, R. and Lamb, M. (2000) 'Scholarship on fatherhood in the 1990s and beyond', *Journal of Marriage and the Family*, 62: 1173–91.

Marsiglio, W., Roy, K. and Fox, G.L. (eds) (2005) *Situated Fathering: A Focus on Physical and Social Spaces*, Lanham, MD: Rowman & Littlefield.

Martin, D.F, Morphy, S., Sanders, W.G. and Taylor, J (2002) 'Making sense of the census: observations of the 2001 enumeration in remote aboriginal Australia', Research Monograph No. 22, Centre for Aboriginal Economic Policy Research, Canberra: The Australian National University.

Maume, D.J. (2006) 'Gender differences in taking vacation time', *Work and Occupations*, 33, 2: 161–90.

McConkie, B. R. (1966) *Mormon Doctrine*, 2nd edn, Salt Lake City, UT: Bookcraft.

McCormack, D. (1999–2002) 'How to teach your child to play catch', Long Island Parent Stuffcom. Online. Available http://www.libabystuff.com/inspire/kids.shtml (accessed October 2003).

McHale, J.P., Lauretti, A., Talbot, J. and Pouquette, C. (2002) 'Retrospect and prospect in the psychological study of co-parenting and family group dynamics', in J. McHale and W. Grolnick (eds), *Retrospect and Prospect in the Psychological Study of Families*, Hillsdale, NJ: Erlbaum.

McHale, J., Khazan, I., Rotman, T., DeCourcey, W., Erera, P. and McConnell, M. (2002) 'Co-parenting in diverse family stories', in M. Bornstein (ed.), *Handbook of Parenting*, 2nd edn, Hillsdale, NJ: Erlbaum.

McKay, J., Messner, M.A. and Sabo, D. (2002) *Masculinities, Gender Relations and Sport*, Thousand Oaks, CA: Sage.

McPhail, A., Kinchin, G. and Kirk, D. (2003) 'Students' conceptions of sport education', *European Physical Education Review*, 9, 3: 285–99.

Mead, G.H. (1934) *Mind, Self, and Society*, Chicago, IL: University of Chicago Press.

Meeks, C. and Maudlin, T. (1990) 'Children's time in structured and unstructured leisure activities', *Lifestyles: Family and Economic Issues*, 11: 257–81.

Melzer, B.N., Petras, J.W. and Reynolds, J.W. (1975) *Symbolic Interactionism: Genesis, Varieties, and Criticism*, London: Routledge and Kegan Paul.

Menning, L.C. (2002) 'Absent parents are more than money: the joint effect of activities and financial support on youth's educational attainment', *Journal of Family Issues*, 23: 648–71.

Merrill, R.M., Lyon, J.L. and Jensen, W.J. (2003) 'Lack of secularizing influence of education on religious activity and parity among Mormons', *Journal for the Scientific Study of Religion*, 42, 1: 113–24.

Merwin, S. (1923, July) 'A father's relation to his children', *Ladies Home Journal*, 40: 15–28.

Messner, M.A. (1992) *Power at Play*, Boston, MA: Beacon Press.

Messner, M.A. (1993) ' "Changing men" and feminist politics in the United States', *Theory and Society*, 22: 723–37.

Messner, M. (1995) 'Ah, ya throw like a girl!', in P.S. Rothenberg (ed.), *Race, Class, and Gender in the United States: An Integrated Study*, New York: St. Martin's, pp. 46–8.

Messner, M. (2002) *Taking the Field: Men, Women and Sport*, Minnesota: University of Minnesota Press.

Miles, M.B. and Huberman, A.M. (1994) *Qualitative Data Analysis*, 2nd edn, Thousand Oaks, CA: Sage.

Miller, Y.D. and Brown, W.J. (2005) 'Determinants of active leisure for women with young children – an "ethic of care" prevails', *Leisure Sciences*, 27, 5: 407–20.

Mkhize, N. (2006) 'African traditions and the social, economic and moral dimensions of fatherhood', in L. Richter and R. Morrell, *Baba: Men and Fatherhood in South Africa*, Cape Town: HSRC Press.

Modood, T., Berthoud, R., Lakey, J., Nazroo, J., Smith, P., Virdee, S. and Beishon, S. (1997) *Ethnic Minorities in Britain*, London: Policy Studies Institute.

Moen, P. (2003) 'Introduction', in P. Moen (ed.), *It's About Time: Couples and Careers*, Ithica, NY: Cornell University Press.

Moen, P. and Sweet, S. (2003) 'Time clocks: Work-hour strategies', in P. Moen (ed.), *It's About Time: Couples and Careers*, Ithica, NY: Cornell University Press.

Morgan, D. (2004) 'Men in families and households', in J. Scott, J. Treas and M. Richards (eds), *The Blackwell Companion to the Sociology of Families*, Malden: Blackwell Publishing, pp. 374–93.

Morrell, R. (2006) 'Fathers, fatherhood and masculinity in South Africa', in L. Richter and R. Morrell (eds), *Baba: Men and Fatherhood in South Africa*, Cape Town: HSRC Press.

Morris, B. (n.d.) 'An enduring game of catch'. Online. Available http://www.legendsmagazine.net/37/endurcat.htm (accessed 16 July 2003).

Morrison, J. (1994) 'Men at leisure: the implications of masculinity and leisure for "househusbands" ', unpublished thesis, Sydney: School of Leisure and Tourism Studies, University of Technology.

Morrow, V. (1998) *Understanding Families: Children's Perspectives*, London: National Children's Bureau/Joseph Rowntree Foundation.

Motherwell, H. (1932, November) 'For fathers only', *Parents Magazine*, 7, 4: 39.

'My dad is way, way cool: Kids tell us why their fathers are best' (2003) *The Columbus Dispatch*. Online. Available http://web.lexis-nexis.com (accessed 20 October 2003).

National Collegiate Athletic Association (2007) '1999–00–2006–07 NCAA Student-athlete race and ethnicity report' Online. Available http://www.ncaapublications.

com/ProductsDetailView.aspx?SKU=RE2008N&AspxAutoDetect
CookieSupport=1 (accessed 8th February 2009).

Nelson, T.S. (2001) 'Quadrant two quadrille: time management as an effective tool for families' [Abstract]. *Journal of Clinical Activities, Assignments and Handouts in Psychotherapy Practice*, 1: 73–7.

Neuman, W.L. (2000) *Social Research Methods Qualitative and Quantitative Approaches*, 4th edn, Sydney: Allyn and Bacon.

Nevile, A. (2001) *State of the Family 2001*, Melbourne, Anglicare Australia.

Nock, S.L. and Kingston, P.W. (1988) 'Time with children: the impact of couples' work-time commitments', *Social Forces*, 67, 1: 59–85.

Obermeyer, C.M. (1992) 'Islam, women, and politics: the demography of Arab countries', *Population and Development Review* 18, 1: 33–60.

O'Brien, M. (2005) *Shared Caring: Bringing Fathers into the Frame*, London: Equal Opportunities Commission.

O'Brien, M. and Shemilt, I. (2003) *Working Fathers: Earning and Caring*, London: Equal Opportunities Commission.

Office for National Statistics (2001) *Population Size, Census, April 2001*, London: HMSO.

Office for National Statistics (2001a) *Social Focus on Men*, London: HMSO.

Office for National Statistics (2001b) *Social Trends 31*, London: HMSO.

Office for National Statistics (2002) *Living in Britain: Results from the 2001 General Household Survey*, London: HMSO.

Office for National Statistics (2003) *Social Trends 33*, London: HMSO.

Office for National Statistics (2008) *Social Trends 38*, London: HMSO.

Oliver, K. (2001) 'Images of the body from popular culture: engaging adolescent girls in critical inquiry', *Sport, Education and Society*, 6, 2: 143–64.

Olson, D.H. (2000) 'Circumplex model of marital and family systems', *Journal of Family Therapy*, 22, 2: 144–67.

Orloff, A.S. and Monson, R. (2002) 'Citizens, workers or fathers? Men in the history of US social policy', in B. Hobson (ed.), *Making Men into Fathers: Men, Masculinities and the Social Politics of Fatherhood*, Cambridge: Cambridge University Press.

Orthner, D.K. (1975) 'Leisure activity patterns and marital satisfaction over the marital career', *Journal of Marriage and the Family*, 37: 91–103.

Orthner, D.K., Barnett-Morris, L. and Mancini, J.A. (1994) 'Leisure and family over the life cycle', in L. L'Abate (ed.), *Handbook of Developmental Family Psychology and Psychopathology*, New York: Wiley, pp. 176–201.

Orthner, D.K. and Mancini, J.A. (1990) 'Leisure impacts on family interaction and cohesion', *Journal of Leisure Research*, 22, 2: 125–37.

Orthner, D.K. and Mancini, J.A. (1991) 'Benefits of leisure for family bonding', in B.L. Driver, P.J. Brown and G.L. Peterson (eds), *Benefits of Leisure*, State College, PA: Venture.

Palkovitz, R. (2002) *Involved Fathering and Men's Adult Development: Provisional Balances*, London: Lawrence Erlbaum.

Parekh, B. (2000) *The Future of Multiethnic Britain: The Parekh Report*, London: Profile Books.

Parke, R.D., Coltrane, S., Borthwick-Duffy, S., Powers, J., Adams, M., Fabricus, W., Braver, S. and Saenz, D. (2004) 'Assessing father involvement in Mexican-American families', in R.D. Day and M.E. Lamb (eds), *Conceptualizing and Measuring Father Involvement*, Hillsdale, NJ: Erlbaum.

Parkinson, P. and Smyth, B. (2003) 'When the difference is night and day: some empirical insights into patterns of parent–child contact after separation', paper presented to the 8th Australian Institute of Family Studies Conference, Steps Forward for Families: Research, Practice and Policy, Melbourne Exhibition Centre, 2003.

Paschal, A. (2006) *Voices of African-American Teen Fathers: I'm Doing What I Got To Do*, New York: Haworth Press Inc.

Pasley, K. and Braver, S.L. (2004) 'Measuring father involvement in divorced non-residential fathers', in R.D. Day and M.E. Lamb (eds), *Conceptualizing and Measuring Father Involvement*, Mahwah: Lawrence Erlbaum Associates.

Patternson, C.J. (2000) 'Family relationships of lesbians and gay men', *Journal of Marriage and Family*, 62/4: 1052–69.

Patternson, C. (2006) 'Children of lesbian and gay parents', *Current Directions in Psychological Science*, 15, 5: 241–4.

Pearce, L.D. and Axinn, W.G. (1998) 'The impact of family religious life on the quality of mother–child relations', *American Sociological Review*, 63: 810–28.

Pennington, B. (2004) 'Baseball's origins: they ain't found till they're found', *New York Times*, September 12, 1, 23.

Percoco, J.A. (1992, summer) 'Baseball and World War II: A study of the Landis–Roosevelt correspondence', *Organization of American History Magazine of History*, 7. Online. Available http://www.oah.org/pubs/magazine/sport/percoco.html (accessed 9 July 2004).

Perry, L.T. (1977 November) 'Father. Your role, your responsibility', *Ensign*, 7: 62–5.

Peterik, A. (1995) 'Women's baseball during World War II', *Illinois History*. Online. Available http://www.lib.niu.edu/ipo/ihy950452.html (accessed 9 July 2004).

Petersen, V. and Steinman, S. (1994) 'Helping children succeed after divorce: a court mandated educational program for divorcing parents', *Family and Conciliation Courts Review*, 32, 1: 27–39.

Phoenix, A. and Husain, F. (2007) *Parenitng and Ethnicity*, York: Joseph Rowntree Foundation.

Pieper, J. (1963) *Leisure: The Basis of Culture*, New York: Random House.

Pilkington, A. (2003) *Racial Disadvantage and Ethnic Diversity in Britain*, Basingstoke: Palgrave.

Piszek, B. (2003) 'The Little League Baseball experience: daddy's memories', *The World of English*. Online. Available http://www.woe.edu.pl/2003/2_03/little league.html (accessed 31 October 2003).

Pleck, J.H. and Masciadrelli, B.P. (2004) 'Paternal involvement by U.S. residential fathers: levels, sources, and consequences', in M.E. Lamb (ed.), *The Role of the Father in Child Development*, New York: Wiley.

Pleck, J.H. and Stueve, J.L. (2004) 'A narrative approach to paternal identity: the importance of parental identity "conjointness" ', in R.D. Day and M.E. Lamb (eds), *Conceptualizing and Measuring Father Involvement*, Hillsdale, NJ: Erlbaum.

Pollack, W. (1999) *Real Boys*, Melbourne: Scribe Publications.

Popenoe, D. (1996) *Life without father: compelling new evidence that fatherhood and marriage are indispensibe for the good of children and society*, New York: Free Press.

Potuchek, J.L. (1997) *Who Supports the Family? Gender and bread-winning in dual-earner marriages*, Palo Alto, CA: Stanford University Press.

Power, T. G. and Woogler, C. (1994) 'Parenting practices and age-group swimming: a correlational study', *Research Quarterly for Exercise and Sport*, 65, 1: 59–66.

Presser, H.B. (2000) 'Nonstandard work schedules and marital instability', *Journal of Marriage and the Family*, 62: 93–110.

Prus, R. (1994) 'Approaching the study of human group life: symbolic interaction and ethnographic inquiry', in M.L. Dietz, R. Prus and W. Shaffir (eds), *Doing Everyday Life: Ethnography as Human Lived Experience*, Chicago, IL: University of Chicago Press.

Putney, Clifford (2001) *Muscular Christianity: Manhood and Sports in Protestant America, 1880–1920*, Cambridge, MA: Harvard University Press.

Pyke, K. (2000) ' "The normal American family" as an interpretive structure of family life among grown children of Korean and Vietnamese immigrants', *Journal of Marriage and Family*, 62: 240–5.

Rademacher, E.S. (1933, August) 'For fathers only', *Parents Magazine*, 8: 6.

Rapoport, R. and Rapoport, R.N. (1975) *Leisure and the Family Life Cycle*, London: Routledge and Kegan Paul.

Raymore, L.A., Godbey, G.C. and Crawford, D.W. (1994) 'Self-esteem, gender and socioeconomic status: their relation to perceptions of constraint on leisure among adolescents', *Journal of Leisure Research*, 26: 99–118.

Renold, E. (1997) ' "All they've got on their brains is football": sport, masculinity and the gendered practice of playground relations', *Sport, Education and Society*, 2, 1: 5–23.

Richter, L. and Morrell, R. (eds) (2006) *Baba: Men and Fatherhood in South Africa*, Cape Town: HSRC Press.

Richter, L. and Smith, W. (2006) 'Children's views of fathers', in L. Richter and R. Morrell, *Baba: Men and Fatherhood in South Africa*, Cape Town: HSRC Press.

Riddick, C.C. and Russell, R.V. (1999) *Evaluative Research in Recreation, Park, and Sport Settings: Searching for Useful Information*, Champaign, IL: Sagamore Publishing Co.

Roberts, H. (2000) 'Listening to children and hearing them', in P. Christensen and A. James (eds), *Research with Children: Perspectives and Practices*, London and New York: Falmer Press.

Roberts, K. (1970) *Leisure*, London: Longman.

Roberts, K. (1999) *Leisure in Contemporary Society*, London: CAB International.

Robertson, B. (1999) 'Leisure and family: perspectives of male adolescents who engage in delinquent activity of leisure', *Journal of Leisure Research*, 31, 4: 335–58.

Robinson, J.P. and Godbey, G. (1993) 'Sport, fitness, and the gender gap', *Leisure Sciences*, 15: 291–307.

Robinson, J.P. and Godbey, G. (1997) *Time for Life: The Surprising Ways Americans Use Their Time*, Pennsylvania: The Pennsylvania State University Press.

Roggman, L.A., Benson, B. and Boyce, L. (1999) 'Fathers with infants: knowledge and involvement in relation to psychosocial functioning and religion', *Infant Mental Health Journal*, 20, 3: 257–77.

Rojek, C. (2005) *Leisure Theory: Principles and Practices*, Hampshire: Palgrave Macmillan.

Rosenblatt, R. (1998, July 13) 'A game of catch', *Time*, 90.

Russell, A. and Saebel, J. (1997) 'Mother–son, mother–daughter, father–son, and father–daughter: are they distinct relationships?', *Developmental Review*, 17: 111–47

Russell, G. (1987) 'Fatherhood in Australia', in: M.E. Lamb (ed.), *The Father's Role: Cross-Cultural Perspectives*, Hillsdale, NJ: Lawrence Erlbaum.

Russell, G. and Radin, N. (1983) 'Increased paternal involvement: fathers' perspectives', in M.E. Lamb and A. Sagi (eds), *Fatherhood and Family Policy*, Hillside, NJ: Lawrence Erlbaum.

Russell, R. (1987) 'The importance of recreation satisfaction and activity participation to the life satisfaction of age-segregated retirees', *Journal of Leisure Research*, 19, 4: 273–83.

Russell, R.V. (1990) 'Recreation and quality of life in old age: a causal analysis', *Journal of Applied Gerontology*, 9: 77–90.

Russell, R.V. (2005) *Pastimes: The Context of Contemporary Leisure*, 3rd edn, Champaign, IL: Sagamore Publishing.

Russell-Chapin, L.A., Chapin T.J. and Sattler, L.G. (2001) 'The relationship of conflict resolution styles and certain marital satisfaction factors to marital distress', *The Family Journal: Counseling and Therapy for Couples and Families*, 9: 259–64.

Sabo, D.F. and Runfola, R. (1980) *Jock: Sports and Male Identity*, Englewood Cliffs, NJ: Prentice-Hall.

Saggers, S. and Gray, D. (1998) *Dealing with Alcohol: Indigenous Usage in Australia, New Zealand and Canada*, Cambridge: Cambridge University Press.

Sasidharan, V. (2002) 'Special issue introduction: understanding recreation and the environment within the context of culture', *Leisure Sciences*, 24, 1: 1–11.

Sayer, L.C (2005) 'Gender, time and inequality: trends in women's and men's paid work, unpaid work and free time', *Social Forces*, 84, 1: 285–303.

Schacher, S.J, Auerbach, C. and Silverstein, L. (2005) 'Gay fathers expanding the possibilities for all of us', *Journal of GLBT Families Studies* 1, 3: 31–52.

Scraton, S., Fasting, K., Pfister, G. and Bunuel, A. (1999) 'It's still a man's game? The experiences of top-level European women footballers', *International Review for the Sociology of Sport*, 34, 2: 99–111.

Shakib, S. (2003) 'Female basketball participation: negotiating the conflation of peer status and gender status from childhood through to puberty', *American Behavioural Scientist*, 46, 10: 1405–22.

Shakib, S. and Dunbar, M. (2004) 'How high school athletes talk about maternal and paternal sporting experiences', *International Review for the Sociology of Sport*, 39: 275–99.

Shannon, C. (2003) 'Mothers and daughters: similarities and differences in work, family and leisure roles', *World Leisure Journal*, 45, 4: 37–43.

Shannon, C. (2006) 'Parents' messages about the role of extra-curricular and unstructured leisure activities: adolescents' perceptions', *Journal of Leisure Research*, 38, 3: 398–420.

Sharpe, S. (1994) *Fathers and Daughters*, London: Routledge.

Shaw, S. (1997) 'Controversies and contradictions in family leisure: an analysis of conflicting paradigms', *Journal of Leisure Research*, 29 (1): 98–112.

Shaw, S. (2008) 'Family leisure and changing ideologies of parenthood', *Sociology Compass*, 2, 2: 688–703.

Shaw, S. M. (1985) 'Gender and leisure: inequality in the distribution of leisure time' [Abstract], *Journal of Leisure Research*, 17: 266–82.

Shaw, S. M. (1992) 'Dereifying family leisure: an examination of women's and men's everyday experiences and perceptions of family time', *Leisure Sciences*, 14: 271–86.

Shaw, S. M. (1994) 'Gender, leisure, and constraint: towards a framework for the analysis of women's leisure', *Journal of Leisure Research*, 26, 1: 8–22.

Shaw, S.M. and Dawson, D.J. (1998) *Active family lifestyles: motivations, benefits, constraints and participation*, Ottawa: Canadian Fitness and Lifestyle Research Institute.

Shaw, S. M. and Dawson, D. (2001) 'Purposive leisure: examining parental discourses on family activities', *Leisure Sciences*, 23, 4: 217–31.

Shaw, S.M., Bonen, A. and McCabe, J.F. (1991) 'Do more constraints mean less leisure? Examining the relationship between constraints and participation', *Journal of Leisure Research*, 23, 4: 286–300.

Shinew, K.J., Floyd, M.F., McGuire, F.A. and Noe, F.P. (1996) 'Class polarization and leisure activity preferences of African Americans: intragroup comparisons', *Journal of Leisure Research*, 28, 4: 228–50.

Silva, E.B. (1996) *Good Enough Mothering? Feminist Perspectives on Lone Motherhood*, London: Routledge.

Skelton, C. (2000) ' "A passion for football": dominant masculinities and primary schooling', *Sport, Education and Society*, 5, 1: 5–18.

Smith, G.T, Synder, D.K., Trull, T.J. and Monsma, B.R. (1988) 'Predicting relationship satisfaction from couples' use of leisure time', *American Journal of Family Therapy*, 16, 3–13.

Smith, K.M., Taylor, S., Hill, B.J. and Zabriskie, R.B. (2004) 'Family functioning and leisure in single-parent families', in W.T. Borrie and D.L. Kerstetter (eds), Abstracts from the 2004 Leisure Research Symposium, Ashburn, VA: National Recreation and Park Association.

Smith, Yevonne. (1992) 'Women of Color in Society and Sport', *Quest*, 44, 22: 228–50.

Smyth, B. (2004a) 'Postseparation fathering: what does Australian research tell us?', *Journal of Family Studies* 10, 1: 20–49.

Smyth, B. (ed.) (2004b) 'Parent–Child Contact and Post-Separation Parenting Arrangements', Research Report No. 9, Melbourne: Australian Institute of Family Studies (AIFS).

Smyth, B. (2005) 'Parent–child contact in Australia: exploring five different post-seperation patterns of parenting', *International Journal of Family Law, Policy and the Family*, 19: 1–22.

Smyth, B., Caruana, C. and Ferro, A. (2003) 'Some whens, hows and whys of shared care', paper presented to the Australian Social Policy Conference, University of New South Wales, July 2003.

Snarey, J. (1993) *How Fathers Care for the Next Generation*, Cambridge, MA: Harvard University Press.

Snyder, K.A. (2007) 'A vocabulary of motives: understanding how parents define quality time', *Journal of Marriage and Family*, 69, 2: 320–40.

Sorenson, E. (2007) 'Non-resident fathers: what we know and what's left to learn', paper presented to The Urban Institute, NICHD Workshop. Washington, DC, January 16–17.

Speaker, T. (1939, April) 'Diamonds in the rough', *Rotarian*, 54: 22–5.

Stacey, J. (2006) 'Gay parenthood and the decline of paternity as we knew it', *Sexualities*, 9,1: 27–55.

Statistics Canada (2001). 'Population by religion, by province and territory', Statistics Canada, Census of Population. Online. Available http://www40.statcan.gc.ca/101/cst01/demo30a-eng.htm (accessed 24 November 2008).

Statistics Canada (2006) 'Census families in private households by family structure and presence of children, by province and territory', 2006 Census of Population, Ottawa: Statistics Canada.

Statistics Canada (2008) Income in Canada, 2006, Catalogue no. 75–202–X, Ottawa: Statistics Canada.

Statistics Canada (1999) Overview of the time use of Canadians in 1998, General Social Survey, Ottawa: Statistics Canada.

Stebbins, R.A. (1999) 'Serious leisure', in E.L. Jackson and T.L. Burton (eds), *Leisure Studies: Prospects for the Twenty-First Century*, State College, PA: Venture.

Steele, J.L. (1904) 'How the national game developed: some baseball reminiscences', *Outing*, 44: 333–6.

Stewart, S.D. (1999) 'Disneyland dads, Disneyland moms: how nonresident parents spend time with absent child(ren)', *Journal of Family Issues*, 20: 539–56.

Stodolska, M. and Livengood, J.S. (2006) 'The influence of religion on the leisure behavior of immigrant Muslims in the United States', *Journal of Leisure Research*, 38, 3: 293–320.

Stolzenberg, R.M., Blair-Loy, M. and Waite, L.J. (1995) 'Religious participation in early adulthood: age and family life cycle effects on church membership', *American Sociological Review*, 60: 84–103.

Strah, D. (2004) *Gay Dads: a celebration of fatherhood*, New York: Penguin.

Strauss, A. and Corbin, J. (1990) *Basics of Qualitative Research: Grounded theory procedures and techniques*, Newbury Park, CA: Sage Publications Inc.

Strauss, A. and Corbin, J. (1998) *Basics of Qualitative Research: techniques and procedures for developing grounded theory*, 2nd edn, Thousand Oaks, CA: Sage.

Strauss, A.L. (1987) *Qualitative Analysis for Social Scientists*, Cambridge: Cambridge University Press.

Such, Elizabeth (2001) 'Leisure, family and work in the lifestyles of dual-earner families', paper presented at the ESRC seminar, Impact of a Changing Labour Market on Families, Children and Mental Health: Building Research–User Alliances, University of Aberdeen, 7 November 2001.

Such, E. (2006) 'Leisure and fatherhood in dual-earner families', *Leisure Studies*, 25, 2: 185–200.

Sullivan, O. (1996) 'The enjoyment of activities: do couples affect each other's well-being? Measuring well-being: the enjoyment of activities within couples', *Social Indicators Research*, 38, 81–102.

Swain, J. (2000) ' "The money's good, the fame's good, the girls are good": the role of playground football in the construction of masculinities', *British Journal of Sociology of Education*, 21, 1: 95–108.

Tamis-LeMonda, C.S. and Cabrera, N. (2002) 'Multidisciplinary perspectives on father involvement: an introduction', in C.S. Tamis-LeMonda and N. Cabrera (eds), *Handbook of Father Involvement*, New Jersey: Lawrence Erlbaum.

Telford, A., Salmon, J., Timperio, A. and Crawford, D. (2005) 'Examining physical activity among 5 to 6 and 10 to 12 year old children: the children's leisure activities study', *Pediatric Exercise Science*, 17, 3: 266–80.

The Church of Jesus Christ of Latter Day Saints (1997) *Teachings of Presidents of the Church: Brigham Young*, Salt Lake City, UT: The Church of Jesus Christ of Latter-day Saints.

The Weekend Australian Magazine, March 25–26, 2006.

Theberge, N. (1981) 'A critique of critiques: radical and feminist writings on sport', *Social Forces*, 60, 2: 341–53.

Thompson, J.A. and Bunderson, J.S. (2001) 'Work–nonwork conflict and the phenomenology of time', *Work & Occupations*, 28, 1: 17–39.

Thompson, S. (1999) *Mother's Taxi: Sport and Women's Labor*, Albany, NY: State University of New York Press.

Thorne, Barrie (1993) *Gender Play: Girls and Boys in School*, New Brunswick, NJ: Rutgers University Press.

Thornton, A. (1985) 'Reciprocal influences of family and religion in a changing world', *Journal of Marriage and the Family*, 47: 381–94.

Thorpe, K. and Daly, K. (1999) 'Children, parents and time: the dialectics of control', in C. Shehan (ed.), Through the eyes of the child: re-visioning children as active agents of family life, Vol. 1, in F. Bernardo (ed.) *Contemporary Perspectives on Family Research*, Stamford, CT: J.A.I. Press.

Thrane, C. (2000) 'Men, women and leisure time: Scandinavian evidence of gender inequality', *Leisure Sciences*, 22, 2: 109–22.

Tirone, S.C. and Shaw, S.M. (1997) 'At the center of their lives: Indo Canadian women, their families and leisure', *Journal of Leisure Research*, 29, 1: 98–112.

'Today's father' (1952, August) *Woman's Home Companion*, 112–14.

Tomlinson, A. and Yorganci, I. (1997) 'Male coach/female athlete relations: gender and power relations in competitive sport', *Journal of Sport and Social Issues (JSSI)*, 21(2): 134–55.

Tomlinson, A. and Ilkay, Y. (1997) 'Male coach/female athlete relations: gender and power relations in competitive sport', *Journal of Sport and Social Issues*, 21, 2: 134–55.

Townsend, N.W. (2002) *The Package Deal: Marriage, Work and Fatherhood in Men's Lives*, Philadelphia, PA: Temple University Press.

UK National Statistics (2006) *Divorces (numbers and rates): Sex and age at divorce, 1999–2000*, Newport: UK Office for National Statistics.

United States Census Bureau (2000) *2000 United States Census*, Washington, DC: United States Census Bureau.

United States Census Bureau (2002) *Children's living arrangements and characteristics: March 2002*, Washington, DC: United States Department of Commerce.

United States Census Bureau (2005) *2005 United States Census*, Washington, DC: United States Census Bureau.

United States Census Bureau (2007) 'Children Characteristics', *2006 American Community Survey*, Washington, DC: United States Census Bureau.

United States Census Bureau (2008) 'Self-described religious identification of adult population: 1990 and 2001'. Online. Available. http://www.census.gov/compendia/statab/cats/population/religion.html (accessed 24 November 2008).

Veal, A.J. and Lynch, R. (2001) *Australian Leisure*, 2nd edn, Sydney: Pearson Education.

Veblen, T. (1994) (originally published in 1899) *The Theory of the Leisure Class*, Toronto, Ontario: General Publishing Company.

Verma, G.K. and Darby, D. S. (1994) *Winners and Losers: ethnic minorities in sport and recreation*, London: Falmer Press.

Voas, D. and Crockett, A. (2005) 'Religion in Britain: neither believing nor belonging', *Sociology*, 39, 1: 11–28.

VonRoenn, S., Zhang, J. and Bennett, G. (2004) 'Dimensions of ethical misconduct in contemporary sports and their association with the backgrounds of stakeholders', *International Sports Journal*, 8, 2: 37–54.

Wade, A. and Smart, J. (2002) *Facing Family Change: children's circumstances, strategies and resources*, York: Joseph Rowntree Foundation.

Walker, Y. (1993) 'Aboriginal family issues', Family Matters 35, August, 51–53. Online. Available http://www.aifs.gov.au/institute/pubs/fm1/fm35yw.html (accessed 18 November 2008).

Wallerstein, J. (1991) 'Tailoring the intervention to the child in the separating and divorced family', *Family and Conciliation Courts Review*, 29, 4 (not paginated).

Wann, D.L., Merrill J., Melnick, G., Russell, W. and Pease, D.G. (2001) *Sport Fans: The Psychology and Social Impact of Spectators*, London: Routledge.

Ward, L. (2003) 'Like father, like son', *Ahwatukee Foothill News*. Online. Available http://www.ahwatukee.com!afn/sports/articles/010502c.html (accessed 6 November 2003).

Warin, J., Solomon, Y., Lewis, C. and Langford, W. (1999) *Fathers, Work and Family Life*, London: Family Policy Studies Centre.

Watton, W. (2005) *Religion and Life*, London: Hodder Education.

Watzlawick, P., Beavin, J. H., Jackson, D. D. (1967) *Pragmatics of Human Communication: A Study of Interactional Patterns, Pathologies, and Paradoxes*, New York: Norton.

Wearing, B. (1984) *The Ideology of Motherhood: A Study of Sydney Suburban Mothers*, Sydney: George Allen & Unwin.

Wearing, B. (1998) *Leisure and Feminist Theory*, London: Sage.

Wearing, B.M. and McArthur, M. (1988) 'The family that plays together stays together: or does it?', *Australian and New Zealand Journal of Sex, Marriage and Family*, 9: 150–8.

Wedgwood, N. (2003) 'Aussie rules! Schoolboy football and masculine embodiment', in S. Tomsen and M. Donaldson (eds), *Male Trouble: Looking at Australian Masculinities*, Melbourne: Pluto Press Australia.

Wedgwood, N. (2004) 'Kicking like a boy: schoolgirl Australian Rules Football and bi-gendered female embodiment', *Sociology of Sport Journal*, 21: 140–62.

West, C. and Zimmerman, D.H. (1987) 'Doing gender', *Gender and Society*, 1, 2: 125–51.

Wilcox, W.B. (1998) 'Conservative Protestant childrearing: authoritarian or authoritative?', *American Sociological Review*, 63: 796–809.

Wilcox, W.B. (2002) 'Religion, convention, and paternal involvement', *Journal of Marriage and Family*, 64: 780–92.

Wilcox, W.B. and Bartkowski, J.P. (2005) 'Devoted dads: religion, class and fatherhood', in W.K. Marsiglio, K. Roy and G.L Fox, *Situated Fathering: a focus on physical and social spaces*, New York: Rowman and Littlefield.

Williams, A. and Bedward, J. (1999) *Games for the girls: the impact of recent policy on the provision of physical education and sporting opportunities for female adolescents*, Winchester: King Alfred's College.

Willming, C. and Gibson, H. (2000) 'A view of leisure and patterns in family life in the late 1990s', *Society and Leisure*, 23, 1: 121–44.

Wimbush, E. and Talbot, M. (eds) (1988) *Relative Freedoms: Women and Leisure*, Milton Keynes/Philadelphia, PA: Open University Press.

Witt, P.A. and Goodale, T.L. (1981) 'The relationships between barriers to leisure enjoyment and family stages', *Leisure Sciences*, 4: 29–49.

Wood, M., Read, J. and Mitchell, R. (2004) 'Do parents still matter? Parent and peer influences on alcohol involvement among recent high school graduates', *Psychology of Addictive Behaviours*, 18, 1: 19–30.

Woods, M. (1999) 'The behaviour and expenditures of non-resident parents during contact visits'. Research Paper No. 75. Canberra: Department of Family and Community Services.

Woodberry, R.D. and Smith, C.S. (1998) 'Fundamentalism *et al.*: conservative Protestants in America', *Annual Review of Sociology* 24: 25–56.

Wright, B.A. and Goodale, T.L. (1991) 'Beyond non-participation: validation of interest and frequency of participation categories in constraints research', *Journal of Leisure Research*, 23: 314–31.

Wright, J. (1997) 'The construction of gendered contexts in single sex and co-educational physical education lessons', *Sport, Education and Society*, 2(1): 55–72.

Wright, J. (1999) 'Changing gendered practice in physical education: working with teachers', *European Physical Education Review*, 5(3): 181–97.

Wuthnow, R. (1991) 'Acts of compassion: Caring for others and helping ourselves', *Review of Sociology*, 24, 25–56.

Yankee Stadium History (n.d.) Online. Available http://newyork.yankees.mlb.com/ NASApp/mlb/nyy/ballpark/stadium_history.jsp (accessed 10 July 2004).

Yeung, W.J., Sandberg, J.F., Davis-Kean, P.E. and Hofferth, S.L. (1999) 'Children's time with fathers in intact families', mimeo, University of Michigan.

Yeung, W.J., Sandberg, J.F., David-Kean, P.E and Hofferth, S.L. (2001) 'Children's time with fathers in intact families', *Journal of Marriage and the Family*, 63: 136–54.

Youth soccer (n.d.) SoccerNova. Online. Available http://www.soccernova.com/ working/youth/youth.htm (accessed 29 October 2004).

Zabriskie, R.B. (2000) 'An examination of family and leisure behavior among families with middle school aged children'. Unpublished doctoral dissertation, Indiana University, Bloomington, Indiana.

Zabriskie, R.B. (2001) 'The validity and reliability of the family leisure activity profile (FLAP)', in M.E. Havitz and M.F. Floyed (eds), *Abstracts from the 2001 Symposium on Leisure Research*, Ashburn, VA: National Recreation and Park Association.

Zabriskie, R.B. and McCormick, B.P. (2001) 'The influences of family leisure patterns on perceptions of family functioning', *Family Relations*, 50: 281–9.

Zabriskie, R.B. and McCormick, B.P. (2003) 'Parent and children perspectives of family leisure involvement and satisfaction with family life', *Journal of Leisure Research*, 35, 2: 163–89.

Zerubavel, E. (1981) *Hidden Rhythms: Schedules and Calendars in Social Life*, Chicago, IL: University of Chicago Press.

Zerubavel, E. (1997) *Social Mindscapes: An Invitation to Cognitive Sociology*, Cambridge, MA: Harvard University Press.

Zinnecker, J. (1995) 'The cultural modernisation of childhood', in L. Chisholm, P. Buchner, H. Kruger and M. Du-Bois-Reymond (eds), *Growing Up in Europe: Contemporary Horizons in Childhood and Youth Studies*, Berlin/New York: Walter De Gruyter.

Index